14 Days

FEB. 1 5 1984

MAY 9 1984

JUN. 1 2 1984

JUN. 1 9 1984   WITHDRAWN

JUL. 2 1 1986

APR. 1 1 1988

SEP 1 1992

MAY 1 2 1994

MAY 2 3 1994

[SEP 1 5 1994

FEB 1 8 1995

AUG 3 0 1997

W9-AYP-526

Midwest
Family Vacation
Book

**225 Great Ideas for
Vacationing Close to Home**

- Ohio
- Michigan
- Indiana
- Illinois
- Wisconsin
- Iowa
- Minnesota
- Missouri

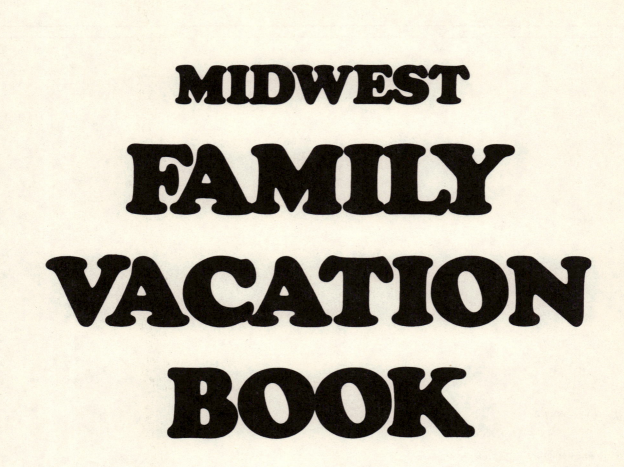

MIDWEST
FAMILY
VACATION
BOOK

Created and Edited by
Jerry L. Nelson

G.L. Nelson Publishing, Inc.
Chicago

Copyright ©1983 by G. L. Nelson Publishing, Inc.
All rights reserved.
Printed and bound in the United States of America.
First edition.

Other books published in this series: **Kids' Guide to Chicago,
Twin Cities Family Fun Guide, Chicagoland Family Fun Guide.**

No part of this book may be reproduced or transmitted in any
form or by any means, including photocopying, recording or by
any information system, without the written permission of the
publisher, except by a reviewer quoting brief passages in a review
written for a magazine, newspaper, or broadcast outlet.

Published by G. L. Nelson Publishing, Inc., KidsLife Books
Division, 664 N. Michigan Ave., Suite 1010, Chicago, Illinois
60611.

Library of Congress Catalog Number 83-90150
ISBN: 0-937416-03-7

Cover Illustration: John Faulkner
Writer/Researchers: Cindy Cooney, Ron Pazola, Linda Wagner,
Susan Smith
Editorial/Production: Richard G. Young
Typesetting: Dennis Halbin, Gabrielle Karras

*We are grateful to the various chambers of commerce, local
tourist bureaus, and publicity agencies for the use of photos.*

917.7
N

36545

CONTENTS

About the Editor

Jerry L. Nelson is a former newspaper writer, publicist and magazine editor who has lived in most of the Midwestern states and traveled extensively in all of them. He's written for many major newspapers and magazines, both as a member of their staffs and as a freelancer. For seven years, he was a staff writer for the *Detroit News*. Among his travel books are *Kids' Guide to Chicago, Twin Cities Family Fun Guide*, and *Chicagoland Family Fun Guide*. Married and the father of two children, he and his wife, Sherry, now live in the Chicago area.

OHIO

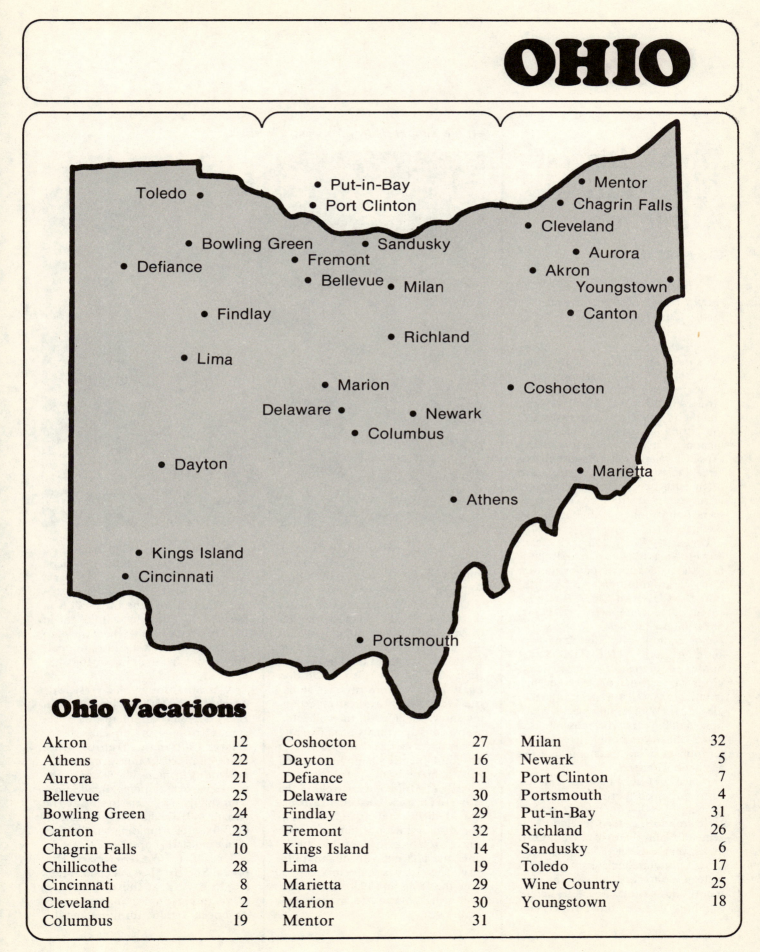

Toledo •

• Put-in-Bay
• Port Clinton

• Mentor
• Chagrin Falls
• Cleveland

• Bowling Green   • Sandusky
• Defiance   • Fremont
          • Bellevue   • Milan

• Aurora
• Akron
  Youngstown •

• Findlay

• Canton

• Richland

• Lima

• Marion

• Coshocton

Delaware •   • Newark
       • Columbus

• Dayton

• Marietta

• Athens

• Kings Island
• Cincinnati

• Portsmouth

Ohio Vacations

1

Ohio

Ohio's Biggest City's Varied Attractions

Cleveland, Ohio

Driving Time: About 3½ hours from Detroit; 8 hours from Chicago

Sprawling out for 50 miles along the shores of Lake Erie, Cleveland, Ohio's largest city, boasts more lakefront property than any metropolitan area in the world. That lakeshore and the 17,500 acres of parks serve as the setting for the city's wide assortment of attractions and activities. Because Cleveland has a reputation as a large industrial center, visitors are often surprised to find such scenic beauty coupled with many entertainment opportunites, from baseball to Bach.

University Circle, four miles from downtown, is the hub of social, cultural, and educational opportunities. The world-famous medical institution, the **Cleveland Clinic**, is also located here, along with museums, parks, and churches.

For example, the **Cleveland Museum of Art** (11150 East Blvd.) houses one of the world's most prestigious collections of 19th-century paintings, as well as Oriental and medieval art. With 41,000 pieces, spanning 5,000 years, the museum is a place where you could spend an afternoon or a few days enjoying the aesthetic wonders.

Nearby, visitors may see another impressive collection of exhibits ranging from live animals to prehistoric dinosaurs at the **Cleveland Museum of Natural History** (Wade Oval at University Circle). It is the state's largest museum dedicated to natural history, conservation, and environmental education, Besides ancient reptilian creatures, other displays in-

At the Natural History Museum, Cleveland

clude gems, geological specimens, birds, mammals, and relics from Ohio and North American Indian cultures.

Don't miss the dazzling shows at the **Ralph Mueller Planetarium**, located in the museum building. In addition, more of nature's creatures are showcased at the **Cleveland Aquarium** (601 E. 72nd St.) in Gordon Park. The numerous varieties of marine life always provide an entertaining show. Included in the collection are various specimens of native and tropical freshwater and saltwater fish, birds, reptiles, amphibians, and aquatic mammals.

Also at University Circle is the **Howard Dittrick Museum of Historical Medicine** (11000 Euclid Ave.). The display includes almost 10,000 objects relating to dentistry, medicine, and pharmacy throughout history. The replicas of doctors' offices from the 1800s and 1930s provide an interesting contrast to modern-day facilities.

With more than 1,300 animals on the 125-acre grounds, the **Cleveland Metroparks Zoo** (Brookside Park, off Fulton Rd.) is one of the largest in the Midwest and the fifth oldest in the nation. Children will delight in the **Children's Farm**, where they can pet and feed domestic farm animals and native wild animals that are tame.

A stroll through the **West Side Market** (W. 25th St. and Lorain Ave.) is always an interesting experience for visitors to Cleveland. There, 130 tenants, representing more than 20 ethnic groups, sell everything from fresh produce to fine meat and bakery items. In addition, your family may want to stop at **The Arcade** (401 Euclid Ave.), a palatial, mall-like 1890 building that houses many unusual shops.

A visit to the **Western Reserve Historical Society Museum and Library** (10825 E. Blvd. at University Circle) is an interesting change of pace. American antique furniture and de-

corative arts are featured in 20 period rooms covering the years 1770 to 1920. Other exhibits show the life and history of the area from the landing of Moses Cleveland in 1796 to the 1870s. One of the most popular displays is the large costume collection.

The performing arts are an important cultural attraction in the city. The Cleveland Orchestra, reputedly one of the world's finest, performs at **Severance Hall** (11001 Euclid Ave.) in fall, winter, and spring. Summer performaces are at **Blossom Music Center**, south of Cleveland (for more information, call [216] 231-1111).

The city features several fine restaurants, such as the **French Connection** (at Stouffer's Inn on the Square), featuring French cuisine, or the Blue Fox (11706 Clifton Blvd.), for a more varied menu.

Sports fans won't want to leave town without attending a football or baseball game at Cleveland's **Municipal Stadium** (Lakeside Ave. and W. Third St.). (For Indians tickets, call [216] 241-5555; call [216] 575-1000 for Browns football tickets.)

While your family is in the area, soak up a little more history in nearby **Burton** (about 15 miles west on Rt. 87). At **Century Village** visitors are invited to learn about pioneer life through exhibits and displays. In 16 restored 19th-century buildings ranging from a railroad station to a blacksmith shop the lifestyle of early American citizens is recreated. (Also, see articles on Sea World and Geauga Lake in Aurora.)

BEST TIME TO VISIT: Summer.
HOURS: Cleveland Museum of Art — 10 a.m.-6 p.m. Tuesday, Thursday, and Friday; 10 a.m.-10 p.m., Wednesday; 9 a.m.-5 p.m. Saturday; 1 p.m.-6 p.m. Sunday. Cleveland Museum of Natural History — 10 a.m.-5 p.m. Monday-Saturday, 1 p.m.-5:30 p.m. Sunday. Cleveland Zoo — 10 a.m.-5 p.m. daily; 10 a.m.-7 p.m. Sunday and holidays in April through October. Cleveland Aquarium — 10 a.m.-5 p.m. Tuesday through Saturday, noon-6 p.m. Sunday. Howard Ditttrick Museum — 10 a.m.-5 p.m. Monday through Friday, 1-5 p.m. Sunday. West Side Market — 7 a.m.-4 p.m. Monday and Wednesday, 7 a.m.-6 p.m. Friday and Saturday. Western Reserve Musuem — 10 a.m.-5 p.m. Tuesday through Saturday, 2-5 p.m. Sunday. Century Village — May through October, 10 a.m.-5 p.m. Tuesday through Saturday, noon-6 p.m. Sunday.
ADMISSION: Cleveland Museum of Natural History — adults, $2; children and teens 6 to 18, $1; free admission Tuesday and Thursday 3-5 p.m. Cleveland Zoo — adults, $2; children 2 to 11, $1. Cleveland Aquarium — adults, $1, children and teens 6 to 18, 50¢.
DIRECTIONS: From Detroit, take I-75 south to Toledo and I-80 east; from Chicago, take I-80 east to Cleveland.
FOR MORE INFORMATION: Call or write Convention and Visitors Bureau of Greater Cleveland, 1301 E. Sixth St., Cleveland, OH 44114; 800 (216) 621-4110.

Ohio

A Full Year Of Festivals In Portsmouth

Portsmouth, Ohio

Driving Time: About 1½ hours south of Columbus

In winter, summer, spring, or fall, visitors to Portsmouth can find festivals and special events focusing on everything from tennis to strawberries.

Beginning with **Statehood Days** in early March, the lineup includes such celebrations as a **Trout Derby** (April), **Scioto River Valley Bike Tour** (May), **Strawberry Festival** (June in Wheelersburg), **Scioto County Fair** (August), **Tennis & Crumpets** (August), **River Days** (Labor Day week), and many more.

The annual **Boneyfiddle Fair,** held in mid-May, is an old-fashioned funfest that offers arts and crafts displays, musical entertainment, dancing, and tasty samples of ethnic foods, all centered around the town's old Market Square. And in the fall, there's the **Oktoberfest/Canal Days** celebration (first weekend in October) and the **Fall Foliage Festival** featuring campouts, bean dinners auto tours, hikes, and hoe-downs.

For a glimpse of pioneer life, visit the **1810 House** (1926 Waller St.). The historic homestead of Aaron and Mary Kinney has been restored to reflect the lifestyle of the family during the very early 19th century. Oak and walnut floors, clay bricks, and the stone foundation of the home were all formed from the land on which the building stands. The 14-inch-thick walls and double thickness doors were built as extra protection against Tecumseh's Shawnee Indian tribes, who were on the warpath when the home was constructed.

Twelve Kinney children were raised around the fires of the great hearth in the large central room, where all meals were cooked. Throughout the house are numerous interesting antiques, including a five-legged cherry table from New London, Connecticut, which survived the Revolutionary War. Clustered around the Jenny Lind bed in the children's room is a collection of miniature period clothing, showing the way boys and girls dressed in America's early days. Children visiting the house are always intrigued with the old schoolroom on the second floor, a remarkable contrast to present-day facilities. Other rooms include the country kitchen, Victorian parlor, master bedroom, library, and costume room.

Civil War buffs should visit the ongoing restoration of the **Boneyfiddle Historic District** in the west end of town, where residences and commercial buildings are being carefully restored to their mid-1800s condition. One of the most popular attractions in the Boneyfiddle area is the **Brewery Arcade,** an 1842 brewery building housing a complex of quaint shops and restaurants.

At the **Southern Ohio Museum and Cultural Center** (825 Gallia St.), tourists find a continually changing array of art and historical exhibits. The museum is one of three community projects that earned Portsmouth the 1980 All-American City award.

BEST TIME TO VISIT: Summer or fall.
HOURS: 1810 House — May through November, 2 p.m.–5 p.m. weekends. Museum and Cultural Center — closed during August; rest of year, noon–5 p.m. Tuesday through Friday, 1 p.m.–5 p.m. weekends. Brewery Arcade — 9 a.m.–6 p.m. Monday through Saturday, 1 p.m.–5 p.m. Sunday.
ADMISSION: Admission to Museum and Cultural Center and the 1810 House is free.
DIRECTIONS: From Columbus, follow U.S. 23 south to Portsmouth, about 91 miles.
FOR MORE INFORMATION: Call or write the Portsmouth Convention and Visitors Bureau, 824 Gallia St., Box 434, Portsmouth, OH 45662; (614) 354-6580.

Exploring an Ancient Indian Culture

Newark, Ohio

Driving Time: About one-half hour northeast of Columbus

Long before the great Shawnee tribes roamed the hills and plains of central Ohio, the area was inhabited by the prehistoric **Moundbuilder Indians.** The remnants and relics of their ancient culture are found in abundance at several locations in Newark. It's well worth the trip to learn about these fascinating people, who were, perhaps, the first native Americans.

First, the **Moundbuilders State Memorial** (S. 21st St. and Cooper) features the **Great Circle Mound,** covering a 26-acre area, which was used for the tribe's ceremonial rites. It has 8- to 14-foot-high walls with burial mounds in the center. Also on the park grounds is the **Ohio Indian Art Museum,** where visitors may view artifacts from all the known prehistoric cultures living in Ohio between 10,000 B.C. and 1,600 A.D. Other locations with mounds remains are the **Wright Earthworks** (two blocks northeast of Great Circle at James and Waldo Sts.) and **Octagon State Memorial** (N. 30th St. and Parkview).

Newark celebrates its history and heritage with the **Land of Legend Festival** during the second week in June. The lively fun-fest includes historic tours, sports events, arts and crafts, flea market, and much more old-fashioned merrymaking.

During your Newark-area visit, you may want to check out the **National Heisey Glass Museum** in Veterans Park (6th and Church Sts.). The museum is housed in the **King House,** built in 1831. Produced in

Newark, from 1895 to 1957, the Heisey glass is famous for its beauty and quality. Also in the park is the **Sherwood-Davidson House,** an elegant Federal-style residence built in 1815. The house showcases period furnishings, paintings, and artifacts from Licking County.

Arts enthusiasts will enjoy browsing at the **Licking County Art Gallery** (391 Hudson Ave.), which features a variety of works by local and regional artists.

Just nine miles east of Newark (on Rt. 146) is the breathtaking natural beauty of **Black Hand Gorge.** Legend has it that the gorge marked the boundary of a sacred Indian territory where no man was to fight another. The 830-acre area surrounding the gorge provides ample opportunites for enjoying the great outdoors with picnics, hiking, bicycling, bird watching, and canoeing.

The **Dawes Arboretum** is another paradise for nature-lovers (five miles south of Newark on Rt. 13). The 315 acres include woodlands, two lakes,

picnic areas, and lovely walking paths, with a collection of 2,000 species of trees and shrubbery.

The **Flint Ridge Memorial and Museum** (five miles east of Newark) focuses on the lives of the Paleo Indians, who lived 8,000 to 10,000 years ago. The Indians used flint, Ohio's official gemstone, to make weapons and implements.

BEST TIME TO VISIT: Summer or early fall.

HOURS: Moundbuilders State Memorial and Flint Ridge State Memorial — 9:30 a.m.–5 p.m. Wednesday–Saturday, Memorial Day through Labor Day; Sunday noon–5 p.m. Dawes Arboretum — daylight hours, daily. Heisey Glass Museum — April–October, 1 p.m.–4 p.m. Wednesday, Saturday, and Sunday; closed holidays. Sherwood-Davidson House— 9 a.m.–4 p.m. daily.

ADMISSION: Moundbuilders and Flint Ridge State Memorials — adults, $1.50; children 6–12 , $1; under 6, free. Sherwood Davidson House — adults, $1; children and teens to 18 years, free. Heisey Glass Museum — adults, $1; under 18 free.

DIRECTIONS: From Columbus, take I-70 east to Rt. 13 exit. Follow Rt. 13 north to Newark.

FOR MORE INFORMATION: Call or write the Newark Area Chamber of Commerce, 50 W. Locust St., Box 702, Newark OH 43005, (614) 345-8224.

Ohio

Cedar Point's Excitement Never Ends

Sandusky, Ohio

Driving Time: About 1 hour west of Cleveland

All the fun, thrills, and adventure at **Cedar Point Amusement Park** have their roots way back in 1870, when a steamboat started transporting passengers from Sandusky to a bathhouse on the Cedar Point peninsula. From then, the reputation of the area as a family recreation center has grown steadily. The first roller coaster was opened six years before the turn of the century, along with a pony track, diving platform, and water trapeze.

Today, the 364-acre park offers an exciting mix of attractions: musical shows, marine life shows, Kiddieland, Jungle Safari, and more, including over 50 rides. New for the 1983 season is the **Demon Drop**, which simulates the sensation of free-falling through space from the top of a 131-foot tower in an open car. The ride, which cost $2.5 million to build, reaches a speed of 55 m.p.h. in approximately two seconds!

Other outstanding rides joining the lineup are **Gemini**, a 125-foot-high double coaster; **Corkscrew**, a triple-looping roller coaster; **White Water Landing**, one of the world's longest water flume rides; and **Space Spiral**, a 285-foot-high observation ride. For the little tots, there is **Kid Arthur's Court** and two other ride areas with pint-sized attractions.

Visitors interested in ocean life should stop at **Oceana**, the 1,600-seat marine life stadium. Shows there feature the frolics and antics of playful dolphins and sea lions. From nine viewing windows, guests may also get a peek at life below the water surface of the above-ground tank. In addition, the area has an inside aquarium filled with king penguins, sharks, and other freshwater and saltwater fish.

More unusual entertainment is on hand at **Jungle Larry's African Safari.** The "Circus Africa" show includes performing lions, tigers, chimpanzees, and other animals.

In addition, there are five different theaters at Cedar Point presenting hits of Dixieland, the Big-Band Era, country, rock, and today's top tunes: the **Frontier Theatre, Lusty Lil's Palace, Centennial Theatre, The Showcase**, and the **Red Garter Saloon**.

While strolling through the park, guests are entertained on the midway with the comedy of the Keystone Kops and Hobo Band. Sometimes, visitors are greeted by the friendly Cedar Pointers, furry animal characters who roam around the park. **Frontier Trail** portrays pioneer life, with demonstrations of glass-blowing, candle-making, woodworking, weaving, and other pioneer skills. There's also a 19th-century grist mill and a replica of Fort Sandusky.

While visiting the Sandusky area, your family may want to see one of nature's wonders in nearby **Castalia** (take Rt. 12 southwest for seven miles). The Blue Hole is an artesian spring 90 feet in diameter with a visible depth of 50-60 feet. The actual depth of the hole is unknown. An underground river is the source of the spring, which maintains a constant temperature of 48 degrees. It's a great place to eat a picnic lunch, too.

BEST TIME TO VISIT: Late spring through summer.

HOURS: Cedar Point Amusement Park — 10 a.m.-10 p.m. daily, mid-May through Labor Day. Blue Hole — 9 a.m.-8 p.m. daily, Memorial Day through Labor Day.

ADMISSION: Cedar Point Amusement Park — adults, teens, and children 5 years and over, $11.95; sr. citzens, $8.75; starlight admission, after 5 p.m. daily, $8.25.

DIRECTIONS: From Cleveland, take the Ohio Turnpike (I-80-90) to Exit 7, follow to Sandusky. In town, follow signs to Cedar Point.

FOR MORE INFORMATION: Call Sandusky Bay Convention and Visitors Bureau, 103 W. Shoreline Dr., Sandusky OH 44870, (419) 625-2984; or Cedar Point Amusement Park, Sandusky OH 44870, (419) 627-2213.

A Bit Of Africa in Ohio

Port Clinton, Ohio

Driving Time: About 1¼ hours from Cleveland

A journey high atop a great, grey beast and a rail ride into the prehistoric past are two of the unusual features that bring families to **Port Clinton.**

At the **African Lions Safari** and the **Prehistoric Forest,** tourists are invited to explore exotic worlds where ferocious creatures roam the wilds, all on the shores of Lake Erie. Of course, there are no real dinosaurs surviving, but visitors to Prehistoric Forest are suprised at the amazingly life-like quality of the animal reproductions. There, a **safari train** takes guests millions of years back to see such awesome animals as the Brontosaurus, sabre-tooth tiger, and giant sloth. Even a cave man and woman! Continuing on the tour, a waterfall thunders at **Old Marbletop Mountain** while visitors investigate the depths of the **Catacomb Caves.**

It's only a short drive from the land of dinosaurs to the wilds of **African Lion Country.** As your family drives through the world-famous wildlife preserve, be prepared for close encounters with a varied assortment of animals brought here from Africa, Asia, and North and South America. Rhinos, gnus, antelopes, giraffes, and zebras are but a few of the beastly characters that wander about on the grounds.

In the petting section of the preserve, guests may touch and feed some of the inhabitants. If an elephant ride sounds a bit too risky, visitors instead can hop aboard a turtle taxi. Finally, at the **Simba Lodge,** African artifacts are displayed. A great way to end the adventure is to try some frosty "jungleberry juice."

Situated on the Marblehead Peninsula, **Port Clinton** offers several more points of interest. Railroad buffs won't want to miss a visit to **Train-O-Rama** (6734 E. Harbor Rd.), where an exciting mini-world comes alive as trains of every imaginable model wind around rivers, mountains, waterfalls, and towns. In addition to the 41 operating pieces, the exhibit includes more than 1,200 pieces of train equipment on display.

Finally, visitors are offered a chance to learn about the art of winemaking at the **Mon Ami Wine Company** (326 W. Catawba Rd.). The winery, which began operation in 1870, is one of the few that still use the classical French method of fermentation known as "methode Champenoise." The Mon Ami Restaurant is widely known for serving superb cuisine.

BEST TIME TO VISIT: Late spring and summer.

HOURS Prehistoric Forest — Memorial Day through Labor Day. African Lion Safari — mid-May through Labor Day, 9 a.m.–6 p.m. daily; Labor Day through early October, 9 a.m.–6 p.m. weekends only. Train-O-Rama — 10 a.m.–7 p.m. daily, Memorial Day through Labor Day; weekends, May, September, and October. Mon Ami Tours — 11 a.m.–4 p.m. Monday through Saturday. Mon Ami Restaurant — 11:30 a.m.–10 p.m., Sunday 1 p.m.–8 p.m.; dinner and winery tours are available with reservations, (419) 797-4445.

ADMISSION: African Lion Safari — adults, teens, children 4 and older, $5.25; under 4, free. Mon Ami Winery — $1.50 per person (includes cheese and wine-tasting).

DIRECTIONS: From Cleveland, take Ohio Turnpike (I-80) to Exit 7. Follow Rt. 250 to Rt. 2, continue west to Port Clinton.

FOR MORE INFORMATION: Call or write the Port Clinton Chamber of Commerce, 111 W. Perry St., Port Clinton, OH 43452, (419) 732-2929.

Ohio

Cincinnati: Charming City On the Ohio

Cincinnati, Ohio

Driving Time: About 1½ hours southeast of Indianapolis and 4½ hours southwest of Cleveland

The big city with small-town charm — that's Cincinnati. Perched high on the bluffs of the Ohio River, Cincinnati is probably one of the most underrated cities in the Midwest. Winston Churchill once called it, "The most beautiful inland city in America." If you're driving near it on a vacation, it's certainly worth a day or two.

Neighborhoods play a very important role in the lifestyle of Cincinnati citizens. One of those unique neighborhoods is **Mt. Adams** (one mile east on Eden Park Dr.), an area of hilly, curving streets and Bohemian-like atmosphere. It offers a potpourri of restaurants, boutiques, art shops, and antique stores.

Nearby, **Krohn Conservatory and Eden Park** (Eden Park Dr.) are worthwhile stops for those interested in flowers, foliage, and the great outdoors. Also in the Eden Park area (1720 Gilbert Ave.) is the **Museum of Natural History and Planetarium.** Here, families will find exhibits focusing on Ohio Indian culture, South Sea Islands, and dinosaurs — even a realistic cavern where visitors may explore its deep, dark interiors.

In the Eden Park area, as well, is the **Cincinnati Art Museum**, reputed to be one of the 10 finest art museums in the United States.

One of the more unusual methods of sightseeing downtown is by horse and buggy. Carriages and surreys provide the transportation for a fascinating, historic tour (call ahead, (513) 431-6600).

At the Museum of Natural History, Cincinnati

The **Cincinnati Fire Museum** (315 W. Court St.) is located in an old restored firehouse, built in 1907. Displays recount the history of the city and firefighting techniques since the early 19th century. Other points of interest include the **William Howard Taft National Historic Site** (2038 Auburn Ave.), birthplace of the 27th U.S. president; **Taft Museum** (Pike and Fourth Sts.), a Federal-style mansion with displays of the Taft family art collection; **Carew Tower** (Fifth and Vine Sts.), the city's tallest building (48 stories with observation deck); and **Harriet Beecher Stowe Memorial** (2950 Gilbert Ave.), the completely restored residence of the famous abolitionist author.

The **Cincinnati Zoo** (3400 Vine St.) is home to more than 5,000 animals. Some of its most popular features are Big Cat Canyon, African Veldt, and the Aquarium. The zoo is world renown for its unique birth record of rare and endangered species, such as the white Bengal tiger, lowland gorilla, and Persian leopard.

Just a few miles north of downtown, **Sharon Woods Village** recreates Ohio Valley life before 1800. (Take I-275 north to the Sharonville exit.) The buildings, brought here from various Ohio locations, include a train station, Greek Revival farmhouse, barn complex, doctor's office, and more. Skilled artisans demonstrating their crafts lend a striking authenticity to the village. Throughout the year, special events are scheduled to add to the old-fashioned fun.

In the summertime, you might want to take in a ballgame at **Riverfront Stadium** (100 Riverfront Stadium), where the Cincinnati Reds hold forth. For ticket information, call (513) 421-4510. The Cincinnati Bengals football team also plays in the stadium; their phone number is (513) 621-3550.

In almost any season of the year, the city (which has been called the "Bluegrass Capital") is alive with song and celebration at one of many festivals. Starting with **Cincinnati Springfest** in mid-May through the

International Folk Festival in November, city dwellers and suburbanites join out-of-towners for arts and crafts displays, music, fireworks, dance, gourmet foods — just to name a few features.

Perhaps one of the most popular festivals is **Oktoberfest Zinzinnati**, a rousing celebration of the city's German heritage attended annually by 500,000 persons. During the festivities, the downtown becomes a German *biergarten* filled with singing, dancing, rides, colorful costumes, and, of course, tons of sauerkraut and weinerschnitzel. Call the Convention and Visitors Bureau for festival information, (513) 621-2142.

At night the busy metropolis is transformed into a glittering jewel on the banks of the Ohio. Enjoy dinner

at one of the city's fine restaurants; only San Francisco boasts a larger concentration of outstanding eateries, per capita, in the United States. Among them are **Pigall's** (127 W. Fourth St.) or **Maisonette** (114 E. Sixth St.) for fine French cuisine; or **The Heritage** (7664 Wooster Pike), specializing in American dishes. In addition, Cincinnati's symphony orchestra, opera and ballet companies attract large audiences annually for their many extraordinary performances.

BEST TIME TO VISIT: Spring, summer, and fall.

HOURS: Cincinnati Art Museum — 10 a.m.-5 p.m. Tuesday through Saturday, 1-5 p.m. Sunday. Carew Tower Observation Deck— 9 a.m. to 5 p.m. Tuesday through Saturday. Cincinnati Fire Museum — 10 a.m.-4 p.m. Tuesday through Friday, noon to 4

p.m. weekends. Museum of Natural History and Planetarium — 9 a.m.-4:30 p.m. Monday through Saturday, 12:30-5 p.m. Sunday. Cincinnati Zoo — 9 a.m.-6 p.m. daily. Krohn Conservatory — 10 a.m.-5 p.m. Monday through Saturday, 10 a.m.-6 p.m. Sunday. Taft National Historic Site — 8 a.m.-4:30 p.m. Memorial Day through Labor Day; open same hours Monday through Friday rest of year. Sharon Woods Village — May through October, 10 a.m.-4 p.m. Tuesday through Thursday, noon-4 p.m. weekends.

ADMISSION: Museum of Natural History and Planetarium — adults and teens, $1.50; children under 12 years, $1. Cincinnati Art Museum — adults, $2; children and teens 12 to 18 years, $1; children 3 to 11 years, 25¢; admission free on Saturday. Sharon Woods Village — adults and teens, $1.50; children under 12, 50¢. Cincinati Zoo — adults and teens, $3.75; children 2 to 12, $1.50.

DIRECTIONS: From Indianapolis, take I-74 southeast to Cincinnati. From Cleveland, take I-71 southwest to Cincinnati.

FOR MORE INFORMATION: Call the Cincinnati Convention and Visitors Bureau, (513) 621-2142.

Ohio

Chagrin Falls: Small Town, U.S.A.

Chagrin Falls, Ohio

Driving Time: One-half hour east of Cleveland

Imagine Hollywood's version of the "perfect" Hometown, U.S.A.: quaint Main Street shops with friendly proprietors; grand Victorian homes with broad, green lawns; shady, tree-lined streets bordered by white picket fences; and, of course, the mandatory gazebo for summer band concerts. Add a tumbling, transparent waterfall right in the center of town — and you have Chagrin Falls, Ohio.

Unfortunately, most people think that towns like this only exist in the movies. But this picture-postcard village is only a short drive from Cleveland. The town has a diverse range of architectural styles — Greek Revival, Queen Anne, Italianate — and simple, but attractive structures that could be called "Midwestern farmhouse."

In the **business district** (Main St., E. Orange St., and River St.), extraordinary merchandise ranging from antiques to fine clothing and Oriental rugs is available. Stroll down Main Street. For antiques, stop in at **Once Upon a House** (corner of W. Washington and N. Franklin), **Ours 'N Yours** (E. Orange and N. Main Sts.), or **Chagrin Falls Antique Shop** (corner of W. Orange and N. Main). Art enthusiasts will want to check out the **River Street Gallery** (River and West Sts.). And for fine clothes, there's the **Shop for Pappagallo** (E. Orange St.), **Peter's Store for Men** (N. Main and Plaza Dr.), the **Whale's Tale** (N. Main and

E. Orange), and many more. Sample Chagrin Falls' sweets at the **Bavarian Pastry** Shop (N. Main St.) or **Cambridge Candies and Popcorn Shop** (corner of Bell and N. Main St).

(For more entertainment ideas in the area, see articles in this section on Cleveland, Mentor and Akron.)

BEST TIME TO VISIT: Any time of year. **DIRECTIONS:** Chagrin Falls is on the far east side of the Cleveland metropolitan area. Take I-480 to east side of town, exit at U.S. 422, and take 422 southeast to Chagrin Falls. **FOR MORE INFORMATION:** Call or write the Chagrin Valley Chamber of Commerce, 13½ N. Franklin St., Chagrin Falls, OH 44022; (216) 247-6607.

Pioneer Life Portrayed In Defiance

Defiance, Ohio

Driving Time: About 45 minutes southwest of Toledo

With the aromas of bubbling sorghum molasses and creamy apple butter wafting over the grounds, Au-Glaize Village, near Defiance, comes alive in celebration of the annual **Johnny Appleseed Festival**. With a lineup of activities that feature pioneer crafts, the festivities are held in mid-October to enhance the restored village's portrayal of pioneer life.

Currently, with 17 new and reconstructed buildings, **AuGlaize Village** (west of Defiance on Krouse Rd.) recreates the life and times of American settlers in the middle and late 19th century. Some of the sites include a cider mill, cane mill, doctor's office, blacksmith shop, church school, railroad station, and more. There's even an old-fashioned broom factory. Two farm museums display early-American farm implements; the military museum showcases various uniforms used at different periods in American history. But that's just a small sampling of the intriguing experiences and good "old-time" fun at AuGlaize Village.

In addition to the Johnny Appleseed Festival, there is an array of entertaining special events at the village from May through December. They include: **Week of Yesteryear** (mid-May), **Maumee Valley Frontier Festival** (early June), **Fort Defiance North-South Skirmish Association Shoot** (mid-July), **Harvest Demonstration** (end of July), **Craft Fair and Transportation Festival** (mid-August), **Cracker Barrel** (early September), **Halloween Lantern Tour** (late October), and **Butchering Demon-**

stration (mid-November). The grand finale to the year's activities is the **Old-Fashioned Christmas** in early December, when the shops are decked out with holly, calico angels, and all their best yuletide items.

(For more entertainment ideas in the area, see articles in this section on Toledo, Bowling Green, Findlay, and Sandusky.)

BEST TIME TO VISIT: During one of the special events. (Check with village for exact dates.)

HOURS: Memorial Day through August, 10 a.m.-5 p.m. Wednesday-Saturday, Sunday 1 p.m.-5 p.m.; September and October, weekends only, 1 p.m.-5 p.m.; closed October 31-Memorial Day, except for Christmas celebration.

ADMISSION: AuGlaize Village — non-event days, adults, $2; teens and children 6 and over, $1. Special events admission: adults, $3; teens and children 6 and over, $1.50.

DIRECTIONS: From Toledo, take U.S. 24 southwest, past Napoleon, to Defiance area. Continue around the city, following U.S. 24. Turn left (south) on Krouse Rd. It's a short distance to the village.

FOR MORE INFORMATION: Call or write Defiance County Historical Society, P.O. Box 801, Defiance, OH 43512; (419) 784-0107.

Ohio

History Comes To Life In Akron

Akron, Ohio

Driving Time: 45 minutes south of Cleveland

Experiencing life as it was in an 1850s farm and village is one of the many attractions families will find while visiting Akron.

The city, home of the University of Akron, features historical sites, museums, outdoor recreational spots, unusual shopping areas, and a great zoo, among other interesting places. Train enthusiasts will definitely want to visit **Railways of America** to view the collection of more than 1,000 scale-model trains.

Lifestyles and customs of the earliest Americans, the American Indians, are recreated through the exhibits of at **American Indian Art Hall of Fame** (5000 Akron-Cleveland Rd.) in Peninsula, Ohio. It's just a few miles north of the city, and well worth a stop. The six museum galleries display the artwork of 300 living Indian artisans from 40 different tribes. Visitors see many fine examples of Pueblo pottery, famous Navajo rugs, bead work, Indian dolls, and much more. Multi-media shows are offered to explain more about Indian culture and art.

In the city, another worthwhile stop is the **Perkins Mansion** (550 Copley Rd.). Built between 1835 and 1837, the large Greek Revival house sits high atop a hill overlooking the city. Colonel Simon Perkins, builder of the home, was a state representative whose father was one of the founders of the Village of Akron in 1825. In 1945, the property was purchased from the Perkins family by the Summit County Historical Society. Surrounded by more than 10 beautifully landscaped acres, the

house features some of the original Perkins furnishings and other historical objects.

Nearby is the **John Brown Home** (Copley and Diagonal Rds.), where the famous abolitionist lived for two years while he was associated with Colonel Perkins in the sheep and wool business.

More Old World charm and a bit of the British is in evidence at the **Stan Hywet Hall and Gardens**, an

authentic English Tudor mansion (714 N. Portage Path). In 1914, F.A. Seiberling, founder of Goodyear and Seiberling Rubber Companies, built the 65-room house. It's filled with furnishings and art objects from the 14th through 18th centuries. Master craftsmen from Europe created the carved woodwork and stained-glass windows. Colorful gardens of various shrubbery and flowers enhance the elegant atmosphere.

Hale Farm and Village in Bath, just north of Akron, offers another look at American history. The Hale House, an 1826 brick farmhouse, is the center of this historic farm. Early American skills and crafts, such as pottery making, weaving, candlemaking, glass blowing, and woodworking, are demonstrated in the barns. Restoration of village buildings, brought here from throughout Ohio, is ongoing. Here, visitors will see the various social, commercial, and residential buildings furnished with artifacts like those used by settlers. During the year, the village holds quilt shows, a harvest festival, and musical events. Many tourists enjoy eating lunch in the picnic area.

More of the area's scenic beauty is exhibited aboard the *Portage Princess* **paddlewheel boat**. Sightseeing tours, which pass charming homes and natural shoreline scenery, begin at the Harbor Inn Restaurant (562 Portage Lakes Dr.).

For more sightseeing outdoors, a trip to the **Akron Zoo** (500 Edgewood Ave.) is recommended. Upon entering the main gate, many visitors are surprised to suddenly leave the bustling city outside and find a relaxing park-like atmosphere where animals roam in their natural habitat. The 28-acre zoo has a petting farmyard with cows, chickens, horses, and pigs, as well as California Big Horn sheep (the only examples of this species east of the Rocky Mountains).

During an Akron visit your family may want to stop at the **Akron Art Museum** (70 E. Market St.), which

Summer activity at Hale Farm and Village

features numerous 20th-century art exhibits and a sculpture garden.

Goodyear Tire and Rubber Company (1202 E. Market St.) offers tours of the **Goodyear World of Rubber**. The displays include a simulated rubber plantation, two Indy 500 race cars, an artificial heart, a moon tire display, and more.

In Akron's downtown area is **Quaker Square** (120 E. Mill St.), a shopping, hotel, restaurant, and entertainment center housed in the original mills and silos of the Quaker Oats Company. The complex offers a myriad of opportunities for family fun (be sure to see the world's largest

collection of railroad memorabilia at the Railway Express Agency). Visitors may eat at the **Depot Restaurant** amidst a collection of mementoes of the railroad era. Outside the building are seven full-size antique railroad cars, a steam engine, and a caboose.

BEST TIME TO VISIT: Spring, summer, or fall.

HOURS: American Indian Art Hall of Fame — 10 a.m.-5 p.m. Tuesday through Saturday; noon-5 p.m. Sunday, April through December only; closed holidays. Akron Art Museum — noon-5 p.m. Tuesday through Friday, 9 a.m.-5 p.m. Saturday, 1-5 p.m. Sunday. Goodyear World of Rubber — 8:30 a.m.-4:30 p.m. Monday through Friday; closed weekends and holidays. Hale Farm and Village — May through October, 10 a.m.-5 p.m. Tuesday through Saturday, noon-5 p.m. Sunday and holidays. Stan Hywet Hall and Gardens — 10

a.m.-4 p.m. Tuesday through Saturday, 1-4 p.m. Sunday; closed holidays. Perkins Mansion and John Brown House — 1-5 p.m. Tuesday through Sunday; closed holidays. Akron Zoo — open end of April to first of October, 10 a.m.-5 p.m. Monday through Saturday, 10 a.m.-6 p.m. Sunday and holidays.

ADMISSION: American Indian Art Hall of Fame — adults, $2; children 6 to 12, $1; family rate, $6. Akron Art Museum and Goodyear World of Rubber, free. Hale Farm and Village — adults, $3.50; senior citizens, $2; children and teens 6 to 16, $2; children under 6, free. Perkins Mansion and John Brown House — adults, $1.50; children and teens to 16, $1 (price includes both houses). Akron Zoo — adults, $1.50; children and senior citizens, 75¢; group rates, 50¢.

DIRECTIONS: Akron is 41 miles south of Cleveland on I-77. The Indian Art Hall of Fame is in Peninsula. From Akron, take I-77 north, exit at Rt. 8. To reach Hale Farm and Village from Akron, take I-77 north toward Cleveland, exit at 138 (Ghent Rd.), turn left to Ira Rd., follow signs to Bath.

FOR MORE INFORMATION: Call Akron Convention and Visitors Bureau, (216) 376-5254.

Ohio

Thrill-A-Minute Action at Kings Island

Kings Island, Ohio

Driving Time: 25 minutes north of Cincinnati

A day at **Kings Island Family Entertainment Center** promises to be a fun-filled jamboree of laughs, adventure, and entertainment. Its six theme areas offer fantasy, thrilling rides, and live shows that feature everything from Broadway to bluegrass. Throughout the park, street performers entertain visitors with magic and song.

A stroll down **International Street**, at the main entrance, includes such wonders as the Eiffel Tower, a replica one-third the size of the original in Paris. On twin elevators, 2,000 guests may ride to the top in 30 seconds. Two observation decks provide visitors with a view of the surrounding countryside from 330 feet up. Along the street, European buildings lend the flavor of Italy, France, Spain, Switzerland, and Germany.

In **Hanna-Barbera Land**, Yogi Bear or perhaps one of the Flintstones will greet you. Or have your picture taken with one of the friendly storybook folks at the Photo Shop. Youngsters will be thrilled with the Hanna-Barbera carrousel, an electric train call Scooby Choo, and a Fool House with tilting floors and mirrored walls. Hungry visitors can stop at **Quick Draw's Cafe** and **Bamm Bamm's Bon Bons**.

For more adventurous guests, the park offers a **Wild Animal Safari**, where more than 350 wild animals from Africa, Asia, and North America roam on a 100-acre preserve. From a monorail train, visitors get a close look at such beasts as lions,

elephants, Bengal tigers, zebras, rhinos, ostriches, giraffes, bison, camels, and more. In the **Nairobi Nursery**, reptiles and small mammals are displayed. And for a real wildlife experience, how about a ride high atop a ponderous pachyderm? There's even breathtaking action in the entertainment section, where the **"Screamin' Demon"** roller coaster transports daring riders forward and backward through a 360-degree loop. The **Congo Curio** has a wide selection of souvenirs from Africa

and India. Stop in at **Kafe Kilimanjaro** for some "elephant ear" pastry (better than it sounds!).

All visitors, whatever their nationality, will enjoy a stop at **Oktoberfest**, Kings Island's version of the famous Bavarian festival. Jolly German music sets the mood for merrymaking as guests ride on the Flying Dutchman, Bayern Curve, or Der Spinnen Keggers. Perhaps the most thrilling ride is the Viking Fury, the world's largest swinging ship. Suspended high above a lake, the 53-foot by 9-foot ship combines speed, a rocking motion, and weightlessness as visitors are carried upward in an 80-foot arc, then suddenly plummeted downward again.

On the banks of the Ohio River, **Coney Island**, a depiction of the famous old amusement park in New York, provides a view of the roaring 20s with rides that were typical of the amusement parks of early days. One of the most popular attractions is "The Bat," the world's first and only suspended roller coaster, closely followed in popularity by "The Shake, Rattle, and Roll," "Tumblebug," and "Flying Carpets," to name only a few. The area also includes game stands, arcades, and galleries. Various foods are available at Cafe Mexicano, Potato Works, and the Transylvania Sausage Works.

Just a short walk from Coney Island takes visitors into quaint **Rivertown**, depicting life as it was in the Ohio riverboat days. Its attractions include the Miami Valley Railroad and boat rides that shoot the rapids (Kenton's Cove Keelboat Canal and Kings Mills Log Flume). The **Beast Roller Coaster** is the highest, fastest, and longest one in the world; it covers 35 densely wooded acres and has a 7,400-foot track. The official speed at the bottom of the 141-foot-long hill is 64.77 miles per hour!

The **Salt Water Circus aqua arena** headlines the lively antics of the sea lion and dolphin show. And at **Columbia Palace**, old-time fun is the attraction with nickelodeon music and a rousing show, "Belly Up to the Bar, Belles."

BEST TIME TO VISIT: Kings Island is open daily from late May through Labor Day and weekends from late April to late May. The Jack Nicklaus Sports Center is open from March through December. The College Football Hall of Fame, Kings Island Resort Inn, and Kings Island Campground are open year round.

HOURS: Kings Island opens at 9 a.m.

ADMISSION: Adults and children over 6, $12.95; children 3 to 6, $6.45; children 2 and under, free.

DIRECTIONS: From Cincinnati, take I-71 20 miles north to Kings Island exit.

FOR MORE INFORMATION: Call Kings Island, (513) 241-5410, or write Kings Island Family Entertainment Center, Kings Island, OH 45034.

Other Attractions

Sports buffs should visit the **College Football Hall of Fame** and the **Jack Nicklaus Sports Center** adjacent to the Kings Island park. However, if visitors are expecting to find only exhibits and displays, they may be surprised to also find ample opportunity for participation at both spots.

At the Hall of Fame, the famous Knute Rockne delivers one of his great inspirational talks. The speech may inspire some members of your team to try their luck at kicking a winning field goal with the "All-Star Kicker." In the strategy room, your team is invited to test football trivia knowledge at computer terminals that pose tough competition.

An hour or two of fairway fun is offered at the Jack Nicklaus Sports Center. The Bruin golf course has 18 three- and four-stroke holes set amidst trees, bunkers, and water hazards.

If tennis is more intriguing, there are five tournament-quality courts. It's a great place for mom and dad to relax while the kids are enjoying Kings Island.

Campers will find ample accommodations at the Kings Island Campground, featuring a swimming pool, playground, and volleyball and basketball courts. The **Kings Island Resort Inn** — (513) 241-5410 — offers excellent accommodations for visitors. The inn features a playground, swimming pool, paddleboat rides, tennis courts, and other fine amenities. Both the campground and the inn provide a free shuttle service to other areas of the Kings Island complex.

Ohio

A City That's A Mecca for Aviation Buffs

Dayton, Ohio

Driving Time: 1 hour northeast of Cincinnati; 3½ hours southwest of Cleveland; 3½ hours east of Indianapolis

From the Wright brothers to the Space Age, the **Air Force Museum** near Dayton contains one of the world's largest exhibitions of aviation history. The museum, located at Wright-Patterson Air Force Base, displays more than 150 major historical aircraft and missiles.

In fact, tourists who are interested in aviation can find a wealth of information and exhibits related to the phenomenon of flying, for Dayton is the home of Orville and Wilbur Wright. Known as the "Birthplace of Aviation," the city focuses attention on its heritage by inviting visitors to travel the **"Aviation Trail."** Through the city and suburbs the trail guides the visitor on a history of flight, starting with a tour of the **Wright neighborhood**, on Dayton's west side. Located there are the **Wright Print Shop and Cycle Shop**. The ancestor of all modern aircraft, the Wright Flyer III is displayed in **Wright Hall at Carillon Park** (2001 S. Patterson Blvd.). The famous brothers called this aircraft "the one in which we learned to fly." In addition, the park features a replica of the last **Wright Cycle Shop**, where the first airplane was built.

Farther along the trail tourists may view Wright family memorabilia from their home, **"Hawthorn Hill,"** an elegant Greek Revival mansion (901 Herman Ave.) that was the home off Orville, his father, and his sister for many years. Wilbur, however, died before the residence was

completed. Other stops on the tour are Woodland Cemetery, where Wilbur, Orville, and sister Katherine are buried; Wright Memorial, located on Huffman Prairie, where the Wrights tested early planes, and South Field, another testing field.

But Dayton offers much more than aviation history. The city's **Art Institute** (Riverview and Forest Aves.) showcases an impressive collection of works that include European and American paintings and sculpture, Asian works, classical and pre-Columbian arts. The **Dayton Museum of Natural History** (2629 Ridge Ave.) also features some intriguing exhibits.

Another delightful area is the **Oregon Historic District**, where visitors are invited to step back into the 19th century. Strolling through the neighborhood, your family will encounter unusual antique shops, artisan boutiques, and novel restaurants.

For some additional adventure, your family will find an enchanting world of fun and frolic at **Americana Amusement Park** (30 miles south, off I-75). Exciting rides such as The Whip, Flying Coaster, and Rock-o-

Plane are among the attractions. In addition, there are lively shows at the **Country Bear Jubilee and Theater House**. Arcades, picnic areas, swimming facilities, and, of course, more rides and shows fill out the agenda. Refreshments are available at the **Beer Garden, Dry Gulch Saloon,** or at the **Calico Confectionary**.

BEST TIME TO VISIT: Summer.
HOURS: Air Force Museum—9 a.m.-5 p.m. Monday through Friday; 10 a.m.-6 p.m. weekends. Carillon Park—May 31 through October 31, 10 a.m.-8:30 p.m. Tuesday through Saturday; 1-8:30 p.m. Sunday; closed Monday except on holidays. Wright Memorial —9a.m.-8 p.m. daily. Americana Amusement Park—mid-June through end of August, 11 a.m.-10 p.m. Tuesday through Friday; 11 a.m.-11 p.m. weekends; weekends mid-April through June and during September. Natural History Museum—9 a.m.-6 p.m. Monday, Wednesday, Thursday, Friday; 9 a.m.-9 p.m. Tuesday and Friday.
ADMISSION: Americana Amusement Park—adults, teens, and children over 5, $5.50; children 3 to 5, $1.50; children under 3, free.
DIRECTIONS: From Cincinnati, take I-75 north to Dayton. To reach Americana Amusement Park (30 miles from Dayton), take I-75 (from either south or north), exit at Monroe-Lebanon (Exit 29), follow to Rt. 63 west, follow Rt. 63 to Rt. 4.
FOR MORE INFORMATION: Call Dayton/Montgomery County Convention and Visitors Bureau, (513) 226-1444; Americana Amusement Park, (513) 539-7339.

Why Toledo, Ohio? Well, Why not?

Toledo, Ohio

Driving Time: 1 hour south of Detroit; 1½ hours west of Cleveland

Why visit Toledo? Because it was named after Toledo, Spain? (It was.) Because it has 400,000 persons and is still alive and kicking? (It does, and it is.) Because John Denver made it famous by satirically singing about "Saturday Night in Toledo, Ohio"? (He did, much to the occasional chagrin of city boosters.)

Let's face it, you probably don't set out for Toledo, Ohio; but while passing through destined for elsewhere, make the most of it. Why? Because the city has its attractions, and they compare well with other cities of its size.

One of your first stops should be the **Toledo Zoological Gardens** (2700 Broadway), which boasts a collection of more than 2,200 mammals, birds, reptiles, and fish. The 33-acre zoo includes a freshwater aquarium, museum of natural science, children's zoo, indoor trout stream, greenhouse, and botanical gardens. Rides on a miniature steam railroad, helicopter, and merry-go-round are also available. During the summer months, the band shell and amphitheater feature musical and theatrical productions.

At the **Wolcott House Museum** (1031 River Rd., S.W., off Rt. 24), visitors get a glimpse of the lifestyle of bygone days. Built by Judge James Wolcott in 1827, this grand Federal Revival house was the scene of several important events in Maumee Valley history. The 19th-century furniture reflects an elegant way of life during our country's early years. The complex also contains a log cabin,

farmhouse, depot, and Greek Revival town house. Just a few miles south of Toledo is **Fort Meigs**, built during the War of 1812 (see article on Bowling Green.)

A visit to the **Toledo Museum of Art** (2445 Monroe St.) provides a look at many intriguing collections from ancient Egypt to the 20th century. Besides paintings, prints, photos, tapestries, and sculptures, the museum has a fine glass collection. Some of the highlights include the galleries of 17th-century Dutch, Flemish, and French art. But don't leave before seeing the Egyptian mummies!

The museum is located in the historic **Old West End** of Toledo, so take a walking tour before moving on to other attractions. The area features the largest collection of 19th-century Victorian architecture in Ohio. The elaborate gingerbread houses, with their gabled roofs, stained-glass windows, towers, and turrets, recall a more leisurely horse-and-buggy era.

During the summer, Toledo visitors are invited to take in more area scenery aboard the *Arawanna II* riverboat. The half-hour trip takes tourists down the Maumee River.

Imagine the Indians who once lurked on the shore! (Board the boat in International Park in East Toledo.)

Crosby Gardens (5403 Elmer Dr.) and the several **Toledo-area Metro-Parks** provide ample opportunities for hiking, picnicking, biking, cross-country skiing, and enjoying the natural surroundings. **Wildwood Preserve**, one of the parks, is on the grounds of **Manor House**, a Georgian Colonial mansion built by a Toledo industrialist. The home is open to the public (see information below). At Pearson and Farnsworth Parks, visitors may rent pedal boats or canoes.

BEST TIME TO VISIT: Summer.
HOURS: Wolcott House Museum—April to December, 1-4 p.m. Wednesday through Sunday. Toledo Zoo—10 a.m.-5 p.m. April 1 to September 30; 10 a.m.-4 p.m. October 1 to March 31. Toledo Museum of Art—9 a.m.-5 p.m. Tuesday through Saturday; 1-5 p.m. Sunday; closed holidays. Arawanna II Riverboat—weekends and holidays, Memorial Day through Labor Day, 1:15, 2:45, 3:30, and 4:15 p.m. Manor House—2-5 p.m. Wednesday through Sunday all year.
ADMISSION: Wolcott House Museum—adults, $1; children and teens under 18, 50¢. Toledo Zoo—adults, $2; children 2 to 11, 75¢. Arawanna II—adults,$1.50; children, $1.
DIRECTIONS: From Cleveland, take the Ohio Turnpike (I-80/I-90) west to Toledo.
FOR MORE INFORMATION: Call the Toledo Area Chamber of Commerce, (419) 243-8191.

Ohio

Youngstown: A Pleasant Surprise

Youngstown, Ohio

Driving Time: About 1¼ hours east of Cleveland

Mill Creek Park, in southwest Youngstown, is said to be Ohio's most beautiful natural park. It probably is, in fact! Established in 1891 by the state legislature and a city vote, the 2,389-acre area includes a six-mile-long gorge, foot trails, scenic drives, and three sparkling lakes. During America's early days, pioneer industries operated along Mill Creek; today, some remnants of these mills, quarries, and homes still remain. The Old Mill, the third flour mill to stand on that site, has displays of early industry in Mill Creek and the surrounding Youngstown area. In addition, the grounds include a log cabin built in 1816 by Dr. Timothy Woodbridge.

From north to south, the park's terrain ranges from steep hillsides, through a gorge, to rolling areas, swamps, and dense woods. Throughout the park, there are areas designated for a wide variety of recreational activities, from boating and fishing to tennis, golf, ice skating, and hiking.

Visitors who wish to know more about the Youngstown area should stop at the **Arms Museum** (648 Wick Ave.). **Greystones**, the lovely, large home of Mr. Wilford P. Arms, is the site of the museum, which contains extensive exhibits of various books, papers, and memorabilia relating to the history of the Mahoning Valley. Rooms on the mansion's main floor remain much the same as they were when the Arms family lived there. The family's furniture and portraits are displayed along with fine collections of silver, china, crystal, Orien-

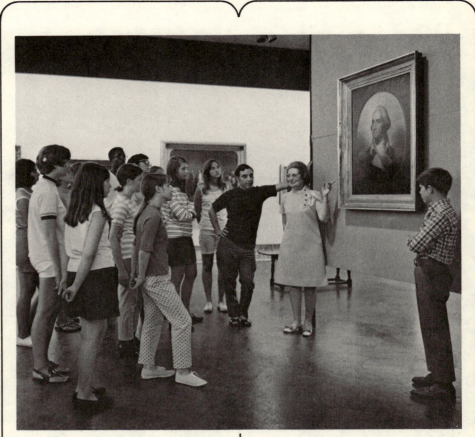

tal rugs, and art objects. On the lower floor there are exhibits of pioneer farm and household tools as well as a gun collection. Throughout the museum, period gowns are displayed on mannequins. Italian stained-glass windows in the mansion date from 1881. On the upper floor of the museum, the history of the valley and its people is depicted through photographs, costumes, and artifacts.

Another interesting stop on a tour of Youngstown is the **Butler Institute of American Art** (524 Wick Ave.). More than 100,000 persons visit here annually to view exhibits of art from colonial days to the present. When the museum opened in 1919, there were 80 items on display; today, the impressive collection numbers well over 4,000 items. As visitors wander leisurely through the Italian Renaissance-style building, they see paintings, sculpture, guns, ceramics, ship models, and even an unusual collection of antique glass bells. During the

year, the Butler Institute sponsors special exhibitions that attract visitors from throughout the country, such as **The Mid-Year Show, Ohio Ceramic and Sculpture Show**, and **Area Artist Annual**.

Perhaps the sweetest way to end a day in Youngstown would be a tour of **Gorant Candies** (8301 Market St.), where the art of chocolate making is demonstrated.

BEST TIME TO VISIT: Summer is probably your best bet, but Mill Creek Park is great for winter sports, too.

HOURS: Arms Museum—1-4 p.m. Tuesday through Friday; 1:30 p.m.-5 p.m. weekends. Butler Institute of American Art—11 a.m.-4 p.m. Tuesday through Saturday; noon-4 p.m. Sunday; closed on major holidays. Gorant Candies—reservations required for tours, which are given 10 a.m.-3 p.m. Monday through Friday; call (216) 726-8821.

ADMISSION: Arms Museum—adults, $2; college students, $1; teens 14 to 18, 50¢; children under 14 and senior citizens, free.

DIRECTIONS: From Cleveland, take I-80 east to Youngstown.

FOR MORE INFORMATION: Call the Youngstown Area Chamber of Commerce, (216) 744-2131.

Space Travel, History, Caverns— All in Lima

Lima, Ohio

Driving Time: About 2½ hours north of Cincinnati; 3½ hours south of Detroit

Intriguing attractions that focus on American history, from pioneer days to the Space Age, are discovered each year by visitors to Lima and the surrounding area.

The **Allen County Museum** (620 W. Market St., Lima) has such diverse residences as a rustic log cabin and an elaborate Victorian mansion. The **MacDonell House** has period rooms furnished in the elegant 1890's style, with parquet floors and carved woodwork of fine mahogany, cherry, and white oak. An unusual aspect of the exhibit is the trophy room's collection of albino birds and mammals. On the museum grounds stands an oil well built for the Bicentennial to commemorate one of Lima's pioneer oil men.

The **railroad exhibit at Lincoln Park** (Shawnee and Elm Sts.) contains the last steam locomotive built in Lima, Nickel Plate No. 779, as well as other railroad cars.

A few miles south on I-75, another popular museum chronicles man's achievements in air and space travel — the **Neil Armstrong Air and Space Museum** (Fisher Rd. at I-75, Wapakoneta). Open since 1972, the museum's architecture reflects the boldness and wonder of space exploration: a futuristic design of concrete topped by a white dome measuring 60 feet in diameter. Inside this extraordinary structure are hot-air balloons and dirigibles, and a recon-

structed aero-boat built and flown by the Wright brothers in 1913.

Next, the **Space Flight Gallery** exhibits the Gemini VIII spacecraft used by Neil Armstrong and Maj. David Scott in 1966. Several items relating to Armstrong's boyhood aviation interests are showcased with a backup spacesuit. In another section, a mini-theater documents America's space progress. For a remarkable experience, step into the 18-foot square infinity cube. Entirely lined with mirrors, the cube simulates a space voyage.

Another stop on a Lima-area tour should be the historic **Piatt Castles** (east of West Liberty on Rt. 245), two 19th-century homes built in Norman French and Flemish styles. Castle Piatt Mac-a-Cheek, named for an Indian tribe, is a three-story Norman structure with a five-story watch tower. Built by General Abraham S. Piatt, the castle features ceilings painted by a French artist. Castle Mac-O-Chee, built a few years later

by General Piatt's brother, sports twin towers crowned by picturesque spires.

Nearby are the breathtaking crystal rock formations of the **Ohio Caverns.** More colorful formations may be seen at **Zane's Caverns** in nearby Bellefontaine.

BEST TIME TO VISIT: Summer.
HOURS: Allen County Historical Society — 1:30-5 p.m. daily except Monday and national holidays. Armstrong Museum — March through November, 9:30 a.m.-5 p.m. Wednesday through Saturday; noon-5 p.m. Sunday. Piatt Castles — Memorial Day through Labor Day, 9 a.m.-5 p.m. daily; April to late May and after Labor Day, 11 a.m.-5 p.m. Ohio Caverns — 9 a.m.-5 p.m. daily, April through October; 9 a.m.-4 p.m. daily, November through March. Zane Caverns — May through September, 10 a.m. to 5 p.m. daily; April and October, weekends only.
ADMISSION: Allen County Historical Society — free. Armstrong Museum — adults and teens, $1.50; children 6 to 12, 75¢; children under 6, free. Ohio Caverns — adults and teens, $4; children 6 to 12, $2. Zane Caverns — adults and teens, $3.50; children 6 to 12, $2.
DIRECTIONS: Lima is located north of Cincinnati and Dayton on I-75. Wapakoneta is south of Lima off I-75. West Liberty and Bellefontaine are southeast of Lima on Rt. 68.
FOR MORE INFORMATION: Call Lima Area Convention and Visitors Bureau, (419) 222-6045.

Ohio

Columbus: Big City With Small-Town Appeal

Columbus, Ohio

Driving Time: About 1½ hours from Cincinnati; 3 hours from Cleveland

Tourists usually find out that Columbus, Ohio's state capital for 150 years, is a city of contrasts. In just minutes, visitors can travel from the hustle and bustle of downtown city streets and towering modern office buildings to an historic old neighborhood where 150-year-old houses grace quiet tree-lined streets. It's a city blending the old with the new — the fruits of modern progress with an apparent reverence for its historic roots.

One of the most popular stops on a city tour is the **Center of Science and Industry** (COSI) (280 E. Broad St.). Visitors can move from a coal mine to a space-travel exhibit to the Street of Yesteryear. Other displays focus on human anatomy and health, chemistry, antique dolls, veterinary medicine, communications, clocks, and oceanography, to name just a few.

A visit to the **Columbus Museum of Art** (480 E. Broad St.) will acquaint your family with works representing many different periods, from 20th-century French and American painting to Oriental, American Indian, and pre-Columbian pieces.

At the **Ohio Village** (I-71 and 17th Ave.) visitors can take a journey back to the days before the Civil War. The 14 restored buildings in the complex represent architectural styles found throughout Ohio. Blacksmiths, printers, weavers, and other crafts people

Bronze Henry Moore Sculpture at the Columbus Museum of Art

in period costumes contribute to the realistic atmosphere of 18th-century America.

In addition, the **Columbus Zoo** always abounds in entertaining and amusing sights as the numerous animals, birds, and fish go about the business of daily life. The typical lions, tigers, and bears are joined by such creatures as jaguars, pandas, camels, otters, eagles, and, of course, elephants.

Another worthwhile place to visit is **The Continent**, "a little city in the corner of town" that features specialty shops, movies, restaurants, and cafes in an Old World, European setting. The **French Market** — 35 shops filled with vintage wines, fine meats, tasty cheeses, colorful produce, and deli treats — is a delightful place to pick up the ingredients for a picnic lunch.

Perhaps a fitting finale to a day in Columbus is a tour of the **Anheuser-Busch Brewery**, where visitors learn about the process of making beer. Producing almost seven million bar-

rels annually, the Columbus brewery is part of the St. Louis-based company, the world's largest beer brewer. A full-size replica of one of the famous Clydesdale horses greets visitors at the brewery entrance.

BEST TIME TO VISIT: Spring ro summer.

HOURS: Center of Science and Industry — 10 a.m.-5 p.m. Monday through Saturday; 1-5:30 p.m. Sunday. Museum of Art — 11 a.m.-5 p.m. Tuesday, Thursday, Friday, Sunday; 11 a.m.-8:30 p.m. Wednesday; 10 a.m.-5 p.m. Saturday; closed Monday. Ohio Village — April 1 through December 23, 9 a.m.-5 p.m. Wednesday through Saturday; 10 a.m.-5 p.m. Sunday. Columbus Zoo — Memorial Day through Labor Day, 10 a.m.-7 p.m.; winter hours, 10 a.m.-5 p.m. The Continent—10 a.m.-9 p.m. Monday through Saturday; noon-6 p.m. Sunday.

ADMISSION: Center of Science and Industry — adults, $3.50; students and senior citizens, $2; family rate, $10. Museum of Art — adults, $1.50; senior citizens, children, and students, 50¢; Tuesday is free admission for all. Ohio Village — parking fee, $2 per car. Columbus Zoo — adults, $3; children 2 to 12, $1.25; children under 2, free; senior citizens, $1.50.

DIRECTIONS: Columbus is located in the center of Ohio, at intersection of I-70 and I-71.

FOR MORE INFORMATION: Call Columbus Convention and Visitors Bureau, (614) 221-6623.

Sea World: Where Whales, Water Skiing Mix

Aurora, Ohio

Driving Time: 30 minutes from Cleveland

A world of performing sea creatures and an amusement park full of chills and thrills can be found in Aurora, just a short drive from Cleveland.

Sea World, mid-America's only marine life park, has as its stars whales and water skiers, pearl divers, Hawaiian revues, and hilarious sea lion shows. The beautiful 85-acre entertainment center features eight exciting shows — 13 entertainment concepts in all — that are delightful and educational.

For example, in "The Shamu Experience," killer whale Shamu stars in a double ballet of whales in which two trainers and two killer whales mirror behavior in graceful, perfectly timed movements. Dolphins join the performance and swim side-by-side with the whales, their natural enemies in the sea.

Nearby, two California sea lions, Clyde and Seamore, perform their "Spooky, Kooky Castle Show" at the seal and otter stadium. Felix the otter and Uncle Smedley the walrus join the line-up of entertainers. However, animals aren't the only performers at Sea World. A ceremonial dragon dance opens the act of the "Chinese Acrobats of Taiwan" as the audience marvels at their agile maneuvers in a gymnastic display.

There's more action at the "Hollywood Stunt Show," including three-story falls, realistic fist fights, and gun duels. In the "Great American Ski Show," world-class skiers and skillful boat drivers exhibit a wide

variety of ballet positions and ski tricks.

Other attractions:

• **Cap'n Kid's World**, where kids can skipper a remote-controlled boat, frolic amidst thousands of multi-colored plastic balls, and climb a net leading to a real pirate ship.

• Master magician Ralph Adams in an **"Arabian Nights"** show of illusions and magic tricks.

• At night, Sea World lights up the skies with fireworks, including a floating parade of Sea World characters.

• The Japanese Village with its pearl divers, white whale feeding and petting pool, and other attractions.

At the nearby **Geauga Lake** amusement park, there are more than 100 rides and features, including costumed characters and a Kiddieland. Other attractions are magic shows and live musical shows performed throughout the day at the Country Music and Palace Theatres; rides on one of the park's supercoasters, the

Double Loop or the Big Dipper; and the unique Cinema 180, where the audience becomes part of the show. Three sit-down restaurants and fast-food stands offer foods ranging from steak to popcorn.

BEST TIME TO VISIT: Both Sea World and Geauga Lake can be very crowded on summer weekends; try to visit during the week or in the spring.

HOURS: Sea World — 9 a.m. daily from the weekend before Memorial Day through early September. Geauga Lake — noon-8 p.m. weekends, early May through late May; 10 a.m.-10 p.m. weekends, late May through Labor Day; 11 a.m.-10 p.m. weekdays, early June through Labor Day.

ADMISSION: Sea World — adults and children 12 and over, $10.95; children 3 to 11, $9.95; children under 3, free; senior citizens, $8.50. Season passes good for unlimited visits during one calendar year are $19.95 for adults and children 12 and older; $17.95 for children 3 to 11. Geauga Lake — adults and children over 3, $9.95; children 3 and under, free; senior citizens, $5.95 Monday through Friday.

DIRECTIONS: From Cleveland, take I-480 east to Solon/Rt. 91 exit; turn right at Rt. 91 and then left on Rt. 43 to Sea World or Geauga Lake.

FOR MORE INFORMATION: Call Sea World, (216) 562-8101; Geaua Lake, (216) 562-9393 for 24-hour information, or (216) 562-7131.

Ohio

Bob Evans: Down on The Farm Experience

Athens, Ohio

Driving Time: About 2 hours from Columbus

A day at **Bob Evans Farms** in Rio Grande, Ohio, will be one full of learning experiences and fun-filled activities for the whole family. From April through October the farm offers a variety of attractions, from craft demonstrations to canoeing. Almost every weekend of the visiting season features a farm event focusing on a different theme, such as the antiques fair, canoe race, or the International Chicken Flying Meet.

Bob Evans, founder and president of Bob Evans Farms, opened a restaurant in nearby Gallipolis, Ohio, shortly after World War II and soon began making the pork sausage that has become famous in American households. In 1953 he bought a farm. As the popularity of the restaurants grew, the company expanded. Now there are more than 90 Bob Evans Restaurants in seven states.

On the farm, visitors are treated to a glimpse of the lifestyle of their ancestors. In the **Craft Barn,** your family will enjoy watching such old-fashioned skills as quilting and spinning. The **Farm Museum** exhibits farm implements like those used by early American pioneers.

Trained guides lead **free wagon tours** and **walking tours** to acquaint visitors with the overall operation and history of the farm. For those who want a closer look at the surrounding countryside, there are miles of **bridle paths**. and for visitors interested in a bit of the Old West lifestyle, **overnight trail rides** are offered Tuesday, Friday, and Saturday evening

during June, July, and August (reservations necessary).

For more outdoor fun, the farm operates the **Raccoon Creek Canoe Livery**, with five different trips on the creek (weekends only in April, May, September, and October; daily between Memorial Day and Labor Day).

In October, the **Bob Evans Farm Festival** features a wide assortment of entertainment from the good old days. More than 125 craftsmen demonstrate their arts, which include weaving, leathermaking, chair caning, candlemaking, and toymaking, just to name a few. Children 8 to 13 years old are invited to join in the rambunctious pig scramble. And visitors have a chance to find out if chickens really can fly at the extraordinary chicken-flying demonstration. (Bob Evans is commander of the International Chicken Flying Association!) During the festivities there is continuous country music on two stages, with old-time clogging and folk dancing.

In the **Athens** area (about 35 miles north of Rio Grande), there are three state parks that offer camping, hiking, boat rentals, and beautiful scenery for outdoor enthusiasts. They are **Strouds Run** (five miles east of Athens off U.S. 50), **Burr Oak** (three

miles north of Athens on U.S. 33, then 14 miles north on Rt. 13), and **Lake Hope** (14 miles northwest of Athens on Rt. 56, then 6 miles south of Rt. 677).

While in the area, you might want to visit **Ohio University** in Athens, founded in 1804. For campus tours, contact the Admissions Office, (614) 594-5511. Also, in nearby **Nelsonville**, the **Hocking Valley Scenic Railway** offers tours on weekends and holidays. Pulled by a steam locomotive, the train travels through beautiful rolling hills for the 1¼-hour round trip.

BEST TIME TO VISIT: Summer or fall.
HOURS: Bob Evans Farm — 9 a.m.–5 p.m. daily, April through October. Hocking Valley Scenic Railway—noon, 2, and 4 p.m. Saturday, Sunday, and holidays, Memorial Day through end of October.
ADMISSION: Bob Evans Farm—free. Hocking Valley Scenic Railway—adults and teens, $4; children 2-11, $2.50.
DIRECTIONS: From Columbus, take U.S. 35 southeast and follow past Jackson to Rio Grande; follow signs to Bob Evans Farm. To reach Athens area from Rio Grande, take U.S. 35 east toward Gallipolis; take Rt. 7 north to junction of U.S. 33; follow north to Athens. For the Hocking Valley Scenic Railway, take U.S. 33 north from Athens 15 miles to Nelsonville.
FOR MORE INFORMATION: Call or write Bob Evans Farm, Box 330, Rio Grande OH 45674, (614) 245-5305; or the Athens County Tourism Bureau, 331 Richland Ave., Athens, OH 45701, (614) 592-1819.

917.7
N

36 545

One, Two, Three, Hike! At the Hall of Fame

Canton, Ohio

Driving Time: 1 hour south of Cleveland

Football, America's most popular sport, is the focus of a modern four-building complex in Canton that includes the **Pro Football Hall of Fame** (2121 Harrison Ave., N.W.). A seven-foot bronze statue of the legendary Jim Thorpe greets visitors, who ascend a spiral ramp to the exhibition area. Even the 52-foot ceiling dome becomes part of the atmosphere — it's shaped like a football!

Some of the displays include a **Pro Football Photo Art Gallery, Enshrinee Mementoes Room**, and **Pro Football Adventure Room**, where photos of all Super Bowl games are posted. The movie theater shows a different action-packed show every hour. One of the favorite activities of tourists is testing their football knowledge at the television monitors placed throughout the museum. Even those who are not football fans enjoy the experience.

But if football is not your game, there's plenty more to keep visitors entertained in Canton. The **Classic Car Museum** (555 Market Ave. S.) features antique, classic, and special-interest autos, many like the ones your grandfather used to drive. The collection includes such treasures as a 1922 Holmes, 1928 Packard Phaeton, 1914 Benham, and even a 1937 art-carved hearse.

Two more points of interest are dedicated to President William McKinley: **the McKinley Monument**, a national historic landmark where President McKinley, his wife,

National Football League Hall of Fame at Canton

and two children are buried, and the **McKinley Museum of History, Science and Industry** (749 Hazlett Ave., N.W.). The museum's collection includes almost 200 years of United States history chronicled in exhibits, displays, and audio-visual presentations. The historical section features four different period room settings, including a pioneer kitchen, toy room, and Victorian parlor. In the **Street of Shops**, visitors travel back in time to see an authentic pioneer house, general store, shops, and offices. In the **Science Hall**, visitors are invited to operate many of the displays themselves, exploring the wonders of scientific progress.

The home of **W.H. Hoover**, founder of the Hoover Company, is another interesting spot. The home is restored with period furniture and various models of early and present-day vacuum cleaners. Canton-area history is depicted in many intriguing displays, documents, and photos of historical significance to the area.

During the warmer months of the year, the **Canton Garden Center** (1615 Stadium Park, N.W.) is ablaze with the vibrant colors of many different flowers.

About 10 miles south of Canton is **Fort Laurens** (Rt. 1, Bolivar), the only American fort built during the Revolutionary War. A re-enactment of the war and a museum of 18th-century memoribilia and artifacts are featured.

BEST TIME TO VISIT: Spring and summer.

HOURS: Pro Football Hall of Fame — Memorial Day through Labor Day, 9 a.m.-8 p.m. daily; rest of the year, 9 a.m.-5 p.m. daily. McKinley Museum and Monument — 10 a.m.-5 p.m. Tuesday through Friday; Saturday, noon-5 p.m.; Sunday, 1:30-5 p.m. Canton Garden Center — daily, 9 a.m.-dusk. Hoover Historical Center — Sunday through Friday, 1-5 p.m. North Canton Heritage Society, 9 a.m.-4:30 p.m. Tuesday through Friday; Saturday, 9 a.m.-noon. Canton Classic Car Museum — 11 a.m.-6 p.m. Tuesday through Saturday, noon-6 p.m. Sunday. Fort Laurens — April through October, 9 a.m.-7 p.m. Tuesday through Sunday.

ADMISSION: Pro Football Hall of Fame — adults, $3; senior citizens, $1.50; children 5 to 13, $1; family group rate, $8. Canton Classic Car Museum — adults, $1.50; senior citizens, $1; children 6 and over, $1; under 6, free. McKinley Museum and Monument — adults, $2; senior citizens, $1; children 5 to 18, $1.

DIRECTIONS: From Cleveland, take I-77 south, past Akron, into Canton. To reach Fort Laurens, take I-77 south out of Canton to Bolivar.

FOR MORE INFORMATION: Call Stark County Convention and Visitors Bureau, (216) 456-7253, or Pro Football Hall of Fame, (216) 456-8207.

Ohio

Bowling Green: A College and The War of 1812

Bowling Green, Ohio

Driving Time: 30 minutes south of Toledo

Bowling Green offers opportunities for sightseeing and entertaining experiences. Children will enjoy a visit to the town's amusement park, while the entire family will learn a bit of Ohio history at Fort Meigs.

Bowling Green is a thriving city of 25,000 and the home of **Bowling Green State University**, founded in 1910. Prospective college students might enjoy a tour of the 1,200-acre campus. It's especially beautiful in the fall.

Fort Meigs, built in 1813 by General William Henry Harrison and named for Governor Return Jonathan Meigs, was first used as a fortified winter camp and supply depot. However, during the War of 1812, 3,000 troops were moved to the fort to defend the area against the British, led by Colonel Henry Proctor. Of course, the Americans did not give up; they successfully held the fort. Today, visitors can learn about Ohio's role in the war through presentations given by costumed interpreters. Brief talks are scheduled at major points of interest: the block houses, cannon batteries, and earthen traverses where Harrison's men withstood the British attack. A diorama depicts life at Fort Meigs as it was in the early 19th century. In one of the block houses is a fascinating display of weapons and artifacts from the war.

On weekends, Fort Meigs becomes even more realistic as costumed soldiers set up camp. And on summer evenings, lantern tours offer an in-

Taking it easy at the African Lion Safari in Port Clinton, Ohio

triguing adventure into the past.

Laughs, thrills, and spills will be the order of the day spent at **Vollmar's Park**. For almost a century families have enjoyed outings at this amusement park. Until 1900 the park site was used by Civil War veterans as a private fishing camp. The old-time atmosphere lends itself to the park's theme, which is plain, old-fashioned fun. Families will enjoy a ride on a miniature steam-powered train and, of course, on the traditional roller coaster. Many visitors bring a picnic lunch to eat while relaxing on the grounds. However, the park midway stands offer cotton candy, hot dogs, and other traditional carnival foods for hungry guests.

There are other sightseeing attractions in Bowling Green that provide both educational and interesting information. **Cain's Potato Chip Factory** offers half-hour tours Tuesday, Wednesday, and Thursday. **WFOB Radio** also welcomes visitors to its station offices. Both of these tours must be arranged in advance (see information below).

In nearby **Waterville**, step back into the days when railroads ruled the country with a trip on **The Bluebird Passenger Train**. The delightful

20-mile excursion travels between Waterville and Grand Rapids (the round trip takes about two hours). The train, powered by a steam locomotive, takes visitors over a section that was once part of the famous "Nickel Plate Road." One of the trip's highlights is a spectacular journey over a 900-foot-long bridge across the Maumee River at Grand Rapids.

BEST TIME TO VISIT: Warmer weather months.

HOURS: Bowling Green State University — tours are given at 11 a.m. and 2 p.m. weekdays, Saturday at 11 a.m.; tours begin at the Admissions Office. Vollmar's Park — 9 a.m.-9 p.m. Sunday through Friday; rides operate from noon until closing. Fort Meigs — 9:30 a.m.-5 p.m. April through mid-June and Labor Day through late October, 10 a.m.-6 p.m. mid-June through Labor Day. Bluebird Passenger Train — rides leave from Waterville at noon, 2:30 and 4:15 p.m. daily except Monday, May through October. Cain's Potato Chip Factory — tours given 9-10:30 a.m. and 12:30-2 p.m. Tuesday, Wednesday, and Thursday. Radio Station WFOB — tours given on weekday afternoons.

ADMISSION: Vollmar's Park — different prices for various rides; no admission fee for entrance to park. Bluebird Passenger Train — adults and children 12 and over, $4.50; children under 12, $2.25; senior citizens, $4.

DIRECTIONS: From Toledo, take I-75 south to Bowling Green. To reach Waterville from Bowling Green, take Rt. 64 north.

FOR MORE INFORMATION: Call Bowling Green Chamber of Commerce, (419) 353-7945; Bowling Green State University, (419) 372-2086; Bluebird Passenger Train, (419) 878-7299; Vollmar's Park, (419) 823-7125.

Bellevue's Impressive Caverns

Bellevue, Ohio

Driving Time: About 1¼ hours southwest of Cleveland; about 1½ hours north of Columbus

With the bottomless "Old Mist'ry River" flowing deep below, the **Seneca Caverns**, in Bellevue, are one of the Midwest's natural wonders. Known as the "earthquake crack," the area is a gigantic split in the earth with some caverns measuring 250 feet long. There are eight different "rooms" on seven levels. One of the unusual aspects of the caverns is that the rock formations of the roofs and floors of each space are juxtaposed so that they would fit together perfectly.

All areas of the caverns are illuminated with colorful lighting effects that enhance the exhibition. Through the years, various artifacts have been uncovered in the caverns. One of the most valuable discoveries was a stone Indian rug needle, dating to a period before 400 A.D., recovered from 80 feet underground.

(For more entertainment ideas in the area, see articles in this section on Sandusky, Port Clinton, Put-in-Bay, and Toledo.)

BEST TIME TO VISIT: Summer or early fall.
HOURS: Seneca Caverns — May 30 to Labor Day, 9 a.m.-7 p.m. daily; May, September, and October, 9 a.m.-5 p.m. weekends only.
ADMISSION: Seneca Caverns — adults and teens over 13, $4; teens and children between 7 and 13, $2.75.
DIRECTIONS: From Cleveland, take the Ohio Turnpike (1-80-90) west to Exit 7 (Norwalk-Sandusky); follow U.S. 250 south, then Rt. 113 west to Bellevue; pick up Rt. 269 south to Seneca Caverns. From Columbus, take U.S. 23 north, past Delaware and Marion; north of Marion, pick up Rt. 4 north; continue on Rt. 4 past Attica, to junction of Rt. 269; follow north to caverns.
FOR MORE INFORMATION: Call or write Bellevue Area Chamber of Commerce, 202 W. Main St., Bellevue, OH 44811; (419) 483-2182.

The "Canadian Lumberjack Show," a typical action-oriented attraction at Sea World in Aurora, Ohio

Visiting Ohio Valley Wine Country

Cincinnati, Ohio

Driving Time: About one-half hour northeast of Cincinnati

With a climate similar to the grape-growing regions of Germany, parts of the Ohio River Valley offer a superb location for wineries. The sandy soil, coupled with just the right amount of rain and snow, produces sweet, succulent grapes — perfect for such wines as Chablis and Rosé.

The **Valley Vineyards Winery** (in Morrow), a short drive from Cincinnati, provides an introduction to the wine-making process. Founded in 1970, the winery offers self-guided tours where visitors may see the vineyards, processing room, storage barrels, and bottling process. At the end of the tour, be sure to stop at the tasting room to sample some of the 12 varieties of wine produced here. Cheese and pizza are also served as tasty accompaniments to the various vintages. One of the most popular kinds is honey wine, made without grapes or sugar.

(For more entertainment ideas in the area, see articles in this section on Cincinnati and Kings Island.)

BEST TIME TO VISIT: Summer or fall.
HOURS: Valley Vineyard Winery — year round, 11 a.m.-8 p.m. Monday through Thursday; 11 a.m.-11 p.m. Friday and Saturday.
ADMISSION: Tours are free.
DIRECTIONS: From Cincinnati, take I-71 northeast to Lebanon-Morrow exit (Rt. 123). Follow Rt. 123 southeast to U.S. 22; turn right and go about two miles to Valley Vineyards.
FOR MORE INFORMATION: Call or write Valley Vineyards Winery, Morrow, OH 45152; (513) 899-2485.

Ohio

History Amid The Beauty Of Nature

Richland County, Ohio

Driving Time: About 1½ hours southwest of Cleveland

Situated in the fertile, rolling countryside of north-central Ohio, Richland County offers numerous points of interest centering on everything from pioneer history to outdoor recreation.

A visit to the **Richland County Museum** (533 Gadfield Rd., Mansfield) provides background on the area, which was first settled by a pioneer named Jared Mansfield. The quaint schoolhouse building, surviving from the 1850s, showcases local memorabilia and artifacts, such as tools, furniture, clothing, and paintings.

Kingwood Center, the estate of the late Charles Kelley (900 Park Ave. W., Mansfield), is a must for nature-lovers. In any season, the 47 acres surrounding the main residence, Kingwood Hall, are picturesque. King, an employee of the Ohio Brass Company in Mansfield, rose through the ranks to become the company's chairman. In 1926, he built the elegant French Provincial mansion, which boasts 27 major rooms. At the time, the house and furnishings were valued at $400,000. Fortunately, most of the original furnishings and fixtures imported from France (hand-painted wallpaper, for example) remain in the home.

But perhaps the most beautiful part of the estate lies outside the walls of the extravagant house. During summer months, gardens burst with colorful blooms of every description. One of the most popular displays is the Dahlia Gardens, exhibiting 200 varieties, from dwarfs to six-foot plants with dinner-plate-sized blos-

Homemade pottery and pewter items are sold at Roscoe Village in Coshocton, Ohio.

soms. If your family visits during April, May, or June, be sure to walk the nature trail to see the vibrant wildflowers native to Ohio. Bird-watchers will be interested to know that about 130 different species of native birds have been identified on the grounds.

More of the great outdoors is in store for your family at **Malabar Farm** (Bromfield and Pleasant Valley Rds.), the former home of noted author and conservationist Louis Bromfield. The restored home is open for tours; free wagon tours of the model farm are offered at 2:30 p.m. each Sunday. The area includes many suitable places for picnicking, hiking, fishing, and horseback riding

(horses not provided).

Another popular attraction in the area is the **Flea Market at the Richland County Fairgrounds** (Lantz Rd.) on the last full weekend of each month, except December and January.

BEST TIME TO VISIT: Spring or summer.
HOURS: Kingwood Center — House, 8 a.m.-5 p.m. Tuesday through Saturday; Sundays 1:30 to 4:30 p.m. Easter to October; closed holidays. Gardens, 8 a.m. to sundown daily. Richland County Museum — 1-4 p.m. weekends, May through October. Malabar Farm — house tours 9 a.m.-5 p.m. daily, March through November; 9 a.m. to 5 p.m. weekdays and Saturday, December, January, and February.
DIRECTIONS: From Cleveland, take I-71 southwest toward Mansfield.
FOR MORE INFORMATION: Call Richland County Tourist and Travel Bureau, (419) 525-1300.

Step Back Into a Real Pioneer Town

Coshocton, Ohio

Driving Time: About 1½ hours northeast of Columbus

In 1816, a man named James Calder crossed the Muskingum River at Coshocton, leaving home and business behind to establish his own town, appropriately named Caldersburg. Today, that site, **Roscoe Village**, stands as a memorial to Calder and other settlers. The village recreates an 1830's Ohio and Erie Canal town, complete with homes, stores, offices, and tavern.

Roscoe Village brings to mind an era when America was a young, expanding country. Tours begin in the visitors center with a slide presentation on the history of the Ohio and Erie Canal system and the Roscoe Village restoration. Visitors opting for a self-guided tour are invited to wander leisurely through the village, imagining what life was like in the early pioneer days. Buildings along the way include the Dr. Maro Johnson House Township Hall, Toll House, Craft House, and the Village Smithy.

At each stop along **Whitewoman Street**, visitors are invited to browse in the shops and businesses, which seem so quaint and primitive when compared with our lifestyle today. The **Village Smithy** features a blacksmith forging wrought-iron items, just like in the old days. At the **Craft House**, the arts of making pottery and pewter are showcased by costumed crafts people. For dinner, a popular spot is the **Old Warehouse Restaurant**, which serves hearty meals to travelers. Light lunches, creamy homemade ice cream, and a wide assortment of confections are available at **Captain Nye's Sweet Shop**.

Special events throughout the year provide additional entertainment, plus a taste of old-time merrymaking. The lineup of celebrations features **Dulcimer Days** in May, **Flea Market Festival** in July, **Coshocton Canal Festival** in August, **Apple Butter Stirrin'** in October, and **Christmas Candelighting** in December.

In good weather visitors may hop aboard a horse-drawn trolley for a short tour of the historic triple locks near the village.

In downtown Coshocton, don't miss the **Johnson-Humrickhouse Museum**'s collections that include Indian arts and artifacts, Oriental pieces, decorative arts, and Americana.

BEST TIME TO VISIT: Summer.
HOURS: Roscoe Village — April through December, 11 a.m.-5 p.m. daily; limited schedule rest of year.
ADMISSION: Johnson-Humrickhouse Museum — adults, $3; children and teens 8 to 18, $1.50; children under 8, free.
DIRECTIONS: From Columbus, take I-70 east toward Zanesville, then take Rt. 60 north to Rt. 16. Follow Rt. 16 northeast to Coshocton.
FOR MORE INFORMATION: Call Coshocton Chamber of Commerce, (614) 622-5411.

Ohio

The Land of Indian Legend Tecumseh

Chillicothe, Ohio

Driving Time: About 1 hour south of Columbus

Tecumseh, the great Shawnee Indian chief, spent much of his life defending the Ohio River area against the advancing white settlers. In an outdoor drama, "Tecumseh!" visitors to **Chillicothe** learn about the legendary Indian warrior and prophet. Presented annually at the Sugarloaf Mountain Amphitheatre, "Tecumseh!" is a sweeping, dramatic musical performance that captures the spirit of the Indians' fight to save their homeland. However, the production is just the beginning of a journey back into Native American history. For Chillicothe is steeped in Indian lore and tradition.

In 1803, the city was designated Ohio's first capital. At the **Ross County Historical Society** (45 W. 5th St.), your family can learn about the area's history from prehistoric Indians to pioneers and the Civil War. The **Franklin House** (80 S. Paint St.) focuses on the role of women in local history.

Adena, the restored plantation home of Thomas Worthington, Ohio's 6th governor, is another worthwhile stop (Allen Ave. off Rt. 104). The grand Georgian-style mansion features elegant antique pieces. The grounds include formal gardens, a smokehouse, a barn, and other service buildings.

More Indian lore is featured on a trip to the **Mound City Group National Monument** on the Scioto River (four miles north, on Rt. 104). The 13-acre area includes 23 burial mounds of the prehistoric Hopewell Indians within an earth wall. Called the "City of the Dead," the area con-

tains a display of ceremonial relics. Another unusual burial site is the **Seip Mound State Memorial**, southwest of Chillicothe (17 miles, on U.S. 50).

Visitors are invited to take the **First Capital Walking Tour** (beginning at Yoctangee Park) for interesting background information on the city. Tour guides point out historical places of interest and many examples of fine 19th-century residences.

A later period of American history, the Civil War, is the subject of another extraordinary performance at Sugarloaf Mountain. "**Shenandoah**," a Tony-award-winning musical, centers on a family's struggle during the death and destruction of the Civil War.

South of Chillicothe, the beautiful **Scioto Trail State Park** beckons with a 30-acre lake and facilities for boating, camping, and hiking. Other area parks include Pain Creek (on U.S. 50, west of Bainbridge), Tar Hollow (east of Chillicothe, off Rt. 327), and Hocking Hills (northeast of Chillicothe, off Rt. 664).

For more enjoyment of the scenic outdoors, follow the **Pain Valley Skyline Drive**, which starts in Bainbridge (southwest on U.S. 50). Routes vary from nine to 38 miles with spectacular views of Ohio's scenic hill country.

BEST TIME TO VISIT: Summer, if you want to attend the Sugarloaf Mountain productions; October is the best time for the skyline drive.

HOURS: Ross County Historical Society — 1-5 p.m. daily except Monday, February through November. Adena — 9:30 a.m.-5 p.m. Wednesday through Saturday; noon-5 p.m. Sunday, Memorial Day through Labor Day only. Mound City — June to Labor Day, 8 a.m.-8 p.m.; rest of year, 8 a.m.-5 p.m. Seip Mound — daylight hours, daily. Thomas Museum — 8:15 a.m.-5 p.m. Monday through Friday, except holidays. "Tecumseh" performances — mid-June to Labor Day, 8 p.m. Monday through Saturday. "Shenandoah" performances — 9 p.m. Sunday, late June to Labor Day, and nightly first two weeks of September.

ADMISSION: Ross County Historical Museum — adults and teens, $1.50; senior citizens, $1; children, 50¢. Adena — adults and teens, $2; children 6 to 12, $1; children under 6, free. Mound City and Seip Mound — free. Walking Tours — adults, $5; teens, $3; children, $1.50-$2.50. "Tecumseh" and "Shenandoah" — adults, $8; children under 10, $6.

DIRECTIONS: From Columbus, take U.S. 23 south, 46 miles to Chillicothe. Sugarloaf Mountain Amphitheatre is five miles north of town, off U.S. 23 (Delano Rd. exit).

FOR MORE INFORMATION: Call the Chillicothe Chamber of Commerce, (614) 772-4539.

Tecumseh, the Shawnee chief who attempted to unite the Indian tribes against white settlers, as played by an actor in an outdoor drama in Chillicothe

An 1800's Ghost Town Near Findlay

Findlay, Ohio

Driving Time: About 2 hours north of Columbus; 2 hours west of Cleveland

Thoughts of old ghost towns usually conjure up images of the Wild West — old mining towns, now long deserted by their inhabitants. But you don't have to go that far to find one.

Only five miles south of Findlay is **Ghost Town**, a replica of an 1880's frontier town. There are 23 buildings in the living museum, including a blacksmith shop, general store, barber shop, cobbler shop, print shop, firehouse, dentist's office — and, of course, a jail, ready and waiting for unruly outlaws. Each building contains artifacts and tools of the period, creating an authentic representation of the times. Additional attractions: the **Black Swamp Railroad** and **Barnyard Louie's Donkey Corral**.

(For more entertainment ideas in the area, see articles in this section on Delaware, Columbus, and Toledo.)

BEST TIME TO VISIT: Summer.
HOURS: Ghost Town — 9:30 a.m.-6:30 p.m. daily, May 30-Labor Day.
ADMISSION: Ghost Town — adults and teens, $2; pre-teens and children 5 and over, $1.
DIRECTIONS: From Columbus, take U.S. 23 northwest toward Findlay. Just outside the city limits, exit at Rt. 68 south; follow to County Rd. 40 and follow signs.
FOR MORE INFORMATION: Call or write Findlay Convention and Visitors Bureau, 118 E. Sandusky St., Findlay, OH 45840; (419) 422-3315. Or Ghost Town, 10936 County Rd. 40, Findlay, OH 45840; (419) 326-5874.

Ohio River Town With Rich History

Marietta, Ohio
Driving Time: About 2 hours southeast of Columbus; 3 hours south of Cleveland

A journey back in time to an early-American Ohio River town becomes reality with a trip to Marietta. Situated on Ohio's eastern boundary, and facing West Virginia across the river, Marietta was the first permanent settlement in the Northwest Territory.

Discover some fascinating information about Ohio and the lifestyle of its first settlers by visiting the **Campus Martius Museum** (Second and Washington Sts.). The settlers named the first fort Campus Martius (field of Mars); the fort superintendent's home is now part of the museum. There, in the restored former home of Rufus Putnam, are furnishings and artifacts from the period, some originally owned by the Putnam family. The museum also contains displays of tools, craft items, primitive oil paintings, and other memorabilia from Ohio's early days.

The state's first office building, the Ohio Land Company Office, is located on the museum grounds, too.

Another fascinating spot in Marietta is the **Ohio River Museum** (Front and St. Clair Sts.), where the history of the "Mighty Ohio" is recounted through multi-media presentations and other fine exhibits.

BEST TIME TO VISIT: Summer.
HOURS: Campus Martius Museum — March through November, 9:30 a.m.-5 p.m. Monday-Saturday; noon-5 p.m. Sunday and holidays. Ohio River Museum — same hours as above.
ADMISSION: Campus Martius Museum — adults and teens, $1.50; children 6 and over, 75¢. Ohio River Museum — same as above.
DIRECTIONS: From Columbus, take I-70 east past Zanesville. In Cambridge, pick up I-77 south and follow to Marietta.
FOR MORE INFORMATION: Call or write Marietta Tourist and Convention Bureau, 310 Front St., Marietta, OH 45750; (614) 373-5178.

Pioneer loom demonstration at Allen County Museum in Lima

A Town Famed For Popcorn And a President

Marion, Ohio

Driving Time: About 45 minutes north of Columbus

Popcorn lovers, unite! The place is Marion, Ohio. Actually, Marion could be called Popcorn, U.S.A., because it is the home of the world's largest popcorn exporter, **Wyandot Popcorn Company**. Marion is also the hometown of President Warren G. Harding.

Each year the town's inhabitants turn out in large numbers for the **Marion Popcorn Festival** (second week in September). The three days of song, celebration, and merriment include a carnival, big-name musical performers, a bike-a-thon, parade, popcorn tours — even a Popcorn Ball and the coronation of a popcorn queen. If you can't attend the festival, pop into the **Popped Right Popcorn Museum** (135 Wyandot Ave.), which

displays more than 40 antique popcorn wagons popcorn poppers, and peanut roasters. Visitors may also view a videotape about popcorn production.

While in town, visit the home of **President Harding**, the 29th president of the United States. The large, 1891 Victorian home (380 Mt. Vernon Ave.) was the residence of President and Mrs. Harding for 30 years before they moved to Washington in 1921. (By the way, did you know that G. — as in Warren G. — stands for Gamaliel?)

(For more entertainment ideas in the area, see articles in this section on Columbus and Delaware.)

BEST TIME TO VISIT: September — for the Popcorn Festival.
HOURS: Popcorn Museum — May-September, noon-6 p.m. Tuesday-Saturday; October-April, noon-6 p.m. Tuesday-Saturday. Harding Home — Memorial Day-Labor Day, 9:30 a.m.-5 p.m. Wednesday-Saturday, noon-5 p.m. Sunday; Labor Day-October, 9:30 a.m.-5 p.m. Saturday, noon-5 p.m. Sunday.
ADMISSION: Popcorn Museum — free. Harding Home — adults and teens, $1; children 6 and over, 50¢.
DIRECTIONS: From Columbus, take U.S. 23 north; get off at Marion-Williamsport exit. Go south about ½ mile on Rt. 423 to reach Popped Right Museum.
FOR MORE INFORMATION: Call or write Marion Area Chamber of Commerce, 206 S. Prospect St., Marion, OH 43302; (614) 382-2181.

Delaware: Indian Caverns, Frontierland

Delaware, Ohio

Driving Time: About 20 minutes north of Columbus

When Ohio was still a wilderness territory and Indians roamed the plains, some of these early Americans dug an unusual series of caves. Once a refuge for the Wyandot Indians, the interconnected limestone caves are on three levels about 105 feet underground. There, visitors may view many different rock formations and fossils formed thousands of years ago.

While visiting the **Olentangy Indian Caverns** (1799 Home Rd., Delaware), also drop in on **Ohio Frontierland** in the adjacent area. The pioneer village recreation recalls 19th-century life in the wide-open spaces; the Indian Village provides further insight into the lifestyle of the people who claimed America before the white man.

(For more entertainment ideas in the area, see article in this section on Columbus.)

BEST TIME TO VISIT: Summer.
HOURS: Indian Caverns and Frontierland — 9:30 a.m.-6 p.m. daily, April-October.
ADMISSION: Combination ticket — adults and teens, $6.25; pre-teens and children 7 and over, $3.25. Caverns only — adults and teens, $4.50; pre-teens and children 7 and over, $2.25. Frontierland only — adults and teens, $2.25; pre-teens and children 7 and over, $1.50.
DIRECTIONS: From Columbus, take U.S. 23 north toward Delaware. The caverns are about seven miles south of Delaware, off U.S. 23.
FOR MORE INFORMATION: Call or write Delaware Area Chamber of Commerce, 27 W. Winter St., Delaware, OH 43015; (614) 369-6221.

Put-in-Bay: An Easy-Going Island

Put-in-Bay, Ohio

Driving Time: About 1¼ hours west of Cleveland

Put-in-Bay — even the name sounds intriguing. This resort town, on South Bass Island in Lake Erie (about three miles from the mainland), is a great place to "get away from it all." Leave your cares — and car — behind, board a ferry boat in Port Clinton and in minutes you'll be enjoying the town's laid-back atmosphere.

Among other attractions, the island claims to have the **best fishing area for smallmouth black bass** — in spring. But, the catches are said to be great any time of year. Other recreation opportunities include boating, swimming, golf, water skiing, bicycling, picnicking, and more.

The town is full of unusual antique and craft shops. In addition, there's a chance to learn a little American history with a visit to **Commodore Oliver Hazard Perry's Cave** (Catawba Ave.), where he reputedly stashed ammunition before the Battle of Lake Erie in the War of 1812.

(For more entertainment ideas in the area, see articles in this section on Port Clinton and Sandusky.)

BEST TIME TO VISIT: Summer.
HOURS: Perry's Cave — 11 a.m.-5 p.m. daily, Memorial Day-Labor Day.
ADMISSION: Adults and teens, $1; children 6 and over, 50¢.
TRANSPORTATION TO ISLAND: Ferry service — leaves from Jefferson St. dock in Port Clinton daily, April-November, every 1½ hours, 7 a.m.-6 p.m. weekdays, to 7 p.m. weekends. Air service — leaves from Island Airlines (2½ miles east of Port Clinton off Rt. 53) mid-May to Labor Day, at 45-minute to one-hour intervals, 8:15 a.m.-7:45 p.m. daily; rest of the year, hours are 8 a.m.-6 p.m. daily.
DIRECTIONS: From Cleveland, take Ohio Turnpike (I-80-90) west to Exit 7. Follow U.S. 250 north to Rt. 2 and continue west to Port Clinton. Take ferry or airplane to Put-in-Bay.
FOR MORE INFORMATION: Call or write Put-in-Bay Chamber of Commerce, Box 76, Put-in-Bay, OH 43456; (419) 285-2832.

Pres. Garfield's Hometown

Mentor, Ohio

Driving Time: About one-half hour east of downtown Cleveland

Lawnfield, in Mentor, was the last home of James A. Garfield before he moved to the White House to become the 20th President of the United States. The first two floors of the large residence are furnished with Garfield family furniture, art objects, and memorabilia. Displayed in the memorial library are Garfield's desk and book collection. The top floor of the structure (8095 Mentor Ave.) contains exhibits of the Lake County Historical Society.

Garfield was born on November 19, 1831, in a log cabin in Cuyahoga County, Ohio. He earned a law degree in 1861 and subsequently served in the Ohio State Senate, U.S. House of Representatives, and U.S. Senate. Inaugurated as president on March 4, 1881, he was shot less than four months later in the Pennsylvania Railroad Station in Washington, D.C. He died 2½ months later in New Jersey.

While visiting Mentor, you might also enjoy a trip to **Holden Arboretum** (on Sperry Rd., five miles southeast of town). The 2,800-acre area includes 7,000 varieties of plants on the grounds. Facilities include hiking trails, picnic grounds, and a wildlife sanctuary.

(For more information on the area's attractions, see articles in this section on Cleveland, Chagrin Falls, and Akron.)

BEST TIME TO VISIT: Summer or fall.
HOURS: Lawnfield — April-November, 9 a.m.-5 p.m. Tuesday-Saturday; 1 p.m.-5 p.m. Sunday and holidays. Holden Arboretum — year round, 10 a.m.-5 p.m. Tuesday-Sunday.
ADMISSION: Lawnfield — adults, $2; teens, $1. Holden Arboretum — adults, $2.50; teens and children 6 and over, $1.75.
DIRECTIONS: From downtown Cleveland, take I-90 east to Exit 615; go south to Mentor Ave. (Rt. 20).
FOR MORE INFORMATION: Call or write Mentor Chamber of Commerce, 7547 Mentor Ave., Rm. 302, Mentor, OH 44060; (216) 255-0263.

Milan: Birthplace of Thomas Edison

Milan, Ohio

Driving Time: About one-half hour west of Cleveland

What would the world be like without the electric light bulb? Most of us, fortunately, will never have the chance to find out — thanks to the famous inventor, Thomas Alva Edison.

Learn more about this extraordinary man with a trip to his birthplace (9 Edison Dr.) in Milan. The three-story structure, which is a National Historic Landmark, is furnished to recreate its appearance in 1847, the year Edison was born. Edison was the youngest of seven children. In an adjoining **museum**, there are displays of unique Edison memorabilia, including models of some of his inventions.

Although most people know that Edison invented the electric bulb, they are not familiar with his other inventions, such as the automatic telegraph system, phonograph, motion picture camera, and more. Among other concepts, he discovered the "Edison Effect," a fundamental principle of electronics.

While visiting Milan, browse in some of the unusual antique shops on Main Street and check out the **Milan Historical Museum** (10 Edison Dr.).

(For more entertainment ideas in the area, see articles in this section on Cleveland, Chagrin Falls, Mentor, Fremont, and Akron.

BEST TIME TO VISIT: Spring or summer.
HOURS: Edison Birthplace — February through May and Labor Day through November, 1 p.m.-5 p.m. Tuesday-Sunday; June-Labor Day, 9 a.m.-5 p.m. Tuesday-Saturday and 1 p.m.-5 p.m. Sunday. Milan Historical Museum — April, May, September, and October, 1 p.m.-5 p.m.; June-August, 10 a.m.-5 p.m.
ADMISSION: Edison Birthplace — adults, $1; children, 50¢. Milan historical Museum — donation requested.
DIRECTIONS: From Cleveland, take I-80-90 west to Exit 7 (Sandusky-Norwalk). Follow U.S. 250 (toward Norwalk) south about two miles; turn left on Rt. 113 and follow to Milan Town Square. Follow signs to Edison Birthplace.
FOR MORE INFORMATION: Call or write Edison Birthplace Museum, 9 Edison Dr., Milan, OH 44848; (419) 499-2135.

Fremont: A President's Hometown

Fremont, Ohio

Driving Time: About 1 hour west of Cleveland

Spiegel Grove, the grand Victorian mansion near Fremont, recalls the elegant lifestyle of the Victorian era, when President Rutherford B. Hayes lived there. The four-story brick residence, with grounds totalling 25 acres, was built in 1863 by Sardis Birchard, an uncle of President Hayes. While he was governor of Ohio, Hayes acquired the estate, which remained in the Hayes family until 1966, when it was opened to the public.

Approximately 25,000 persons visit **Spiegel Grove** annually to view the elaborate furnishings in the mansion and historical memorabilia housed in the adjoining museum. Two stories of the residence are open to the public; most of the furnishings are original pieces belonging to the Hayes family. The museum has various interesting displays, including an extensive gun collection, Civil War battle scenes, information on Hayes' political campaigns, Lincoln memorabilia, and more. Hayes served as president from 1877 to 1881; he lived at Spiegel Grove until his death in 1893.

(For more entertainment ideas in the area, see articles in this section on Toledo, Sandusky, Port Clinton, and Cleveland.)

BEST TIME TO VISIT: Summer.
HOURS: Hayes State Memorial (house and museum) — year round, 9 a.m.-5 p.m. Tuesday-Saturday; 1:30 p.m.-5 p.m. Sunday, Monday, and holidays.
ADMISSION: Adults, $1.50; children, 75¢.
DIRECTIONS: From Cleveland, take I-80-90 west. In Fremont, exit at Rt. 53 south to Rt. 20 west. Spiegel Grove is located just a few blocks away at 1337 Hayes Ave. at Buckland Ave.
FOR MORE INFORMATION: Call or write Spiegel Grove, Hayes State Memorial, 1337 Hayes Ave., Fremont, OH 43420; (419) 332-2081 or (419) 332-4952.

MICHIGAN

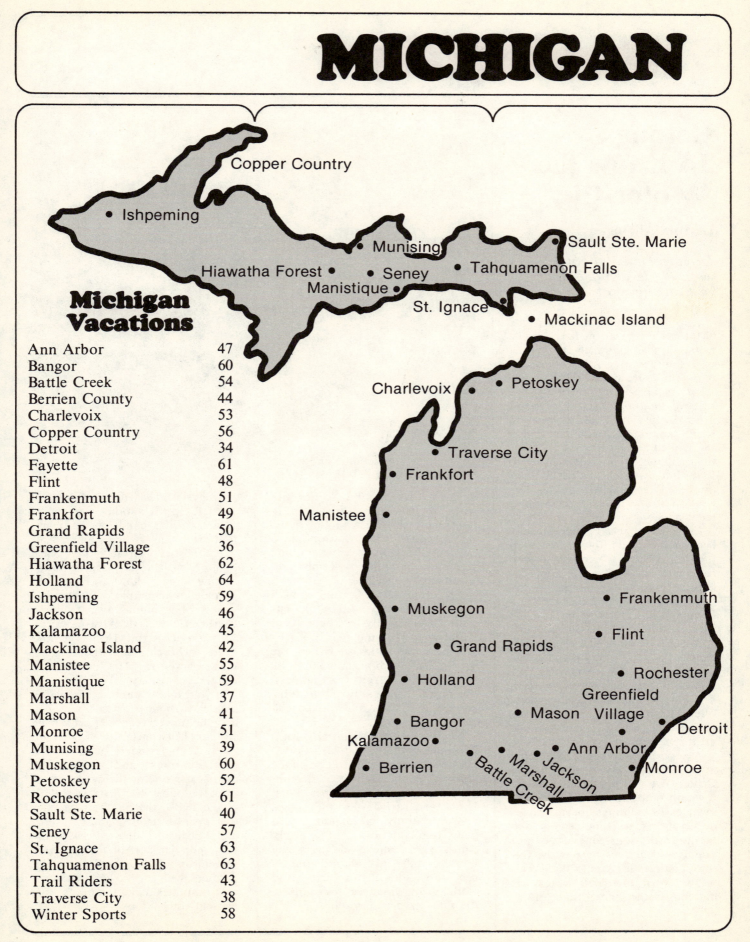

Copper Country

Ishpeming

Sault Ste. Marie

Munising

Hiawatha Forest   Seney   Tahquamenon Falls

Manistique

St. Ignace

Mackinac Island

Michigan Vacations

Charlevoix   Petoskey

Traverse City

Frankfort

Manistee

Muskegon

Frankenmuth

Flint

Grand Rapids

Rochester

Holland

Greenfield

Mason   Village

Bangor

Detroit

Kalamazoo

Ann Arbor

Berrien

Battle Creek   Marshall   Jackson   Monroe

Michigan

Getting To Know the "Motor City"

Detroit, Michigan

Driving Time: About 3 hours west of Cleveland; 6 hours east of Chicago

Known for years as America's "Motor City," Detroit had humble beginnings as a French fur-trading post and frontier fort. The city's name comes from the French phrase *le place du detroit*, meaning "the place of the strait." Each year Detroit produces 23% of all the automobiles, trucks, and tractors manufactured in the United States. For the auto enthusiast, there's no better place to visit. But even if your family isn't interested in motorized vehicles, Detroit offers a wide array of entertainment possibilities.

Detroit is unusual geographically because it is one of the few places in the United States where a person can look straight south into Canada! (While your family is visiting Detroit, it's possible to have lunch in a foreign country and be back in the United States in time for supper!) Another little-known fact is that Detroit is the potato chip manufacturing capital of the world; also, the home of the nation's oldest state fair. Those who think that the city merely offers lots of factories and thousands of cars will be missing out on some great experiences.

A good place to begin sightseeing in the "Motor City" is the **Cultural Center** (five minutes north of downtown on Woodward Ave.). The area includes 18 buildings housing museums, schools, teaching centers, and service institutions. One of the most popular attractions here is the **Detroit Institute of Arts** (5200 Woodward Ave.). The fifth largest art museum in the United States, it in-

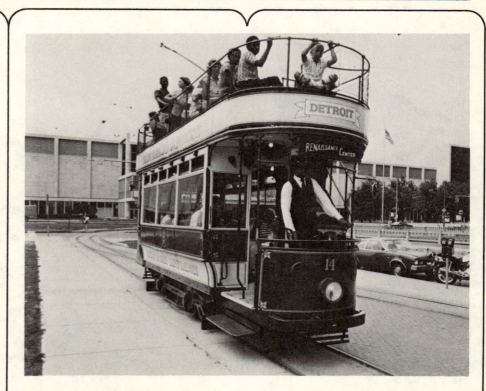

cludes more than 100 galleries with works by American, African, Flemish, Dutch, British, and Italian artists. Diego Rivera's "Detroit Industry" murals are displayed in addition to famous paintings by Rembrandt, Van Gogh, and Picasso.

Children will be fascinated with some of the extraordinary exhibits planned especially for them at the **Children's Museum** (67 E. Kirby Ave.). At the entrance, visitors are greeted by Silverbolt, a nine-foot-tall horse sculpted from car bumpers. There are also exhibits on dolls, science, and toys, and foreign cultures are explored.

Nearby, at the **Detroit Historical Museum** (5401 Woodward Ave.), guests are invited to stroll down the "Streets of Old Detroit." The cobblestone streets recall the 1840s, 1870s, and early 1900s with shops and institutions that long have been gone from American life: the blacksmith shop, nickelodeon movie house, and the old-fashion 5- and 10-cent store. Antique furniture, period clothing, and vintage autos complete the 19th-century atmosphere.

The **Detroit Science Center** (5020 John R. St.) is another worthwhile stop, featuring "hands-on" participation exhibits in virtually all areas of scientific study. The incredible space theater, with its 180-degree wraparound screen, allows the visitor to become an actual part of the show.

Just a few minutes away from the Cultural Center is the **Afro-American Museum of Detroit** (1553 W. Grand Blvd.), where documents and artifacts relating to black culture and history are displayed.

If your family wants to experience and learn about America's early history, be sure to visit the **Fort Wayne Military Museum** (6325 W. Jefferson Ave.). With its underground tunnels, moats, barracks, and ramparts, the complex is one of the nation's best preserved Civil War fortresses. Built in the 1840s, the fort now includes displays of Detroit's military history and Michigan Indians. Perhaps the most popular part of the tour is a recreation of a Civil War battle. Soldiers, women, and children in period costumes make the drama surprisingly realistic.

The transition from the 19th century to the skyscrapers of a modern 20th-century city is easy to achieve in a short drive to **downtown Detroit**. Your family won't want to miss the fabulous **Renaissance Center** on the riverfront. The seven-tower complex includes the world's tallest hotel — the 73-story Detroit Plaza with its own indoor lake. Throughout the center there are unusual restaurants and intriguing specialty shops that sell such interesting items as hand-blown glass, art objects, chocolates, toys, and designer clothes.

For a change of pace, visit the **Eastern Market** (Russell St. at Fisher Freeway). In the open-air setting, there are more than 300 stalls and shops featuring an almost infinite assortment of fresh produce, meats, fish, poultry, cheeses, and other delicacies. (Sample world-famous Michigan cherries and the sweet apple cider from local orchards.)

Another quaint downtown neighborhood is **Harmonie Park** with its Detroit Artists Market. During the summer it's a great place just to stroll down the street and absorb the atmosphere. There are frequent art fairs and impromptu concerts on the sidewalks.

And in **Greektown**, there's Old World music and merrymaking in this one-block ethnic enclave (Monroe St. between Beaubien and St. Antoine). Small shops and tempting restaurants are plentiful. For a real Greek treat, try the saganaki (flaming cheese) at the **Old Parthenon** (579 Monroe St.) or the **New Hellas Cafe** (583 Monroe St.) — both among Detroit's most popular eateries.

The **Detroit Zoo** (10 Mile Rd. at Woodward Ave. in Royal Oak) was the first "cageless" zoological park in the United States. The zoo features 5,000 animals with extraordinary exhibits of reptiles, apes, bears, and penguins.

Other creatures are featured at the **Children's Zoo** at scenic **Belle Isle Park** (take MacArthur Bridge to island in middle of Detroit River). The 1,000-acre island, known to the Indi-

ans as Wah-na-be-zee or "white swan," offers countless opportunities for fun and recreation. With its lakes, ponds, picnic groves, woods, and golf course, the island attracts visitors for nature walks, swimming, fishing, canoeing, horseback riding, picnicking, tennis, and more. On the grounds is **Whitcomb Conservatory**, with year-round flower shows and a quarter-million plants. One of the nation's largest orchid collections is located here.

The nation's oldest freshwater aquarium is another favorite spot on Belle Isle. Open since 1904, the aquarium includes 5,000 live fish and a 4,500-gallon shark tank.

Children in your family will certainly enjoy a trip to **Boblo Island Amusement Park** (18 miles south in middle of Detroit River). An interesting way to reach Boblo is to hop aboard the *Columbia* or *Ste. Claire* steamers and take a leisurely ride down the river (board steamers at 661 Civic Center Dr.). After passing

18 miles of beautiful shoreline of the United States and Canada, your family will arrive at the park, with its 32 rides and attractions. The **Carousel Theater** features lively on-stage revues. And one of the best outdoor attractions is the **Acapulco High Divers** show, in which performers plunge from 85-foot heights.

Detroit is a great town for sports. Even though the Detroit Tigers have won few World Series titles, it's hard to find more loyal fans. (For information on baseball tickets, call **Tiger Stadium** [Trumbull at Michigan Ave.] — [313] 963-9944.) Detroit Lions football and Piston basketball games are played at the 80,000-seat **Pontiac Silverdome** (1200 Featherstone, Pontiac; for information on football or basketball tickets, call [313] 857-7700).

BEST TIME TO VISIT: Summer.

HOURS: Eastern Market — 5 a.m.-noon Monday through Friday; 5 a.m.-6 p.m. Saturday. Boblo Island — May through Labor Day, 11 a.m.-8:30 p.m. Monday through Friday; 11 a.m.-10:30 p.m. Saturday. Boat transportation from Detroit to Boblo Island — 9:30 and 11 a.m., 2, 3:30 and 6 p.m. Monday through Friday and 8 p.m. on Saturday and Sunday (board at 661 Civic Center Dr. in Detroit). Whitcomb Observatory (Belle Isle) — 9 a.m.-6 p.m. every day. Aquarium (Belle Isle) — 10 a.m.-5 p.m. daily. Detroit Zoo — mid-May to Sunday after Labor Day, 10 a.m.-5 p.m. Monday through Saturday, 9 a.m.-6 p.m. Sunday; rest of the year, 10 a.m.-5 p.m. Wednesday through Sunday. Detroit Institute of Arts — 9:30 a.m.-5:30 p.m. Tuesday through Sunday. Detroit Historical Museum — 9:30 a.m.-5 p.m. Tuesday through Saturday. Detroit Science Center — 9 a.m.-4 p.m. Tuesday through Friday, 10 a.m.-5 p.m. Saturday, noon-8:30 p.m. Sunday; also 7 to 9:30 p.m. Friday and Saturday. Children's Museum — 1-4 p.m. Monday through Friday; 9 a.m.-4 p.m. Saturday, May through October only. Afro-American Museum — 9 a.m.-5 p.m. Tuesday through Friday; 10 a.m.-4 p.m. Saturday. Fort Wayne — 9:30 a.m.-5 p.m. Wednesday through Saturday; 11:30 a.m.-7 p.m. Sunday.

ADMISSION: Boblo Island (for boat trip, island admission, and shows) — adults, teens, $8.50; children 4 to 11 years, $7.50; children under 4 years, free; for unlimited rides only, $6 per person. Detroit Zoo — adults and teens, $2; children 6 to 12 years, 75¢. Detroit Institute of Arts — admission donation voluntary. Detroit Historical Museum — adults, $1; children, 50¢. Detroit Science Center — adults, $2.50; children under 6 years, 75¢. Fort Wayne — adults, $1; teens, 50¢. Afro-American Museum — adults and teens 16 years and over, 50¢; children and teens under 16 years, 25¢.

FOR MORE INFORMATION: Call or write Metropolitan Detroit Convention and Visitors Bureau, 100 Renaissance Center, Suite 1950, Detroit, MI 48253; (313) 259-4333.

Michigan

Incredible Collections Of Americana

**Greenfield Village
Dearborn, Michigan**

Driving Time: About 1¼ hours north of Toledo; about 6 hours east of Chicago

The **Henry Ford Museum and Greenfield Village** in Dearborn, near Detroit, offers 260 acres of exhibits, shows, and homes that document the past 300 years of America's progress. Founded by Henry Ford in 1929, the indoor-outdoor museum tells the story of America's early rural life through the modern industrial age of today. Its numerous collections, restored buildings, festivals, theatrical productions, and crafts demonstrations feature something for everyone in the family.

Within the museum are unique collections documenting America's lifestyle in home, workplace, farm, and factory. Visitors will see the world's largest assortment of 19th-century agricultural tools. Daily tours describe how the various farming processes have changed over the years to increase America's productivity. In another section, displays of pottery, glass, musical instruments, and kitchen appliances are showcased.

One of the most popular areas is the **Transportation Hall**, which includes approximately 180 vehicles tracing the history of Ford cars from the Quadricycle to the Thunderbird. Also on display is an impressive exhibit of race and show cars that once belonged to famous Americans, world leaders, and, of course, the Ford family.

In Greenfield Village, the open-air museum, your family will enjoy a rare opportunity to stroll through a bit of American history. The wide

array of buildings and exhibits demonstrate changes in American life, as well as what has remained the same throughout the centuries. A highlight of the village is the restoration of **Thomas Edison's laboratory**, where he invented the light bulb. The structure, one of the world's first research and development laboratories, was moved from Menlo Park, New Jersey, to the Dearborn site. Another exciting attraction is the **Wright Cycle Shop**, transported from Dayton, Ohio, where Orville and Wilbur planned and built the first airplane.

In addition, the village includes the 19th-century farmhouse where Henry Ford was born; the house of Noah Webster, who wrote the famous dictionary; the Logan County Courthouse, where Abraham Lincoln was a circuit-riding attorney; and much more.

Throughout the area, blacksmiths, millers, potters, and other artisans demonstrate their crafts. And visitors are invited to experience early transportation by riding in a horse-drawn carriage, steamboat, or steam train.

For lunch, stop at the **Eagle Tavern** on the village green and try some food prepared from recipes of the 1850s.

Henry Ford's 56-room mansion, **Fair Lane**, is nearby (4901 Evergreen Rd.). Built in 1915, the house exhibits simplicity and functionalism, which were very important to Ford.

Another interesting stop is the **Dearborn Inn, Colonial Homes and Motor House** (20301 Oakwood Blvd.). The Georgian-style inn and motor house were built to represent Henry Ford's concept of a unique inn. The cottages were constructed to represent the exteriors of houses belonging to five famous Americans: Walt Whitman, Barbara Fritchie, Edgar Allen Poe, Patrick Henry, and Governor Oliver Wolcott. Overnight guests are welcome.

While your family is in the area, there are many more attractions in and around Detroit (see article in this section.)

HOURS: Henry Ford Museum and Greenfield Village — 9 a.m.-5 p.m. daily, year round; closed Thanksgiving, Christmas, and New Year's. Fair Lane — 1-4:30 p.m daily.
ADMISSION: Henry Ford Museum and Greenfield Village — each charge adults $8; children 6 to 12 years, $4; under 6 years, free. Fair Lane — adults and teens, $2; children under 12 years, $1.
DIRECTIONS: From Toledo, Ohio, and areas south of Detroit, take I-75 north toward Detroit. Follow I-75 within Detroit metropolitan area to junction of U.S. 24 north. Follow U.S. 24 north to Dearborn and then follow signs to Greenfield Village. From Grand Rapids, take I-96 southeast to Detroit area; exit at I-275 south. Follow I-275 south to junction of I-96 east. Follow to Rt. 24 exit, then go south to Dearborn.

In Marshall, The 'Old Ways' Continue

Marshall, Michigan

Driving Time: About 3½ hours east of Chicago, 1¾ hours west of Detroit; 15 minutes east of Battle Creek

Shady streets with Victorian homes, quaint shops with intriguing collectibles, and an old-fashioned friendly hospitality. If it sounds like something out of the past, it is. But all these old-time charms can be found in Marshall, just a short drive from Detroit.

As visitors cross the Marshall city limits, they journey into yesteryear. It's easy to imagine the days when horses and buggies were a common sight on Marshall's streets, which seem to have escaped the 20th century.

Each year the **Marshall Historical Society** sponsors the **Annual Home Tour** (weekend after Labor Day), which attracts about 14,000 persons from throughout the Midwest. The picturesque 19th-century homes range in style from classical Greek Revival to elaborate Italianate and elegant Queen Anne, all contributing to the charming and gracious atmosphere.

One of the most popular points of interest during spring and summer months is the **Honolulu House Museum** (107 N. Kalamazoo Ave.). The grand Italianate house, built in 1860, was the residence of the former U.S. consul to the Sandwich Islands. Listed in the National Register of Historic Places, the restored home features period furnishings and art treasures. The rather small Greek Revival-style **Governor's Mansion** was built in 1839, when Marshall citizens had hoped their town would be

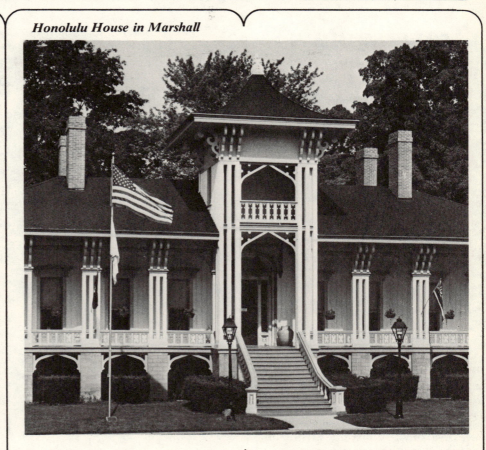

Honolulu House in Marshall

chosen as the state capital. The **Capitol Hill School**, built in 1860, is a Gothic Revival two-room schoolhouse.

But, historic places and homes are only part of the story, for a Marshall shopping spree adds another measure of old-fashioned fun: antique shops filled with furnishings and decorative objects abound. **Marshall Antiques**, **Attic Trunk Antiques**, and **Cupboard Antiques** (all located on 200 block of Michigan Ave.) are a few of the shops.

Christmas in Marshall is a special time of year, when holly wreaths and glowing candles appear in windows all over town. Groups of carolers stroll down the snow-covered streets, and the town is invaded by about 10,000 visitors for its **Christmas parade** (first Monday after Thanksgiving).

Another point of interest for families is the **American Museum of Magic** (107 E. Michigan Ave.). The

135-year-old building displays a dazzling assortment of historical memorabilia and props relating to magic. Visitors even get the chance to see items that once belonged to Houdini. Other exhibits include historic magicians' posters (some dating back to more than 100 years ago), magic toys, magicians' diaries, newspaper clippings, and a display on magic used in commercial advertising.

BEST TIME TO VISIT: Summer.
HOURS: Honolulu House — mid-May to September 30, 1 p.m.-4 p.m. weekdays, noon-5 p.m. weekends; closed holidays and Tuesday. Shops — daily 10 or 11 a.m. to 5 p.m. American Museum of Magic — 1 p.m.-5 p.m. Tuesday-Friday; 8 a.m.-5 p.m. Saturday.
ADMISSION: Honolulu House — adults, $1; children, 50¢.
DIRECTIONS: From Detroit, take I-94 toward Jackson and Ann Arbor. Exit at Marshall sign; follow road southwest to town. From Battle Creek or west of Battle Creek, take I-94 east to I-69 south. Follow I-69 south to Marshall exit.
FOR MORE INFORMATION: Call or write Marshall Area Chamber of Commerce, 308 E. Michigan Ave., Marshall, MI 49068; (616) 781-5163.

Michigan

Traverse Bay: Festivals, Sports, Fun

Traverse City, Michigan

Driving Time: About 3 hours north of Grand Rapids; about 6 hours northwest of Detroit

Cherries — and lots of them. That's what you'll find on a trip to Traverse City.

Known as the "Cherry Capital of the World," the city and its surrounding area produce a phenomenal one-third of the world's cherry crop annually.

And, in homage to that mighty little fruit, the town and toursts turn out each July to celebrate at the fabulous **Cherry Festival**. For one week following the Fourth of July, Traverse City bursts with excitement and festive spirit for parades (three of them!), pageants, music, sports, children's special events, arts and crafts fairs, food, and much more. It's incredible to think that all this activity would stem from a tiny red berry — but that's what attracts the festival's half-million participants.

Each day of the week-long extravaganza features a whole assortment of activities. Following the **Heritage and Junior Royale Parades**, the town hosts a chicken barbeque and ice cream social. Also, the **Cherry Royale Parade** features more than 50 floats, 20 bands, and 30 marching units. Other highlights of the week include brunch and lunch fashion shows, jazz concerts, boat and canoe races, sand-sculpture contest, bike races, and, of course, a fun-filled cherry pie-eating contest.

However, even if your family can't attend the Cherry festival, a trip to **Traverse City** will be well worthwhile. For years, the city has been the

Action at the National Cherry Festival

hub of a popular summer recreation area. Recently, too, visitors have been coming to Traverse City in increasing numbers for winter sports.

Swimming, sunning, sailing, and water skiing are favorite activities of summer tourists to the area. For a change of pace, however, how about trying your luck at **hang gliding**?

When the snow falls in Traverse City, popular pastimes are downhill skiing, snowmobiling, cross-country skiing, and tobogganing. Two great ski resorts in the area are **Sugar Loaf Mountain** (18 miles northeast of town on U.S. 31) and **Hickory Hills** (two miles west of town on Randolph Rd.).

Don't overlook Traverse City in the fall, when the landscape is ablaze with vibrant red, yellow, and orange hues. Your family might want to take the **scenic drive** (north from Traverse City on Rt. 37) fo some dramatic views of the countryside. There are many other routes for color tours that include historic sights, wineries, or antique shops, depending on individual interest. (For more information, contact the Chamber of Commerce.)

Another popular activity in Traverse City is shopping. Quaint and unusual shops abound, with merchandise ranging from art and antiques to designer clothes for men, women, and children.

About 15 miles from Traverse City is the renowned **Interlochen Center for the Arts** (13 miles southwest on U.S. 31, then two miles south on Rt. 137). Each summer almost 2,000 students assemble here to study music, theater, art, and dance. Performances are scheduled throughout the season.

There are numerous fine restaurants in Traverse City and the surrounding area. Your family might try **J.R.R.'s Warehouse Restaurant** (Lake and Cass Sts., Traverse City), **Harvest Table** (420 Munson, Traverse City), or **Great Lakes Steak Co.** (1796 Garfield, Traverse City).

BEST TIME TO VISIT: Summer
DIRECTIONS: From Grand Rapids, take Rt. 37 straight north to Traverse City.
FOR MORE INFORMATION: Call or write Traverse City Area Convention and Visitors Bureau, 202 E. Grandview Pkwy., Box 387, Traverse City, MI 49684; (800) 421-5204.

Michigan

Pictured Rocks: Nature's Palette

**Pictured Rocks National Lakeshore
Munising, Michigan**

Driving Time: About 2 hours north of Mackinac City area

Overlooking the azure waters of Lake Superior on Michigan's Upper Peninsula, are the spectacular "Pictured Rocks." With rock formations that seem to be nature's castles and fortresses, the **Pictured Rocks National Lakeshore Park** offers some of the most breathtaking scenery anywhere in the upper Midwest.

Some visitors come to Pictured Rocks just to see the terrain and exquisite works of art that nature has sculpted 50 to 200 feet above the glistening lake. Actually, the extraordinary cliffs seem to rise out of the depths of the lake, standing guard over the peaceful waters that lap at the impenetrable bases. Stretching for about 15 miles northeast of Munising, the rocks are constantly transformed by the continually changing lights and shadows cast on them. With each passing year, the ice, wind, and weather leave their marks that alter the rocky facade.

The national park offers many unique points of interest. For example, **Sable Falls**, just west of Grand Marais, is a beautiful cascade; nearby is one of the park's pebble-covered beaches. Farther west and south along the lakeshore is the white sandy stretch of Twelvemile Beach, where picnicking, camping, and hiking facilities are available. Be sure to see the 500-foot log slide (near Grand Sable Banks). Constructed of wood, the slide was built in the late 1800s. This site provides a picturesque view of the Au Sable Point Light Station.

Pictured Rocks National Lakeshore

Listed in the National Register of Historic Places, the lighthouse began guiding boats on the lake way back in 1874.

At the **Beaver Basin**, your family can explore woodland trails or enjoy motorless boating on the area's rivers and smaller lakes. And of course, in the famous Pictured Rocks area is the marvelous Miners' Castle formation, as tall as an eight-story building.

Pictured Rocks National Lakeshore can be visited at any time of year. In the spring, wildflowers enhance the park's beauty; in the fall, the golden and red leaves are gorgeous. When the winter snows fall, the park is transformed into a white wonderland. The average annual snowfall is 150 inches, making a great base for cross-country skiing or snowshoeing. All park roads, except the Lakeshore Trail, are well suited to these wintertime activities. Along the lake, though, there are often very deep (and steep) drifts.

A Michigan fishing license is required for fishing in Lake Superior and the park's other lakes and streams. Some of the catches might include lake trout, whitefish, sunfish, perch, bass, pike, and brook and rainbow trout.

Before leaving the area, your family might want to stop by the town of Christmas, Michigan (just west of Munising on Rt. 28). It's not far enough north to be the North Pole — but it may seem like it in winter!

(For more entertainment ideas in the area, see articles on the National Ski Hall of Fame in Ishpeming and such other U.P. places as Fayette State Park, Hiawatha National Forest, and Toonerville Trolley to Taquamenon Falls.)

BEST TIME TO VISIT: Any time.
TRAVEL TIP: During the summer, from June through early September, the park sponsors an interpretive program, designed to acquaint visitors with the many wonders of Pictured Rocks. Some of the topics and events include Lighthouse and Shipwrecks Walk, Man and the Lake Campfire Program, An Evening at the Dunes, The Wildlife and Times of Beaver Basin, and more. (Check with the National Lakeshore Headquarters for schedule — see information below.)
HOURS: Pictured Rocks National Lakeshore is open daily, year round. The park headquarters on Sand Point in Munising is open weekdays from 8 a.m. to 4:30 p.m. The visitors centers outside Grand Marais and Munising entrances are open daily from 9 a.m. to 6 p.m.
DIRECTIONS: The park can be reached on the east from Grand Marais and on the west from Munising. From the Mackinac City area, take I-75 north to Rt. 123 northwest. Follow Rt. 123 past Trout Lake to Rt. 28 west; continue west to intersection of Rt. 77 at Seney. Follow Rt. 77 north to Grand Marais. To reach Munising area, continue west on Rt. 28, past Seney, and follow into town.
FOR MORE INFORMATION: Call or write Pictured Rocks National Lakeshore, P.O. Box 40, Sand Point, Munising, MI 49862; (906) 387-2607.

Michigan

The Locks: Fascinating Technical Feat!

Sault Ste. Marie, Michigan

Driving Time: About 1 hour north of Mackinac City area; about 7 hours north of Detroit

Perched on the northernmost border of the United States, the Soo Locks in Sault Ste. Marie are one of the world's engineering feats. Before the locks were built in the mid-19th century, there was no way for cargo vessels and ships to pass from Lake Superior to Lake Huron and the lower Great Lakes. This situation was an obvious handicap to the mining industry of Michigan's Upper Peninsula, as there was no way to transport goods by water to ports south and east. But in 1852 Congress passed an act giving 750,000 acres to the State of Michigan to use as payment to any company that would build locks. The next year, 1853, the Fairbanks Scale Co., which had a large mining business in the U.P., accepted the challenge.

Each year, thousands of visitors to the Soo Locks are amazed by the fascinating system that raises and lowers gigantic lake- and ocean-going vessels 21 feet in an amazingly short time period of just six to 15 minutes! The spectacular sight of huge ships being shifted from one water level to another provides a striking contrast to the image of early Ojibway Indian inhabitants who had to carry their canoes and chattels around the rapids to reach the opposite lake.

The history of the locks is an interesting one. When settlers came to the Northwest Territory, their belongings had to be unloaded from boats, carted around the rapids, and loaded

on boats on the other side. The Northwest Fur Co. first constructed a small lock on the site about 1797, but it was destroyed in the War of 1812. Years later, when construction began on the present system, an old Chippewa Indian burial ground had to be moved, and the tribe began beating its drums in warning to the white trespassers.

When the completed locks were turned over to the State of Michigan in 1855, the toll was four cents per ton. In 1881, when the U.S. government took over the locks, the fee was discontinued. Now about 13,000 vessels travel through the locks annually without paying a toll. This traffic represents more total tonnage than all the world's other canals combined, including Panama and Suez. That's quite a statistic for a system once ridiculed by Henry Clay: "Build a canal up at the end of nowhere? The federal government might just as well build a canal on the moon!"

Today, there are four American locks and one Canadian. The Poe Lock, belonging to the United States, has the largest capacity in the facility.

This lock, which took six years to construct, is the only one ever built between two operating locks.

Start your exploration of the locks at the **Visitors' Information Center** in the upper park area. There, your family will get an overview of the background and operation of the locks by seeing a movie, scale model, and various informative exhibits. From the observation towers, there are various views of the vessels going through the locks with accompanying information over a public address system.

In addition, your family might enjoy a **boat tour** through the American and Canadian locks. The 2½-hour trips take guests through the locks, past the great St. Mary's rapids, and along the waterfront of the twin cities of Sault Ste. Marie, Michigan, and Sault Ste. Marie, Ontario (*Sault* is the French word for "cascade"). The excursions leave from the docks at 1155 East Portage Avenue and 500 East Portage Avenue. Should you prefer a tour with a foreign flavor, your family can take a cruise from the Canadian side. Boats depart from docks of Lock Tours Canada (southeast of the Canadian lock, off Foster and Elgin Sts.).

More sightseeing fun is on hand at the **Soo Locks Tour Train**, leaving from the Haunted Depot (Osborn Blvd. near W. Portage Ave.). The train takes its riders on the 2.5-mile International Bridge, which is 135 feet above the great lock system. During the 1¼-hour trip, visitors view several historical spots, such as the location of the first French fort, site of Father Marquette's first mission, and the first Indian mission. The **Haunted Depot** has a number of believe-it-or-not-type features, including a gravity-defying "mystery bed room," an eerie cemetery, and a breath (and head) taking guillotine.

While in the Sault area, sea-lovers might check out the **SS Valley Camp Marine Museum** (five blocks east of the locks). The facility includes the Great Lakes Marine Hall of Fame with numerous interesting exhibits on maritime history and accomplishments. Also, visitors may tour a Great Lakes freighter.

BEST TIME TO VISIT: Summer or fall.
HOURS: Soo Locks Information Center — mid-May through mid-September, 8 a.m.-9 p.m.; mid-September through mid-November, 9 a.m.-5:30 p.m. Soo Locks Boat Tours (Michigan side) — late May through mid-June and early October, trips leave at 9 a.m., 11 a.m., 1:30 p.m., and 4 p.m.; mid-June through end of June and Labor Day through September 30, trips leave at one-hour intervals from 9 a.m. to 4 p.m.; from July 1 through Labor Day, trips leave throughout the day from 8 a.m. to 6 p.m. Soo Lock Boat Tours (Canadian side) — late May through end of June and Labor Day through mid-October, trips leave at 11 a.m., 1:30 p.m., 4 p.m. and 6:30 p.m.; July 1 through Labor Day, trips leave from 9:30 a.m. to 6:30 p.m. (eight trips daily); after September 21, the last trip leaves at 6 p.m. Soo Locks Tour Trains — July and August, trains leave daily at half-hour intervals from 9 a.m. to 7:30 p.m.; late May to June and after Labor Day to early October, daily from 9 a.m. to 5 p.m.
ADMISSION: Soo Locks admission is free. Boat Tours (Michigan side) — adults and teens, $1; children 6 years and over, 50¢. Train Tours — adults, $3.25; students, $1.75.
DIRECTIONS: From Mackinac City, take I-75 northwest to Sault Ste. Marie. From Detroit, take I-75 north, past Mackinac, to Sault Ste. Marie.
FOR MORE INFORMATION: Call or write Sault Ste. Marie Area Chamber of Commerce, 2581 I-75 Business Spur, Sault Ste. Marie, MI 49783; (906) 632-3301.

The Soo Locks at Sault Ste. Marie

Mason: World of the Fur Traders

Mason, Michigan

Driving Time: About 1½ hours north of Grand Rapids; 5 hours northeast of Chicago; 5 hours west of Detroit

French explorers came to the Lake Michigan shoreline in Mason County, Michigan, in the 18th century seeking animal skins for the fur trade. The home of the first white settler, Burr Caswell, became the focal point for a Bicentennial restoration project recalling pioneer days. That 1976 project, **White Pine Village** (1687 S. Lakeshore Dr., Ludington), is now a growing collection of reconstructed buildings that recreate the lifestyle of early American settlers: a blacksmith shop, general store, trapper's cabin, town hall, school, hardware store, and more.

While in the area, visit the **Rose Hawley Museum** (305 E. Filer St., Ludington), where Indian artifacts, historical information, and collections from early settlement days are displayed. The Marine Exhibit focuses on early shipping history.

(For more entertainment ideas in the area, see the article in this section on Manistee.)

BEST TIME TO VISIT: Summer, during one of the special events. Check with White Pine Village office for schedule (phone number below).
HOURS: Village and Museum — Memorial Day to Labor Day, 11 a.m.-5 p.m. Monday-Saturday. Village is also open Sunday, 1 p.m.-7 p.m.
ADMISSION: Village — adults and teens 18 and over, $1; teens 13-17, 50¢. Museum is free.
DIRECTIONS: From Grand Rapids, take I-96 northwest toward Muskegon; pick up U.S. 31 north and follow to Ludington.
FOR MORE INFORMATION: Call or write White Pine Village, 1687 S. Lakeshore Dr., Ludington, MI 49431; (616) 843-4804.

Michigan

An Historic Island—With No Cars!

Mackinac Island, Michigan

Driving Time: About 7 hours north of Detroit, 8 hours northeast of Chicago

The long-ago days of the horse and buggy are still preserved in glorious style on Mackinac Island in northern Michigan. Here, just at the point where Lake Michigan meets Lake Huron, is the historic island offering thousands of visitors a place to relax, see the sights and explore to their hearts' content. No motorized vehicles are allowed on the island so you'll have to take a ferry boat from Mackinaw City or St. Ignace.

A good way to begin your vacation is to take a carriage tour, which lasts about an hour. The tour will give you an overall view of the many intriguing spots that you may miss if you go on your own. At Fort Mackinac, which was occupied by the British from 1780 to 1895, you may leave the carriage tour to investigate the historic old fort. All the buildings are open for inspection, including barracks, officers' quarters, hospital, storeroom, etc. There are also cannon salutes and musket firings, lending a note of authenticity to the visit. Nearby points of interest include a mission church, Indian dormitory, blacksmith shop and Biddle House, the home of a 19th-century fur trader, restored to the 1820's period style.

Outdoor enthusiasts will enjoy the many island routes marked for hiking, biking and

horseback riding. For example, on the **Natural History Tour** you will see lofty pines, Sugar Loaf Rock and Arch Rock, which rises 146 feet above the water and spans 50 feet at its widest point. On another tour of the middle section of the island, you will see Skull Cave, Fort Holmes, British Landing, military battlefields and old cemeteries. Each route offers magnificent views of the island and surrounding straits, as well as scenic terrain. (Information is available from the Visitor Cen-

ter on Fort Street.)

But back on **Main Street** there are more attractions for each family member. Everyone will be delighted by the quaint 19th-century charm of the area, which abounds with unusual shops with all sorts of articles from cornhusk dolls to that fabulous fudge. Thousands of pounds of fudge are sold each year to tourists, who may watch the candy prepared in huge copper kettles—part of Mackinac's tradition.

Michigan

Just across the straits in Mackinaw City is **Fort Michilimackinac**, a Revolutionary War fortified town built by the French in 1715. There you may tour the buildings and watch craftsmen and military demonstrations. At the church of Ste. Anne there is a light and sound program each hour featuring history of the fort. For overnight accommodations, there are many hotels on the island, including, of course, the famous **Grand Hotel**.

HOURS: Carriage Tours: 8:30 AM to 5 PM daily, July through Labor Day; 8:30 AM to 2:30 PM daily, mid-May to early June and after Labor Day to mid-October; 8:30 AM to 4 PM mid-June to June 30; no tours rest of year. Fort Mackinac: 9 AM to 6 PM daily, mid-June to Labor Day; 10 AM to 4 PM daily, late May to mid-June and after Labor Day to Oct. 15. Indian Dormitory, Biddle House, Benjamin Blacksmith Shop: 11 AM to 5 PM daily, June 15 through Oct. 15. Fort Michilimackinac: 8 AM to 8 PM daily, mid-June through Labor Day; 8 AM to 5 PM mid-May to mid-June and after Labor Day to mid-October.

FOR MORE INFORMATION: Call Mackinac Island State Park Commission, (906) 847-3328, or Greater Mackinaw City Chamber of Commerce, (906) 436-5396.

ADMISSION: Carriage Tours: Adults, $5, children and pre-teens 5 to 11 yrs., $2.50; children under 5 yrs., free. Historic Mackinac Island ticket includes Fort Mackinac, Indian Dormitory, Blacksmith Shop, Mission Church, Fort Holmes and Biddle House: Adults, $2.50; teens 13 to 17 yrs., $1.50; pre-teens and children, free with adult. (Prices subject to change.)

DIRECTIONS: From Twin Cities, take U.S. Rt. 8 north and east across Wisconsin. At Iron Mountain, Michigan, pick up U.S. Rt. 2 (toward Escanaba) and continue east to Mackinaw City and St. Ignace. Take ferry to Mackinac Island.

Saddle Up! Across Michigan On Horseback

Want to relive the "good old days," when the Midwest was wilderness and Indians roamed the plains? The **Michigan Trail Riders Association** welcomes you to do so on any of its three annual rides across the state. During the year, there are rides to accommodate various riding skills and needs in June, September, and October.

Ranging in age from five to 80 years, club members welcome newcomers who wish to saddle up and ride off into the proverbial sunset. If your family wants to join the group, just write for a family membership (it's only $10), and you are well on your way to an extraordinary adventure in the scenic area called Top O' Mich.

The **June trip**, which attracts 200 to 300 riders, is the most popular. Following the official trail stretching from Lake Michigan on the west to Lake Huron on the east, the riders tackle the 225-mile distance, covering 20 to 25 miles per day. Although it's a considerable distance, the route is planned for leisurely travel with many stopover points in the two-week period.

Each year, the trip alternates between an east-west route starting in Traverse City, and a west-east course originating in Empire City. At dawn, the day begins with feeding the horses and moving vehicles to the next camp. The ride starts about 9 a.m., with a parade of Appaloosas, Palominos, and Arabians. The next stop is about three to six hours away.

The trail is open year round, but two other group rides are held in the fall. During the second half of September, there's a nine-day ride that's intended for those who want a fast-paced, challenging journey. Later, during the first week of October, there's a seven-day trip that is less strenuous.

Families interested in taking a weekend ride can contact any of several stables near the trail, where horses and guides can be obtained: **Ranch Rudolph**, Brown Bridge Rd., Traverse City, MI 49684, (616) 947-9529 (guided group rides are offered at $8 per hour for each horse); and **Karefree Ranch**, Fairview, MI 48621, (517) 848-5771 (weekend pack trips are available for $100 per person, hourly and daily rentals are $8 an hour or $30 per day).

FOR MORE INFORMATION: Call or write Mrs. Ilma Flannery, Michigan Trail Riders Association, 1650 Ormond Rd., Highland, MI 48031; (313) 887-5402. Send $10 for maps, guide book, and family membership.

Michigan

Wine Tours In Western Michigan

Berrien and Van Buren Counties, Michigan

Driving Time: About 1½ hours east of Chicago

Chablis, chardonnay, burgundy, rosé — four different kinds of wine. Unfortunatley, many people believe that the only variation among them is whether the wine is red or white. Each wine, however, has its own personality or character. One can be soft, flowery, and sweet; another, full, robust, and dry; or somewhere in between.

One of the best ways to learn about wines and the art of winemaking is to take a trip to the southeastern tip of Lake Michigan — in Michigan. There, the naturally sandy soil, lake-influenced weather, and winter snows combine to create one of America's better wine-producing regions. Several of the wineries offer fine tours of their facilities.

Perhaps the best spot to start is at the south end of the wine country in **Berrien County**. At **Tabor Hill Vineyard and Winecellar**, near Buchanan, visitors are invited to take a walking tour in the vineyard to see the grapes ripening on the vine. Inside the wine cellar, the winemaker is hard at work surrounded by the huge vats and old oaken casks, where the wine is aged. Next, bottles are filled with selections ranging in color from deep, rosy red to clear, sparkling white. At the end of the free tour, guests may stop for wine and cheese in the wine-tasting rooms.

The Tabor Hill Vineyard was started years ago with a collection of hybrid grape vines transplanted from France. And in 1977, Tabor's 1974 Baco wine was named the best Baco in the nation at the First Annual

American Wine Competition. One year later, every variety of wine produced there received an award at one of the wine competitions. (To reach Tabor Hill, take I-94 and exit at Exit 16 in Bridgman.)

Nearby is **Frontenac Vineyards** (3418 W. Michigan, Paw Paw), another worthwhile stop. Frontenac is the home of peach and honey wine. Here, especially in winter, one of the favorite drinks is Skier's Delight, a mixture of spiced peach with honey wine.

From Tabor Hill, take I-94 to Exit 12 (at Sawyer) for a visit to the **Lakeside Winery** (13581 Red Arrow Hwy., Harbert). This is the home of Molly Pitcher wines, so guides are appropriately dressed in colonial garb. From June through August, the outdoor Wine Garden is open for wine-tasting. In colder weather, guests may sample the delicious vintages in the Wine Barrel. Throughout the year, Lakeside Vineyard hosts special events that include: New Wine Festival (last weekend in May),

Frontier Days (third weekend in July), Art Fair (third weekend in August), and October Winefest (first weekend in October).

For the next vineyard area, continue north and east on I-94 (past Benton Harbor) toward Paw Paw. Michigan's largest winery, **Warner Vineyards** (706 S. Kalamazoo St., Paw Paw), is located just north of I-94 at Exit 60. The free tour begins at the Wine Haus. From there, guests move to a remodeled 1919 Grand Trunk railroad car, where they view an audio-visual presentation on the history of winemaking and modern wine production. The walking tour exhibits the various steps in wine production. A tour highlight is the demonstration of two Old World winemaking methods: Methode Champenoise, in which champagne is fermented in its own bottle; and the Solera system, aging in oak casks to produce premium sherry or port. Of course, visitors are invited to taste the Warner products at the end of the tour.

Down Home In Michigan's Farm Country

Near Kalamazoo, Michigan

Driving Time: About 3 hours northeast of Chicago and west of Detroit

All the attractions of an old-fashioned Midwestern farm can be found near Kalamazoo, at the **Bee Hive Farm**. Located just off U.S. 131 between Gobles and Kendall, the farm offers experiences that are well suited to families. In the farmland section, children may meet nose-to-nose with real farm animals that include donkeys, goats, lambs, pigs, turkeys, rabbits, and chickens.

In the farm's growing center, visitors may purchase seeds, trees, shrubs, and tools to tend their lawns and gardens. In seasons, visitors can also pick such vegetables as tomatoes, green beans sugar snap peas, rhubarb, and wild huckleberries. Other fresh produce available from local farms include asparagus, strawberries, cherries, broccoli, peaches, pumpkins, and more. A complete line of natural foods, from nuts and cheese to bakery goods and fresh cider, is available.

BEST TIME TO VISIT: Summer.
HOURS: Bee Hive Farm — year round, 8 a.m.-7 p.m. Tuesday, Wednesday, Thursday, and Sunday; 8 a.m.-8 p.m. Friday and Saturday.
ADMISSION: To petting farmland, 75¢ per person.
DIRECTIONS: From Chicago, take I-94 northeast around the tip of Lake Michigan, past Michigan City and Benton Harbor, continuing toward Kalamazoo. Exit (west of Kalamazoo) at Rt. 40 north (Paw Paw). Follow Rt. 40 north to Gobles, turn right on D Ave. (County Rd. 388) and follow to Bee Hive Farm (2½ miles). From Detroit area, take I-94 west past Jackson and Kalamazoo. On west side of Kalamazoo exit at U.S. 131 north; continue to D Ave. (County Rd. 388) and turn left (west). Continue on D Ave. through Alamo and Kendall to Bee Hive Farm.
FOR MORE INFORMATION: Call or write Bee Hive Farm, 8997 E. 16th Ave., Gobles, MI 49055; (616) 628-2854.

St. Julian Wine Co. (716 S. Kalamazoo St., Paw Paw) is the oldest winery in the state. Founded in 1921, St. Julian is Michigan's largest and oldest producer of prize-winning premium table wines and champagne. The winery, founded by Mariano Meconi, was originally located in Windsor, Ontario, Canada. With the repeal of the prohibition laws, the winemaker moved the facility across the river to Detroit, and three years later to Paw Paw.

If you've never heard of onion wine (and most people haven't), make sure to visit the **Vendramino Winery** (off I-94 at Exit 56).

While in the area, your family might also want to check out the **Bronte Champagne and Wine Co.**, about 20 miles west of Paw Paw (take I-94 to Exit 46). The vineyards are located on land that was once a harness horse racing track. Free tours and wine sampling are offered here.

Each fall, the wineries in the area participate in the **Kalamazoo-Paw Paw Wine and Harvest Festival** (early September, after Labor Day). The festival celebration features, among other activities, a carnival, parade, arts and crafts fair, and, of course, a grape stomp.

BEST TIME TO VISIT: Spring, summer, or fall.
HOURS: Tabor Hill — 10 a.m.-8 p.m. Monday through Saturday, noon-8 p.m. Sunday, May through October; closed at 6 p.m. November through April. Lakeside — March through October, 9:30 a.m.-4 p.m. Monday through Saturday; noon-4:30 p.m. Sunday. Warner — year round, 9 a.m.-5 p.m. Monday through Saturday; noon-5 p.m. Sunday; summer hours are extended to 6 p.m. Frontenac — year round, 9 a.m.-5 p.m. Monday through Saturday; noon-5 p.m. Sunday. St. Julian — year round, 9 a.m.-5 p.m. daily. Vendramino — mid-May through October, 9 a.m.-5 p.m. daily. Bronte — 10 a.m.-4 p.m. Monday through Saturday; noon-4 p.m. Sunday all year.
ADMISSION: All tours are free
DIRECTIONS: From Chicago and points west, take I-94 east, past Michigan City, Indiana, and into Berrien County. From Detroit, take I-94 west (start in Paw Paw-Kalamazoo area, then go to Lakeside and Tabor Hill). From Grand Rapids, take U.S. 131 south to Kalamazoo area and pick up I-94 west.
FOR MORE INFORMATION: Call or write Southwestern Michigan Tourist Council, Napier Professional Building, 151 E. Napier, Benton Harbor, MI 49022; (616) 925-6301.

Michigan

Space Museum In the Middle Of Michigan

Jackson, Michigan

Driving Time: 2 hours west of Detroit; 4½ hours east of Chicago

The story of space exploration is vividly told at the **Michigan Space Center** in Jackson (2111 Emmons Rd.). The museum building — a large, golden, geodesic dome — is a sight in itself. Inside, the fantastic voyage into outer space unfolds with exhibits and souvenirs of U.S. space flights.

The **Apollo 9** command module is displayed, along with astronaut suits, a Mariner spacecraft, an early lunar rover, satellites, moon rocks, giant rocket engines, and more. A special exhibit allows visitors to view a stereo picture of the moon through 3-D glasses — an astronaut's eye-view. In another area, museum guests are invited to put on space helmets and watch themselves in a mirrored lunar landscape. Space food, with its unusual form and consistency, is an additional attraction, providing such a contrast to the food we eat on earth. And in the **Astrotheatre**, movies on space exploration enhance the museum's exhibits.

During a visit to Jackson, it's worth seeing the breathtaking shows at the **Sparks Illuminated Cascade Waterfalls** (on S. Brown Ave. in Sparks County Park). The nighttime spectaculars feature 2,000 gallons of water per minute cascading over 16 waterfalls, with constantly changing combinations of light, color, and music. Surrounding the falling water are six fountains that literally explode with colored lights. In addition, the park includes the **Cascades-Sparks Museum**, showcasing the falls early history and the life

Lunar Surveyor spacecraft mock-up at the Michigan Space Center in Jackson

of its creator, Captain William Sparks. Original drawings, models, and audio-visual displays are featured.

A visit to the **Ella Sharp Museum** (3225 Fourth St.) provides a close look at life in pioneer days. Listed on the National Register of Historic Places, the Merriman Sharp family farmhouse is the center of the complex. The restored residence, with its large front portico framed by grand white pillars, exhibits 19th-century Victorian antiques and elegant furnishings. Other buildings include the **Tower Barn**, where farm implements and carriages are shown; the **Woodworking Shop**, showcasing early craftsmen's tools; the **General Store**, filled with a potpourri of old-fashioned goods; and the **Log Cabin**, exhibiting pioneer lifestyle in the mid-19th century. The one-room schoolhouse is a memorial to the pioneer's high regard for education.

Each year, Jackson County is host to numerous tourists who seek outdoor recreational opportunities at the county's 601 natural lakes. Just 10 miles south of Jackson (off U.S. 127) is **Clark Lake**, surrounded by 500 acres of sandy beaches and shady woodlands. There are facilities for swimming, sailing, fishing, riding, golf, and more.

BEST TIME TO VISIT: Summer.
HOURS: Michigan Space Center — 8 a.m.-5 p.m. Monday-Friday. 11 a.m.-5 p.m. weekends. Sparks Cascade Waterfalls shows — Memorial Day-Labor Day, 7 p.m.-11 p.m. Wednesday-Sunday. Ella Sharp Museum — 10 a.m.-5 p.m. Tuesday-Friday, 1:30 p.m.-5 p.m. weekends; closed January.
ADMISSION: Michigan Space Center — adults, $3; students and sr. citizens, $2; family rate, $9. Sparks Cascade Waterfalls — adults, teens, and children over 5 years, $1.50. Ella Sharp Museum (farmhouse) — adults and teens, $1; children, 50¢.
DIRECTIONS: From Detroit, take I-94 west past Ann Arbor to Jackson.
FOR MORE INFORMATION: Call or write Jackson Chamber of Commerce, 401 S. Jackson, Box 80, Jackson, MI 49203; (517) 782-8221.

Ann Arbor Life: Football, U. of M., Museums, Fairs

Ann Arbor, Michigan

Driving Time: About 1 hour west of Detroit

Ann Arbor's claim to fame is that it's the home of the **University of Michigan**, one of the nation's leading educational institutions with an enrollment of 35,000 students. Perhaps the best time of year to visit is the fall, when the whole town gears up for Michigan football games.

The U. of M. campus, which was originally located in Detroit, boasts several fine museums with national reputations. The **A.G. Ruthven Museum** features numerous exhibits focusing on natural history, from dinosaurs to minerology. Some of the displays include early reptiles, prehistoric mammals, amphibians, Michigan wildlife, plants, and astronomy.

The **Kelsey Museum of Archeology** showcases intriguing relics from ancient civilizations. Other campus points of interest are the **Museum of Art**, **Nichols Arboretum**, and the **Botanical Gardens**. Even if your family does not attend a Wolverines game, see **Memorial Stadium**; seating more than 100,000 persons, it's the country's largest college-owned football stadium. **Campus walking tours** are available September through April at 10 and 11 a.m., 1 and 2 p.m., Monday through Friday (tours begin at Alumni Center, 200 Fletcher St.).

In the campus area there are also many intriguing shops: the **Nickels Arcade**, an unusual European-style shopping mall built in 1915 that in-

Burton Memorial Tower at the University of Michigan in Ann Arbor

cludes unique little shops and galleries; and **Kerrytown** (415 N. 5th Ave.), another quaint shopping area with a wide assortment of such merchandise as antiques, gourmet items, furniture, wine, and seafood. Also, each Saturday (and Wednesday in summer), the area outside Kerrytown is host to the popular **Farmers' Market**. Fresh produce, bakery goods, and arts and crafts are offered in the open-air setting.

Several festivals and special events are held annually in Ann Arbor. The **May Festival** (first week) features the Philadelphia Orchestra performing a series of concerts with famous soloists. Then, in mid-July Ann Arbor is the setting for the state's most well-known **Art Fair**, where local and regional artists exhibit works ranging from traditional painting to unusual modernistic expressions. The **Greek Ya'ssoo Festival** is held the first weekend in June at St. Nicholas Greek Orthodox Church. The **Antiques Market** (Farm Council Fairgrounds) is reputedly one of the Midwest's finest antiques displays, with more than 200 participating dealers (third Sunday of the month, May through October).

BEST TIME TO VISIT: Fall.
HOURS: Ruthven Museum and Museum of Art — 9 a.m.-5 p.m. Monday-Saturday, 1 p.m.-5 p.m. Sunday; closed major holidays. Kelsey Museum of Archeology — September-June, 9 a.m.-5 p.m. Monday-Friday; July and August, 11 a.m.-4 p.m. Tuesday-Friday; 1 p.m.-5 p.m. weekends all year. Kerrytown shops — 9:30 a.m.-5:30 p.m. weekdays; 9 a.m.-5 p.m. Saturday. For football tickets, call (313) 764-7268.
ADMISSION: Free to all U. of M. museums.
DIRECTIONS: From Detroit, take I-94 west to Ann Arbor.
FOR MORE INFORMATION: Call or write Ann Arbor Conference and Visitors Bureau, 200 E. Washington St., Ann Arbor, MI 48104; (313) 995-7281.

Michigan

Huckleberry Railroad Adventure

Flint, Michigan

Driving Time: About 1 hour north of Detroit

With humble beginnings as an American Bicentennial project, **Huckleberry Railroad and Crossroads Village** in Flint has grown to become a popular visitor attraction, brimming with old-time charm. Guests at the village (on Bray Rd., six miles northeast of town) are invited to turn the clock back and step into another time and place.

A trip on the **Huckleberry Railroad** (named after Huckleberry Finn, of course) takes riders on a scenic, 10-mile trip through Genessee County. The old-fashioned wooden passenger coaches, pulled by a steam-powered locomotive, recall the leisurely 19th-century life. (But watch out for the train robbers lurking in the woods to snatch valuable gold shipments!)

At the village depot, visitors step into a town of 100 years ago. Featuring 19 buildings, the village reproduces in meticulous detail the various elements of life in the mid-19th century.

Michigan's oldest **grist mill**, at the village, demonstrates the method of grinding corn and wheat with gigantic grindstones. Take home a souvenir bag of flour, the freshest you'll ever find. And at the **blacksmith shop**, a village smithy forges ironwork for appreciative audiences. Nearby, other early-American industries are operating, such as the **cider mill**, where apples are pressed to make sweet cider, and the **saw mill**, where steam-powered machinery cuts logs into rough-hewn lumber.

Even on vacation, children are always delighted to attend classes at the **Crossroads Village School** —

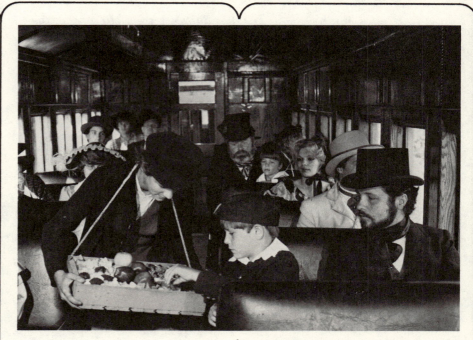

they notice quite a difference as compared to the present methods. Other buildings with many unusual sights to offer include the **doctor's office**, **general store**, **Post Office**, and, of course, a pioneer home, complete with costumed women working on craft projects and household tasks.

For a break, picnic in the **village park** on the lovely shore of Mott Lake. But don't leave before witnessing the trickery and mystery of the magic show at the **opera house**.

Adjacent to Crossroads Village is **Stepping Stone Falls**, a unique concrete structure with water cascading over the various levels. It's especially pretty at night, when the cascades are flooded by multi-colored lights.

Michigan's third largest city, Flint is the home of the **General Motors Buick and Chevrolet plants**. In automobile production, Flint is second only to Detroit. Free tours are available at the Buick Motor Division of GM (902 E. Hamilton); the plant shows the final steps in the assembly of cars.

Your family can learn more about that intriguing machine, the automobile, at the **Sloan Museum** of the **Flint College and Cultural Center** (1221 E. Kearsley St.). Antique autos

and carriages are featured along with presentations of American history.

Another worthwhile stop, especially for art enthusiasts, is the **Flint Institute of Art** in the **DeWaters Art Center** (1120 E. Kearsley). The collection showcases fine examples of diverse periods and cultures, including Renaissance, Oriental, 19th- and 20th-century American painting, and sculpture. Also, in the cultural center area is the **Robert T. Longway Planetarium** (1310 E. Kearsley). Sky shows there explore planets, stars, ancient mythology, science fiction, and space travel.

BEST TIME TO VISIT: Summer.
HOURS: Crossroads Village — end of May-Labor Day, 10 a.m.-5:30 p.m. Monday-Friday, 11 a.m.-6:30 p.m. weekends and holidays. Stepping Stone Falls — end of May-early September, noon-11 p.m. Monday-thusday; noon to midnight Friday, weekends, and holidays. GM tours — 9:30 a.m. Monday-Friday. Sloan Museum — 10 a.m.-5 p.m. Tuesday-Friday, noon-5 p.m. weekends. Institute of Art — 10 a.m.-5 p.m. Tuesday-Saturday, 1 p.m.-5 p.m. Sunday. Longway Planetarium shows — 7:30 p.m. Friday; 1 p.m., 2:30 p.m., and 4 p.m. weekends.
ADMISSION: Crossroads Village — adults, $5.75; children 3 years and over, $3.25. Sloan Museum and Longway Planetarium — adults, $1; students and sr. citizens, 50¢.
DIRECTIONS: From Detroit, take I-75 northwest to Flint.
FOR MORE INFORMATION: Call or write Flint Convention and Visitors Bureau, 1 Northbank Center, Flint, MI 48502; (313) 232-8900.

Sleeping Dunes: Getting Close To Nature

Frankfort, Michigan

Driving Time: About 2½ hours north of Grand Rapids

.Formed by the residue of the giant glaciers that once carved out the Great Lakes, **Sleeping Bear Dunes National Lakeshore Park**, near Frankfort, is a terrific place to commune with nature. Besides the natural beauty of the forest, dunes, and lake, the area offers countless opportunities for recreation in both winter and summer.

The story behind the park's name is an intriguing one. A Chippewa Indian legend tells of another bear and her cubs who tried to swim across Lake Michigan from Wisconsin. Although the mother bear reached safety, her cubs did not. And today she can still be seen watching for her offspring as the "sleeping bear," a solitary dune covered with dark foliage. Her cubs are the **North and South Manitou Islands**, forever stranded out in the lake.

The park's terrain includes a sandy shoreline, hills and valleys, small lakes, forests, swamps, and bogs. The area encompasses 34 miles of lakeshore, with various dune formations. The vegetation supported by the dunes serves as an obstacle to the wind, thus creating and maintaining the sand formations. Some of the earliest plants there that still remain today are beachgrass, sandy cherry, and cottonwood.

A visit to the **Philip A. Hart Visitor Center** (open mid-May through October) is an excellent way to get acquainted with all the park has to offer. Exhibits on the area's maritime and natural history and a slide presentation on the park are available there.

Spectacular vistas of the **Sleeping Bear landscape** are featured on the **Pierce Stocking Scenic Drive**. The 7.6-mile route over dunes and into forests has numerous spots overlooking Lake Michigan, the Manitou Islands, Glen Lake, and, of course, the Sleeping Bear. (Open early May through early November; closed in wet weather.)

A popular activity for hearty hikers is tackling the **Dune Climb**, which rises 130 feet above the shoreline. Throughout the park, hiking is permitted on public grounds.

Visitors are invited to swim at **Glen Lake, Platte Bay, Good Harbor Bay,** and **Glen Haven beaches**. But beware: Lake Michigan waters are *cold* until late summer. For relaxation, your family might try canoeing on the **Platte** or **Crystal Rivers**, or fishing in the lake (Michigan fishing license required). There are also many facilities for camping near the Platte River, Dune Climb, and on South Manitou Island.

A boat taking visitors to **South Manitou Island** operates mid-spring through mid-fall from the Leland dock. Island guests are allowed about three hours to explore the area before returning to the mainland. (North Manitou Island is privately owned and closed to the public.)

For longer stays there are **camping facilities** available. There are more than 5,000-island acres of dune, beach, forest, and field containing an area of virgin white cedar trees that are about 500 years old. Other points of interest there are magnificent dunes, an historic lighthouse, and even a shipwreck that is easily seen from shore.

.In winter, the **Sleeping Bear area** attracts numerous cross-country skiers, taking advantage of the snow-covered expanse with breathtaking views. Ski trails abound in various locations, including Platte Bay, Empire Bluff, Alligator Hill, and Good Harbor Bay.

BEST TIME TO VISIT: Summer, fall, winter.
HOURS: Sleeping Bear Dunes is open daily, year round. Visitors Center — 9 a.m.-5 p.m. daily, mid-May to mid-October; weekends the rest of year. Boat trip to South Manitou — 10 a.m. daily from Leland dock.
FEE: Camping fee is $6 per site, each night.
DIRECTIONS: From Grand Rapids, take I-96 northwest to junction with U.S. 31 north. Follow U.S. 31 north past Manistee to Benzonia on Crystal Lake. At Benzonia, pick up Rt. 115 west to Frankfort. Follow Rt. 22 north to Sleeping Bear Dunes National Lakeshore.
FOR MORE INFORMATION: Call or write U.S. Department of the Interior, National Park Service, Sleeping Bear Dunes National Lakeshore, 400 Main St., Frankfort, MI 49635; (616) 352-9611.

Michigan

Visiting A President's Home Town

Grand Rapids, Michigan

Driving Time: About 3 hours west of Detroit; 3 hours east of Chicago

Former United States President Gerald R. Ford was raised in Grand Rapids, Michigan's second largest city. Over the past few years since he left office, Ford's memorial museum has become one of the most popular tourist attractions in the area. Located on the banks of the Grand River, the **Gerald R. Ford Presidential Museum** contains numerous displays that trace the life and accomplishments of the 38th president. A tour of the facility begins with a half-hour movie, "Gerald R. Ford: The Presidency Restored."

Showcased in the second-floor exhibit hall are Richard M. Nixon's resignation letter and Ford's subsequent letter pardoning Nixon for his involvement in the Watergate scandal. Other videotape presentations focus on Congress, the vice-presidential office, and the 1976 presidential campaign. One of the favorite attractions is a full-scale reproduction of the Oval Office as it appeared during the Ford administration. Another highlight is a multi-media show, "An American Celebration: The Bicentennial," featuring music performed by the University of Michigan symphony orchestra.

Another of the town's attractions is the **John Ball Zoological Gardens** (Fulton St. and Valley Ave. S.W.). The Adventureland section contains a children's petting zoo, a 60-foot waterfall, and an alpine climb. Two of the newer exhibits feature playful monkeys and intriguing otters.

Gerald R. Ford Museum in Grand Rapids

A journey back to Grand Rapids as it was a century ago is a favorite part of the **Grand Rapids Public Museum** (54 Jefferson Ave., S.E.). Be sure to see Gaslight Village to learn about the old days. Other areas of the museum showcase Indian artifacts, old-fashioned costumes, period furniture, Michigan mammals and plants, and more. In mid-May the museum sponsors a Pioneer Days Arts and Crafts Festival. Demonstrations are given of such pioneer crafts as tinsmithing, woodworking, candle-dipping, and weaving.

The **Roger B. Chaffee Planetarium**, part of the Public Museum, attracts numerous visitors annually for its spectacular sky shows.

The **Grand Rapids Art Museum** (155 N. Division St.) is housed in the renovated, historic Federal Building, built in 1909 and listed in the National Register of Historic Places. Renaissance, American and German paintings are included in the permanent collection, with various changing exhibits.

A charming collection of unusual shops is found at **Gaslight Village** (2100 Wealthy St., S.E.). Items sold in the quaint establishments range from designer clothes to antiques, art, and homemade candies.

Just a few miles northwest of the city is **Blandford Nature Center** (1715 Hillburn Ave., N.W.). The 113-acre area abounds in wooded sections, fields, and ponds where your family can enjoy the many wonders of the great outdoors. Also, there is a furnished pioneer farm with gardens and an old-time, one-room schoolhouse.

BEST TIME TO VISIT: Summer or fall.
HOURS: Ford Museum — 9 a.m.-4:45 p.m. Monday through Saturday, noon-4:45 p.m. Sunday year round; closed New Year's Day, Thanksgiving Day, and Christmas Day. Grand Rapids Public Museum — 10 a.m.-5 p.m. Monday through Friday; Saturday and Sunday, 1 p.m.-5 p.m. John Ball Zoo — mid-April through September, 10 a.m.-7 p.m.; rest of year to 4:30 p.m. Grand Rapids Art Museum — 10 a.m.-5 p.m. Tuesday through Saturday, 1 p.m.-5 p.m. Sunday. Blandford Nature Center — 9 a.m.-5 p.m. weekdays; 2 p.m.-5 p.m. Sunday.
ADMISSION: Ford Museum — adults and teens 16 years and over, $1. Grand Rapids Public Museum — adults and teens over 15 years, $1; seniors, children, and teens to 15 years, 50¢. Planetarium — adults and teens over 15 years, $1.50; children over six and teens to 15 years, $1.
DIRECTIONS: From Detroit, take I-96 northwest, past Lansing, to Grand Rapids.
FOR MORE INFORMATION: Call or write the Grand Rapids Area Chamber of Commerce, 17 Fountain St., N.W., Grand Rapids, MI 49503; (616) 459-7221.

A Bit of Old Germany In Michigan

Frankenmuth, Michigan

Driving Time: About 1-1/3 hours north of Detroit

Weinerschnitzel, beer gardens, craft shops, and the Old World atmosphere of Germany bring numerous tourists annually to Frankenmuth. Originally settled by Lutheran missionaries from Germany in 1845, the Bavarian-style town recalls the heritage of its first inhabitants.

A first stop might be the **Frankenmuth Historical Museum** (613 S. Main St.), with its folk art and period rooms. Just a few blocks away is **Carling National Breweries** (926 S. Main St.), where guided tours tell the story of malt beverage manufacturing. (After all, what would Germany be without beer?)

From one end of Main Street to the other, Frankenmuth is full of shops selling everything from stylish apparel to gourmet food and craft items. At **Rapunzel's** (Main St. near the river), weaving demonstrations are given daily. And at the **Schnitzelbank Shop**, the local woodcarver creates intricate designs just like they do in the Old Country. Each shop makes a special contribution to the town's enchanting environment. Don't miss **Bronner's Christmas Wonderland**, with its dazzling assortment of decorations for Christmas and other seasons. (The address — 25 Christmas Lane, of course!)

Hearty German food is available at **Zehnder's** (730 S. Main St.) or the **Bavarian Inn** among other spots. These two restaurants are linked by the Holz-Brucke (covered bridge).

(For more information on other attractions in the area, see articles in this section on Detroit and Flint.)

French and English re-enactment at Old Au Sable Days in Ludington

BEST TIME TO VISIT: Summer (Town Pola-fest is in mid-August; Bavarian Festival is second week in June).

HOURS: Frankenmuth Historical Museum — June through August and October, 10:30 a.m.-5 p.m. daily; rest of year, except January and February, same hours Wednesday-Saturday; year round, Sunday 12:30-5 p.m. Carling National Breweries — weekdays year round, tours at 10 a.m., 11 a.m., 1 p.m., 2 p.m. and 3 p.m. Most shops in town are open daily, year round, from 9 or 10 a.m.-5 p.m.

ADMISSION: Historical Museum — 75¢; children under 12, free.

DIRECTIONS: From Detroit, take I-75 northwest, past Flint. Exit at Rt. 54-83 east (Frankenmuth-Birch Run exit). Follow Rt. 83 north to Frankenmuth.

FOR MORE INFORMATION: Call or write Frankenmuth Chamber of Commerce, 635 S. Main St., Frankenmuth, MI 48734; (517) 652-6106.

Monroe: Gen. Custer's First Stand

Monroe, Michigan

Driving Time: About 45 minutes south of Detroit, Michigan, and north of Toledo, Ohio

With the glistening waters of Lake Erie lapping at its eastern edge, Monroe is one of the oldest cities in Michigan. The best way to get acquainted with the town is to take a walking tour.

Founded in 1785, the city was originally called Frenchtown; it was renamed Monroe in 1817. One of Monroe's famous residents was **General George Armstrong Custer** (of "Custer's Last Stand" fame), who spent his school years here.

At the **Monroe County Historical Museum** (126 S. Monroe St.), there is a nationally recognized collection of Custer memorabilia, in addition to Indian artifacts and other special changing exhibits. Particularly interesting are the museum's dioramas of the Massacre at River Raisin — the War of 1812 battle that had the highest mortality rate.

(For more information on attractions in the area, see the articles on Detroit and Greenfield Village, Michigan, and on Toledo, Ohio.)

BEST TIME TO VISIT: Summer or fall.

HOURS: Monroe County Historical Museum — May through October, 10 a.m.-5 p.m. daily, except Monday; November through April, 1 p.m.-5 p.m. daily, except Monday.

ADMISSION: Free.

DIRECTIONS: From Detroit, take I-75 (or I-275 to I-75) south to Monroe. From Toledo, take I-75 north to Monroe.

FOR MORE INFORMATION: Call or write Monroe County Chamber of Commerce, 22 W. Second St., Monroe, MI 48161; (313) 242-3366.

Michigan

Picturesque Petoskey: A Michigan Gem

Petoskey, Michigan

Driving Time: About 1 hour south of Mackinac City; 4½ hours north of Lansing

Petoskey is the state stone of Michigan. It's also a fabulous resort town perched on limestone bluffs high above **Little Traverse Bay**. Deriving its name from a Chippewa Indian chief, Pet-o-sega, this photogenic city draws flocks of tourists and summer inhabitants who come to enjoy its glorious scenery, sparkling blue waters, and white, sandy beaches. In recent years, Petoskey has also become the center of a thriving ski area.

Swimming, water skiing, sun bathing, boating, and fishing are the major summertime activities here. Many fishermen are attracted to the Little Traverse Bay waters, which are brimming with lake trout.

However, one of the most popular outdoor activities is searching along the beautiful beaches for petoskey stones, a coral fossil. The stones, which wash ashore constantly, were formed about 300 million years ago when the area was a saltwater lake.

For the shopper, the bayside town features an assortment of fine apparel shops and antique stores in its **Gaslight District**. The merchandise includes china, crystal, jewelry, craft items, and fashionable designer clothing for men, women, and children. Originally, many of the shops were located only in such posh places as Palm Beach and Naples, Florida.

While in the area, make sure to visit nearby **Harbor Springs**, an exclusive resort community of grand homes, golf courses, and unusual gift

shops. Years ago, several of the Midwest's famous families, such as the Fords and Libbys, built elegant "summer cottages" high on the bluffs in the Harbor Point area. The town's friendly atmosphere is apparent when visitors browse through the unusual shops or dine at one of the charming restaurants. For a tasty meal in Harbor Springs, try **Stafford's Pier Restaurant** (102 Bay St. at the waterfront) or the **Arboretum** (2½ miles west, on Rt. 119).

The shore drive along Route 119 is certainly one of the most beautiful in the country. Perhaps autumn is the best time for breathtaking scenery. Besides the magnificent views, the drive features such other sites as the **Old Council Tree**, where Indian chiefs made a peace treaty designed to last "as long as these trees shall stand," and **Devil's Elbow and Springs**, a spot Indians believed was haunted by evil spirits.

(For information on ski areas near Petoskey, see article on Michigan skiing in this section.)

BEST TIME TO VISIT: Summer or winter, for skiing.

DIRECTIONS: From Lansing, take Rt. 27 north to junction of I-75; follow I-75 north to Rt. 32 west. Take Rt. 32 to Rt. 131 north; follow to Petoskey. From Mackinac City area, take I-75 south to Rt. 68 west; follow southwest to Petoskey. Harbor Springs is only a few miles north of Petoskey; follow Rt. 119 along the shore.

FOR MORE INFORMATION: Call or write Petoskey Regional Chamber of Commerce, 401 E. Mitchell St., Petoskey, MI 49770; (616) 347-4150.

Michigan

Blue Waters, Elegant Homes In Charlevoix

Charlevoix, Michigan

Driving Time: 1½ hours south of Mackinac City; 4½ hours north of Lansing

"Charlevoix the Beautiful." That's what the residents of this Michigan resort community call their town — and, indeed, Charlevoix is true to its name. Overlooking Lake Michigan on the west and Lake Charlevoix on the east, this charming city offers almost an endless menu of sightseeing and recreation.

For years, Charlevoix has enjoyed the reputation of being one of Michigan's most prestigious summer retreats. Many of the town's summer inhabitants at the turn of the century were Chicago or New Orleans residents who built grand summer homes overlooking the sparkling lake waters. Today, many visitors still come to this lakeshore city for the scenery and sporting activities.

Along miles of white sandy beaches bordering Lakes Michigan and Charlevoix there is plenty of space to soak up the sun, after a swim in the brilliant blue waters.

The best way to get acquainted with the city is to drive through the streets lined with elegant old homes, quaint shops, and parks.

Antique buffs will find a wealth of shops to explore. American and Oriental furniture is featured at the **Norman and Judy Brunn Showroom** (U.S. 31, south of airport). An abundance of country collectibles can be found at **Lake Charlevoix Farm Antiques** (on Boyne City Rd.). Arts and crafts are available at several places, including **Godwin Pottery** (230 Antrim), and **Off Bridge Street Artists** (104 Clinton St.). Visitors looking for a sweet treat should stop in the

Yellow Submarine Bakery (307 Bridge St.) or **Murdick's Famous Fudge** (230 Bridge St.).

Throughout the year, Charlevoix holds many celebrations and special events: the **Winter Cup Festival** in mid-February; the **Annual Lakeside Hobbycraft Show** in early July; **Venetian Festival** in late July; **Waterfront Art Fair** in mid-August; **Fall Color Cruises** and the **Apple Festival** in October. Two of the most popular events are the **Venetian Festival** — with parades, street dancing, sports, food, and fireworks — and the **Waterfront Art Fair**, considered to be one of the state's best.

The brilliant red, orange, and yellow hues of autumn leaves attract many visitors annually for the **Fall Color Cruises**. Aboard the **Beaver Islander Motorship**, the views along the lakeshore are spectacular.

When the snow falls, the Charlevoix area and its surroundings become a winter wonderland. There are several fine ski lodges nearby (see "Michigan Skiing" article in this section), including **Boyne Mountain Lodge** (off U.S. 31 in Boyne Falls), one of the nation's leading winter resorts. Facilities feature 14 ski runs and eight chairlifts, with accommodations for 850 guests.

BEST TIME TO VISIT: Summer.
DIRECTIONS: From Lansing, take Rt. 27 north to junction of I-75. Follow I-75 north; exit at Rt. 32 west; follow Rt. 32 to junction of Rt. 66; follow Rt. 66 north to Charlevoix. From Mackinac City area, follow I-75 south to Rt. 68 west; pick up Rt. 31 southwest to Charlevoix. To reach Boyne Falls from Charlevoix, take Rt. 66 south out of town to County Rd. 48 Follow C-48 east to Boyne Falls.
FOR MORE INFORMATION: Call or write Charlevoix Chamber of Commerce, 408 Bridge St., Charlevoix, MI 49720, (616) 547-2101; or Boyne Mountain Lodge, (616) 549-2441.

Michigan

The City of Breakfast Cereals

Battle Creek, Michigan

Driving Time: About 2 hours west of Detroit; 3 hours east of Chicago

For years, Tony the Tiger has been extolling the virtues of Kellogg's breakfast cereals and publicizing his home base in Battle Creek. On a visit to that city, your family will have a unique opportunity to find out just how that famous American breakfast food is made — from start to finish.

Towering statues of Tony the Tiger (and Tony, Jr.) welcome tourists at the entrance to Kellogg's, the world's largest manufacturer of ready-to-eat cereals. Almost six million packages of cereal are produced daily at the plant, which includes 56 acres of floor space and employs 4,300 persons. Daily, Kellogg's uses 330,000 pounds of rice and ships 70 freight carloads of cereal.

Each year, the **Battle Creek plant** (235 Porter St.) is host to approximately 200,000 persons, who come to learn about the processes that transform farmers' grain to crispy flakes and puffs, all boxed on grocers' shelves. In fact, your family might even learn the secret of producing that famous "snap, crackle and pop"! The tour is routed to allow observation of different stages of cereal processing. The various viewing locations include the cooking room, toasting ovens, conveyor-transport systems, and packing operations. At the end of the tour, each person receives a free gift package as a souvenir of his Kellogg's visit.

Another interesting spot in Battle Creek is the **Binder Park Zoo** (7500 Division Dr.). Children and adults will enjoy a trip on the Z.O.&O. Railroad, winding through the scenic

grounds. Some of the more unusual animals on exhibit are bison, prairie dogs, and giant tortoises, just to name a few.

While visiting Battle Creek, your family might check out another attraction, the **Kingman Museum of Natural History** (W. Michigan Ave. and 20th St.). A chance to discover our world — past, present, and future — awaits museum visitors. Displays there feature fossils and rocks, Michigan's Ice Age history, astronomy and space science, ecology, birds and reptiles, and more.

Nature enthusiasts will want to wander around on the grounds of the **Leila Arboretum**, which surround the Kingman Museum. The large park, totaling more than 70 acres, features beautiful plants, shrubbery, and flowers indigenous to the area.

Just north of Battle Creek is another nature-lover's paradise, the **Kellogg Bird Sanctuary** of Michigan State University (13 miles northwest on Rt. 89). On Wintergreen Lake and

nearby ponds there, visitors may feed many species of waterfowl. In addition, the sanctuary offers an unusual opportunity to see birds of prey that are on loan from the U.S. Fish and Wildlife Service.

But back in town, there are several other attractions to keep visitors busy. The **Art Center of Battle Creek** (265 E. Emmett St.) displays many fine examples of arts and crafts by Michigan artists.

A bit of Civil War history is recalled at the gravesite of **Sojourner Truth** (Oak Hill Cemetery), a well-known freedom fighter of the mid-19th century. Formerly a slave herself, Truth carried her campaign against slavery from town halls to the U.S. Congress and even to the office of Abraham Lincoln. Each year hundreds of persons visit the gravesite to pay homage to her courage and steadfast spirit of justice.

More history is offered at the **Kimball House Museum** (196 Capital Ave.), where Victorian-period pieces and furnishings are exhibited in a late 19th-century atmosphere. One of the exhibits shows the changes in tools, appliances, and medical instruments over the past 100 years. A country store and an old-fashioned herb garden are also part of the tour.

BEST TIME TO VISIT: Spring and summer.

HOURS: Kellogg's tours — 9 a.m. and 4 p.m. Monday-Friday, year round. Kingman Museum of Natural History — 9 a.m.-5 p.m. Tuesday-Saturday, 1 p.m.-5 p.m. Sunday. Kellogg's Bird Sanctuary — 8 a.m. to dusk, year round. Binder Park Zoo — 10 a.m.-5 p.m. weekdays, 10 a.m.-6 p.m. weekends and holidays. Kimball House Museum — 1 p.m.-4:30 p.m. Tuesday, Thursday, and second Sunday of each month; closed January.

ADMISSION: Kingman Museum of Natural History — adults, 50¢; children, 25¢. Binder Park Zoo — adults, 75¢; children, 50¢. Kimball House Museum — adults, 50¢; children and teens, 25¢. Kellogg's Bird Sanctuary — adults, $1; children and teens, 50¢.

DIRECTIONS: From Detroit, take I-94 west (past Jackson and Ann Arbor) to Battle Creek. From Grand Rapids, take U.S. 131 south to Kalamazoo, and pick up I-94 east to Battle Creek.

FOR MORE INFORMATION: Call or write Battle Creek Visitor and Convention Bureau, 172 W. Van Buren, Battle Creek, MI 49016; (616) 962-2240.

Fishing, Boating In Manistee

Manistee, Michigan

Driving Time: About 2½ hours north of Grand Rapids; 6 hours northwest of Detroit; 5 hours north east of Chicago

"Spirit of the Woods" — that's the translation of the Indian word "Manistee," a city and county bordering on the eastern shores of Lake Michigan. Once the home of more than 1,000 Indians, Manistee was formerly a busy center of Michigan's lumbering industry. Centuries before that, the great glaciers that covered the land carved out gorges, valleys, and hills in the Manistee area. Today, the only traces of that Ice Age are the glistening, azure lakes and scenic landscapes that abound through the county.

Outdoor recreation, from fishing to hiking, is the major attraction of **Manistee**. Its many rivers, streams, and lakes, including Lake Michigan, draw hundreds of fishermen annually who try their luck in the well-stocked waters. In fact, the Manistee area is reputed to be one of the best fishing locations in the country!

Summer catches include perch, northern pike, walleye, steelhead, and lake trout. In the late summer and early fall, the waters offer fighting coho and chinook salmon. And in winter, ice fishing produces smelt, perch, northern pike, steelhead, and rainbow trout. Some of the best spots are **Portage Lake, Bear Lake, Manistee Lake**, or the **Big and Little Manistee Rivers**. But beware of crowds seeking salmon in early September. Local people say that fishing boats at that time are so thick on Manistee Lake that you could cross the lake by stepping from one boat to another, and never worry about wet feet!

Canoeing is another popular sport in Manistee. By canoe, your family has a chance to see the rivers and unspoiled banks just the way the Indians did. The **Coho Bend Campground** (5025 River Rd., Manistee) offers planned canoe trips of any length along the beautiful Manistee River. (Call [616] 723-7321 for more information.)

Perhaps the best place to go for those who are unfamiliar with the area is **Manistee National Forest** (south and east of town via U.S. 31 and Rt. 55). With more than 500,000 acres, the forest contains ample facilities for virtually unlimited outdoor fun. Some of the recreational possibilities are camping, picnicking, boating, hiking, swimming, fishing, and hunting. Of course, in winter there are terrific spots for both downhill and cross-country skiing and snowmobiling.

In early July, the area comes alive with song and celebration for the annual **Manistee National Forest Festival** (in Manistee). Commemorating the lumbering heritage, the festivities include an arts and crafts fair, fish boil, pancake breakfast, tennis tournament, raft races, dances, lumberjack contests — even an ox roast. A parade and traditional fireworks on the Fourth of July are the grand finale to this special event.

To learn about Manistee history, your family may want to visit the **Manistee County Historical Museum** (425 River St., Manistee). The building, constructed in the 1870s, contains a collection of artifacts and furnishings used during the town's lumbering heyday. Part of the museum is an old-fashioned general store with items ranging from soap to cotton chintz. Just like the days of yesteryear!

Other relics of days gone by are exhibited at the **Old Holly Waterworks Building** (W. First St.), in the **Victorian Village** shopping district of Manistee. This charming section of town has been restored to recall the 19th century with fine examples of vintage Victorian architecture. Sailboats and yachts docked on the river lend another dimension of picturesque beauty to the quaint neighborhood.

Don't miss the historic **Ramsdell Theatre** (First and Maple Sts.), a classical Renaissance structure built in 1901 by Thomas Jefferson Ramsdell, a pioneer Manistee attorney. Listed in the National Register of Historic Places, the building has several features that were very unusual for playhouses of that period, such as the nine trap door platforms on stage and the stage curtain painting of an outdoor scene. Performances are presented by the Manistee Civic Players there from April through October. (See information below.)

BEST TIME TO VISIT: Summer.
HOURS: Manistee County Historical Museum — June-September, 10 a.m.-5 p.m., Monday through Saturday. Holly Water Works — June-Labor Day, 11 a.m.-4 p.m. Monday through Saturday. Ramsdell Theatre — tours available upon request; for performance information, call or write Manistee Civic Players, Box 32, Manistee, MI 49660; (616) 723-9948.
ADMISSION: Manistee County Historical Museum and Holly Water Works — 50¢ per person.
DIRECTIONS: From Grand Rapids, take I-96 northwest toward Muskegon; pick up U.S. 31 north and follow to Manistee.
FOR MORE INFORMATION: Call or write Manistee Chamber of Commerce, Box 608, Manistee, MI 49660; (616) 723-2575.

Michigan

Forts, Islands, Wilderness In Michigan

Driving Time: 9 hours north-east of Minneapolis/St. Paul; 12 hours north of Detroit

Copper Country: Isle Royale, Michigan

Just imagine the natural beauty of a crystal-clear waterfall cascading over a cliff or a blazing sunset over the calm waters of Lake Superior and you'll have a good idea of the attraction of Copper Country in Michigan's Upper Peninsula. From the forest land wilderness of Isle Royale National Park to the picturesque towns on the mainland, the area is sure to offer many new sights and experiences.

First, the unspoiled wilderness of **Isle Royale** is a nature lover's paradise. The island, which is only accessible by boat or floatplane, features sparkling inland lakes, rugged scenic shores and, of course, all sorts of wild creatures who live in the surrounding woodlands. The sure-footed hiker will delight in exploring the island's foot trails, which twist and turn for 160 miles. And for fishermen, there couldn't be a better place; the waters are full of pike, perch, walleye and trout. Overnight accommodations are available at **Rock Harbor Lodge** on the east end of the island.

Back on the northernmost point of the peninsula is **Copper Harbor**, once the center of the shipping and mining industries. There you may visit the **Fort Wilkins Historic Complex**, an army post built in 1844 on the

shores of Lake Fanny Hooe. The 190-acre state park includes 15 buildings restored to their appearance during the copper boom: bakehouse, hospital, ice house, company barracks, officers' quarters, etc. Also, there are facilities for camping, picnicking, hunting and fishing. And at the east end of the park are the abandoned mine shafts of the Pittsburgh and Boston Company. Nearby, at the **Copper Harbor Marina**, you can take an hour boat trip and tour of the Copper Harbor Lighthouse, built in 1866. Before moving on, stop at the **Astor House Museum**, which features antique doll and toy collections, Indian relics and railroad and nautical memorabilia. For some breathtaking scenery, take the **Brockway Mountain Drive** for 10 miles through lush forests

along the Lake Superior shore. (Start the drive one-quarter mile west of U.S. 41 and MI 26 junction.)

Heading south again on U.S. 41, stop in **Calumet** and take a step back in time. The quaint town of 1,000 persons was once a prosperous mining center. A walking tour of the town provides a look back to the days of "copper glory." Pick up a guide book at the visitors' center on Fourth St. and Red Jacket Rd. so you won't miss anything.

More fragments of the old mining days are on display in **Hancock, Michigan** (about 10 miles south of Calumet). The **Quincy Mine** on U.S. 41 boasts the world's largest steam hoist. In fact, an actual underground tour of a copper mine is offered at the **Arcadian Copper Mine** in Ripley (just east of Hancock).

Forts, Islands, Wilderness

Continued

Comfortable overnight accommodations on the peninsula are available at **Keweenaw Mountain Lodge** in Copper Harbor. For dinner, the **Harbor Haus** in Copper Harbor serves good food with homemade pastry. The specialties are lake trout, weiner schnitzel and sauerbraten; children's portions are available.

HOURS: Fort Wilkins Historic Complex: 8 AM to 10 PM daily; closed in winter. Lighthouse Boat Tour: 10 AM to 5 PM daily, June through Labor Day. Arcadian Copper Mine: 9 AM to 5 PM daily, June 1-18 and Sept. 17-Oct. 15; 8 AM to 6 PM daily, June 19-Sept. 16. Quincy Mine: 9 AM to 5 PM daily, mid-June through Labor Day. Astor House Museum: 9 AM to 6 PM daily, May 15-Oct. 15; closed rest of year.

FOR MORE INFORMATION: Call Isle Royale National Park, (906) 482-3310, or Copper Country Chamber of Commerce, (906) 482-5240.

ADMISSION: Lighthouse Boat Tour: Adults, $2; pre-teens and children 12 yrs. and under, $1. Arcadian Copper Mine: Adults, $1.50; children and teens 7 to 15 yrs., $1; children under 7 yrs., free. Quincy Mine Steam Hoist: Adults, $1.50; children and teens 6 to 17 yrs., 75c; children under 6 yrs., free. Astor House Museum: Teens and adults, $1; pre-teens end children, free.

DIRECTIONS: From the east (Chicago), take I-94, I-43 and Rt. 141 north. From Minneapolis/St. Paul, take U.S. 8 northeast through Wisconsin, pick up U.S. 45 north into Michigan, pick up Rt. 26 north at Rockland and continue to Houghton. The ferry to Isle Royale takes about six hours from Houghton.

NOTE: If you only wish to visit Isle Royale—not Copper Country, Michigan—you may take a passenger ferry from Grand Portage, Minnesota, a 1½-hr. ride. From Twin Cities, take U.S. Rt. 61 and head north along Lake Superior to Grand Portage.

Seney Refuge: Close-Up View Of Wildlife

Seney, Michigan

Driving Time: About 1½ hours northwest of the St. Ignace-Mackinac area; about 4 hours east of the northern Wisconsin border

Located in the wide-open spaces and woodlands of Michigan's Upper Peninsula, **Seney National Wildlife Refuge** is a terrific place to absorb the sights, sounds, and smells of the great outdoors. From fishing and canoeing in summer to snow shoeing and cross-country skiing in winter, Seney is brimming with recreational opportunities. Some visitors, however, come to Seney just to relax amid natural surroundings on the 95,000 acres.

The best way to get acquainted with the wildlife refuge is to stop at the **Visitors Center** (open April 1 through Sept. 30). There, dioramas, exhibits, and conservation information assist visitors in pinpointing their major points of interest at the refuge.

Taking the **Marshland Wildlife Drive** is an excellent way to observe the many forms and species of wildlife that inhabit the area. (The tour takes one or two hours; make sure you have at least one-quarter tank of gas.) Numbered sign markers point out special interest areas along the trail, which is open from dawn to dusk.

For those who would rather travel on foot, the **Pine Ridge Nature Trail** starts at the Visitors Center and takes a 1.4-mile course around one of the pools. The wildlife includes birds (such as Cape May warblers, eastern kingbirds, woodpeckers, brown thrashers, song sparrows, grouse, ring-necked ducks, and woodcock) and mammals (beaver, deer, black bears, chipmunks, and more).

Other areas of the refuge are designated for fishing, picnicking, boating (only on Driggs and Manistique Rivers), hunting, camping, ice fishing, and cross-country skiing.

Seney's history began with the advent of the lumber industry in the Upper Peninsula during the 1860s. The **town of Seney** had become a thriving lumber center by the late 19th century. However, when the forest resources had been largely over-used, after the turn of the century, the area's economic base collapsed. Many attempts were made to convert the ground to farm land, but to no avail. Then, in 1935 the U.S. Department of the Interior designated the large expanse of land as Seney National Wildlife Refuge.

The area around **Manistique** (southwest of the refuge) features three fine state parks. They are **Indian Lake** (seven miles west on Rt. 149), **Palms Book** (12 miles northwest on Rt. 149), and **Fayette** (15 miles west on U.S. 2, then 17 miles south on the county road to Fayette). Palms Book features the state's largest spring (200 feet wide by 40 feet deep), with 16,000 gallons of water per minute pouring into Indian Lake. Fayette Park contains the remnants of the ghost town of Fayette. All three areas have facilities for picnicking, fishing, swimming, camping, hiking; other recreational activities are offered at Indian Lake Park and Fayette.

BEST TIME TO VISIT: Summer.

HOURS: Seney Wildlife Refuge is open during daylight hours daily all year. Marshland Wildlife Drive — daylight hours, mid-May through Sept. 30. Visitors Center — mid-May through September 30, 8 a.m.-4 p.m. daily. State parks — open year round.

DIRECTIONS: From St. Ignace-Mackinac City, take U.S. 2 west along Lake Michigan to Rt. 77 north. Follow signs to Seney National Wildlife Refuge.

FOR MORE INFORMATION: Call or write Seney National Wildlife Refuge, Seney, MI 49883; (906) 586-9851.

Michigan

Where to Enjoy Winter Sports In Michigan

With the first snowfall, the hills and valleys of Michigan are transformed into a winter wonderland. And without a moment wasted, the state's skiing enthusiasts don their down jackets and stocking caps, take up their ski poles, and head for the hills.

But even for those who are not brave enough to try the slopes, there is winter fun throughout the state, with many excellent areas for cross-country skiing or snowmobiling. Here's a guide to some of the best winter sport spots in the state:

West Michigan

Boyne Mountain (near Charlevoix-Petoskey area)
Boyne Falls, MI 49713
(800) 632-7174
(Off U.S. 131, one mile south of Boyne Falls

Schuss Mountain (between Charlevoix and Traverse City)
Mancelona, MI 49659
(616) 587-9162
(U.S. 131 and intersection of Rt. 66 and 88)

Crystal Mountain (Traverse City area)
Thompsonville, MI 49683
(616) 378-2911
(On Rt. 115, southwest of Traverse City)

Boyne Highlands (Petoskey area)
Harbor Springs, MI 49741
(616) 549-2441
(Off Rt. 119 and Pleasant View Rd.)

Nub's Nob (Petoskey area)
Harbor Springs, MI 49741
(616) 526-2131
(On Pleasant View Rd., northeast of Harbor Springs)

Royal Valley Ski Resort (north of South Bend, Ind.)
Buchanan, MI 49107
(616) 695-5862
(On Main St., three miles north of town)

Timber Ridge (Kalamazoo area)
Gobles, MI 49055
(616) 694-9741
(Off Rt. 40, northwest of Kalamazoo)

Sugar Loaf Mountain Resort (near Traverse City)
Rt. 1
Cedar, MI 49621
(On U.S. 31, 18 miles northeast of Traverse City)

Swiss Valley Ski Area (Kalamazoo area)
Three Rivers, MI 49093
(616) 244-5635
(Off Rt. 60, 10 miles west of Three Rivers)

Hilton Shanty Creek Resort (between Charlevoix and Traverse City)
Bellaire, MI 49615
(616) 533-8621
(Two miles southeast of Bellaire, off Rt. 88)

Eastern Michigan

Alpine Valley Ski Resort (near Pontiac)
6775 E. Highland Rd.
Milford, MI
(313) 887-4183
(12 miles west of Pontiac on Rt. 59)

Apple Mountain Ski Resort (near Saginaw)
4535 N. River Rd.
Freeland, MI
(517) 781-0170
(Four miles west on Rt. 46, then six miles north on Rt. 47, near Freeland)

Michigan

Upper Peninsula

Mont Ripley Ski Area (Hancock-
Houghton area)
   Houghton, MI 49931
   (906) 487-2340
   (On Rt. 26, half-mile east of town)

Pine Mountain Lodge (near Wisconsin state line, central U.P.)
   Iron Mountain, MI 49801
   (906) 774-2747
   (North of town, off U.S. 2-141)

Blackjack Mountain Ski Resort
(near Ironwood, far west U.P.)
   Bessemer, MI 49911
   (906) 229-5115
   (Off U.S. 2, eight miles east of
Ironwood)

Mount Zion Ski Resort (Ironwood,
far west U.P.)
   Ironwood, MI 49938
   (906) 932-9879
   (Three miles north of U.S. 2)

Big Powderhorn Mountain Ski Re-
sort (Ironwood, far west U.P.)
   Ironwood, MI 49938
   (906) 932-3100
   (Two miles northeast off U.S. 2 on
Powderhorn Rd.)

Indianhead Mountain Resort (near
Ironwood, far west U.P.)
   Wakefield, MI 49968
   (906) 229-5181k
   (Two miles west of Wakefield, off
U.S. 2)

Ski Brule (near Iron Mountain, west
U.P.)
   P.O. Box 165
   Iron River, MI 49935
   (906) 265-4957
   (Five miles southwest of Iron
River, off Rt. 189)

Cliffs Ridge Ski Area (near Marquette, central U.P. on Lake Superior shore)
   Marquette, MI 49855
   (906) 225-1155
   (Three miles southwest of town on
County Rd. 553)

Ishpeming: Skiers' Paradise

Ishpeming, Michigan

Driving Time: About 3 hours west of Mackinac City area; about 1 hour northwest of Escanaba

With its abundance of ski resorts and scenic winter sports spots, Michigan is appropriately the home of the **National Ski Hall of Fame**. Situated in the northwestern section of the Upper Peninsula, in Ishpeming, the museum is the perfect place for ski buffs to explore the roots and soak up the history of their favorite sport. One of the most extraordinary exhibits is a replica of the oldest known ski and pole, dating from 4,000 years ago (no mention made of broken limbs).

Operated by the United States Ski Association, the facility houses various displays relating to skiing around the world as well as historical data and records of world-class skiers. The museum was dedicated in 1954.

(Also, see articles in this section on Pictorial Rocks National Lakeshore and Hiawatha National Forest.)

BEST TIME TO VISIT: Anytime.
HOURS: Hall of Fame — mid-June to Labor Day, 9 a.m.-4 p.m. daily; rest of year, 10 a.m.-4 p.m. weekdays, 1 p.m.-4 p.m. weekends; closed major holidays.
ADMISSION: Hall of Fame requests donation.
DIRECTIONS: From Mackinac City area, take I-75 north to junction of Rt. 123. Follow Rt. 123 northwest to intersection of Rt. 28. Follow Rt. 28 west, past Munising and Marquette, to Ishpeming (becomes Rt. 28-41). The National Ski Hall of Fame is about two blocks north of U.S. 41 at Mather Ave. and Poplar St., Ishpeming. From Escanaba, take U.S. 35 north to junction of U.S. 28-41. Follow west to Ishpeming.

A Remarkable Spring and Bridge

Manistique, Michigan

Driving Time: About 1½ hours northwest of Mackinac City area

Early Indians called it Kitch-iti-kipi or "Mirror of Heaven." Today, it is simply called the **Big Spring in Palms Book State Park,** near Manistique. But, whatever its name, the spring is a fascinating natural wonder: 45 feet deep, 200 feet across, with a constant water temperature year around. The water is so clear that visitors can see fish, unusual formations, and 16,000 gallons of water per minute that appear to erupt from the depths of the spring. Picnicking is allowed on the grounds, but no camping.

While in the area, see another remarkable attraction, the **Siphon Bridge** (on Rt. 2 in Manistique). Supported by water that is atmospherically forced under it, the bridge is listed in Ripley's "Believe It or Not." Built in 1919, the 300-foot-long bridge has a roadway that is actually four feet below water level! You have to see it to believe it.

(For information on other attractions in the area, see articles in this section on Fayette State Park and Hiawatha National Forest.)

BEST TIME TO VISIT: Summer.
HOURS: Palms Book is open daily, except in winter.
DIRECTIONS: From Mackinac City area, take U.S. 2 northwest to Manistique. To reach Palms Book State Park, continue on U.S. 2 to junction of Rt. 149. Follow Rt. 149 about 12 miles northwest to park.
FOR MORE INFORMATION: Call or write Manistique Area Chamber of Commerce, Rm. 207, Courthouse, Manistique, MI 49854; (906) 341-5010.

Michigan

All Aboard! Kalamazoo's Toy Train Works

Bangor, Michigan

Driving Time: About 3 hours east of Chicago and west of Detroit

With their swift-moving, brightly colored cars speeding through miniature villages, over "mountains" and under pint-sized bridges, model railroads have long fascinated old and young alike. With a trip to the **Kalamazoo Toy Train Works**, in Bangor, you'll have an opportunity to see how model trains are made.

Each year, this unusual factory is host to visitors from around the world. Even the President of the United States isn't immune to the toy train mystique; one year President Reagan called to order a train for the White House. Not after that, a six-foot-long long Virignia Truckie train was delivered to 1600 Pennsylvania Avenue.

All trains made at the Toy Train Works are Gauge One size and operate on brass rails with a track gauge of 1¾ inches. Each car measures about 14 inches long, with the locomotive about 24 inches long.

(For more entertainment ideas in the area, see articles in this section on Berrien County and Van Buren County winery tours and on Bee Hive Farm in Gobles.)

BEST TIME TO VISIT: Any time of year.
HOURS: Toy Train Works— 8:30-4:30 p.m., weekdays; 10 a.m.-3 p.m. Saturday, year round.
ADMISSION: Free.
DIRECTIONS: From Chicago, take I-94 northeast around the tip of Lake Michigan. Continue past Michigan City; north of Benton Harbor pick up I-196 north. Exit at Rt. 43 east to Bangor. Train works is at 541 Railroad St. From Detroit, take I-94 west. Just west of Kalamazoo pick up U.S. 131 north and follow to Rt. 43 west. Continue west on Rt. 43 to Bangor.
FOR MORE INFORMATION: Call or write Kalamazoo Toy Train Works, 541 Railroad St., Bangor, MI 49013; (616) 427-7927.

President and Mrs. Reagan with toy train from the Kalamazoo Toy Train Works

An Amusement Park With Animals for The Kids

Muskegon, Michigan

Driving Time: About 45 minutes north of Grand Rapids

Muskegon's **Deer Park Funland** (eight miles north of Muskegon, at 4750 Whitehall Rd.) is more than just a name; it does have live deer, the kind you usually only see for moments in your car's headlights. The deer here are tame, so approachable that kids get a thrill out of petting and feeding them.

When the novelty of that wears off, take the youngsters over to the adjacent amusement park — not the biggest amusement park around but nice for a side trip. The park has rides for the adventurous and tamer ones for the younger children, plus a miniature railroad. There are picnic grounds, too, and concession stands with a variety of food.

(For more information on attractions in the area, see articles in this section on Grand Rapids and Holland.)

BEST TIME TO VISIT: Weekdays, during the summer (weekends can get crowded).
HOURS: Deer Park Funland — Memorial Day-Labor Day, 11 a.m.-5 p.m. weekdays; 11 a.m.-6 p.m. weekends and holidays.
ADMISSION: Deer Park Funland— $5 per person.
DIRECTIONS: From Grand Rapids, take I-96 northwest to Muskegon. Pick up U.S. 31 north and exit at Russell Rd. Follow signs to Deer Park Funland.
FOR MORE INFORMATION: Call or write Deer Park Funland, 4750 Whitehall Rd., Muskegon, MI 49441; (616) 766-3377.

Michigan

Michigan's 'Garden' Peninsula

Fayette, Michigan

Driving Time: About 1 hour northeast of Escanaba

In the late 1860s, a man named Fayette Brown discovered the Garden Peninsula of Upper Michigan, with its dense growth of hardwood trees — perfect for use in iron smelting. Soon after, the town of **Fayette** was founded. Boasting a population of about 800 persons at its peak, Fayette thrived for about 22 years.

Today, the little iron-smelting village is being restored on the grounds of **Fayette State Park**. About 22 buildings are being reconstructed. Now, visitors may see the finished company office, doctor's and foreman's houses, and exhibits depicting the villagers' lifestyle in four other buildings. A videotape at the Visitors' Center and a scale model of the town help guests to visualize the early community.

The park also offers a harbor, beach, picnic area, and an 80-site campground (fee $5 per night).

(For more information about the area's attractions, see articles in this section on Hiawatha National Forest and Palms Book State Park.)

BEST TIME TO VISIT: Summer.
HOURS: State parks are open year round.
DIRECTIONS: From Escanaba, take U.S. 2-41 north to Rapid River and continue east on U.S. 2. Turn right (south) on County Rd. 483 and follow south on Garden Peninsula to Fayette State Park (about 17 miles).
FOR MORE INFORMATION: Call or write Fayette State Park, Fayette, MI 49835; (906) 644-2603.

Fayette State Park

An Auto Baron's Elegant Lifestyle

Rochester, Michigan

Driving Time: About 1 hour north of Detroit

Meadow Brook Hall, an elaborate 100-room, Tudor-style mansion in Rochester (30 miles north of Detroit, provides a glimpse of the wealthy lifestyle of the early 20th century. The building, which was begun in 1926 and took three years to construct, was once the home of Mrs. John F. Dodge, wife of the renowned auto pioneer.

Fortunately, almost all of the original furnishings and art works from the home have survived. Meadow Brook Hall features a beautiful ballroom with beamed ceilings, antique needlepoint draperies, and 24 fireplaces. Today, the stately mansion serves as the cultural and conference center for Oakland University.

(For more entertainment ideas in the area, see the articles in this section on Detroit and Greenfield Village.)

BEST TIME TO VISIT: Summer.
HOURS: Meadow Brook Hall — year round, Sunday 1 p.m.-5 p.m.; July-August, 10 a.m.-5 p.m. daily.
ADMISSION: Meadow Brook Hall — adults and teens, $3.50; children under 12, $2.
DIRECTIONS: From Detroit, take I-75 north to Rochester exit, about three miles north of Pontiac. Follow the signs to Oakland University; Meadow Brook Hall is on university grounds.
FOR MORE INFORMATION: Call or write Metropolitan Detroit Convention and Visitors Bureau, Oakland County Branch, 47 W. Huron St., Pontiac, MI 48058; (313) 259-4333.

Michigan

Explore The Land Of Hiawatha

Hiawatha National Forest Upper Peninsula, Michigan

Driving Time: About 20 minutes west of St. Ignace to eastern section; about 20 minutes east of Escanaba to western section

Nature at its best — beautiful, colorful, rugged. That's what visitors find in the wide-open spaces of Michigan's Upper Peninsula in any season.

Remember Henry Wadsworth Longfellow's celebrated poem, *Song of Hiawatha*? The famous American poet wrote of the "Shining Big Sea Water" and he took his inspiration from Lake Superior. Along the shoreline of those sparkling blue waters is Hiawatha National Forest, which was named after the poem. "By the Shores of Gitche Gumme," this 860,000-acre area offers almost infinite possibilities for sports, nature enjoyment, and relaxation — far away from the pressures and problems of everyday life.

The boundaries of Hiawatha's western section stretch from Lake Superior on the north to Lake Michigan on the south, covering the entire north-south length of the Upper Peninsula between Bay de Noc State Forest on the west and south, and Manistique and Grand Sable State Forests on the east.

Hiawatha's eastern section stretches from Lake Superior on the north to Lake Michigan and Lake Huron on the south, extending down to St. Ignace. Thus, from almost any location on the Upper Peninsula, it's not too far to some part of this national forest. In fact, considering this impressive land expanse, it's not surprising that Michigan (including

Point Iroquois Lighthouse at the Hiawatha Forest

state and national forest lands) has the largest area of public forest ownership of any state east of the Rockies.

Perhaps one of the best things about the great northern forest lands is the peaceful and relaxing atmosphere they offer. Here nature is virtually unspoiled by 20th-century civilization and cities. While your family is on the Hiawatha grounds, take time to quietly enjoy the sights and sounds of nature around you.

However, "communing" with nature is only one pastime in the great wilds of Hiawatha. For example, visitors in the western section may take canoe trips along the Indian, Sturgeon, AuTrain, Carp, and Whitefish Rivers. Explore the way the Indians used to do. In addition, there are lighthouses at Point Peninsula, Point Iroquois, Round Island, and Bay

Furnace, each of them an historic landmark.

Campsites at developed areas are offered on a first-come, first-served basis. Swimming is allowed in the eastern section at Brevoort Lake, Monocle Lake, and Soldier Lake. In the western section your family may swim at AuTrain Lake, Camp 7 Lake, Colwell Lake, Corner Lake, and Pets Lake. Fishing and boating are allowed at many locations throughout both sections of Hiawatha.

BEST TIME TO VISIT: Summer.
HOURS: Forest is open year round.
DIRECTIONS: To reach the eastern section, take I-75 north from St. Ignace, just a few miles to Hiawatha. To reach the western section from Escanaba, take U.S. 2-41 north toward Rapid River.
FOR MORE INFORMATION: Call or write Forest Service, U.S. Department of Agriculture, 2727 N. Lincoln Rd., Escanaba, MI 29829; (906) 786-4062.

A Museum Dedicated to Pere Marquette

St. Ignace, Michigan

Driving Time: About 10 minutes north of Mackinac City on north side of Straits of Mackinac; about 7 hours north of Detroit

Dedicated to the famous French Jesuit explorer, Pere Jacques Marquette, the 53-acre park named for him in St. Ignace brings alive the early history of the Mackinac-St. Ignace area. The **Father Marquette National Memorial Museum** depicts the missionary's life and travels, with scenic walking trails. An outlook spot features an impressive view of the Mackinac Bridge spanning the Straits of Mackinac. The area also includes picnic grounds.

In 1671, Father Marquette founded a mission at St. Ignace, starting with about 200 Huron Indians converted to Christianity. He left the area two years later for his famous explorations of the Mississippi River with Louis Jolliet.

(For more on attractions in the area, see articles in this section on Mackinac Island, Soo Locks, and Hiawatha National Forest.)

BEST TIME TO VISIT: Summer
HOURS: Memorial Museum— daily during the summer, 8:30 a.m.-9 p.m.
DIRECTIONS: From Mackinac City, take I-75 north across the Mackinac Bridge; the park is at junction of I-75 and U.S. 2. From Detroit, take I-75 north across Mackinac Bridge.
FOR MORE INFORMATION: Call or write St. Ignace Area Chamber of Commerce, S. State St., St. Ignace, MI 49781; (906) 643-8717 or (906) 643-8620.

Toonerville: A Great Way To See the Falls

Tahquamenon Falls, Michigan

Driving Time: About 1 hour northwest of Mackinac City area

When your family climbs aboard the **Tonnerville Trolley** and hears the conductor shout "All aboard," it's the beginning of an adventure that climaxes with one of Michigan's natural wonders — **Tahquamenon Falls**. During the 6½-hour trip via railroad and riverboat, you'll take in one of the most breathtaking vistas of Michigan's Upper Peninsula. There is a 1¼-hour stopover at the falls.

The thundering waterfall (the Upper Falls) is the largest east of the Mississippi River. And the Lower Falls consist of beautiful falls and cascades flowing around an island.

Michigan's Upper Peninsula boasts more than 150 waterfalls, varying in size and depth. (See information on the Upper Peninsula Travel and Recreation Association. (For more information on the Upper Peninsula, see the articles in this section on Mackinac Island, St. Ignace, and Hiawatha National Forest.)

BEST TIME TO VISIT: Summer.
HOURS: Toonerville Trolley and Riverboat Trips — mid-June and September through early October to the end of June one trip daily, 10:30 a.m.; July and August, two trips daily, 10 and 11:30 a.m., Monday-Thursday, and one trip daily, 10:30 a.m. Friday, Saturday, and Sunday.
ADMISSION: Toonerville Trolley and Riverboat Trip — adults and teens, $8; children 5 and over, $4.
DIRECTIONS: From Mackinac City area, take I-75 north to Rt. 123 northwest. Follow Rt. 123 northwest to junction of Rt. 28. Turn right (west) on Rt. 28 and continue to sign for Soo Junction and Toonerville Trolley (just north of Rt 28).

Michigan

Holland, Michigan: A Dutch Treat

Driving Time: About 3 hours northeast of Chicago, 5 hours west of Detroit

Holland, Michigan

Wooden shoes, windmills, scenic waterways and fields of vibrant tulips. If Holland, Michigan, sounds like a lovely Dutch holiday, you're right. On any day from May through September, Windmill Island (7th and Lincoln St.) will take you back to the picturesque Netherlands of 200 years ago.

The main attraction: the magnificent 12-story-high, 200-year-old windmill, "De Zwaan." Tours of the windmill are offered—and you can buy some of the whole wheat flour that the mill grinds. You can also ride on an authentic old Dutch carousel, and see the traditional Dutch "klompen" dance performed by girls in authentic costumes.

Other island sights include a mechanized mini-model of Old Holland, an antique collection and a film about windmills. Back on the mainland, visit the Dutch Village (1 mile north of Holland at Rt. 31 and James St.) and hear the sounds of a huge Amsterdam street organ, ride on a "Zweefmolen" (unique swing imported from Holland), or shop in the many Dutch stores offering imported clocks, dolls, wooden shoes and more. Then stroll through the village, have your picture taken aboard a horse-drawn wagon, and stop for a lunch or dinner of Dutch cooking at the Queen's Inn Restaurant at the Dutch Village.

Only a few miles south (U.S. 31 by-pass at 16th St.) is Holland's original Wooden Shoe Factory, where craftsmen make the famous footwear. You might even see Fred Oldemolders the oldest maker of wooden shoes in the United States. The Deklomp Wooden Shoe and Delft Factory (257 E. 32nd St.) features wooden shoemaking and Delftware decorating demonstrations.

In mid-May for four days Holland comes alive with the annual "Tulip Festival," celebrating the customs of the Dutch homeland.

HOURS: WINDMILL ISLAND—9 a.m. to 5 p.m., daily May through Labor Day; 10 a.m. to 4 p.m. off-season. DUTCH VILLAGE—9 a.m. to 4:30 p.m., April, June, September, October; 9 a.m. to 6:30 p.m., May, July, August. WOODEN SHOE FACTORY—8 a.m. to 6 p.m., spring and fall. DeKLOMP WOODEN SHOE AND DELFT FACTORY—9 a.m. to 5:30 p.m., daily; 8 a.m. to 10 p.m. during Tulip Time. Closed Sundays except during May.

FOR MORE INFORMATION: Call the Tulip Time office, (616)396-4221.

ADMISSION: Windmill Island: Adults, children over 12 yrs., $1.75; Children 6 to 12 yrs., $1; Children under 6 yrs., free. Dutch Village: Adults, children over 11 yrs., $1; Children under 3 yrs. free.

DIRECTIONS: See map included in this section. (We suggest also calling ahead or writing for exact directions and time and price changes, if any.)

INDIANA

Indiana Vacations

Map of Indiana with locations:

Indiana Dunes
South Bend
La Porte
Mishawaka
Crown Point
Goshen
Amish Acres
Chain O'Lakes
Lake Wawasee
Fort Wayne
Peru
Indiana Beach
Lafayette
Mounds State Park
Indianapolis
Rockville
Cataract Falls
Nashville
Bloomington
Spring Mill
Lincoln City
Vincennes
Marengo Park
Clifty Falls
St. Meinrad
Santa Claus Land
Jeffersonville
New Harmony
Wyandotte Caves
Evansville
Corydon

Indiana

Indianapolis: Fun in the Hoosier Capital

Indianapolis, Indiana

Driving Time: 3 hours south of Chicago; 3½ hours west of Columbus, Ohio

Indianapolis, the largest city in Indiana, is a great place for families to visit. Located near the geographical center of the state, the city has activities and attractions that appeal to young and old.

The hub of the city is **Monument Circle**, adorned with the lofty Soldiers and Sailors Monument, which has an observation platform at the top.

Downtown Indianapolis boasts the state's tallest building, the 504-foot-high Indiana National Bank Tower, as well as the elegant gold-domed state capitol, built in the late 1800s with the finest Indiana limestone.

Near the city's hub lies the **War Memorial Plaza**, a five-block area honoring Indiana's dead in two World Wars.

A must-see is the **Children's Museum** (30th and Meridian Sts.). Billed as the largest children's museum in the world, it is also the third-oldest children's foundation in existence, founded in 1925. The exhibits include a spectacular layout of working toy trains, a 19th-century log cabin, a simulated Indiana limestone cave, an operating turn-of-the-century carousel, an 1890's firehouse with hand-drawn and motorized fire-fighting equipment, and a 55-ton Reuben Wells locomotive alongside a Victorian railway depot. There's also a gigantic Tyrannosaurus and other replicas of prehistoric beasts, an "Emergence of Man" gallery, and a 2,600-year-old mummy. A new performing arts theater brings drama,

music, dance, puppets, films, and other entertainment to museum visitors. And the newly opened **Science Spectrum** allows children to perform many scientific experiments.

A historic landmark worth seeing is the **Anthenaeum** (401 E. Michigan St.). Built in 1893, it is home for Indiana's only resident theater, the Indiana Repertory Theater, and includes a photographic exhibit of all past productions.

Another landmark, the **President Benjamin Harrison Memorial Home** (1230 N. Delaware), honors the nation's 23rd president. Sixteen rooms have been restored, and the third-floor ballroom serves as a museum where many artifacts of the Harrisons' personal and professional lives are exhibited.

Another "must" stop, the **Museum of Indian Heritage** (6040 De Long Rd.), is a treasure house of Indian America. The building houses rare

and ancient pottery, stone sculpture, clay figurines, costumes, bead- and quill work, weapons, ritual objects, tomahawks, pipes, war bonnets, and blankets.

The **Indianapolis Museum of Art** (1200 38th St.) includes European and American paintings, Egyptian figures, and Oriental exhibits. There are winding trails and manicured gardens in the spacious "art park." Separate from the museum building is the **Lilly Pavilion of Decorative Arts**, a French chateau that contains rare tapestries, period furniture, and antique porcelains.

If your family wants to learn more about the natural and cultural history of Indiana, then the **Indiana State Museum** (202 N. Alabama St.) is the place to go. The museum is housed in the former Indianapolis City Hall, a Roman-classic structure featuring exquisite architecture, marble columns, and inlaid marble walls and floors.

Indiana

In **Holocomb Gardens** (4600 Sunset Ave.), lilies, lilacs, peonies, gladiolas, Japanese crab trees, and more than 600 other species of trees flourish on 20 acres of property.

For a journey into the past, visit **Hook's Historical Drug Store and Pharmacy Museum** at the Indiana State Fairgrounds (1200 E. 38th St.), where 1853 furnishings, medical antiques, and an operating soda fountain can be seen.

The attractive 25-acre **Indianapolis Zoo** (3120 E. 30th St.) houses animals in settings resembling their natural habitat. Domestic animals, reptiles, and exotic and native birds are part of the more than 450-member zoo family.

The busy **City Market** (227 E. Market St.) has the sights, sounds, and aromas of an Old World marketplace. More than 50 vendors operate colorful stalls with meat, fish, poultry, fresh fruit and vegetables, cheeses, and ethnic specialties in a renovated building constructed in 1886.

Just north of the city, in Noblestown, the **Connor Prairie Pioneer Settlement** offers a look at Hoosier frontier life. This 55-acre pioneer village, located on a rolling hillside, has grown with the addition of log houses typical of the 1830s. More than 125 costumed interpreter-guides act as blacksmith, housewives, school teachers, potter, farmer, and doctor.

Indianapolis' main annual attraction, however, is a 2½-mile oval, the **Indianapolis Motor Speedway**, which plays host to the largest single sports event in the world — the Indy 500 (held each Memorial Day). Crowds of 400,000 and more come to see the fastest cars in the world race around the track.

The **Auto Racing Hall of Fame** contains racing memorabilia and more than 50 race cars, along with classic and antique cars from around the globe, including the *Texaco Star*, driven by Janet Guthrie, the first woman race driver to qualify for the famous race.

During the **500 Festival Month**, 30 days of hoopla preceding the big race, the city bursts with civic activities: a parade, coronation ball, Festival of the Arts, and much more. During **State Fair time**, usually 10 days before Labor Day, Indianapolis also swings at a faster tempo.

BEST TIME TO VISIT: Year round, but especially in May when the Indianapolis 500 and the 500 Festival Memorial Parade are held.

TRAVEL TIPS: If you come for the Indy 500, be prepared to deal with noisy, jostling crowds. Also, be prepared to pay for a place to stay since motels and hotels charge higher rates during this time of the year. And it's a good idea to make reservations well in advance.

HOURS: Children's Museum — 10 a.m.-5 p.m. Tuesday-Saturday, noon-5 p.m. Sunday, closed January 1, Thanksgiving, December 25. Anthenaeum — 11 a.m.-10 p.m. Monday-Friday, 6-12 p.m. Saturday and Sunday. Benjamin Harrison Memorial — 10 a.m.-4 p.m. Monday-Saturday, 12:30-4 p.m. Sunday, closed January 1, Thanksgiving, December 25. Museum of Indian Heritage — 11 a.m.-5 p.m. Tuesday-Sunday, June 15-Labor Day; 1-5 p.m. Monday-Friday, 10 a.m.-5 p.m. Saturday and Sunday, Labor Day-June 15. Museum of Art — 11 a.m.-5 p.m. daily, closed Monday, January 1, Thanksgiving, December 25. Indiana State Museum — 9 a.m.-5 p.m. daily, closed holidays. Holcomb Gardens — daylight hours daily. Hook's Historical Drug Store and Pharmacy Museum — 11 a.m.-5 p.m. daily, closed December 25. Indianapolis Zoo — 10 a.m.-4 p.m. daily; October-Easter, 10 a.m.-6 p.m. Saturday-Sunday. City Market —6 a.m.-6 p.m. Tuesday, Thursday-Saturday, 7 a.m.-3 p.m. Monday-Wednesday, closed holidays. Connor Prairie Pioneer Settlement — 10 a.m.-5 p.m. Tuesday-Sunday, May-October, Wednesday-Sunday, April, November-December 19; closed Easter, Thanksgiving. Auto Racing Hall of Fame — 9 a.m.-5 p.m. daily, closed December 25.

ADMISSION: Children's Museum — free. Anthenaeum — admission charged for special events. Benjamin Harrison Memorial — adults, $1.50; students, 75¢. Museum of Indian Heritage — adults, $1.25; under 4, free. Museum of Art — free except for special exhibits. Indiana State Museum — free. Holcomb Gardens — free. Hook's Historical Drug Store and Pharmacy Museum — free; Indianapolis Zoo — adults, $2; sr. citizens and children 2-11, $1; under 2, free. City Market — free. Connor Prairie Pioneer Settlement — adults, $4.50; sr. citizens, $3.75; children 6-18, $2.50; under 6, free. Auto Racing Hall of Fame — free except in May: practice days, $1; time trial days, $5; race day, $10; bus ride around track, $1.

DIRECTIONS: From Chicago, take I-90 to I-65 south to Indianapolis.

FOR MORE INFORMATION: Call the Convention and Visitors Bureau, (317) 635-9567, or write 100 S. Capitol Ave., Indianapolis, IN 46225.

Indiana

Fort Wayne: Gateway to Indiana's Lakelands

Fort Wayne, Indiana

Driving Time: 3½ hours southeast of Chicago

Fort Wayne's location at the confluence of the Maumee, St. Mary's, and St. Joseph's Rivers has contributed to the growth of Indiana's second-largest city. This industrial center is located in a rich agricultural region and is the gateway to eastern Indiana's lakelands. It derived its name from the fort established there by General "Mad" Anthony Wayne at General George Washington's direction.

Historic Fort Wayne (211 S. Barr) is considered the finest military fort reconstruction in the Midwest. Within the 11 log buildings in the complex, visitors can view the lives of soldiers and settlers in 1816. The fort is garrisoned by accurately costumed personnel who demonstrate crafts, daily living activities, and military drills. A museum in the Enlisted Barracks depicts the colorful history of Fort Wayne and northern Indiana from the Ice Age to 1819 and contains displays of important artifacts from this period, including personal possessions of Chief Little Turtle and General Wayne.

Visitors can also take historic river cruises of the city, which depart from the dock located on Superior Street in downtown.

Famed for its outstanding landscaping and cleverly designed exhibits, the **Children's Zoological Gardens** (3411 Sherman St.) is residence for animals from around the world. Miniature safaris are offered on 22 acres of the property that have been

landscaped like Africa's southland. There's a contact area for animal feeding. Train, pony, and horse rides are also available.

The **Museum of Art** (1202 W. Wayne St.) features exhibits from its permanent collection of Greek, Roman, Egyptian, medieval, and contemporary works as well as important exhibits from outside collections. Also featured is a children's wing, with hands-on workshops in various art media.

Lakeside Rose Garden (Lakeside Park and Lake Ave.), the largest rose garden in Indiana, was made to order for flower enthusiasts. More than 5,000 rose plants thrive in formal gardens that cover approximately three acres along lagoon banks.

History buffs will enjoy the **Louis A. Warren Lincoln Library** (1300 S. Clinton). The building houses a collection of original manuscripts autographed by Abraham Lincoln, Matthew Brady photographs, prints, paintings, and books. The 10,000 books and pamphlets comprise one

of the nation's top Lincoln collections and is rated as the one best suited for research.

Six miles southwest of Fort Wayne lies **Fox Island**, a 448-acre nature preserve for the protection of unique flora, fauna, and geological features.

BEST TIME TO VISIT: Spring, summer.
HOURS: Historic Fort Wayne — 9 a.m.-5 p.m. daily, mid-April to October. Historic River Cruises — noon-7 p.m. Saturday and Sunday, mid-May to mid-October. Children's Zoological Gardens — 9 a.m.-5 p.m. daily, late April to mid-October; also July till dark. Museum of Art — 1-5 p.m. Friday, 10 a.m.-5 p.m. Saturday. Lakeside Rose Garden — 8 a.m.-11 p.m. daily. Louis A. Warren Lincoln Library — 8 a.m.-4:30 p.m. Monday-Thursday, 8 a.m.-12:30 p.m. Friday, 10 a.m.-4:30 p.m. Saturday, May-November. Fox Island — 8 a.m.-8 p.m. Tuesday-Saturday, noon- 5p.m. Sunday.
ADMISSION: Historic Fort Wayne — adults, $3; 13-18, $2; 6-12, $1; under 6, free. Children's Zoological Gardens — adults, $2; children, $1. Museum of Art — free. Lakeside Rose Garden — free. Louis A . Warren Lincoln Library — free.
DIRECTIONS: From Chicago, take I-90 to South Bend, Ind. At South Bend, pick up U.S. 30 east to Fort Wayne.
FOR MORE INFORMATION: Call the Fort Wayne Chamber of Commerce, (219) 424-1435, or write 826 Ewing, Fort Wayne, IN 46802.

All-Seasons Resort At La Porte

La Porte, Indiana

Driving Time: 1½ hours southeast of Chicago; 4 hours north of Indianapolis

La Porte is a popular resort in both winter and summer. Seven lakes with fishing and boating facilities border the town on the north and west.

Ski Valley on Forrester Road is a great place to ski, and **Gateway Snowmobile Trail** (three miles east on School Road at County Road 150 N) offers snowmobiling and many other winter recreational facilities.

A bygone age comes to life at the **La Porte County Historical Steam Society**, where one of the most varied collections of steam equipment in the country is on display. Tourists can stroll among machines that once furnished the power for a growing America's transportation and industry. Your family can ride a scenic railroad powered with vintage locomotives, or they can hike through the rustic countryside.

Boulder Hill Vineyard (3366 W. Road 400 N) provides the only all-French hybrid vineyard in northern Indiana. Pick your own grapes and have them crushed.

La Porte County is noted for its lucious red strawberries. **Johnson Farm Produce** in nearby Hobart is only one of the great strawberry-picking spots in the area. Also, here you can pick blueberries and red and black raspberries when they are in season.

BEST TIME TO VISIT: Summer, winter, spring.

TRAVEL TIPS: If your family decides to go strawberry picking, be sure to bring old clothes; berry picking can be dusty work. Also, try to start early enough to avoid the mid-day heat and bring a thermos of your favorite cold drink to quench your thirst.

HOURS: Ski-Valley — December-March, 6-10 p.m. Monday-Friday, Saturday from 10 a.m., Sun. to 6 p.m. La Porte County Historical Steam Society — 1-6 p.m. Saturday and Sunday May 15-October. Boulder Hill Vineyard — 3-7 p.m. Monday, Tuesday, Friday; 9 a.m.-5 p.m. Saturday; noon-5 p.m. Sunday, November-August; 9 a.m.-7 p.m. daily, September-October.

ADMISSION: Ski Valley — call for exact fee. La Porte County Historical Steam Society — free. Boulder Hill Vineyard — free.

DIRECTIONS: From Chicago, take I-90 to the Indiana Toll Road, then U.S. 35 to La Porte.

FOR MORE INFORMATION: Call the Greater La Porte Chamber of Commerce, (219) 362-3178, or write Box 486, La Porte, IN 46350.

Indiana

Back to the Simple Life

Driving Time: About 3 hours southeast of Chicago, 5 hours west of Detroit, 3 hours from Indianapolis

Amish Acres, Nappanee, Indiana

Thirty miles from South Bend, Ind., in Nappanee, stands a monument to the traditional and hardworking lifestyle of the Amish people. Within the boundries of 80 acres, a 100-year-old German farming community has been reproduced down to the last detail. Teams of horses plow the land, black buggies move along the back roads and beautiful, simple Amish farmhouses dot the countryside.

The plain and simple life of the Amish is evident everywhere: from the W.H. Best Meat and Cheese Store to the clapboard farmhouse built in 1847 by one of Nappanee's first settlers. Inside are all the old-fashioned utensils, including wood-burning stoves, antique spinning wheels, oil lamps and butter churns. The plain, simple clothes typically worn by the Amish are on display, also. Outside you may visit the milk house, wash house, open well and summer kitchen. You may also want to take a buggy ride around the farmland.

Nineteen different buidings are scattered throughout the grounds, each contributing to the faithful recreation of the Amish lifestyle. Demonstrations of daily tasks include soap-making, candle-making, horseshoeing and meat preservation. In the fall the cider mill operates; maple syrup is made in the spring.

Every element of the Amish tradition is exhibited to help the visitor experience the simple life. And true to that lifestyle, visitors will want to end their tour with a hearty family-style meal at the Amish Acres Restaurant.

HOURS: Amish Acres: 9 a.m. to 8 p.m., Monday through Saturday, and 11 a.m. to 6 p.m., Sunday, May through October; 11 a.m. to 8 p.m., Saturday, 11 a.m. to 4 p.m. Sunday, April through November.

FOR MORE INFORMATION: Call Amish Acres, (219) 773-4188. Guided tours of the Notre Dame campus are available: 9 a.m. to 5 p.m. daily in summer; by appointment the rest of the year. Call (2190 283-2211.

ADMISSION: Amish Acres: Adults, $2.75; pre-teens and teens 12 to 18 yrs., $2; Children 6 to 11 yrs., $1.50; children under 6 yrs. free. (Prices subject to change)

DIRECTIONS: From Chicago, take I-90 or I-80 east to Indiana Toll Road. Past South Bend, take exit No. 9 (Rt.19) south to Rt. 6. Amish Acres is 1 mile west.

The Dunes: Sun, Sand and Nature

Indiana Dunes

Driving Time: 1½ hours from Chicago

The Indiana Dunes on Lake Michigan's southern shores offer opportunities for exploration, adventure and enjoyment. Whether you're a swimmer, hiker, historian, or simply a sun-lover, a trip to the Dunes will be a great experience.

There are sandy beaches, sparkling waters, and, of course, the dunes. On the hiking trails you can see plants and animals in their natural habitat. In dense forests that cover part of the Indiana Dunes, you'll encounter rare plant species and deer, raccoon, opossum, woodchuck, squirrel and chipmunk. There are also trails for biking and horseback riding.

There are two areas of the Dunes: the federally administered **Indiana Dunes National Lakeshore** and an area it surrounds, the **Indiana Dunes State Park**. (There's a fee for entrance to the State Park; none for the National Lakeshore area.)

While at the Dunes, you should learn to figure out the ages of the dunes by identifying the plant and animal life that exists there. The newest dunes are just behind the beach with no soil, and few insects and vegetation such as cottonwood trees, goldenrod, marram grass, and sand-cherry bushes. Pine dunes are the next oldest; they have little soil and have plant life like blueberries, poison ivy, Jack pine and juniper. The beech-maple dunes, the oldest at 10,000 years, are covered with deep soil and grow beech and maple trees. Year after year, wind and water push the sand hills farther back from the beach where they eventually attract wildlife and vegetation.

Several sections compose the total Indiana Dunes National Lakeshore area; it may be hard to choose which part to visit. The Bailly area (off Mineral Springs Road) has hiking trails and the Joseph Bailly Homestead, a 150-year-old pioneer home. In the Furnessville-Tremont section, you'll find parts of two ancient dune ridges formed when Lake Michigan was at a higher level. In the Mount Baldy area (west of Michigan City), you may climb the huge 135-foot dune. If you make it to the top, you'll have a breath-taking view of the bright blue water. Obtain information booklets and maps at the Visitor Center in the Furnessville-Tremont area (Kemil Road and Route 12, three miles east of Route 49).

HOURS: Vary for different areas of the dunes.
FOR MORE INFORMATION: Call the Indiana Dunes National Lakeshore at (219) 926-7561 or the Indiana Dunes State Park at (219) 926-4520.
DIRECTIONS: From Chicago, take I-90 or I-80 east to junction of I-94. Take I-94 north and exit on Route 12 or Route 20 to reach main dune area.

Indiana

Goshen/ Nappanee: Land of The Amish

Goshen, Indiana

Driving Time: 3 hours south of Chicago

Many quaint Amish farms dot the countryside surrounding Goshen and Nappanee. In September, Goshen hosts the annual **Michiana Mennonite Relief Sale**, held at the 4-H Fairgrounds, with thousands of hand-crafted articles (see write-up on festivals).

Families can easily spend the morning or afternoon exploring the pastoral countryside around Goshen. In town is the **Mennonite Historical Library** on the campus of Goshen College. The library boasts the largest collection in the world of historical books and reference works dealing with the Mennonite religion. More than 200 rare books, some dating back to the 16th century, are among the collection of 29,000 items that include pamphlets, maps, photographs, and paintings.

North of Goshen, 2½ miles east of Bristol, stands **Bonneyville Mill**, a restored gristmill with adjacent nature trails, picnic areas, fishing pond, and arboretum.

Nature-lovers and sportsmen will enjoy **Goshen Millrace and Dam**, a shady retreat along the Elkhart River.

At Nappanee, just south of Elkhart on U.S. 6, is **Amish Acres**, an 80-acre working Amish farmstead that provides a day of recreation and education for the whole family. Horse-and-buggy rides and historic lecture tours of a furnished 12-room

Amish house are followed by an Amish family-style dinner. The settlement has farm buildings, stores, a cider mill, a smokehouse, an outdoor brick oven, a bakery, and a restaurant.

In all, 19 different buildings are scattered throughout the grounds, each contributing to the faithful recreation of the Amish lifestyle. Demonstrations of daily tasks include soap making, candle making, horseshoeing, and meat preservation. In the fall, the cider mill operates; maple syrup is made in the spring.

BEST TIME TO VISIT: Year round.
HOURS: Mennonite Historical Library — 8 a.m.-noon, 1-5 p.m. Monday-Friday, Sat. to noon, closed most holidayss. Bonneyville Mill — 10 a.m.-5 p.m. daily, late May-October. Goshen Millrace and Dam — 24 hours daily. Amish Acres — 10 a.m.-6 p.m. daily, May-October, till 8 p.m. July and August.
ADMISSION: Mennonite Historical Library — free. Bonneyville Mill — free. Goshen Millrace and Dam — free. Amish Acres — adults, $3.50; children 6-11, $2; under 6, free.
DIRECTIONS: (Goshen is about 30 miles east of South Bend, Indiana.) From Chicago, take I-90 or I-80 east to Indiana Toll Road. Past South Bend, take Exit 9 (Rt. 19) south to Rt. 6 to Nappanee. From Nappanee, take Ind. 15 north to Goshen.
• **FOR MORE INFORMATION:** Call Chamber of Commerce, (219) 533-2102, or write E. Clinton St., Gohen, IN 46526.

Rockville: Land of Covered Bridges

Rockville, Indiana

Driving Time: 1½ hours west of Indianapolis; 5 hours south of Chicago

One way to start touring southern Indiana out of Indianapolis is by heading west into **Parke County**, Midwest stronghold of that fast disappearing symbol of rural America, the covered bridge. There are more than 35 of these picturesque roofed structures, located mostly on back roads. A free map showing the location of every bridge is distributed at the Tourist Information Center in Rockville, the county seat.

One such structure, the century-old **Mecca Covered Bridge** just south of Rockville, spans Little Raccoon Creek. A restored old-time school-house stands nearby as a reminder of the area's tranquil past.

More than 100,000 people from all over the nation descend on the county during the ten-day **Annual Covered Bridge Festival** held in mid-October to coincide with the peak of the fall color season. There are narrated bus tours for those who do not wish to drive to the many bridges, chicken and barbecue dinners, antique sales, and a Farmers' Market.

Billie Creek Village (east on U.S. 36) is a recreation of a turn-of-the-century village and working farmstead. There's also a one-room schoolhouse, county store, blacksmith shop, and log cabin.

Located within the border of Parke County is **Turkey Run State Park**, a 2,382-acre tract of beautiful virgin woods. Within the park are deep, rock-walled prehistoric can-

yons and winding streams that twist through solid rock. Vacationers can go canoeing or they can fish in Sugar Creek for bluegill, crappie, and rock bass. (Swimming is not allowed, however, because the creek can be treacherous.) There are 13½ miles of hiking trails and four miles of bridle paths through canyons, along cliffs, and into forests.

Raccoon Lake State Recreation Area (nine miles east on U.S. 36), a favorite spot among the locals, provides boating, fishing, water skiing, swimming, picnicking, and camping.

BEST TIME TO VISIT: Fall.

TRAVEL TIPS: As you drive along the scenic countryside, be sure to watch for scarecrows. They are along covered bridge routes as part of an annual contest. Be sure to pick up a ballot to vote for the scarecrow of your choice.

HOURS: Billie Creek Village — noon-5 p.m. Thursday-Sunday, late May to mid-October, 9 a.m.-5 p.m. daily third week in October. Turkey Run State Park — open all year.

ADMISSION: Billie Creek Village — adults, $2; children 6-13, $1; under 6, free. Turkey Run State Park — standard fees.

DIRECTIONS: From Indianapolis, take U.S. 36 west to Rockville.

FOR MORE INFORMATION: Call Tourist Information Center, (317) 569-5226, or write Box 165, Rockville, IN 47872.

Indiana

Exploring Pres. Lincoln's Home Turf

Lincoln City, Indiana

Driving Time: 3 hours southwest of Indianapolis; 7 hours south of Chicago

Here is the grave of Nancy Hanks Lincoln, mother of Abraham Lincoln. She died at the age of 35, when Abraham was nine years old. Abraham Lincoln spent 14 years of his boyhood in this vicinity, reading books, working as a clerk for a nearby merchant, and helping his father with farm work. When Lincoln was 21, his father and stepmother moved to Illinois, where Lincoln's political career began.

The **Nancy Hanks Lincoln Memorial** consists of Nancy Lincoln Hall, Abraham Lincoln Hall, and an interpretative museum. The one-story building is constructed of Indiana limestone and sandstone. On the original Thomas Lincoln tract is the **Lincoln Living Historical Farm**, consisting of a log cabin similar to the one the Lincolns lived in, a smokehouse, stable, chicken house, and workshop. The fields of the Lincoln farm have been cleared and planted with crops of the period. In the **Visitor Center** is a museum and a bookstore. A film is shown depicting the early life of Lincoln.

Across the road from the memorial is **Lincoln State Park**, a 1,730-acre area that has camping, hiking, fishing, swimming, picnicking, and naturalist services.

BEST TIME TO VISIT: Summer.
HOURS: Year round.
DIRECTIONS: From Indianapolis, take Ind. 67 southwest to U.S. 231 to the park.
FOR MORE INFORMATION: Call Lincoln State Park, (812) 937-4710, or write Box 216, Lincoln City, IN 47552.

Queen's Palace at Marengo Cave

Exploring An Old-Time Brewery

Mishawaka, Indiana

Driving Time: 1¾ hours from Chicago

The **100 Center Complex** is an exciting restoration of the 125-year-old **Kamm's Brewery**. Preserving the charm of its setting along the St. Joseph River, the brewery now contains a variety of unusual specialty shops, three restaurants, two art galleries, and twin theaters. Restored buildings in the complex include the old brick and masonry brewery, the ice house, boiler house, stable, and worker's quarters. The complex also has a modern motel and an old-fashioned beer garden located on a five-acre island behind the main brewery building. The *Island Queen*, a paddlewheel boat reminiscent of those on the Mississippi River, makes trips on the St. Joseph River during spring, summer, and fall.

BEST TIME TO VISIT: Summer.
HOURS: 10 a.m.-9 p.m. Monday-Saturday, noon-6 p.m. Sunday.
ADMISSION: Free.
DIRECTIONS: From Chicago, take the Indiana Toll Road to U.S. 33 to Mishawaka.
FOR MORE INFORMATION: Call 100 Center Complex, (219) 259-7861, or write 700 Lincoln Way West, Mishawaka, IN 46544.

Mounds State Park

Anderson, Indiana

Driving Time: 30 minutes north of Indianapolis

Mounds State Park consists of 259 acres of rolling woodlands; it has facilities for picnicking, camping, hiking, and swimming. There is also fishing and canoeing (rentals) in the White River. Vacationers can enjoy cross-country skiing in the winter.

Within the park are several well-preserved earth formations constructed many centuries ago by a prehistoric race of moundbuilders. On bluffs overlooking the **White River** are earth structures that once were an important center of an ancient civilization of which very little is known. The largest earth structure is nine feet high and nearly one-quarter mile in circumference. Smaller structures nearby include a conical mound.

BEST TIME TO VISIT: Summer.
HOURS: Year round.
ADMISSION: Standard fees.
DIRECTIONS: From Indianapolis, take I-69 north to Ind. 109 to Ind. 232 to the park.
FOR MORE INFORMATION: Call Mounds State Park, (317) 642-6627, or write Anderson, IN 46015.

Prehistoric Wyandotte Caves

Harrison-Crawford State Forest, Indiana

Driving Time: 3 hours southwest of Indianapolis

Since prehistoric times, when Indians used the caves for shelter and a burial place, the beauty of **Wyandotte Caves** has attracted people. In addition to approximately 25 miles of undiscovered passages, the caves include the largest underground room and underground mountain of any known cave in the world. Wyandotte is designated as state forest property and is located in Harrison-Crawford State Forest.

BEST TIME TO VISIT: Year round.
HOURS: Two-hour guided tours 9 a.m.-6 p.m. daily, May-October; last tour at 4 p.m. Memorial Day-Labor Day; 10 a.m., noon, and 2 p.m. rest of the year except Monday; closed January 1, Thanksgiving, December 25.
ADMISSION: Adults, $3; children 4-12, $1.50.
DIRECTIONS: From Indianapolis, take I-65 south to I-64 west. Exit at Corydon-Palmyra (Exit 105) and follow signs to the caves.
FOR MORE INFORMATION: Call Wyandotte Caves, (812) 738-2782, or write RR #1, Box 60A, Leavenworth, IN 47137.

Cave Country: Marengo Park

Marengo, Indiana

Driving Time: 2 hours south of Indianapolis

Beneath the scenic Lincoln Hills of southern Indiana is one of America's most beautiful caves. The new **Dripstone Trail Tour**, which opened in 1979, covers a one-mile walk through a section of the cavern known for its delicate beauty and numerous totem pole stalagmites. The tour emerges into Indiana's largest known cavern passage, big enough for a highway.

The **Crystal Palace Tour**, open since 1883, takes 35 to 40 minutes while covering one-third mile of the cave. This tour is noted for its huge flowstone formations and is climaxed by a special underground pageant in the world-famous "Crystal Palace." A swimming pool, signed nature trails, wooded campsites, and picnic areas are located in a 75-acre park over the cavern.

BEST TIME TO VISIT: Summer.
HOURS: 9 a.m.-5 p.m. Monday-Friday, 9 a.m.-6 p.m. Saturday and Sunday.
ADMISSION: Fee charged.
DIRECTIONS: Take U.S. 37 south past Bloomington to the park.
FOR MORE INFORMATION: Call Marengo Cave Park, (812) 365-2705, or write Box 217, Marengo, IN.

Indiana

Nashville: Log Cabin Country

Nashville, Indiana

Driving Time: 1½ hours from Indianapolis

This isn't the Nashville of country music fame, but it's situated in one of Indiana's most scenic areas, Brown County. The county is best remembered for its forested hills crowding the eastern shores of Lake Monroe, the state's largest lake.

The heart of the county, **Nashville**, has been called "Log Cabin Country" because of its many historic log cabins. Beautiful and quaint, this area is also noted for its art, antiques, and collectibles.

Brown County Art Gallery (One Artist Dr.) contains paintings by members of the Brown County Art Gallery Association, a permanent collection of the works of early Brown County and Hoosier artists, and a collection of the works of Glen Cooper Henshaw.

The **Brown County Log Cabins** form a complex of buildings that includes the Old Log Jail, the Log Community Building, the Historical Society Museum, the David Family Log Cabin, and an 1890's doctor's office.

One of Nashville's more peculiar contributions to culture is the **John Dillinger Historical Museum** (corner of Franklin and Van Buren Sts.), containing mementos and wax figures of Prohibition-era gangsters. Gangster buffs will appreciate the recreation of Dillinger's funeral and the "original tombstone" from his grave in Indianapolis' Crown Point Cemetery. The collection is reputed to have cost $100,000.

The **John Hook 1900 Drug Store** (Salt Creek Valley Park Shopping Center) contains the original fixtures from John Hook's first drug store in Indiana. The antique pharmacy and carved wooden fixtures are preserved as they were at the turn of the century.

Nashville House (corner of Van Buren and Main Sts.) is built of native sandstone and log timbers. The building contains the Old County Store, which sells cookware, straw brooms, curios, and housewares. Inside, there's also a bakery and a restaurant.

Bean Blossom, just a short drive from Nashville, hosts in June the annual Bluegrass Festival, regarded nationally as one of the best events of its kind.

Two miles south of town, visitors will find **Brown County State Park**, the largest and one of the most beautiful parks in Indiana. There are 15,000 acres of hilly drives; a wildlife game sanctuary; a wildlife exhibit of Indiana's once plentiful elk, bear, and buffalo; and several artificial lakes. For a sweeping view of the countryside, climb the observation tower atop **Weed Patch Hill**. The park offers naturalist lectures, hiking over miles of trails, swimming, boating, and horseback riding. Families can stay in furnished cottages or in **Abe Martin Lodge**, which also has a swimming pool and a restaurant.

Five miles west on Ind. 46 is **Yellowood State Forest**, with boating, fishing, camping, hiking, picnicking, and horseback riding.

T.C. Steele State Memorial, eight miles south on Ind. 46, is the home and studio of the late artist, Theodore Steele, who did much to spread the fame of Brown County. The 11-room home overlooks 211 acres of picturesque forest land.

Spice Valley musicians

The **Nashville Alps Ski Resort** (four miles west via Ind. 46) has two chair lifts, two rope tows, ski rentals, a snow-maker, and a concession area.

Visitors can taste and buy various types of wine at **Possum Trot Vineyards** (8310 N. Possum Trot Rd., 12 miles northwest).

At **Sorghum Hill** (Ind. 46 near Gnaw Bone), families can watch farmers bring in cane and press it to make sorghum. Roadside stands sell sassafras root, maple sugar candy, popcorn, melons, pumpkins, and sorghum.

BEST TIME TO VISIT: Summer, fall. People visit the Nashville countryside especially to see the beautiful color of leaves in autumn.
TRAVEL TIPS: Pick up a map at the Chamber of Commerce in Nashville and tour the striking scenery on some of the back roads, such as Greasy Creek Road, Railroad Road, or the Sweetwater Trail.
HOURS: Brown County Art Gallery — 10 a.m.-5 p.m. daily, April-November; closed Thanksgiving. Brown County Log Cabins — 10 a.m.-5 p.m. daily, all year. John Dillinger Historical Museum — 10 a.m.-6 p.m. daily, March-November; 1-5 p.m. December-February. John Hook 1900 Drug Store — 9 a.m.-10 p.m. Monday-Saturday, 9 a.m.-7 p.m. Sunday and holidays. Nashville House — restaurant open 11:30 a.m.-8 p.m. Wednesday-Monday, 11:30 a.m.-8 p.m. daily in October. T.C. Steele State Memorial — 9 a.m.-noon, 1-5 p.m. Tuesday-Saturday, 1-5 p.m. Sunday only. Nashville Alps Ski Resort — 10 a.m.-10 p.m. Monday-Thursday, late December-early March; 8 a.m.-midnight Friday-Sunday, holidays; closed December 24 evening. Possum Trot Vineyards — 10 a.m.-6 p.m. Monday-Saturday, April-December.
ADMISSION: Brown County Art Gallery — adults and children, 50¢. John Dillinger Historical Museum — adults, $2; children 6-12, $1; under 6, free. John Hook 1900 Drug Store — free. T.C. Steele State Memorial — adults, 50¢; under 12, free.
DIRECTIONS: From Indianapolis, take I-65 south to the Columbus exit. Drive east on State Hwy. 46 all the way to Nashville.
FOR MORE INFORMATION: Call the Brown County Chamber of Commerce, (812) 988-4920, or write Box 164, Nashville, IN 47448.

Santa Claus Land

Santa Claus, Indiana

Driving Time: 3 hours south of Indianapolis

Santa Claus Land (seven miles south of I-64 on Ind. 162) is the oldest theme park in the United States, celebrating Christmas all year round. It's a fantasyland with 200 acres of rolling, wooded hills filled with rides, museums, live shows, a petting zoo, House of Dolls, Hall of Famous Americans, game room, arcade, gift and souvenir shop, restaurant, and even Santa Claus. Adjacent to the park are 220 modern campsites on **Lake Rudolph**, with fishing, swimming, and a playground for campers. "Live" dolls and clowns roam the amusement park roads.

BEST TIME TO VISIT: Summer.
HOURS: 10 a.m.-dusk daily, Memorial Day-Labor Day, Saturday and Sunday other months.
ADMISSION: Adults, $4.25; children 2-11, $3.25; children under 2, free.
DIRECTIONS: From Indanapolis, take I-65 south to I-64 west to Ind. 62, south to Santa Claus Land.
FOR MORE INFORMATION: Call Santa Claus Land, (812) 937-4401, or write Santa Claus, IN.

Indiana Beach Amusement Park

Indiana Beach, Indiana

Driving Time: 1 hour north of Indianapolis; 2½ hours east of Chicago

An amusement boardwalk extending along the shore of Lake Shafer is a favorite attraction at Indiana Beach, the state's largest privately owned summer resort. The amusement park contains motels, cottages, a multitude of rides, miniature golf courses, shops, and restaurants. The *Shafer Queen*, a paddlewheel cruise ship, leaves the dock daily for sightseeing tours. Professional ski shows are performed at the **Aqua Theater** during the summer.

BEST TIME TO VISIT: Summer.
HOURS: 9 a.m.-11 p.m. daily, May 16-September 1.
ADMISSION: Call for prices.
DIRECTIONS: From Indianapolis, take I-65 north. Exit at Ind. 43 and pick up U.S. 24 east to Indiana Beach.
FOR MORE INFORMATION: Call Indiana Beach, (219) 583-4441, or write 306 Indiana Beach Dr., Monticello, IN 47960.

Indiana

South Bend: Home of the Fighting Irish

South Bend, Indiana

Driving Time: 2½ hours east of Chicago

South Bend has almost become synonymous with the **University of Notre Dame** — and its famous football team. From almost every vantage point in the city, visitors can see the golden dome of the university's administration building. During summer, tours of the 1,250-acre campus are offered. The many sights include the **Memorial Library**, one of the largest college libraries in the world; the paintings and art exhibitions at **O'Shaughnessy Hall**; the **Grotto of Lourdes**; and **Sacred Heart Church**.

Knute Rockne's name is closely linked to Notre Dame, and the great coach is buried not far from his beloved university in **Highland Cemetery** on Portage Avenue. His grave is marked with a simple stone.

The **Discovery Hall Museum** depicts the industrial history of the area from the 19th through 20th centuries. The museum houses the **Studebaker Vehicle Collection**, which includes a Conestoga wagon as well as the Lincoln carriage.

The colorful **Farmers' Market** (7600 Eddy St.) has more than 125 stalls offering a wide range of produce and other goods. Vendors include plain-frocked Amish farmers from outlying settlements.

Another interesting bazaar is the **Thieves Market**. This bright-red-barn structure houses almost 50 interesting small shops offering quality antiques and collectibles.

Indian Dunes National Lakeshore, north of South Bend

Potato Creek State Park (seven miles south on U.S. 31, then six miles west on state route 4) has 3,815 acres where families can go camping, picnicking, bike riding, swimming, cross-country skiing, and fishing on Lake Worster.

BEST TIME TO VISIT: Summer, fall.
TRAVEL TIPS: There's nothing more exciting than a good football game, especially when Notre Dame is playing. Make sure that your family catches at least one game when in town.

HOURS: University of Notre Dame — office hours 8 a.m.-noon and 1-5 p.m. Monday-Friday. Discovery Hall Museum — 10 a.m.-4:30 p.m. Tuesday-Friday, 10 a.m.-4 p.m. Saturday, 1-4 p.m. Sunday. Farmers Market — 7 a.m.-2 p.m. Tuesday, Thursday; Saturday to 3 p.m. Thieves Market — 10 a.m.-6 p.m. Saturday and Sunday. Potato Creek State Park — naturalist service, May-August.
ADMISSION: Discovery Hall Museum — free. Farmers Market — free. Thieves Market — free.
DIRECTIONS: From Chicago, take I-90 to the Indiana Toll Road. Exit at Angola and head west on U.S. 20 to South Bend.
FOR MORE INFORMATION: Call the South Bend-Mishawaka Convention and Visitors Bureau, (219) 234-0051, or write 230 W. Jefferson Blvd., Box 1677, South Bend, IN 46634.

Spring Mill State Park

Mitchell, Indiana

Driving Time: 1½ hours from Indianapolis

In this 1,319-acre park, an abandoned **pioneer village** has been restored in a small valley among wooded hills. Built around an 1816 gristmill are the log-constructed shops and homes of a pioneer trading post. The village's Main Street is flanked by a tavern, cobbler's shop, distillery, boot shop, post office, apothecary shop, and a pottery. A small stream trickling through the valley turns an overshot waterwheel at the gristmill and furnishes power for a sawmill. The reconstructed homes of the pioneers have been furnished with household articles of a century ago.

The **Virgil I. Grissom Memorial**, dedicated to the Indiana astronaut who was the second American in space, includes a memorial room, space exhibits, and a visitor center.

In the surrounding forest, which includes 80 acres of virgin woods, are some of the largest oak and tulip trees in Indiana. Some of the many caverns in the park have underground streams with rare species of blind fish. In **Twin Caves**, boat trips may be taken on underground rivers (April-October). The park has excellent hiking trails. Recreation facilities include an Olympic-size pool, tennis, fishing, and boating (rentals, no motors) in a 30-acre manmade lake. The park also has a saddle barn, a naturalist service, and camping and picnic areas.

BEST TIME TO VISIT: Summer.
HOURS: Year round.
ADMISSION: Standard fees.
DIRECTIONS: From Indianapolis, take Ind. 37 to Mitchell to Spring Mill State Park.
FOR MORE INFORMATION: Call Spring Mill State Park, (812) 849-4129, or write Mitchell, IN.

Lakes Galore: Chain O'Lakes State Park

Albion, Indiana

Driving Time: ?

This park derives its name from the presence of nine natural, connecting lakes situated in Indiana's lake country. Two smaller, nonconnecting lakes make a total of 11 in the park. It is located five miles southeast of Albion, in Noble County, on Indiana 9 in the northeast corner of the state. **Chain O'Lakes State Park** offers a wide variety of facilities, such as family housekeeping cabins, campground, beach, boat rentals, fishing, hiking trails, and picnic areas.

BEST TIME TO VISIT: Summer, winter. The park offers seasonal naturalist service and an old two-room, red-brick schoolhouse that has been converted into a nature center. Throughout the summer season, a variety of cultural arts programs are offered for the enjoyment of park visitors. During the winter, ice fishing is available and skiing equipment can be rented. One cross-country ski trail is three-quarters of a mile in length and the other is two miles longer.
TRAVEL TIPS: In summer, bring insect repellent because mosquitoes can be a problem.
HOURS: Open all year round.
ADMISSION: Free.
DIRECTIONS: Take Rt. 33 northwest from Fort Wayne, then north on Rt. 9.
FOR MORE INFORMATION: Call Chain O'Lakes State Park at (219) 636-2654 or write Route 2, Albion, IN 46701.

High, Mighty Clifty Falls State Park

Madison, Indiana

Driving Time: 1½ hours southeast of Indianapolis

From a high, wooded plateau, **Clifty Falls State Park** offers a striking view of 1,360 acres, the Ohio

River and its traffic, and hills on the Kentucky shore. It also contains waterfalls of Clifty Creek and Little Clifty Creek, bedrock exposures, and a deep boulder-strewn canyon reached by the sun at high noon only.

There are wildflowers and a variety of wildlife throughout the park. The grounds also has a playground, picnic areas, shelters, fireplaces, camping facilities, a swimming pool, tennis courts, a concession area, a naturalist service, and a nature center.

BEST TIME TO VISIT: Summer.
HOURS: The Inn in the Park has year-round accommodations.
ADMISSION: Standard fees.
DIRECTIONS: From Indianapolis, take I-65 to the Taylorville exit. Get on U.S. 31 to Columbus, then take Ind. 7 to Madison and then to the park.
FOR MORE INFORMATION: Call Clifty Falls State Park, (812) 273-5495, or write 1501 Green Rd., Madison, IN 47250.

Indiana

New Harmony: Enduring Utopia

New Harmony, Indiana

Driving Time: 1 hour west of Evansville on the Wabash River

Located in southwest Indiana, at the Illinois state line on U.S. 160, the town of **New Harmony** was founded in 1814 by the Harmony Society (separatists from the Lutheran Church). Graceful and sturdy structures from this period remain to tell the saga of those skilled, dedicated settlers who thought that they could build a utopian community.

The **New Harmony State Memorial Tour** traces the town's history from early frontier days to its modern reemergence as a cultural center; the tour includes the Athenaeum and Theatrum, West Street Log Structures, David Lenz House, Robert Henry Fauntleroy Home, Workingmen's Institute, Murphy Auditorium, George Kepler House, 1830 Owen House, John Beal House, Theater Museum and Workshop, Solomon Wolf House, and Dormitory No. 2 and Kitchen.

Originally an apple orchard, the **Harmonist Burial Ground** (West St. between North and Church Sts.) has 230 members of the Harmony Society buried here in unmarked graves dating from 1814 to 1824. The site also includes several mounds of prehistoric Woodland Indians.

The paths of life and the rewards for the correct choices are symbolized by the **Labyrinth**, a restoration of the original Harmonist landscaped maze and hedge garden. Visitors can discover their own path to the center.

Designed by architect Philip Johnson, the interdenominational **Roofless Church** commemorates New

The "Roofless" Church in New Harmony, a community that was an experiment in communal life.

Harmony's religious heritage. Jacques Lipchitz's sculpture, "Descent of the Holy Spirit," is located in the center of the church under an unusual dome.

The **New Harmony Gallery of Contemporary Art** (Owen Block, Main St.) showcases regional artists. Special traditional and contemporary exhibits are featured monthly.

Famous theologian Paul Tillich is buried in **Tillich Park**. Engraved stones contain selections of Dr. Tillich's writings.

Harmonie State Recreation Area, three miles south of New Harmony, includes 200 campsites on 32 acres of land along the Wabash River.

BEST TIME TO VISIT: Year round.
HOURS: Harmonist Burial Ground — daylight hours daily. Labyrinth — daylight hours daily. Roofless Church — daily. New Harmony Gallery of Contemporary Art — 9 a.m.-5 p.m. daily, 1-5 p.m. Sunday, until 8 p.m. on days of evening theater performances. Tillich Park — daily.
ADMISSION: Harmonist Burial Ground — free. Labyrinth — free. Roofless Church — free. New Harmony Gallery of Contemporary Art — free. Tillich Park — free.
DIRECTIONS: From Evansville, take Ind. 66 west to New Harmony.
FOR MORE INFORMATION: Call New Harmony Visitor Reception, (812) 682-4474, or write North and Arthur Sts., New Harmony, IN 47631.

Bloomington: Gateway to Southern Indiana

Bloomington, Indiana

Driving Time: 1½ hours south of Indianapolis

Bloomington is the home of **Indiana University**, cultural center for thousands of Hoosiers and visitors who attend the numerous concerts, operas, and plays performed by students and world-renowned artists. Tours of the campus are available; among buildings not to miss are the **University Museum**, **Musical Arts Center**, the **Lilly Library** of rare books, the **Museum of Art**, and the large, new assembly hall.

More than 50 **historic homes** dot the Bloomington countryside. A tour originates at the home of Andrew Wylie, Indiana University's first president, and concludes at the Monroe County Historical Society Museum.

The **Woolery Stone Company** provides small group tours of its facilities, including demonstrations of stone cutting. Participants should be prepared to walk through rocky terrain.

Eight miles south of Bloomington lies **Lake Monroe**, Indiana's largest manmade lake. Families can go boating, swimming, skiing, and fishing in 24,000 acres of water and recreation areas. Some of the region's best bass fishing is here.

McCormick Creek State Park (12 miles northwest on Ind. 46) is a must-see for vacationers. The creek plunges headlong through a limestone canyon in this 1,833-acre park to join the White River at its border. Foot trails, bridle paths, and roads lead through beech and pine forests, steep

ravines, and stone gullies. **Wolf Cave** and the stone bridge over **McCormick's Creek** are attractions worth seeing. Accommodations are available in a 60-room inn and in rustic cabins. Tourists can enjoy swimming in an Olympic-size pool in summer and go horseback riding, play tennis, fish, or hike. A naturalist is on duty in summer, and there is a fine new **Nature Center**.

Oliver Winery (seven miles north on Rt. 37) provides free wine tasting and a tour of the facility, complete with an explanation of the wine-making process. Assorted meats, cheese, and breads are on sale, as well as bottled Oliver wines.

BEST TIME TO VISIT: Summer, fall.
TRAVEL TIPS: A splendid vacation retreat, Bloomington is in the heart of the state's most picturesque region — an area of rolling wooded hills, transformed into a wonderful mosaic of color in fall. Make a point to visit the campus of Indiana University, which is great for strolling.
HOURS: Musical Arts Center — daily and weekends, closed holidays. Lilly Library — 9 a.m.-5 p.m. Monday-Friday, 6-10 p.m. Monday-Thursday, 9 a.m.-noon and 2-5 p.m. Sunday. Museum of Art — 9 a.m.-5 p.m. Tuesday-Saturday, from 1 p.m. Sunday. Wylie House — 1:30-5 p.m. Wednesday, Friday. Oliver Winery — 11 a.m.-6 p.m. Monday-Saturday, closed January 1, Thanksgiving, December 25, election days; tours, noon-5 p.m. Saturday.
ADMISSION: Musical Arts Center — free. Lilly Library — free. Museum of Art — free. Wylie House — admission charged. Oliver Winery — free.
DIRECTIONS: From Indianapolis, take Ind. 37 to Bloomington.
FOR MORE INFORMATION: Call Convention and Visitors Bureau of Monroe County, (812) 334-8900, or write 441 Gourley Pike, Bloomington, IN 47401.

Indiana

Lafayette: Feast of the Hunter's Moon

Lafayette, Indiana

Driving Time: 1 hour from Indianapolis

Lafayette is a good travel destination or stopping-off spot, with historic sights, a wildlife preserve, a major university, and art and music attractions.

Hugging the east bank of the Wabash River in western Indiana, this friendly city is the county seat of historically famous Tippecanoe County. Its namesake is Marquis de Lafayette, a Frenchman who served as a general under George Washington in the Revolutionary War.

Four miles south of Lafayette lies one of the state's most interesting and oldest historic sites, **Fort Ouiatenon**, named after the group of Wea Indian villages located there. The fort was established by the French in 1747 to protect their fur trade. The present blockhouse, a replica of a frontier fortress, was built in 1930 and is a part of the rich history of the trading era. An **interpretive museum** and **gift shop** are housed on the ground of Fort Ouiatenon Historical Park.

Once a year in early fall, Fort Ouiatenon is the scene of a colorful festival, the **Feast of the Hunter's Moon**. The accent is decidedly French, with costumed military units, bubbling caldrons of onion and pea soup, and French ballads. Other nationalities are also represented, with recreated units of British redcoats and American Revolutionary Army forces. The festival commemorates life 200 years ago, when the fort's soldiers, Canadian traders, Indians, and backwoodsmen gathered to trade and celebrate the fall season.

Other annual events include the **Fiddlers' Gathering**, held at the Tip-

pecanoe Battlefield in mid-July, and the **Wabash River Canoe Race** at Digby Park in late June.

The **Tippecanoe Battlefield** is located in Battle Ground, Indiana, approximately eight miles north of Lafayette. It's a 90-acre park with a museum, picnic areas, historic and scenic trails, and educational programs.

For an unusual experience, visit **Wolf Park** and see 22 wolves in several packs. Guides will explain their behavior and introduce them by name.

Tippecanoe County Historical Museum is an English Gothic house built in 1850 and now listed in the National Register of Historic Places. It contains an extensive collection of articles representing life in the area over the past few centuries. Relics from the Battle of Tippecanoe, lusterware, glass, Dresden porcelain, and metal items are featured in the collection.

Nearby, **Clegg Memorial Garden** forms an attractive 20-acre botanical garden in a rugged setting. Families can stroll through expansive woodland, criss-crossed by a mile of marked trails in the deep woods and ravines, as well as a five-acre pond and meadow area.

Horticulture Park, Westwood Trails, on the campus of Purdue University, consists of a 40-acre wilderness area where visitors will find a variety of annuals, a rose garden, shrubs, and other greenery in the park.

Another popular outdoor site is **Columbian Park**, where a zoo, a lagoon with pedal boats, an amusement park, a game arcade, a swimming pool, and lots of picnic area can be found.

BEST TIME TO VISIT: Summer, fall.

TRAVEL TIPS: If your family plans to participate in the Feast of the Hunter's Moon, be sure to make reservations well in advance. Accommodations are plentiful, but the festival — one of Indiana's most popular — is always well attended.

HOURS: Fort Ouiatenon Historical Park — 1-5 p.m. daily, closed Monday, mid-April to mid-November. Feast of the Hunter's Moon — weekend, late September or early October. Tippecanoe County Historical Museum — 1-5 p.m. daily, closed Monday, holidays, and January. Clegg Memorial Garden — 10 a.m.-sunset daily. Wolf Park — 1-5 p.m. Saturday and Sunday, mid-April-November. Horticulture Park — dawn-dusk daily. Slayter Center of the Performing Arts — daily for viewing.

ADMISSION: Fort Ouiatenon Historical Park — adults, 25¢; children, 10¢. Feast of the Hunter's Moon — adults, $3; children 4-12, $1; under 4, free. Tippecanoe County Historical Museum — free. Clegg Memorial Garden — free. Wolf Park — adults, $1.50; children 6-13, 50¢. Horticulture Park — free.

DIRECTIONS: From Indianapolis, take I-65 to U.S. 52 to Lafayette.

FOR MORE INFORMATION: Call Convention and Visitors Center, (317) 423-5551, or write Box 348, Lafayette, IN 47902.

Peru: Circus Capital of The World

Peru, Indiana

Driving Time: 2½ to 3 hours from Chicago

Once known as the **Circus Capital of the World**, Peru formerly provided winter headquarters for some of America's foremost circuses.

The spirit of the circus still lives on in Peru, however. Taught by old-time circus pros, local school children train for the annual **Circus Festival** each July.

The **Circus Museum** (154 N. Broadway) has one of the finest collections of circus relics in the country. Miniature circuses, furniture from the Wallace Circus Train, a wild animal cage, photographs and lithographs, costumes of famous performers, trapeze, rigging, and harness gear are colorful remembrances of the many great circuses that wintered in Peru.

At the junction of U.S. 24 and 31, travelers can visit the **Miami County Historical Museum** in the fourth floor of the County Courthouse. The building contains Indian and pioneer relics, circus mementos, a military display, blacksmith and cobbler shops, musical instruments, and doll exhibits.

In the **Puterbaugh Museum** (11 N. Huntington St.) are war relics, circus mementos, Indian and pioneer artifacts, and period clothing exhibits. There's also a replica of a pioneer home.

Your family can visit **Cole Porter's birthplace** (still privately owned) on the old **Skokum Indian Trail**.

Drive seven miles southeast via state route 19, then east on County Road 40 south to see **Mississinewa Lake**, which has public recreational facilities, water skiing, swimming, picnicking, and camping.

BEST TIME TO VISIT: Summer.
HOURS: Circus Museum — 9 a.m.-5 p.m. daily. Miami County Historical Museum — 9 a.m.-noon, 1-4 p.m. Monday-Saturday, May-September. Mississinewa Lake — daily, May 15-September 15.
ADMISSION: Circus Museum — adults, 25¢, children, 10¢. Miami County Historical Museum — free. Puterbaugh Museum — free. Mississinewa Lake — $1.25/car.
DIRECTIONS: From Chicago, take I-90 to the Indiana Toll Road. Head west on U.S. 20 to South Bend, Ind. From South Bend, pick up U.S. 31, then turn east on U.S. 24 to Peru.
FOR MORE INFORMATION: Call the Peru Chamber of Commerce, (317) 472-1923, or write 154 N. Broadway Peru, IN 46970.

Indiana

Evansville: Rivertown USA

Evansville, Indiana

Driving Time: 3½ hours southwest of Indianapolis; 9 hours south of Chicago

Evansville, the largest city in southern Indiana, is a stone's throw from Kentucky, just across the Ohio River. Families should find the tourist attractions here quite enjoyable.

Mesker Zoo, on the northwest edge of town, is an exceptionally large, fine zoo with more than 500 animals in natural surroundings without cages. A replica of Columbus' flagship, the *Santa Maria*, is the summer home of monkeys. There's an unusual open-air cage for birds and a **Children's Contact Area**, where youngsters can feed and touch animals. Visitors can also ride the Zoo Train around the grounds.

Travelers will want to stop off at **Angel Mounds State Memorial** (8215 Pollack Ave.). The Chief's Mound is one of the largest pre-Columbian structures in eastern America. A ritual temple building and a portion of the stockade wall have been reconstructed on the grounds. The **Interpretive Center** shelters artifacts, a simulated excavation site, and pictorial displays.

The **Evansville Museum of Arts and Science**, on the Ohio River in Sunset Park, is an attractive three-story structure that contains permanent and monthly exhibits of art, history, and science. The museum also includes a planetarium, a library, two sculpture gardens, a steam railroad train, and **Rivertown USA**, a recreation of a turn-of-the-century village.

An **Old Evansville Walking Tour**, starting at Riverside Drive and First Street (between Walnut and Adams

Historic Evansville Reitz Home

Sts.), is great for those who want to learn about 19th-century Evansville at a leisurely pace.

One example of the city's early architecture is the **John Augustus Reitz Home**. The 1872 structure is ringed by a wrought-iron fence and has space aplenty with 17 rooms and no less than 10 fireplaces. The house was accepted for the National Register of Historic Places in 1973.

Families will especially enjoy **Wesselman Park Nature Center** (551 N. Boethe Rd.). Two hundred acres of virgin hardwood forest are laced with marked trails for secluded walks in the midst of native trees and wildflowers. A one-way glass in the visitor's center provides a unique view of bird and other animal activity. A remnant section of the old **Wabash Erie Canal**, used from 1832 to 1875, runs along the northern boundary.

The *Spirit of Evansville* (Dress Plaza on the riverfront), a 150-passenger sternwheel paddleboat, offers charter cruises on the Ohio River.

Burdette Park, six miles southwest of the city, provides fishing, picnicking, RV camping, cabins, a swimming pool, skating, tennis courts, and a bicycle moto-cross race track.

The Swiss chalet-like **Golden Rain Tree Winery** (eight miles northwest of Evansville on Winery Rd.) has a tasting room and underground wine cellar. Visitors can sample the wine and purchase it by the glass, bottle, or case.

BEST TIME TO VISIT: Year round.
HOURS: Mesker Park Zoo — 9 a.m.-5 p.m. daily, mid-April to mid-October, rest of the year to 4 p.m.; closed January 1, December 25. Angel Mounds State Memorial — 9 a.m.-5 p.m. daily, November-March; Sunday from noon; closed holidays. Museum of Arts and Science — 10 a.m.-5 p.m. Tuesday-Saturday, Sunday from noon; closed January 1, Thanksgiving, December 24, 25, 31. Old Evansville Walking Tour — guided tours after 4:30 p.m. Reitz Home — 1-4 p.m. Friday-Sunday, March 14-December 14; rest of year by appointment only; closed January 1, December 25. Wesselman Park Nature Center — 9 a.m.-5 p.m. Tuesday-Saturday, noon-5 p.m. Sunday and holidays. Burdette Park — Memorial Day-Labor Day. Golden Rain Tree Winery — 11 a.m.-10 p.m. Mon.-Thurs., 11 a.m.-11 p.m. Fri. and Sat.
ADMISSION: Mesker Park Zoo — adults, $2; children 3-12, $1; sr. citizens, 75¢; under 3, free. Angel Mounds State Memorial — adults, 50¢; under 11, free. Museum of Arts and Science — free. Reitz Home — adults, $1; children 7-12, 50¢; under 7, free. Wesselman Park Nature Center — adults and children, $3 Monday-Friday; weekends and holidays, $3.50. Burdette Park — pool: adults, $1; under 5, free. Golden Rain Tree Winery — free.
DIRECTIONS: From Indianapolis, take I-70 west to Terre Haute. Pick up U.S. 41 south to Evansville.
FOR MORE INFORMATION: Call the Convention and Visitors Bureau, (812) 425-5402, or write 715 Locust St., Evansville, IN 47708.

The Bonnie Belle riverboat at Jeffersonville, Indiana. The Wave-tek Water Park, which creates oceanlike waves for Midwest surfers, is also there. Another Jeffersonville attraction is the Howard Steamboat Museum.

Lake Wawasee

Syracuse, Indiana

Driving Time: 3 hours south of Chicago

Named after an Indian chief—also referred to as Old Flat Belly—**Lake Wawasee** (south on Ind. 13 near Syracuse) has 21 miles of shoreline and the Wawasee Fish Hatchery, one of the oldest in Indiana. Lake Wawasee is the largest natural lake in Indiana and has long been a popular summer resort. It is joined by Lake Syracuse to the north and Lake Papakeechee to the southwest. Winter sports are enjoyed at nearby Mt. Wawasee.

BEST TIME TO VISIT: Summer.
DIRECTIONS: Take I-90 or I-80 east to Indiana Toll Road. Pass South Bend, take Exit 9 (Rt. 19) south to Rt. 6 to Syracuse to Lake Wawasee.
FOR MORE INFORMATION: Call Goshen Chamber of Commerce, (219) 533-2102, or write E. Clinton St., Goshen, IN 46526.

Steamboat Paradise In Indiana

Jeffersonville, Indiana

Driving Time: 2 hours south of Indianapolis

Jeffersonville, one of Indiana's oldest Ohio River towns, was built according to plans by that jack-of-all-trades and master-of-many, Thomas Jefferson.

The **Howard Steamboat Museum** (1101 E. Market St.) is a 22-room Victorian mansion that contains 15 types of wood, stained glass, and leaded windows in a Moorish-style music room. The museum is crammed with the stuff of river lore: navigational equipment, paddlewheels, small steamboat relics, and photographs of the Yukon Gold Rush steamboats.

The **Colgate Clock** atop the Clarksville Colgate-Palmolive plant is said to be the second-largest clock in the world (40 feet in diameter). (Let us know if it's accurate.)

For an old-fashioned river ride, take the **Bonnie Bell**, an authentic sternwheeler with a maximum capacity of 160 persons. Cruises are regularly scheduled.

Visitors will also enjoy a tour of **Jeffboat, Inc.** (E. Market St. on the Ohio River), the nation's largest inland shipyard, where river and ocean-going barges and towboats are built.

The **Steamboat Days Festival**, on the first weekend in September, includes a parade, entertainment, talent shows, and arts and crafts.

BEST TIME TO VISIT: Year round.
TRAVEL TIPS: During Kentucky Derby time in adjacent Louisville, hotel and motel rates may be higher.
HOURS: Howard Steamboat Museum— 10 a.m.-4 p.m. Monday-Saturday, from 10 a.m. Sunday. Jeffboat, Inc. — tours by appointment only.
ADMISSION: Howard Steamboat Museum — adults, $1.50; sr. citizens, college and high school students, 75¢; children 7-12, 50¢.
DIRECTIONS: From Indianapolis, take I-65 south to Jeffersonville.
FOR MORE INFORMATION: Call the Clark-Floyd Convention and Tourism Bureau, (812) 282-6654, or write Box 608, Jeffersonville, IN 47130.

Indiana

Corydon: Old State Capital

Corydon, Indiana

Driving Time: 3 hours from Indianapolis

Lying in relative anonymity near the southernmost center of Indiana, not far from the Ohio River, is **Corydon**. As the story goes, the town's name came from William Henry Harrison, who was inspired by a popular song of the day. It enjoyed a brief day in the sun as the first state capital from 1813 to 1835.

The city was the scene of the only battle fought on Indiana soil during the Civil War, when a Confederate raiding party occupied the town briefly on July 9, 1863. Otherwise, life has continued at a leisurely pace in this Indiana backwater — and that's the way they like it.

The **Corydon Capitol State Memorial** (Old Capitol Ave.), a blue limestone building erected in 1812 as a courthouse, served as the seat of the Indiana territorial government from 1813 to 1816, when the state's first constitutional convention assembled here. Following Indiana's admission to the Union in 1816, the building was the state capitol until 1825. It has been carefully restored to resemble the days when the pioneer lawmakers met there.

Governor Hendricks Headquarters (202 Walnut St.) was the former home of Thomas A. Hendricks, Indiana's third governor. A recent restoration project by the State of Indiana portrays Indiana's homelife in three distinct time periods between 1820 and 1880.

Another interesting building for those with a bent for history is the **Posey House** (Walnut and Oak Sts.), home of Col. Thomas Lloyd Posey

The George Rogers Clark Memorial, in Vincennes

when Corydon was the state capital. The house is an example of early 1800 architecture and has been restored as a museum.

Visitors to the **Zimmerman Art Glass Company** (Beech St.) can see individually blown glass novelties and art objects, paperweights, vases, and perfume bottles.

Squire Boone Caverns (12 miles south on state route 135) is a fantastic subterranean world of colorful stalactites and stalagmites, waterfalls, rivers, towering pillars, and the world's largest travertine dam formation. Squire Boone, Daniel Boone's brother, discovered the cave in 1790 and is buried deep in its interior. Above ground, there are nature trails, picnic groves, crafts shops, and a campground.

BEST TIME TO VISIT: Summer.
HOURS: Corydon Capitol State Memorial — 9 a.m.-noon and 1-5 p.m. daily. Governor Hendrick's Home — 9 a.m.- 5 p.m. daily; 1-5 p.m. Sunday, winter. Posey House — 1-4 p.m. Monday-Friday. Zimmerman Art Glass Co. — 8 a.m.-4 p.m. daily; closed Tuesday and holidays. Squire Boone Caverns — 9 a.m.-6 p.m. daily, May-October; 9:30 a.m.-5 p.m. daily, November-December, March-April; 10 a.m.-5 p.m. Saturday and Sunday, January-February; 9 a.m.-7 p.m. holidays; closed Thanksgiving and December 25.
ADMISSION Corydon State Capitol Memorial — adults, 50¢; under 12, free. Gov. Hendrick's Home — adults, $1; under 12, free. Posey House — admission charge. Zimmerman Art Glass Co. — free. Squire Boone Caverns — adults, $4; children 6-11, $2.50; under 6, free.
DIRECTIONS: From Indianapolis, take I-65 south to I-64, then take State Highway 62 into Corydon.
FOR MORE INFORMATION: Call the Harrison County Chamber of Commerce, (812) 738-2137, or write 225 N. Oak St., Corydon, IN 47112.

Vincennes: Historic Frontier Town

Vincennes, Indiana

Driving Time: 3 hours southwest of Indianapolis

Three flags — French, British, and American — have flown over Vincennes, the oldest city in Indiana. Located on the banks of the Wabash River, French fur traders roamed through the region as early as 1683.

Each May, Vincennes sponsors the annual **Spirit of Vincennes Rendezvous**, a reenactment of the Revolutionary War battle. Also included in the event are musical entertainment, dancing, arts and crafts, and an antique show.

The **Trailblazer Train** (First and Harrison Sts.) in Harrison Historical Park relives history by passing various points of interest in the city.

One such site is **George Rogers Clark National Historical Park** (downtown off U.S. 50 and U.S. 41), where the Clark Memorial and Visitor Center stands. A circular Doric building commemorates Clark's conquest of the Old Northwest during the Revolutionary War. This massive structure of granite, marble, and limestone, erected at a cost of almost $2 million, was officially dedicated by President Franklin Roosevelt in 1936.

Brouillet House (525 N. First St.) is an original 1790 French house, constructed of logs and mud.

The first brick building in Vincennes is **Grouseland**. Built in 1803-04 and set in a grove of walnut trees near the Wabash River, the structure was once the home of William Harrison, 9th president of the U.S. and first governor of the Indiana territory. The house is furnished with original Harrison possessions.

The George Rogers statue

The largest Indian mound in Indiana is the **Sonotabac Prehistoric Indian Mound** (2401 Wabash Ave.). Archaeologists call the moundbuilders Hopewellian People; they used the mound to worship their sun god. Indian life and prehistoric cultures are interpreted in the museum center.

The **Old Cathedral** (207 Church St.), built in 1826, stands on the site of the oldest parish in the state. Parish records date back to the French occupation of the 1740s, and four early bishops of the diocese are buried in the church basement. The **Old Cathedral Library** next to the church contains more than 11,000 books and rare documents, many dated before 1700.

The **Indiana Territory State Memorial** (Harrison and First Sts., on Vincennes University campus), a small two-story building built in the late 1700s, served as the territorial capitol from 1800 to 1812. The memorial includes Elihu Stout's print shop, where Indiana's first newspaper, *The Indiana Gazette*, was published. The **Log Cabin Visitor Center** provides tourists with information, guides, and tickets to various attractions.

BEST TIME TO VISIT: Year round.

TRAVEL TIPS: History buffs should follow the "Old Post Trail" markers, which point out 26 of Vincennes' 42 historic sites.

HOURS: Trailblazer Train — 10 a.m.-4 p.m. daily, April-May, September-October, Memorial Day-Labor Day. Rogers Clark National Historical Visitor Center — 8:30 a.m.-5 p.m. daily; closed January 1, Sunday, May-October; November-May by appointment. Grouseland — 9 a.m.-5 p.m. daily. Sonotabac Prehistoric Indian Mound and Museum — 10 a.m.-5 p.m. daily, May-October. Old Cathedral Complex — 9 a.m.-5 p.m. daily. Indiana Territory State Memorial — 9:30 a.m.-4:30 p.m. daily, March 1-November 1.

ADMISSION: Trailblazer Train — adults, $1.50; children, 50¢. Rogers Clark National Historical Visitor Center — free. Brouillet House — adults, 50¢; children, 25¢. Grouseland — adults, $1; children 6-12, 25¢; under 6, free. Sonotabac Prehistoric Indian Mound — adults, 50¢; children, 25¢. Indiana Territory State Memorial — adults, $1; children, 50¢.

DIRECTIONS: From Indianapolis, take State Highway 67 to U.S. 50 to Vincennes.

FOR MORE INFORMATION: Call the Knox County Chamber of Commerce, (812) 882-6440, or write Box 553, Vincennes, IN 47591.

Indiana

A Medieval-Style Abbey In Indiana

St. Meinrad, Indiana

Driving Time: 3 hours southwest of Indianapolis

St. Meinrad's medieval-styled archabbey, poised high atop a southern Indiana hill, provides inspiration to visitors when they experience the feeling of religious dedication and hospitality prevailing in the **Abbey Complex**.

St. Meinrad is today one of the largest Catholic seminaries in the nation, with more than 400 students studying for the priesthood. Take time to stroll through the beautifully landscaped grounds, paying close attention to the graceful architectural styling. The archabbey, founded by monks in 1854, exhibits a stark interior in contrast to its ornate sandstone exterior. The 100-year-old **Chapel of Monte Cassino** contains a handsome "Statue of Our Blessed Mother" (carved in Switzerland) and fine stained-glass work.

BEST TIME TO VISIT: Year round.
TRAVEL TIPS: Although the archabbey is not a vacation site, it is listed as one of Indiana's top 10 manmade attractions and worth a look.
HOURS: 8 a.m.-5 p.m. daily; guided tours by appointment 1-3 p.m. Sunday.
ADMISSION: Free.
DIRECTIONS: From Indianapolis, take I-65 south to I-64 west and exit at Birdseye-Bristow. Follow signs to St. Meinrad.
FOR MORE INFORMATION: Call News Information Development Office. St. Meinrad Archabbey, (812) 357-6611, or write St. Meinrad, IN 47577.

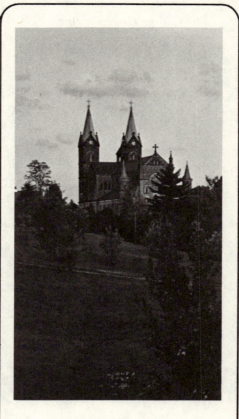

Beautiful Cataract Falls

Cloverdale, Indiana

Driving Time: 1 hour southwest of Indianapolis

Cataract Falls, Indiana's largest natural waterfall, tumbles and gushes into the southern end of 1,500-acre Cataract Lake near Cloverdale. Both upper and lower falls offer rugged beauty in picturesque surroundings that visitors and camera buffs won't want to miss.

BEST TIME TO VISIT: Summer.
HOURS: Year round.
ADMISSION: Lieber State Recreation Area—$1 entrance fee.
DIRECTIONS: From Indianapolis, take I-70 southwest to Cloverdale to U.S. 231. Follow signs to Lieber State Recreation Area and the falls.

Crown Point: Gangsters and Good Guys

Crown Point, Indiana

Driving Time: 30 minutes south of Chicago

Families with a yen for 1920s and 1930s nostalgia should make a point to visit the **Old Lake County Jail** in Crown Point. This 96-year-old structure, which retains its original interior, gained national notoriety on March 3, 1934, when John Dillinger made his daring escape here using a gun carved from soap.

The jail is surrounded by 12 interesting specialty shops and a 1930s-style restaurant. A small museum containing jail memorabilia and prisoner art is located in the jail.

In the years after World War I, the **Lake County Courthouse** came to be known as the "marriage mill" of the Midwest. Among the many notables who got married here were Tom Mix, "Red" Grange, Ronald Reagan, and Rudolph Valentino.

Today, the huge red-brick building also houses a series of shops and boutiques, including a bookstore and an ice cream parlor.

BEST TIME TO VISIT: Year round.
HOURS: Old Lake County Jail—10 a.m.-5:30 p.m. daily.
ADMISSION: Fee charged.
DIRECTIONS: From Chicago, take I-80 east to I-65 south.
FOR MORE INFORMATION: Call the Chamber of Commerce, (219) 663-1800, or write Box 343, Crown Point, IN.

ILLINOIS

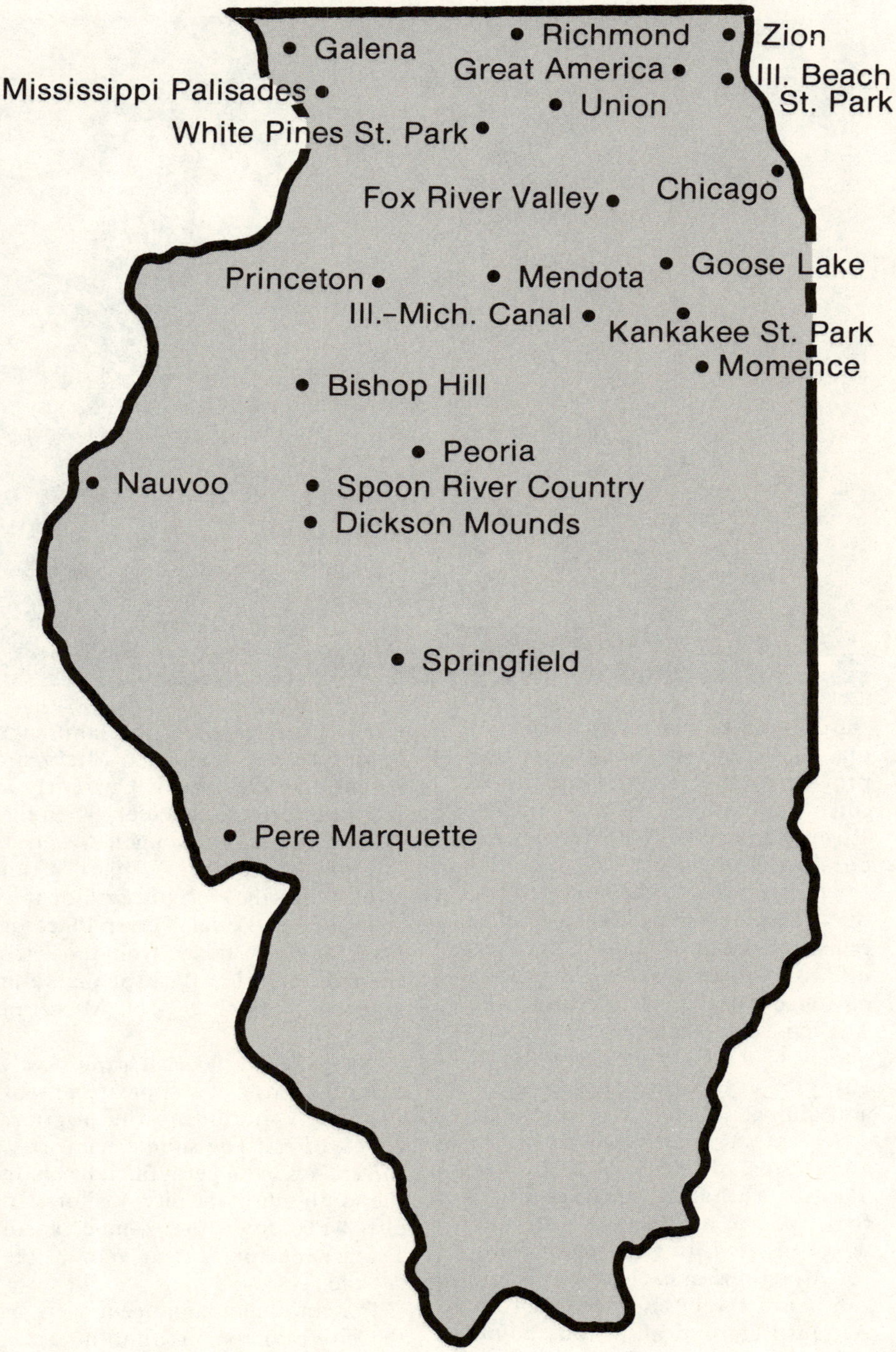

Map of Illinois with the following locations marked:

- Galena
- Richmond
- Zion
- Mississippi Palisades
- Great America
- Ill. Beach St. Park
- White Pines St. Park
- Union
- Fox River Valley
- Chicago
- Princeton
- Mendota
- Goose Lake
- Ill.-Mich. Canal
- Kankakee St. Park
- Momence
- Bishop Hill
- Peoria
- Nauvoo
- Spoon River Country
- Dickson Mounds
- Springfield
- Pere Marquette

Illinois Vacations

Illinois

Chicago: Your Kind Of Town, The 'Windy City'

Chicago, Illinois

They call it the "Windy City," not because of its weather, although an "occasional" breeze does pipe in from Lake Michigan, chilling local bones. Rather, the city got its nickname from a turn-of-the-century newspaper columnist who mocked the boastful style of the city's politicians. The name stuck despite — or perhaps because of — the fact that the columnist was from New York.

Windy or not, Chicago need not take a back seat to any city in terms of what if offers visitors: a shoreline of sandy beaches stretching from its shopping district to its fashionable north suburbs, tall buildings, chic shops, thriving ethnic enclaves such as Chinatown, world-famous museums, and dozens of theaters big and small are just a few of its attractions.

Downtown, there are such architectural wonders as **Sears Tower**, the world's tallest building, and the **John Hancock Building**, one of the world's tallest. The lakefront has 29 miles of grassy parks, sandy beaches, bike paths, and museums — all of which can be seen by driving along Lake Shore Drive.

Downtown Chicago, sometimes called the "Loop" because of the elevated railroad that winds around it, is just a short walking distance from the lake. The area is brightened by the newly developed **State Street Mall** (no cars, only buses are permitted on famous State Street, "that great street").

Sightseeing in Chicago can be done by bus or boat. The **Wendella Excursion Boats** (400 N. Michigan Ave., at the north end of the Michigan Ave. bridge, next to the Wrigley

The Old Water Tower one of the few buildings to survive the Great Chicago Fire. The John Hancock Center, one of the world's tallest buildings, is to the left.

Bldg.) give passengers a choice of one-, 1½-, and two-hour tours that provide a good view of the downtown area from both the Chicago River and the lake. The **Mercury Excursion Boats** (Wacker Dr. and Michigan Ave., at the south end of the Michigan Ave. bridge) also offer cruises. The **Clipper Line** (Navy Pier, off Lake Shore Dr. at Ohio St.) offers passengers a chance to cruise Lake Michigan on a steamship that affords a view of the Chicago skyline while enjoying entertainment, dancing, and dining.

A great way to see the city is to take advantage of the **CTA (Chicago Transit Authority) Culture Buses** that operate on north, south, and west routes, visiting the major cultural attractions in each area. Visitors can board the buses in front of the Art Institute and at various points throughout the city. (The buses operate on Sunday and holidays, Memorial Day to fall.) Start a **Chicago tour** by visiting a survivor of the 1871

Great Chicago Fire, the landmark **Water Tower**, on North Michigan Avenue at Delaware. Currently a tourist information center, it's in the middle of North Michigan Avenue's "Magnificent Mile". Visitors can stroll across the street for fashionable shopping at **Water Tower Place** or for a look at Chicago from the 94th-floor observation deck of the **John Hancock Center** (835 N. Michigan Ave.).

Navy Pier (600 E. Grand Ave.) hosts a variety of visitor attractions each year, including the popular ChicagoFest. The submarine *U.S.S. Silversides* has a permanent berth on the south side of the pier. Visitors can also walk down the ¾-mile North Promenade for a great view of the skyline.

For another magnificent view of the city and its surrounding area, head up to the skydeck on the 103rd floor of the **Sears Tower** (233 S. Wacker Dr.), where observers can see more than 20 miles away.

Chicago's scenic Lake Michigan shoreline

A large, first-class museum is the **Chicago Historical Society** (North Ave. and Clark St.), where families can see exhibits on city and state history, including many Lincoln and Civil War artifacts, and an audio-visual presentation of the Great Chicago Fire.

The **DuSable Museum of African American History** (740 E. 56th Pl. and Cottage Grove) offers a variety of permanent and special exhibitions as well as programs dealing with black history and culture.

If members of your family like fish and are fascinated by the world of the sea, they'll enjoy the **John G. Shedd Aquarium** (1200 S. Lake Shore Dr.), with its dazzling display of fishes, mammals, reptiles, and invertebrates. The spectacular 90,000-gallon Coral Reef exhibit puts you nose-to-nose with sharks and other inhabitants of the deep. (Come during feeding times and watch the scuba diver enter the tank and feed the fish; this happens at 11 a.m., 2 p.m., and 3 p.m. in summer months; at 11 a.m. and 2 p.m. from September to April.)

The **Adler Planetarium** (1300 S. Lake Shore Dr.) takes you up into the heavens with its Universe Theatre, sky shows, and outstanding exhibits on astronomy. Moon rocks, NASA space suits, and other outerspace objects and oddities are on display, and the "Sky Show" is a particularly striking multi-screen sound-and-light show that's well worth seeing.

Buckingham Fountain (lakefront in Grant Park) is twice the size of the Latona Fountain in Versailles, which it resembles. A nighttime light show transforms the fountain into a many-colored, glittering water sculpture.

The **Chicago Public Library Cultural Center** (Michigan Ave. and Washington St.) is a landmark with Tiffany glass domes, mosaics, and marble walls and stairs. Programs are scheduled on an almost daily basis and exhibits are changed frequently.

The **Prairie Avenue Historic District** (Prairie Ave. between 18th and Cullerton Sts.), where millionaires lived during the 1800s, is being restored to its original appearance with cobblestone streets and gaslights. Tours are available in Glessner House, one of the most interesting mansions in the area.

Travel farther south in the city for a visit to **Chinatown** (Cermak Rd. and Wentworth Ave.), one of the country's most interesting ethnic areas with fascinating shops and dozens of fine Chinese restaurants. Then take a guided tour through historic **Pullman Village** (11111 S. Forrestville Ave.), the 1880's company town-within-a-town that was supposed to be a worker's "Utopia."

One of the city's two major zoos, the **Lincoln Park Zoo**, is located on the city's North Side (west entrance, Webster Ave. and Stockton Dr.; east entrance, off Fullerton Ave.). A special Children's Zoo houses smaller animals for children to hold and pet. And the Farm-in-the-Zoo provides a

continued

Illinois

Chicago Attractions ... continued

rural farm atmosphere complete with dairy barn, beef barn, and horse and poultry buildings. The **Brookfield Zoo** (1st Ave. and 31st St., Brookfield) has 24 major exhibits on more than 200 acres. Divided by moats and natural-looking barriers, this is one of the most modern zoos in the country — and one of the best.

For garden and flower-lovers, the **Lincoln Park Conservatory** (Stockton Dr. near Fullerton) has four glassed buildings of tropical plants, formal and rock gardens, and an extensive collection of orchids. There are four major flower shows held here annually. The **Garfield Park Conservatory** (300 N. Central Park Blvd.) features 4½ acres of horticultural exhibits with more than 5,000 species and varieties of plants.

Baseball fans can see the Chicago Cubs play at **Wrigley Field** (1660 W. Addison) or the Chicago White Sox at **Comiskey Park** (35th and Shields) — two historic ballparks with colorful histories. (The Cubs play only during the day at home because Wrigley Field has no lights.)

Chicago is rich in museums. Among them are:

• The **Museum of Science and Industry** (lakefront at 57th St.), one of the world's great museums, where visitors can tour a working coal mine, walk through a captured German submarine, and push the buttons of more than 2,000 exhibits that explain how science and technology work in our everyday lives. (The museum has more than four million visitors yearly and is a busy place, so expect lines for some exhibits at the most popular hours.)

• The **Field Museum of Natural History** (Roosevelt Rd. at Lake Shore Dr.), complete with dinosaurs, Stone Age men, Egyptian mummies, wildlife exhibits, and a full-sized walk-in Pawnee earth lodge, among hundreds of exhibits and curiosities of nature.

• Not to be missed is the **Art Institute of Chicago** (S. Michigan Ave. and E. Adams St.), where art-lovers can view such treasures as French Impressionist paintings, Oriental drawings and sculptures, and primitive, decorative, and modern arts.

• Chicago's oldest museum, the **Chicago Academy of Science** (2001 N. Clark St.), features natural history in life-like dioramas.

Buckingham Fountain in Chicago

The Art Institute of Chicago

BEST TIME TO VISIT: Year round.

TRAVEL TIPS: Getting around in Chicago is fairly easy. The Loop is considered the center of the city, with State St. running north and south, and Madison St. east and west as the bases. Driving and parking in Chicago are no more difficult than any other major city and easier than some. Take advantage of Chicago's public transportation system, which will take your family anywhere in the city and to some suburbs. Taxis are plentiful.

HOURS: Wendella — 10 a.m.-9 p.m. daily, mid-April to mid-September. Mercury — daily, May-September. Clipper Line — 10 a.m.-2 p.m. Monday-Saturday, May 15-September; Sunday from noon. CTA Culture Buses — 11 a.m.-5 p.m. every 5 minutes, Sundays and holidays, Memorial Day-fall. Water Tower — 9 a.m.- 5 p.m. daily. Water Tower Place — shopping hours, 10 a.m.-7 p.m. Monday, Thursday; to 6 p.m. Tuesday, Wednesday, Friday, Saturday; noon-5 p.m. Sunday; closed holidays. John Hancock Center Observation Deck — 9 a.m.-midnight daily. Sears Tower — 9 a.m.-midnight daily. Chicago Public Library Cultural Center — 9 a.m.-7 p.m. Monday-Thursday; Friday to 6 p.m.; Saturday to 5 p.m.; closed holidays. Glessner House — 11 a.m.-4 p.m. Tuesday-Friday, May-October. rest of year Tuesday and Thursday;

Saturday and Sunday to 5 p.m. all year. Lincoln Park Zoo — 9 a.m.-5 p.m. daily. Lincoln Park Conservatory — 9 a.m.-5 p.m. daily. Garfield Park Conservatory — 9 a.m.-5 p.m. daily. Brookfield Zoo — 10 a.m.-6 p.m. daily, May-October; rest of year to 5 p.m. Adler Planetarium — 9:30 a.m.—9 p.m. daily, mid-June to August; to 4:30 p.m. Monday-Thursday; to 9 p.m. Friday; rest of the year, to 5 p.m. Saturday, Sunday, holidays. Art Institute — 10:30 a.m.-4:30 p.m. Monday-Wednesday, Friday; to 8 p.m. Thursday; 10 a.m.-5 p.m. Saturday; noon-5 p.m. Sunday, holidays; closed December 25. Chicago Academy of Science — 10 a.m.-5 p.m. daily; closed December 25. Chicago Historical Society—9:30 a.m.-4:30 p.m. Monday-Saturday; noon-5 p.m. Sunday; closed January 1, Thanksgiving, December 25. DuSable Museum — 9 a.m.-5 p.m. Monday-Friday; from noon Saturday, Sunday; closed January 1, Easter, December 25. Field Museum — 9 a.m.-5 p.m. daily; closed January 1, Thanksgiving, December 25. Museum of Science and Industry — 9:30 a.m.-5:30 p.m. Monday-Friday, Memorial Day-Labor Day; rest of year, to 4 p.m.; 9:30 a.m.-5:30 Saturday, Sunday, holidays all year; closed December 25. Shedd Aquarium — 9 a.m.-5 p.m., Saturday-Thursday, May-August; from 10 a.m.-4 p.m. November-February; to 9 p.m. Friday all year; closed January 1, December 25.

ADMISSION (all prices subject to change): Wendella — adults, $4-$6; children under 12, $2-$3. Mercury — phone 332-1353 for fees. Clipper Line — adults, $3; children 5-11, half fare; under 5, free. CTA Culture Buses — $1.40. Water Tower — free. John Hancock Center Observation Deck — adults, $2.25; sr. citizens and students, $1.50; under 5, free. Sears Tower Observation Deck — adults, $2; children 2-12, $1; under 2, free. Chicago Public Library Cultural Center — free. Glessner House — admission charge for guided tours. Lincoln Park Zoo — free. Lincoln Park Conservatory — free. Garfield Park Conservatory — free. Brookfield Zoo— adults, $2; sr. citizens and children 6-11, 75¢; under 6, free with adult. Adler Planetarium — free. Art Institute of Chicago — suggested donation: adults, $3; sr. citizens, students, and children, $1.50; Thursday, free. Chicago Academy of Science — free. Chicago Historical Society — adults, $1; sr. citizens, 25¢; 6-17, 50¢; under 6, free; Monday, free. DuSable Museum — adults, 50¢; children, 25¢; Monday, free. Field Museum — adults, $2; 6-17, students, $1; sr. citizens, 50¢; family, $4; Thursday, free. Museum of Science and Industry — free. Shedd Aquarium — adults, $2; 6-17, $1; sr. citizens, 50¢; family, $4; Thursday, free.

FOR MORE INFORMATION: Call the Chicago Convention and Tourism Bureau, (312) 225-5000, or write the Bureau at McCormick Place on the Lake, Chicago, IL 60616.

Illinois

Great America: A Great Park For a Great Time

Gurnee, Illinois

Driving Time: About 1 hour northwest of Chicago

There's literally something for everyone in the family at Great America: fun, laughs, thrills, excitement. The park continues to be one of the finest amusement offerings in the nation, and especially so since last year's debut of the American Eagle roller coaster and the 1983 appearance of the Edge.

The Edge is destined to become one of the park's most popular rides. It's unique, thrilling, and guaranteed to take your breath away (see the accompanying feature). Suffice to say that the Edge provides an unrestricted free fall of 60 feet in two seconds—enough to leave your heart in your throat.

The American Eagle, meanwhile, shares the spine-tingling headlines, with its 147-foot vertical drop and its screaming twists and turns. It rates among the world's great roller coasters and, for the thrill-seeker, should not be missed.

The park has also added an entertainment package that includes magical illusions, a rock-and-roll revue, and an animal acrobatics show. The rock show is held in the Grand Music Hall, the "It's a Magic World" show in the Theatre Royale, and the animal show (starring, among others, the dolphin duo of Nemo and Neptune) in the "Wilderness Theatre."

Getting around the park is an easy, fun experience. Just beyond the entrances lies the beautiful Carousel Plaza, where you can either ride to the top of the Sky Trek Tower or take a leisurely ride on the double-decker carousel. A trolley can take you around Hometown Square and to Orleans Place for great jazz music and shopping. All along the way you'll be serenaded by the Marching Band, the Barbershop Quartet, or the Country Music Band (hear the latter while eating at the Farmer's Market).

For younger children, too, there are a number of special attractions. Rides tailored to younger sisters and brothers are found in the Midwest County Fair, in the acre of attractions called Fort Fun, and in Buzzy Been in Yankee Harbor and David's Le Bumpe in Orleans Place (miniature bumper cars).

Youngsters will also enjoy the passel of characters who stroll around the park, including Sylvester the Cat, Foghorn Leghorn, and Daffy Duck. Children can have their pictures taken with them in the photo booth in Hometown Square.

On the grounds, there are more than 30 different restaurants and food stands featuring everything from fresh fruit juices to tacos to fried chicken.

The park in recent years has shaved its admission price to just over $13 per person (ages 4 to 54, subject to change, of course). The single price covers all rides. Great America is popular, however, so expect large crowds and lines for rides. The park provides these tips for getting the most out of a trip to Great America:

• Arrive at the park by 9 a.m. If you are in a group, have a specific place to meet in case your group separates.

• Beat the rush and eat before noon or after 2 p.m.

• Put off trying the major rides until after 5 p.m., when they are usually less busy.

• Visit the park on Thursday and Friday, the least busiest days; Sunday and Monday are second best. Saturday, Tuesday and Wednesday are the busiest.

• If you want to rest at mid-day, have your hand stamped, return to your hotel and come back that night. The admission includes a full day of fun.

FOR MORE INFORMATION: Call Great America at (312) 249-1776.
SEASON: May 7 to October 10.
HOURS: May 7-22, weekends only, 10 a.m. to 8 p.m. May 23-September 5, open daily, generally 10 a.m. to 10 p.m. on weekends and weekdays in summer (closes at 8 p.m. on weekdays in early and late summer). September 10-October 10, open weekends only, 10 a.m. to 8 p.m.
ADMISSION: $13.20 per person (ages 4 to 54), regular price. $8 for adults 55 and over. Children three years and under, free. Special rates for groups of 25 or more. Call for information on low-priced season pass. (Based on 1983 prices, subject to change.)
DIRECTIONS: From Chicago, take I-94 north to Route 132 (Grand Avenue east).

Facts on Great America's Top Attractions

The American Eagle

The double-tracked wooden roller coaster made its debut in May 1981, and remains one of the world's great amusement park attractions.

Track length: 4,650 feet per track; 9,300 total feet of track

No. of trains: 6

No. of cars: 5 cars per train

No. of passengers: 30 passengers per train

No. of guests per hour: Estimated 3,200

Greatest height: 127 feet (first incline)

Length of first vertical drop: 147 feet

Angle of first drop: 55 degrees

Length of first lift: 330 feet (chain speed: 9 feet per second)

Maximum speed: 66.32 m.p.h.

Length of ride: Estimated at 2 minutes, 23 seconds

No. of helix: 3

Gravity forces: Up to 1.65 Gs in the dips

Other interesting facts: 2,000 concrete footings (average of 18" in diameter, 4.5 feet in depth), 1,060,000 board feet of lumber used, 60,720 bolts, 30,600 lbs. of nails (between 15 and 16 tons), 9,000 gallons of white paint, over 20,000 man hours to build.

The Edge

Great America's new ride, the Edge, provides the spine-tingling thrill of a free fall. It was built for $2.5 million and made its debut in May 1983.

Track length—complete cycle: 450 feet

No. of cars: 8

No. of passengers: 4 passengers per car

No. of guests per hour: 1,200

Highest point: 131 feet

Length of free fall including curve: 99 feet (80 feet per second)

Maximum speed: Approximately 55 m.p.h.

Time of ride: Estimated at 45 seconds

Time of free fall: 1.8 seconds

Gravity forces: Acceleration—force into turn, 5.5 Gs; deceleration—3.5 Gs

Illinois

Springfield: Where Old Abe Got His Start

Springfield, Illinois

Driving Time: 4 hours southwest of Chicago; 3 hours northeast of St. Louis

If you're a history buff and a fan of Abe Lincoln, the country lawyer turned president and Great Emancipator, then Springfield, Illinois, should be in your travel plans. The 12th president of the United States lived here for a quarter century, making his name in state politics before moving on to Washington.

Seemingly everywhere that Lincoln slept, ate, drank, practiced law, or kibbitzed with the local pols is commemorated in this town, which also happens to be the state capital. One of the first places that tourists should stop at is the **Lincoln Home Visitors Center** (426 S. 7th St.), which offers films, exhibits, and information about the four-block Lincoln area. From there, you'll probably go on to these Lincoln landmarks:

• The **Lincoln Tomb State Historical Site** (Oak Ridge Cemetery), the memorial resting place of Lincoln and his family.

• The **Lincoln Home National Historic Site** (8th and Jackson Sts.). Purchased at a cost of $1,500, this was the only home Lincoln ever owned. The house and its interior have been faithfully preserved.

• The **Lincoln Wax Museum** (400 S. 9th St.), where life-sized wax figures depict Lincoln's life.

• The **Lincoln Depot** (Monroe, between 9th and 10th Sts.), from which the soon-to-be president bade farewell to his beloved Springfield and boarded a train for Washington, D.C. There are restored waiting rooms, an exhibit area, and a multi-media presentation.

The Abraham Lincoln home at 8th and Jackson in Springfield, Illinois. Lincoln bought it for $1,500; it was the only home he ever owned.

• The **Lincoln Family Pew** at the First Presbyterian Church (7th St. and Capitol Ave.). The pew is marked.

• The restored **Lincoln-Herndon Building** (6th and Adams Sts.), where Lincoln practiced law for a decade. The structure, which also housed the old Federal Court, is now a museum that offers a multi-media presentation on "Lincoln the Lawyer."

• The **Lincoln Memorial Garden and Nature Center**, which shows visitors the Illinois landscape as Lincoln knew it. There are five miles of rambling trails and rustic scenery. The Nature Centure Building contains exhibits and a gift shop.

• The reconstructed village where Lincoln spent his early years can be seen at **Lincoln's New Salem State Park** (20 miles northwest on Rt. 97). Among the 23 log cabins, there are the Rutledge Tavern (where Lincoln boarded), a gristmill, sawmill, schoolhouse, post office, and several shops where a variety of craftsmen give demonstrations of their work. Picnic areas and campsites are also avail-

able in the 500-acre park. And near New Salem, you can ride on the Sangamon River in a replica of the steamboat *Talisman*.

The **Clayville Rural Life Center** (14 miles west on Rt. 125) is a stagecoach inn and farmhouse that recreates life of the 1880s. An outdoor museum features exhibits and resident craftspeople.

The **Illinois State Capitol** (2nd St. and Capitol Ave.) is one of the tallest buildings in central Illinois, with an immense dome and an elaborately decorated rotunda that rest on bedrock. The Renaissance-style building has murals in its stairways and halls.

The **Illinois State Museum** (Spring and Edwards Sts.) contains excellent exhibits of natural history, geology, anthropology, and Illinois prairie life.

Visitors shouldn't miss the **Old State Capitol** (downtown mall), reconstructed in the style of the period of Lincoln's legislative years. This building contains an original copy of the Gettysburg Address and is the site of the Illinois State Historical Library.

The **Governor's Mansion** (5th and Jackson Sts.) contains beautiful antiques and historic artifacts.

The **Thomas Rees Memorial Carillon** (Washington Park) is one of the largest carillons in the world and home of the International Festival held in mid-June. The **Horticultural Center** (also in Washington Park) has floral displays in a domed conservatory and a nearby rose garden.

The **Parks Telephone Museum** (529 S. 7th St.) contains more than 90 antique telephones dating from 1882. There is also modern and futuristic telephone equipment, including the picturephone.

Youngsters will especially enjoy the **Henson C. Robinson Children's Zoo** (1100 E. Lake Dr.), a menagerie that has 70 different species of animals. The zoo also has a petting arena.

The **Vachel Lindsay Home** (663 S. 5th St.) is the historic residence of the nationally known poet.

The store that Abraham Lincoln once co-owned in New Salem Village. Now restored, the village is 20 miles northwest of Springfield, Illinois, on Route 97. The village contains log cabins, stores and museums.

Near Springfield, **Lake Springfield** (south on U.S. 66) offers picnicking, fishing, and boating, Lifeguards are available at the Center Park.

BEST TIME TO VISIT: Summer.

TRAVEL TIPS: If your family is traveling by car, they may want to take the 325-mile Lincoln Heritage Trail, which passes many points of interest. A map of the trail can be obtained at the Springfield Convention and Visitors Center.

HOURS: Lincoln Home Visitors Center — 8 a.m.-5 p.m. daily. Lincoln Tomb State Historic Site — 9 a.m.-5 p.m. daily; closed January 1, December 25. Lincoln Wax Museum — 9 a.m.-5 p.m. daily; closed January 1, Thanksgiving, December 25. Lincoln Depot — 9 a.m.-5 p.m. Monday through Saturday, noon-5 p.m. Sunday, April through October. Lincoln Family Pew (First Presbyterian Church) — 9 a.m.-5 p.m. daily. Lincoln-Herndon Building — 11 a.m.-5 p.m. Monday through Saturday. Lincoln Memorial Garden and Nature Center — 10 a.m.-4 p.m. Monday through Saturday; 1-5 p.m. Sunday; closed December 23 through January 1. Lincoln's New Salem State Park — 9 a.m.-5 p.m. daily; no guide service January 1, Thanksgiving, December 25. Clayville Rural Life Center — 10 a.m.-5 p.m. Wednesday through Sunday, May through October; closed holidays. Illinois State Capitol — 8 a.m.-4 p.m. daily. Illinois State Museum — 8:30 a.m.-5 p.m. Monday through Saturday; Sunday from 1:30 p.m.; closed holidays. Old State Capitol — 9 a.m.-5 p.m., closed holidays. Governor's Mansion —

9:30-11 a.m., 2-3:30 p.m. Tuesday and Thursday. Thomas Rees Memorial Carillon — guided tours 2-8 p.m. Tuesday through Sunday, Memorial Day through Labor Day. Parks Telephone Museum — 9 a.m.-4:30 p.m. daily. Robinson Zoo — 10 a.m.-4 p.m. Monday through Friday, April through October; 10 a.m.-5 p.m. Saturday, Sunday, holidays. Vachel Lindsay Home — 45-minute guided tour by appointment only. Talisman River Boat — 10 a.m.-5 p.m. daily, May through Labor Day; Saturday and Sunday only after Labor Day.

ADMISSION: Lincoln Home Visitors Center — free. Lincoln Tomb State Historic Site — free. Lincoln Home National Historic Site — free. Lincoln Wax Museum — adults, $1; children 8-12, 50¢; under 8, free. Lincoln Depot — admission charged. Lincoln Family Pew (First Presbyterian Church) — free. Lincoln-Herndon Building — adults, $1; family, $2; sr. citizens and students, 50¢. Lincoln Memorial Garden and Nature Center — free. Lincoln's New Salem State Park — free. Clayville Rural Life Cneter — free. Illinois State Capitol — free. Illinois State Museum — free. Old State Capitol — free. Governor's Mansion — free. Thomas Rees Memorial Carillon — adults, $1; students, 50¢. Robinson Zoo — adults, $1.25; 13-17, 75¢; 3-12, 50¢; under 3, free. Talisman River Boat — adults, $1.50; under 3, free.

DIRECTIONS: From Chicago, take I-55 southwest to Springfield.

FOR MORE INFORMATION: Call the Springfield Convention and Visitors Bureau, (217) 789-2360, or write 219 S. 5th St., Springfield, IL 62701.

Illinois

Union, Illinois: Railroads and The Wild West

Union, Illinois

Driving Time: 1¼ hours from Chicago

The mighty steam locomotive and the clanging trolley car have disappeared from American life. But the railroad life of the old days still exists at the Illinois Railway Museum in Union, Illinois. It's the world's largest operating railroad museum, with more than 140 steam engines and railway, street and trolley cars on 46 acres. All that equipment would make a train more than 1½ miles long. You can ride on the steam-powered trains and electric cars of the museum's railway, or visit an 1851 railway depot, the oldest west of Pittsburgh.

More of America's past is on display at the **Seven Acres Antique Village and Museum** (8512 S. Union Road). You'll really think you're in the Wild West as you explore this completely rebuilt western town of the early 1900s. In the corner of the village stands the town gallows, originally built in 1886. The Pioneer Kitchen, the Print Shop, the Old Union Jail, General Store, Blacksmith Shop, Arcade, Village Peddler, Phonograph Store and an 1881 saloon, complete with a Belgium jazz orchestra complete the picture.

In the museum area, on the 1890s Street, you can peek in windows of the antique toy shop, the 1890s Barber Shop, Western Union Telegraph Office, doctor's office, and more. For a meal, you might try the Shady Lane Farm (3½ miles west of Marengo on Route 20).

HOURS: ILLINOIS RAILWAY MUSEUM—10 a.m.-5 p.m. daily, Memorial Day through Labor Day; 11 a.m.-5 p.m. Saturday and Sunday, May to mid-June and after Labor Day in September; open Sundays in March, April, October and November. Closed December, January, February and holidays.

SEVEN ACRES ANTIQUE VILLAGE AND MUSEUM—10 a.m.-6 p.m. daily, April through October; 10 a.m.-5 p.m. weekends, November through March. Closed January.

ADMISSION: Illinois Railway Museum — adults, $3.50; children 5 and over, $2; children under 5, free; special group rates available for 15 or more (for group information, write: Illinois Railway Museum, Box 431, Union, IL 60180). Seven Acres Antique Village and Museum — adults, $3; children 6-12, $1.50; children under 6, free.

FOR MORE INFORMATION: Call the Illinois Railway Museum, (815) 923-4391 or (312) 262-2266; Seven Acres office, (815) 923-2214; Marengo-Union Chamber of Commerce, (815) 568-6680.

DIRECTIONS: From Chicago, take I-90 northwest, exit at Rt. 20 (Marengo exit). Drive northwest on Rt. 20 to Union Rd.

Galena, Illinois: A President's Home Town

Driving Time: About 4 hours west of Chicago, 7 hours southeast of Minneapolis

Galena, Illinois

Widely known as the home town of President Ulysses S. Grant, picturesque Galena sits on the rolling countryside of northwestern Illinois. Once a thriving center of steamboat trade and mining, Galena slowed down around the early 1900s. But today it brims with activity. Thousands of tourists come annually to find out what life was like a century ago. One of the most popular sights is President

Grant's family home on Bouthillier Street. The brick is restored along with the 19th-century furnishings. Mom and dad may be interested in the town's numerous antique shops (Main St. or Hwy. 20). Galena boasts several other restored houses, including the Dowling House, Galena's oldest building, which was built in 1826 as a miner's trading outpost. It is finished just as it was back in those days.

Another interesting spot, for girls especially, is Jan's Gallery (128 S. Main St.), where you can buy, trade, sell or just appreciate old-fashioned dolls like the kind your great-grandmother had. From there, it's a short distance to The Old Stockade (Main and Perry Sts.), an 1832 fort built during the Black Hawk War that contains an Indian artifacts collection. To finish off the day, don't miss the Vinegar Hill Historic Lead Mine and Museum (six miles north of town, Hwy. 84). Early mining methods are demonstrated with many old-

time tools. Your family might want to have dinner at The Log Cabin (201 N. Main St.), Galena's oldest restaurant. There are also several scenic parks for picnicking, and horseback riding is offered at the Palace Campground and Resort (Hwy. 20). Should your family decide to spend the night before returning home, the Chestnut Mountain Lodge (eight miles south of town on Blackjack Rd.) features excellent rooms with a nice view of the Mississippi River.

HOURS: Grant's Home: 9 a.m. to 5 p.m. daily. Shops: Summer, 10 a.m. to 5 p.m. daily; off-season, 10 a.m. to 4 p.m. daily. The Belvedere: 10 a.m. to 5 p.m. daily, May to December. Dowling House and Old Stockade: 9 a.m. to 5 p.m. daily, May to November. Vinegar Hill Lead Mine Museum: daily June through August; weekends only May, September and October.

FOR MORE INFORMATION: Contact the Galena Chamber of Commerce, (8150 777-0203. Guided tours are available.

DIRECTIONS: From Chicago, take HWY. 20 west, or take I-90 to Rockford and pick up Rt. 20 west to Galena.

Illinois

The Old State Capitol building in Springfield

Illinois Beach State Park

Zion, Illinois

Driving Time: 1 hour north of Chicago

Three miles of white beach on Lake Michigan between Waukegan and Zion make Illinois Beach State Park a busy summer playground for thousands. Lifeguards are present all along the 1,000-foot shoreline.

The park has a 900-acre preserve threaded with hiking trails. More than 500 species of plants have been recorded in the dunes area. The park is also an important refuge for wildlife, especially migrating birds.

There are modern campgrounds and a comfortable 96-room lodge that is only 100 yards from the shoreline. The lodge has a restaurant, tennis courts, and a swimming pool.

Beachhouses, an interpretive center, a playground, concession stands, and shaded picnic areas are also available in the park. Fishing for coho is also popular here.

BEST TIME TO VISIT: Summer.
DIRECTIONS: From Chicago, take I-94 north to U.S. 41 to the park.
FOR MORE INFORMATION: Call Illinois Beach State Park, (312) 662-4811, or write Zion, IL 60099.

Princeton: Throwback to Victorian Age

Princeton, Illinois

Driving Time: 3 hours west of Chicago

Princeton is a charming old town that still has many brick-paved streets lined with attractive Victorian mansions. Many antique shops stand on Main Street.

The **Owen Lovejoy Homestead** (east of town on U.S. 6) was the home of the famous abolitionist preacher and a station on the underground railroad.

Near the courthouse square, with its Civil War monument, is the **Bureau County Historical Museum** (109 Park Ave. W.), an elegant Victorian mansion with four floors of local and Midwestern historical exhibits.

Just north of town (on the other side of I-80, off Rt. 26) is the Red Covered Bridge. Built in 1863, it spans Big Bureau Creek.

Nearby City-County Park is a good picnicking spot and a marked hiking trail. There is also a children's playground.

BEST TIME TO VISIT: Summer.
HOURS: Owen Lovejoy Homestead — 1 p.m.-4:30 p.m. daily, June-September. Bureau County Historical Museum — 1 p.m.-5 p.m. Thursday, Saturday, Sunday; closed holidays. City-County Park — daily, May 15-early October.
ADMISSION: Owen Lovejoy Homestead — adults, $1; children, 50¢. Bureau County Historical Museum — donation. City-County Park — free.
DIRECTIONS: From Chicago, take I-55 to I-80 west to Princeton.
FOR MORE INFORMATION: Call the Princeton Chamber of Commerce, (815) 875-2616, or write 435 S. Main St., Princeton, IL 61356.

Learning About The Original Americans

Driving Time: 3½ hours south of Chicago

Dickson Mounds Museum Lewistown, Illinois

If you'd like to learn about the history of Illinois Indians, visit the Dickson Mounds Museum in Lewistown, Ill. The museum, devoted to the prehistoric Indian, sits on an Illinois River bluff. Founded in 1927, the museum has grown to a 161-acre complex, including an archeological preserve, nature trail and picnic grounds. Exhibits feature evidence of prehistoric and early man in the New World, artifacts, ceramics and human pathology, enhanced by slide-and-sound shows. Maps of the Indian routes, artifacts and animal replicas tell the story of America's first inhabitants, who were Indians. Outside the museum building, archeological sites showing remains of the early history of man may be explored. And in the museum's south wing, you can see 234 skeletons and accompanying grave offerings unearthed in the area. In nearby Peoria, there are many other attractions worth exploring. Excursions on the kind of high paddlewheel steamboats you read about in *Tom Sawyer* are offered during the summer, an excellent way to see the sights along the Illinois River banks. The Glen Oak Botanical Gardens (2218 N. Prospect Rd.) feature beautiful floral and green plant displays. And aspiring farmers will enjoy a tour of the Caterpillar Tractor Co. (100 N.E. Adams). You can stay overnight and eat at Jumer's Castle Lodge (117 N. Western Ave.).

HOURS Dickson Mounds Museum: 8:30 a.m. to 5 p.m. daily; picnic grounds open until sundown. Museum and grounds closed New Year's Day, Easter, Thanksgiving Day and Christmas Day. Glen Oak Botanical Garden: 8 a.m. to 4 p.m. Monday through Friday, Saturday and Sunday from noon. Caterpillar Tractor Co. (tour by appointment).
ADMISSION: Dickson Mounds Museum and Glen Oak Botanical Garden are free. Julia Belle Swain: Adults, $4; Children $1.
FOR MORE INFORMATION: Call Dickson Mounds Museum, (309)547-3721, or the Peoria Chamber of Commerce (309)676-0755.
DIRECTIONS From Chicago, take I-55 southwest to Bloomington; exit on I-74 west to Peoria. Take Rt. 24 west to Lewistown, junction of Rt. 78 and 97. Go south five miles to Dickson Mounds.

Bishop Hill: A Town Founded by Swedes

Bishop Hill, Illinois

Driving Time: 3 hours west of Chicago

Bishop Hill, founded as a communal colony by Swedish immigrants amidst the rich Illinois farmland in the mid-1800s, looks much today as it did 100 years ago.

That's because the historically rich town has retained some of its old ways and has lovingly restored the priceless old structures that were important to its past. The Swedish film, "The Immigrants," was shot on location near the town, recapturing much of the area's atmosphere and portraying the difficulties the original settlers had in coming to this land.

Bishop Hill was founded in 1846 by Swedish dissenters who came to America in search of religious freedom. The first settlers arrived on this stretch of the Illinois prairie in that year, having walked 160 miles from Chicago. They bought the land and dug in for the winter, but nearly 100 died for lack of adequate food and shelter.

But more immigrants arrived from Sweden to expand the colony and to lay the groundwork for remarkable economic gains during the 15 years that Bishop Hill existed. Twenty large commercial buildings were erected and 15,000 acres of land were put into farm production.

The village is now both a state and a national historic site. Most of the old buildings still survive, including a church, a blacksmith shop, a carriage and wagon shop, a dairy building, a store and post office, residence buildings, a hotel, a school, and a hospital.

The **Colony Church**, the first permanent building, is a large barnlike structure with a gambrel roof, and the sanctuary is unadorned except for the black walnut pews. A center divider separates the men's and women's pews. Each of the two lower floors originally contained 10 apartments with fireplaces. A museum in the lower rooms currently contains objects that settlers brought with them from Sweden, implements and utensils that they made themselves, and examples of their simple but fine handcrafted furniture.

Also in the church are the **paintings of Olaf Krans**, who chronicled life in the colony through his artwork.

The **Steeple Building**, the tallest structure in town, was completed in 1855. The wooden steeple has a clock with only one hand! Legend has it that the colonists were too busy working to worry about minutes. The building has various rooms furnished in 19th-century style and a collection of memorabilia from the 1800s.

The **Bjorkland Hotel** was once an important stagecoach stop. It has recently been restored, and the first floor and one guest room have been furnished in the style of the 1860s.

Various annual events are held in town. One of the most popular is *Jordbruksdagarna* (**Harvest Days**), held on a weekend in late September. Visitors are invited to join costumed workers in the fields as they pick corn and harvest flax and broomcorn. There is also entertainment and plenty of Swedish food.

BEST TIME TO VISIT: Spring, summer, fall.
TRAVEL TIPS: For overnight lodgings, stay at Galesburg, which is only 29 miles southwest of Bishop Hill.
HOURS: Colony Church — 9 a.m.-5 p.m daily; closed January 1, Thanksgiving, December 25. Steeple Building — 10 a.m.-5 p.m. daily, May-October. Bjorkland Hotel — 9 a.m.-5 p.m. daily.
ADMISSION: Colony Church — free. Steeple Building — adults, $1; children under 12, free. Bjorkland Hotel — free.
DIRECTIONS: From Chicago, take I-55 southwest to I-80 west. Then get on U.S. 34 to Bishop Hill.
FOR MORE INFORMATION: Call Bishop Hill Historic Site, (309) 927-3520, or write Bishop Hill, IL 61419.

Nauvoo: Town With a Fascinating History

Nauvoo, Illinois

Driving Time: 6 hours southwest of Chicago; 4 hours east of Des Moines

Believe it or not, Nauvoo was once the biggest city in Illinois. Yes, this rural town in western Illinois was once bigger than Chicago.

You'd think a town that could make that claim to fame *must* have a colorful history. In fact, you're right. Nauvoo does boast of a past that puts many larger, and duller, cities to shame. For example, Joseph Smith and his Mormon followers trekked here in 1839 to escape persecution in Missouri, and in quick order put up 8,000 houses and began to build a gigantic temple. Everything dissolved, though, when Smith and his brother were killed by a mob. Brigham Young then became leader of the Nauvoo Mormons and took his followers to Utah.

Nauvoo fell into disfavor and became a ghost town until the Icarians, a band of French communalists, called it home for a while. They, too, soon left, however.

Next — and — last came the Germans, who stayed to develop a wine and cheese business in the town and to establish it as a somewhat more conventional Illinois community.

Today, there are barely 1,000 residents in Nauvoo, but many of the homes built by Smith, Young, and other leaders of the Mormon Church still remain. Three visitors centers provide tour information, and Mormon missionary guides are on hand to explain the history of the church and the town.

The **Nauvoo Restoration, Inc., Visitor Center** (Young and Main Sts.) shows a movie describing the sites of the town. Tour maps are also available.

Some of the attractions include the Times and Seasons Buildings, the Herbert C. Kimball Home, the Brigham Young Home, and the Wilford Woodruff Home. Also, there are the Nauvoo Temple Site, the Montrose Crossing Monument, the Webb Blacksmith and Wagon Shop, and an 1840 theater.

The Joseph Smith Historic Center is located in the Colonial-style **Joseph Smith Mansion**. A 50-minute tour includes a slide presentation, a tour of the mansion, and a visit to the graves of Joseph Smith and his family.

Hotel Nauvoo in the center of town was originally a Mormon residence built in 1840. Currently, it is a restaurant that has a few rooms and suites for overnight guests.

The **Old Carthage Jail** (12 miles south on Rt. 96) is the site where Smith and his brother died.

In **Nauvoo State Park** (south on Rt. 96) stands a restored home that houses the museum of the Nauvoo Historical Society. There is also a lake for fishing, picnic areas, and campsites. The adjacent vineyard is more than 100 years old.

BEST TIME TO VISIT: Summer.
HOURS: Restoration Visitor Center — 8 a.m.-9 p.m. daily, May-October; to 7 p.m. November-April. Joseph Smith Historic Center — 8 a.m.-8 p.m. daily, Memorial Day-Labor Day; 8:30 a.m.-5 p.m. rest of the year. Old Carthage Jail — 8 a.m.-7 p.m. daily, May-September; 9 a.m.-5 p.m., October-April.
ADMISSION: Nauvoo Restoration Visitor Center — free. Joseph Smith Historic Center — free. Old Carthage Jail — free.
DIRECTIONS: From Chicago, take I-55 to I-80 west to Moline. Then head south on I-74 to U.S. 34 to U.S. 67 south to Rt. 94 east to Dallas City. Then take Rt. 96 south to Nauvoo.
FOR MORE INFORMATION: Call the Nauvoo Chamber of Commerce, (217) 453-6648, or write Muholland St., Nauvoo, IL 62354.

Chain O'Lakes: Outdoor Fun, Antiques, Old Towns

Richmond, Illinois

Driving Time: 1½ hours north of Chicago

The Chain O'Lakes recreational area, in northeastern Illinois, just south of the Wisconsin line, is one of the Midwest's most popular outdoor vacation sites.

Additionally, the village of **Richmond**, just west of the area, has old Victorian houses, sidewalk hitching rings for horses, and old wooden bridges crossing the railroad tracks. There are at least 30 antique shops in this town, including the **Emporium** (10310 Main St.) and the old **Columbian Hotel** (10331 Main St.).

At Antioch, east of Richmond, is **Chain O'Lakes State Park** (six miles west on Rt. 173), which contains the state's largest concentration of freshwater lakes, making the area one of the most popular year-round fishing spots in Illinois. The park borders on three of 10 lakes in the Fox River chain: Grass, Marie, and Bluff. The 10 lakes have a combined total of 5,465 acres of water and 488 miles of shoreline. In addition to fishing, there are hunting, boating, picnicking, winter sports, and seven camping areas. There are also many motels and restaurants in the area.

Fishing buffs may want to visit the **Illinois State Fish Hatchery** in nearby Spring Grove. The property contains a 15-acre lake, seven outdoor ponds, and indoor tanks. A trail about one mile in length circles the lake.

Moraine Hills State Park in McHenry is a 1,667-acre park with picnic areas, boat rentals, fishing, hiking, and a refreshment stand.

There are four small lakes in the park but no camping area.

Woodstock (south of McHenry) has been called the "grand capital of mid-Victorianism in the Midwest." The Victorian charm has been preserved, especially in the town square with its ornate gazebo, wooded parks, cobblestone streets, and many historic homes and buildings that now house antique shops.

The **Old Volo Museums and Village** (five miles east on Rt. 120 in Volo; see accompanying article) contains a display of more than 70 antique autos. There's a 19th-century general store museum, a 1930s game room, antique popcorn machines, an animal pet farm, a playground, a pavillion, and a country store.

The **Volo Bog** (one mile south on Brandenburg Rd.) gives families a chance to inspect and learn something about the ecology of a bog. There are boardwalks here that extend over the vegetation so visitors can observe successive stages in bog development.

Still farther south is the charming village of **Long Grove**. The town has been designated a historic district. An authentic replica of a New Hampshire covered bridge stands at the entrance to the town. The shops here are fascinating, and there are many fine restaurants.

BEST TIME TO VISIT: Summer.
HOURS: Old Volo Museums and Village — 10 a.m.-5 p.m. daily; closed holidays.
ADMISSION: Old Volo Museums and Village — adults, $3.25; children 4-12, $1.75; under 4, free.
DIRECTIONS: From Chicago, take I-90 west to Rt. 59 north to Chain O'Lakes area.
FOR MORE INFORMATION: Call the Antioch Chamber of Commerce, (312) 395-2233, or write 880 Main St., Antioch, IL 60002.

Illinois

Spoon River: Captivating Rural Illinois Landscape

Spoon River Valley Drive, Illinois

Driving Time: 3½ hours southwest of Chicago

The Edgar Lee Masters country along the Spoon River provides some of the most beautiful rural scenery to be found anywhere in Illinois. The scenic **Spoon River Drive** covers 65 miles of byways and backroads over rolling hills along the Spoon River, past 19th-century farms and through rustic villages. The route is well marked with signs. (A map and a brochure of the various sites are also available. See the end of this section.)

The north entrance to the drive is at London Mills, where visitors can see **Ross Hotel Museum**, a turn-of-the-century lodging.

Ten miles down the valley, travelers will come to **Ellisville**, a picturesque country village and location of the first mill on Spoon River. **Fairview** is the site of a Dutch Reformed Church that was built in 1837; it is the oldest Dutch Reformed Church west of the Allegheny Mountains. A newly developed, year-round campsite is located at **Mt. Pisgah**, about one-half mile south; it offers a great view of the valley.

In **Babylon**, you'll find the famous Babylon Gristmill, a fascinating bit of history worth the few miles drive. A few miles south lies **Cuba** and Putnam Township Park, site of the first strip mine in Fulton County (early 1920s) and also part of the underground railroad that runaway slaves used to escape to freedom.

The drive follows the west side of the Spoon River Valley for the next

10 miles and brings travelers to Seville, where Indian trails used to cross. The only dam on the Spoon River, at Bernadotte, is a favorite fishing spot for vacationers.

The next and final leg of the trip follows the river very closely, crossing at Elrod Bridge then onto a blacktop road to Lewistown and to Dickson Mounds.

Lewistown, the county seat, has been dubbed the "capital" of the Spoon River Valley. It has several interesting attractions that include Edgar Lee Masters' home, Fulton County Jail (the oldest county jail still in use), Rasmussen Blacksmith Shop, and famous Oak Hill Cemetery.

At **Dickson Mounds State Museum** (off Rts. 97 and 98, near Havana), exhibits explain how prehistoric Illinois Indians used to live. The museum has been built over an old burial ground where 234 skeletons have been uncovered.

The drive continues past **Norris Farms** (one of the largest farms in the state), through the Fulton County Conservation Area, past Canton, Spoon River College, and finally Farmington (eastern entry of the drive), where slaves were once harbored during the Civil War.

The **Spoon River Valley Festival** is held during the first or second weekend in October. Residents of the communities along the route of the drive greet visitors in turn-of-the-century costumes as they give various demonstrations and show their wares.

BEST TIME TO VISIT: Spring, summer, fall.
DIRECTIONS: From Chicago, take I-55 to Bloomington, then I-74 west to Peoria. From there, take Rt. 24 into Lewistown.
FOR MORE INFORMATION: Call the Spoon River Scenic Drive, (309) 486-3315, or write Box 59, Ellisville, IL 61431.

Illinois

Quaint Towns Along the Fox River

Fox River Valley, Illinois

Driving Time: 1½ hours west of Chicago

The idyllic Fox River Valley is the setting for a string of towns west of Chicago, each of which has its own placid place aside the broad Fox River and each of which has something to offer visitors — whether it's shopping, antiques, boating, outdoor sports, or fine restaurants. Taken individually or together, they make a nice day's trip or a great stopping-off place between destinations.

Eleven dams have converted the Fox River into a gentle, recreational source for fishing, canoeing, hiking, and biking, all popular pursuits in the river towns — East and West Dundee, Elgin, St. Charles, Geneva, Batavia, and Aurora.

Founded in the 1830s by Scottish and Irish farmers, **Dundee** is now the home of the world's largest art pottery center. The **Haeger Potteries** (7 Maiden Lane) is open for tours and sales. On display is the vase that made the *1983 Guinness Book of Records* as the world's tallest art pottery vase.

Children will especially enjoy **Three Worlds of Santa's Village** in West Dundee (at the junction of Rts. 25 and 72), where everyday is Christmas. There's Santa's house, a petting zoo, live shows, and a picnic area. South on Rt. 25 is the **McGraw Wildlife Center**, a lush wooded game farm. The Milk Pail Restaurant is a popular eating place for families, and visit the Fin and Feather Farm situated on the preserve.

Elgin, just a few minutes to the south, is a prosperous city with excellent recreational and cultural facilities. Downtown, the impressive **Hemmen Memorial Building** rises above the Fox River. It is the home of the Elgin Symphony Orchestra.

Anyone interested in creative crafts and needle arts should be sure to stop at **Lee Wards** (840 N. State, just south of the Northwest Tollway). It bills itself as the world's largest creative crafts center and features frequent demonstrations.

In **South Elgin**, the **Fox River Trolley Museum** (south on Rt. 31) offers a 30-minute ride along the scenic Fox River on turn-of-the-century interurban cars and trolleys. There are other old cars that may also be viewed, a gift shop, and a picnic area.

St. Charles, the central city of the Fox Valley, began in 1834 as Charleston. The most striking building here is the Municipal Center, on the east bank of the Fox River. Featuring a tower of white marble, illuminated at night by changing colored lights, the Art Deco architecture is in a parklike setting with formal gardens, terrazzo walkways, and fountains. **Pottawatomie Park** (N. 2nd Ave.) is an outdoor recreational center that has an Olympic-size swimming pool, wading pool, nine-hole golf course, boat rentals miniature train ride, paddlewheel boat trips on the Fox River, and tennis courts.

A few minutes south on Rt. 25 is the town of **Geneva**, which has more than 200 landmark buildings within its boundaries. **Mill Race Inn** (4 E. State St.) is a quiet, elegant restaurant on the banks of the Fox River. Visitors can dine by candlelight in the Stone Room, built in 1842.

Bikers can follow the newly paved path trailing the river from St. Charles to Batavia. (The county hopes to build the path along both sides of the river from St. Charles to Batavia.)

Just north of **Batavia**, the Fabyan Forest Preserve is the site of Riverbank, an impressive three-story mansion with Japanese gardens and a windmill. River Square, in the heart of town, has become a shopping center carved from old buildings. The Depot Museum, on the west bank of the Fox River, is a showcase for displays on Batavia's history (kids will like the red caboose on the nearby tracks).

The **Fermi National Accelerator Laboratory** (east on Wilson Rd. then south on Kirk Rd.) is the home of the world's largest nuclear particle accelerators. A herd of buffalo on the

6,800-acre range greets visitors to the laboratory and the cultural center.

The largest of the Fox River cities, **Aurora**, offers theater buffs a renowned national landmark: the stunning Paramount Arts Center, an Art Deco movie house built in 1931. It's now an entertainment center, having been carefully restored to its original splendor.

Another attraction in the neighborhood is **Blackberry Historical Farm Village** in 54-acre Pioneer Park (Galena Blvd. at Barnes Rd.). Old Engine No. 9, a replica steam train, takes passengers to an 1840 functioning farm and a turn-of-the-century village.

The **Aurora Historical Museum** (304 Oak Ave. at Cedar St.) contains early household items, pioneer portraits, and historical mementos exhibited in a house built in 1857.

BEST TIME TO VISIT: Year round.
HOURS: Haeger Potteries — 8 a.m.-4:30 p.m. Monday-Friday; Saturday, Sunday, and holidays from 10 a.m.; closed January 1, Easter, Thanksgiving, December 25. Three Worlds of Santa's Village — 10 a.m.-6 p.m. Monday-Friday, 11 a.m.-dusk Saturday and Sunday, mid-June to Labor Day; Saturday and Sunday only, mid-May to mid-June, rest of September. McGraw Wildlife Center — 11 a.m.-9 p.m. Monday-Friday; 11 a.m.-10 p.m. Saturday; 9 a.m.-8 p.m. Sunday. Fox River Trolley Museum — trolley rides 11 a.m.-6 p.m. Sunday, Memorial Day-July; 1-5 p.m. Saturday, 11 am.-6 p.m. Sunday, August-October. Pottawatomie Park — open year round. Mill Race Inn — 11:45 a.m.-3 p.m. and 5:30-8:30 p.m. Tuesday-Thursday, to 9 p.m. Friday and Saturday; 11:45 a.m.-8:30 p.m. Sunday. Fermi Lab — 8:30 a.m.-5 p.m. daily; closed holidays. Blackberry Historical Village — 10 a.m.-4 p.m. Monday-Friday, May-September; Saturday and Sunday to 5 p.m. Aurora Historical Museum — 2 p.m.-4:30 p.m. Wednesday and Sunday; closed Easter, December 25 to mid-February.
ADMISSION: Haeger Potteries — free. Three Worlds of Santa's Village — adults, $5.95; children under 3, free. Fox River Valley Trolley Museum — adults, $1.50; children 3-11, 75¢. Pottawatomie Park — non-residents, 50¢/person Monday-Friday; $1/person weekends and holidays. Blackberry Historical Farm Village — adults, $3; sr. citizens, $1.50; children under 12, $2.50; family, $10. Aurora Historical Museum — donation.
DIRECTIONS: From Chicago, take the East-West Tollway (Rt. 5) or the Northwest Tollway (I-90) to the Fox River Valley area.
FOR MORE INFORMATION: Call the Kane County Forest Preserve Commission, (312) 232-2400, or write 719 Batavia Ave., Geneva, IL 60134. Also, call the Fox Valley Park District, (312) 897-0516, or write 712 S. River, Aurora, IL 60506.

Chicago's scenic Lake Michigan shoreline

Mendota's 'Time Was' Museum

Mendota, Ilinois

Driving Time: 2½ hours southwest of Chicago

The **Time Was Village Museum** (four miles south of Mendota on U.S. 51) bills itself as "12,000 yesterdays" housed in nine buildings. Families will see a miniature circus under canvas, an old-time barber shop, printshop, firehouse, sawmill, blacksmith shop, carriage house, and a garage containing more than 40 antique automobiles. The museum's displays include toys, 300 dolls, bottles, bells, glassware, china, music boxes, clocks, antique fire-fighting equipment, and old farm implements. There are also period rooms and old-time shops.

BEST TIME TO VISIT: Summer.
HOURS: 10 a.m.-5 p.m. daily, May through October.
ADMISSION: Adults, $3; children 6-14, $1.50; under 6, free.
DIRECTIONS: From Chicago, take U.S. 34 southwest to Mendota, then U.S. 51 south to the museum.
FOR MORE INFORMATION: Call the museum, (815) 539-6042, or write Mendota, IL 61342.

Momence: Gladiola Capital

Momence, Illinois

Driving Time: 2 hours southeast of Chicago

Momence is the place to go if you like gladiolas. Gladiola fields abound in the village of **Wichert** (south of Momence, off Rt. 1), where there are 500 acres of these spectacular flowers.

Several major growers, including Miedema Brothers Gladiolus Farms, produce about 60 varieties.

The **Gladiolus Festival** is held each year in mid-August, with a daily flower show and a big weekend parade. The Old Car Show, which is part of the festivities, is the largest antique auto show in Illinois.

BEST TIME TO VISIT: Summer
DIRECTIONS: From Chicago, take I-57 south to Rt. 17 east to Momence.
FOR MORE INFORMATION: Call the Momence Chamber of Commerce, (815) 472-4620, or write Momence, IL 60954.

Illinois

Peoria: Riverboating And Lincoln's Courthouse

Peoria, Illinois

Driving Time: 4 hours southwest of Chicago; 3 hours northeast of St. Louis

Everyone in the national media and politics seems to mention Peoria at one time or another, usually in the context of the city being middle class, "middle America," and midway between east and west. The idea is that what's accepted in Peoria will probably be OK with the rest of middle America — whether it's TV shows, political candidates, or soap.

If you've never met a Peorian or seen the city, you owe it to the pollsters and pundits to drop in the next time you're in the area. Considered to be the oldest city in the state, Peoria is a pleasant surprise: relaxed, low-keyed, friendly, and scenic — with its surroundings of wooded hills, soaring bluffs, and ridges.

A relaxing way to begin a sojourn in Peoria would be aboard the *Julia Bell Swain*, a 1,000-passenger sternwheel paddle steamer that offers 1½-hour daytime cruises on the Illinois River, Friday and Saturday evening cruises with dancing, Sunday dinner trips, and special one- and two-day excursions to Starved Rock State Park and Dickson Mounds. Peoria's annual **Steamboat Days**, held in June, features riverboat and canoe races, concerts, a carnival, and Dixieland jazz.

Glen Oak Park (Prospect and McClure Aves.) has a zoo, picnic areas, baseball diamonds, tennis courts, a playground, and an excellent conservatory with tropical plants and seasonal floral displays. There are amphitheater concerts in the summer.

Tower Park (off Rt. 150 via Prospect Rd.) offers visitors awe-inspiring, 360-degree vistas from a spiralling observation tower.

The **Lakeview Museum of Arts and Science** (1125 W. Lake Ave. at University St. N.) contains permanent and changing exhibits in the arts and sciences. A planetarium offers multi-media shows and constellation programs.

Another interesting attraction is the **Metamora Courthouse State Historic Site** (15 miles northeast on Rt. 116 at 303 N. Hanover), where Abraham Lincoln practiced law while traveling the old 8th Circuit. There is a guide service and a museum.

The Caterpillar Tractor Co. (100 Adams) offers 1½-hour guided tours of its giant earth-moving equipment plant.

Flanagan House (942 E. Glen Oak Ave.) is the oldest home in the city and the current headquarters for the

Peoria Historical Society. The furnishings predate the Civil War. Maps, guides, and bus tour information are available in the building.

Another old house worth a visit is the **Pettengill-Morron Mansion** (1212 W. Moss). Built around 1868, this elegant Victorian structure contains interesting 19th-century furnishings, china, and glassware.

If you like the outdoors, take advantage of the **Forest Park Nature Center** (¼ mile off Rt. 29); it's a natural science museum with five miles of trails.

A definite must-see is the **Wildlife Prairie Park** (10 miles west on Taylor Rd.), where bears, wolves, cougars, elk, and bison roam 1,000 acres of natural prairie. Six walking trails let visitors observe these animals in a natural habitat. The Pioneer Homestead Area has a working farm from the late 1800s. (Don't miss the Bald Eagle Aviary.)

BEST TIME TO VISIT: Summer.

HOURS: Flanagan House — 2 p.m.-4 p.m. Sunday. Petengill-Morron House — 2 p.m.-4 p.m. Sunday. Julia Belle Swain — daily, May 30-Labor Day. Glen Oak Park — zoo, 10 a.m.-4 p.m. daily; conservatory, 8 a.m.-4 p.m. Monday-Friday, from noon Saturday and Sunday. Lakeview Museum of Arts and Science — 10 a.m.-5 p.m. Tuesday-Saturday; Wednesday also 7-9 p.m.; from noon Sunday; closed holidays. Metamora Courthouse State Historic Site — 9 a.m.-5 p.m. daily. Caterpillar Tractor Co. — tours Monday-Friday by appointment only; closed July 18-29 and December 26-30. Forest Park Nature Center — 9 a.m.-5 p.m. Monday-Saturday; from noon Sunday. Wildlife Prairie Park — 9 a.m.-6:30 p.m. daily, June-August; 9 a.m.-4:30 p.m. Monday-Friday, May, September-October; to 6 p.m. Saturday and Sunday.

ADMISSION: Flanagan House — adults, $1.50; students, 50¢. Pettengill-Morron House — adults, $1.50; under 13, 50¢. Julia Belle Swain — afternoon sightseeing trips: adults, $4; children, $1. Glen Oak Park — zoo, April-September: adults, $1.75; children, 50¢; family, $5. under 4, free; October-March: adults, $1.50; children, 35¢; under 4, free; conservatory, free. Lakeview Museum of Arts and Science — free. Metamora Courthouse State Historic Site - free. Caterpillar Tractor Co. — free. Forest Park Nature Center — free. Wildlife Prairie Center — adults, $3; 13-17, $1.50; 5-12, $1; under 5, free.

DIRECTIONS: From Chicago, take I-55 to U.S. 24 west to Peoria.

FOR MORE INFORMATION: Call the Peoria Convention and Visitors Bureau, (309) 676-0303, or write 331 Fulton, Suite 625, Peoria, IL 61602.

Pere Marquette State Park: Illinois' Largest

Grafton, Illinois

Driving Time: 6½ hours south of Chicago

Pere Marquette State Park, at 8,000 acres the largest state park in Illinois, offers scenic views from bluffs overlooking the Illinois River. The Park was named after Father Jacques Marquette, who passed the site with Louis Joliet in 1673, the first Europeans to enter Illinois at the confluence of the Mississippi and the Illinois Rivers. A large white cross, east of the park entrance alongside Route 100, marks where these two famous men landed.

Boating, fishing, hunting, hiking, horseback riding, picnic areas, and camping are available. Also located here are a playground, museum, interpretive center, and lodge.

BEST TIME TO VISIT: Summer.

DIRECTIONS: From Chicago, take I-55 southwest to Rt. 100 to Grafton and the park.

FOR MORE INFORMATION: Call Pere Marquette State Park, (618) 786-3785, or write Box 325, Grafton, IL 62037.

Illinois

Illinois' White Pines State Park

Mount Morris, Illinois

Driving Time: 3 hours west of Chicago

White Pines Forest State Park (eight miles west of Oregon and 12 miles north of Dixon) is a beautiful 385-acre preserve where families can hike through a pine forest, picnic in a meadow beside a winding creek, or sleep and eat in a timbered park lodge.

Pine Creek, which cuts through the park, is filled with bluegills, crappies, smallmouth bass, and catfish.

Miles of hiking trails wind through virgin white pines and along the crest of the bluff in the west end of the park.

Sliding, cross-country skiing, and ice skating are popular in the winter.

A nearby attraction popular with children is **White Pines Deer Park**, the largest deer refuge in the Midwest. The park-zoo is home to nearly 100 types of animals, including six species of deer.

BEST TIME TO VISIT: Summer.
HOURS: White Pines Deer Park — 10 a.m.-7 p.m. daily, Memorial Day-Labor Day.
ADMISSION: White Pines Deer Park — adults, $3; children 6-12, $2; under 6, free.
DIRECTIONS: From Chicago, take I-90 west to Rt. 72 to Mount Morris and the park.
FOR MORE INFORMATION: Call White Pines Forest State Park, (815) 946-3717, or write R.R. 1, Mount Morris, IL 61054.

Illinois-Michigan Canal Trail

Morris, Illinois

Driving Time: 2 hours southwest of Chicago

The **Illinois and Michigan Canal State Trail**, once a busy waterway of commerce, is now a fine recreational resource. Canoeists have about 28 miles of canal at their disposal, with launch facilities at Channahon, Aux Sable, Gebhard Woods, and LaSalle.

Originally, the canal stretched 96 miles, linking Lake Michigan with the Illinois River at LaSalle. The canal was directly responsible for the beginning of Chicago's growth and for the development of Lockport, Joliet, and other towns along its western stretches.

For **hiking and bicyling**, there is a 15-mile section of marked trail between Channahon and Morris and a five-mile segment between LaSalle and Utica. The longer section has water facilities, toilets, and parking space along its course.

At Morris, the trail connects with **Gebhard Woods State Park**, which has shaded picnic areas with tables and grills. The park's slightly rolling terrain is dotted with wildflowers and many old shade trees.

Children can go fishing in several small ponds, while adults can fish in Nettle Creek and the Illinois and Michigan Canal.

The trail also offers 10 miles of cross-country ski paths between Morris and Seneca. Snowmobiling trails are also available.

BEST TIME TO VISIT: Spring, summer, fall.
DIRECTIONS: From Chicago, take I-55 southwest to U.S. 6 to the canal.
FOR MORE INFORMATION: Call Illinois and Michigan Canal State Trail, (815) 942-0796, or write P.O. Box 272, Morris, IL 60450.

Spectacular Mississippi Palisades

Savanna, Illinois

Driving Time: 3 hours northwest of Chicago

Mississippi Palisades State Park, near the confluence of the Apple and Mississippi Rivers in northwestern Illinois, is four miles north of Savanna in Carroll County. The 1,717-acre state park has scenic beauty as well as plenty of recreational opportunities: steep limestone bluffs, hillside prairies, and wooded uplands provide a haven for outdoor lovers.

The view of the Mississippi River from the palisades is spectacular. Travelers who want a closer look at the river can drive two miles below Savanna to watch tugboats nudging barges through the river locks.

The area, once inhabited by Indians, has numerous burial mounds within the park boundary.

The park is located in a region that escaped the huge drifts of the Ice Age. As a result, many unusual rock formations are found in the park. **Indian Head** is a large rock outcropping from the bluff line; the rock face, with its aquiline features, was sculpted by the natural process of wind and water erosion. Equally popular is **Twin Sisters**, a pair of tall columns with the general outlines of human figures rising from a huge rock base.

Lookout Point, easily accessible by car or hiking trail, has an observation platform nested atop the bluffs.

Plant life thrives in the park. The deep ravines are filled with ferns, and the bases of the cliffs are covered with rare and interesting plants, shrubs, and trees. Eleven miles of **well-marked trails** lead hikers from the Mississippi River floodplain to the top of the palisades. **Fishing** in the

Mississippi and its backwaters remains one of the park's most popular activities. The waters are filled with bluegill, crappie, and bass.

There are 250 **campsites**, 100 of which have electrical hook-ups. Several private campgrounds are available at Savanna, including **Shady Inn**, which offers year-round camping as well as horseback riding.

Visitors can also enjoy picnicking, boating, and winter sports. The park also offers a year-round program of nature walks and outdoor education.

A special summer recreational program is available for children.

Ice fishing is permitted at the boat-launch area if the ice is thick enough. Sledding and cross-country skiing on the hills are popular winter pastimes.

Century Craft Days, held in the park in mid-July, offers pioneer crafts, entertainment, and exhibits.

BEST TIME TO VISIT: Spring, summer.
DIRECTIONS: From Chicago, take I-290 northwest to Rt. 64 west to the park.
FOR MORE INFORMATION: Call the Savanna Chamber of Commerce, (815) 273-2722, or write 127 Main St., P.O. Box 315, Savanna, IL 61074.

Illinois

Illinois' Goose Lake State Park

Morris, Illinois

Driving Time: 2 hours southwest of Chicago

Goose Lake Prairie State Park, one of the last remnants of prairie life in Illinois, is in Grundy County, about 25 miles south of Joliet and two miles south of the Illinois River.

The park is a reminder of the environment with which Illinois' Indians and white settlers had to contend: a place of grasses, wildflowers, and seemingly endless prairie winds.

The park is a haven for wildlife. Wild ducks and geese concentrate on the vast marshlands in spring and fall. Rare species, such as the Henslow's sparrow, are common here. The plains pocket gopher inhabits the area as well as much larger mammals, such as deer and coyote.

BEST TIME TO VISIT: Spring, summer.
DIRECTIONS: From Chicago, take I-55 southwest to the park.
FOR MORE INFORMATION: Call Goose Lake Prairie State Park, (815) 942-2899, or write 5010 N. Jug Rd., Morris, IL 60450.

Kankakee State Park For Fishing

Kankakee, Illinois

Driving Time: 1½ hours south of Chicago

The city of Kankakee gets its name from the Kankakee River, which runs through it. Approximately 60 miles south of Chicago, the Kankakee has some of the best river fishing in the area; bass, sunfish, bluegill, and crappie abound in the waters.

Kankakee River State Park (eight miles northwest on Rt. 102) is great for family vacations. There are woodlands on both sides of the river. Dunes, meandering streams, and canyons also fill the park. Don't miss Rock Creek, which flows at the foot of a deep canyon with precipitous walls of limestone. There are picnic areas and two campgrounds, one of them at the old village of Altorf, at the east end of the park, where a gristmill once operated. Fishing, boating, hiking, hunting, snowmobiling, and cross-country skiing are also available.

Head over to **Gladiola Fields** (east on Rt. 1), where more than 150,000 flowers are harvested here from early summer to the first frost.

The **Kankakee Historical Society Museum** (Water St. and 8th Ave., in Small Memorial Park) contains molds of 12 George Gray Barnard sculptures. In 1936, the famous sculptor donated the molds to Central School, where he was a former student. The building also houses Indian artifacts, Civil War relics, toys, costumes, dishes, and an historical library.

BEST TIME TO VISIT: Summer.
HOURS: Kankakee County Historical Society Museum — 1-4 p.m. Sunday and by appointment; closed holidays and January.
ADMISSION: Kankakee County Historical Society Museum — free.
DIRECTIONS: From Chicago, take I-57 south to Kankakee.
FOR MORE INFORMATION: Call the Kankakee Chamber of Commerce, (815) 933-7721, or write P.O. Box 905, Kankakee, IL 60901.

WISCONSIN

Wisconsin Vacations

Map labels: Hayward, Door County, Green Bay, Wisconsin Dells, Green Lake, Baraboo, Horicon Marsh, Blackhawk Ridge, Elkhart Lake, Spring Green, Sauk City, Blue Mounds, Milwaukee, Kettle Moraine, Prairie du Chien, Eagle, Mineral Point, Janesville, Racine County, Green County, Lake Geneva

Wisconsin

A Door-Way to Lake Views, Village Life

Door County, Wisconsin

Driving Time: 3 hours from Milwaukee to Sturgeon Bay

For those who love fresh air, a cozy cottage, and the company of peaceful people, there is no better region than the **Door County peninsula**. Jutting into Lake Michigan on the east and Green Bay on the west, this narrow strip of land is punctuated at its north end by several small islands that offer a pleasant refuge from the hectic pace of everyday life. The terrain features gentle slopes inland, while the coastline provides dramatic views of sharp cliffs, limestone bluffs, and sandy beaches.

Fishing villages nestle into the natural surroundings of Door County, whose regular residents welcome visitors to the area's resort cottages, motels, and lodges. The summer months boast of top-quality entertainment. At **Fish Creek**, the country's oldest professional summer stock company, the Peninsula Players, perform every night but Monday during July and August. Just north of Fish Creek, in **Peninsula State Park**, the Heritage Ensemble provides family musical entertainment during those same summer months. A series of symphony concerts also graces Fish Creek during August, with the **Peninsula Music Festival** at Gibraltar Auditorium.

But visitors need not stay right in Fish Creek to take part in the summer shows. Dozens of nearby communities, each with its own special attractions, have facilities for visitors. **Sturgeon Bay**, in the southern part of the region, is set among huge rolling hills covered with cherry and

Cana Island in Door County

apple orchards that display their full blossoms in May and are harvested in July and August. The city itself is a center for the shipbuilding industry and features one of the world's largest dry docks. Sturgeon Bay spans a canal that connects Green Bay and Lake Michigan, and it offers an excellent protected harbor for all boating.

There are 250 miles of shoreline to explore in Door County, making summer water sports its most unparallelled attraction. **Fishing, boating,** and **swimming** are the obvious activities, but the numerous shipwrecks lying beneath the waters at the peninsula's northern tip make it fascinating for **skin diving** also. **Bicyclists** will thrill to a tour of Door County roads, which wind through villages where many artists and craftsmen have found their homes and opened shops

that delight the buyers and browser.

A **fish boil** feast is a culinary treat not to be missed when you visit this region. The fish boil (white fish and lake trout, tossed with potatoes and onions into an open boiling pot) is a ceremonious outdoor tradition and a delicious meal that can be found at many Door County restaurants.

For those who want to avoid all traces of civilization, **Newport State Park** and **Rock Island** (which can be reached by ferry) provide backpackers with primitive camping near wooded trails and sandy beaches. Nature-lovers will also want to stop at the **Ridges Sanctuary** in Bailey's Harbor to view its rare native wildflowers.

Door County is becoming popular as a winter vacationland, too. Four state parks and a 17-mile state trail combine with private trails into a terrific network of paths for **cross-country skiing** and **snowmobiling**. The county's western shoreline opens onto the frozen waters of Green Bay during the cold winter months. There, **ice fishing "safaris"** and **ice sailing** have become favorite activities. In autumn, when tourist traffic is thin, brilliant hues of maples, oak, and birch trees lend a calm to the Door County countryside, and the brisk fall air invigorates those who wander there.

BEST TIMES TO VISIT: Summer, winter.
TRAVEL TIPS: Arrange for accommodations well in advance. July, August, and winter holidays are very popular periods, and it's not uncommon to find lodges, cottages, and even campgrounds booked several months ahead.
ACCOMMODATIONS, SHOPS, EQUIPMENT RENTAL: The Door County Chamber of Commerce publishes an excellent annual guide with a clear map and dozens of business listings. Their address is below.
ANNUAL FESTIVALS: Maifest in Jacksonport on Memorial Day weekend features dancing, rides, horse show; Fyr Bal Festival in Ephraim in mid-June features Scandinavian folk arts; Olde Ellison Bay Days in late June features a talent show, fish boils, contests; Belgian Days in Brussels, mid-July, features dancing, rides, feasts; Door County Fair in Sturgeon Bay, early August, features fireworks, tractor pull, horse and car races; Fall Festival in Sister Bay, early October, features fish boils, carnival, auction.
COUNTRY INNS: A homey way to stay for small groups. The Griffin Inn, Ellison Bay, WI 54210, (414) 854-4306. The Proud Mary, Box 193, Fish Creek, WI 54212, (414) 868-3442. White Gull Inn, Box 175, Fish Creek, WI 54212, (414) 868-3517. Hotel Du Nord, 11000 Bay Shore Dr., Box 68, Sister Bay, WI 54234, (414) 845-4221. Bay Shore Inn, Bay Shore Dr., Stugeon Bay, WI 54235, (414) 743-4551.
DIRECTI)NS: From Chicago, take I-94 to Milwaukee, then I-43 north to Manitowoc, then Rt. 42 north into Door County. Or from Milwaukee, take I-43 north to Green Bay, then Rt. 57 to Door County.
FOR MORE INFORMATION: Call or write to Door County Chamber of Commerce, Box 219, Sturgeon Bay, WI 54235, (414) 743-4456. Visitor Information Center located just south of Sturgeon Bay where Highways 52 and 57 intersect. For snow report December 15-March 15, call (414) 743-7046. Newport State Park, (414) 854-2500; Peninsula State Park, (414) 868-3258; Potawatomi State Park, (414) 743-5123; Rock Island State Park, (414) 847-2235.

Life on an Old World Wisconsin Farm

Eagle, Wisconsin

Driving Time: 1½ hours from Chicago; 40 minutes from Milwaukee; 1 hour from Madison

The rolling hills of **Eagle, Wisconsin**, were farmed by Finns, Germans, Danes, Norwegians and Yankees during the last century. The barns and granaries they built now stand on a 576-acre site called **Old World Wisconsin**. All the traditional chores are demonstrated and celebrated there annually at festivals like Spring on the Farm in April, Scandinavian Midsummer in June, Summer on the Farm in August, and a Thresheree in September.

Each season has its own preparations, and people at Old World Wisconsin relive the lives of the ethnic pioneers. They plant the fields; put up the hay; make soap; and card, weave, and dye their wool. Scattered farmsteads and a rural village are all part of this Old World museum, the only one of its kind in the world.

A hush falls over Old World Wisconsin with the snow in winter, when the farm is shut down. But the grounds are open to cross-country skiers, with ski rentals available at the **Ramsey Barn**, and refreshments at a heated rest stop in the **Raspberry School** or in the **Clausing Barn Restaurant**.

Eagle is just outside the southern unit of the **Kettle Moraine State Forest**. The activities there are very similar to those in the northern unit, profiled in one of this book's longer features. Backpackers in Kettle South take the **Ice Age Trail**, hikers often favor the **Scuppernong Trail**, and cross-country skiers love the **Nordic Trail**. The autumn colors of the forest are most brilliant during October.

BEST TIME TO VISIT: Summer, fall.
HOURS: Old World Wisconsin farm—open May 1-October 31. Cross-country ski trails—open December 19-March 8. Admission fee.
DIRECTIONS: From Chicago, take I-94 toward Racine, then exit at Rt. 20 (near Racine) and go west along 20 past East Troy to Rt. 67; take 67 north into Eagle. From Milwaukee, take I-94 west, exit at Waukesha, and take Rt. 59 south into Eagle. From Madison, take I-94 east to Delafield, then take Rt. 67 south into Eagle.
FOR MORE INFORMATION: Old World Wisconsin, Rt. 2, Box 18, Eagle, WI 53119, (414) 594-2116. Kettle Moraine State Forest-South, Eagle, WI 53119, (414) 594-2135.

Wisconsin

Circus World: Fun Under The Big Top

Driving Time: About 4 hours northwest of Chicago

**Circus World Museum
Baraboo, Wisconsin**

Lions and tigers and bears are only some of the spectacular attractions at the **Circus World Museum** in Baraboo, Wisconsin. Within a short drive from the Twin Cities, the magic of the big top comes alive from mid-May through September. The 40-acre museum, built on the original site of the Ringling Brothers' winter quarters, features displays of old-time circus equipment, such as 152 colorfully decorated circus wagons. From dawn to dusk there are continuous performances, parades and music. The day begins with a concert of unique circus instruments. Next, professional trainers explain and demonstrate how llamas, camels, ponies, dogs and tigers are trained. Finally, the highlight of the day: the **Big Top Circus Performance** featuring trapeze artists, tightrope walkers, elephants and clowns—all the exciting, fun things you expect at a circus.

In early afternoon, you'll see an old-fashioned circus street parade or younger children may opt for a mini-train ride behind the steady pace of a friendly goat. Or if you're brave, take a leisurely ride on an elephant! There's also a menagerie where you can feed and pet the animals. Before you go, see the animated miniature replica of the Ringling Brothers Barnum and Bailey Circus of the 1920s, constructed on a scale of one-half inch to one foot. The show ends with an ear-splitting, melodious Steam Calliope Performance. If you're not quite ready to go home, you might check out **Devil's Lake State Park** for more outdoor activity (three miles south on WI-123).

HOURS: Circus World: 9:30 AM to 6 PM daily, mid-May through September.

FOR MORE INFORMATION: Call the museum, (608) 356-8341.

DIRECTIONS: From Twin Cities, take I-94 east and south toward Baraboo. Exit at Baraboo exit (Hwy. 33).

Green County, Wisconsin: A Bit of Switzerland

Green County, Wisconsin

Driving Time: About 8 hours from Chicago; 2 hours from Milwaukee

Green County, Wisconsin is known as "America's Little Switzerland." If you like spectacular scenery, Wisconsin cheese, and outdoor recreation, this is the place to go. Pretty green foliage, peaceful farmlands and the lovely Sugar River are characteristic of Green County. Named for Nathaniel Green, Revolutionary War hero, it's one of the smallest counties in Wisconsin—593 square miles and only 30,000 persons.

Begin your tour in Monroe, a charming town of 5,900 residents. Throughout the town the Swiss influence is evident. Monroe, called "the Swiss Cheese capital of the U.S." has the largest cheese and gourmet pastry mail order house. You might stop in the Swiss Colony Store (west side of downtown Square) and sample the delicacies. Don't miss the Swiss chocolates! The art of cheesemaking is demonstrated at the Swiss Cheese Shop (¼ mile north of Monroe on Highway 69). For supper, visit the Idle Hour Mansion (1 mile north of town on Route 69), a restored 19th-century residence containing rare antiques.

Eighteen miles north of Monroe on Route 39 is **New Glarus**, a cozy village settled by Swiss immigrants from Canton Glarus in Switzerland. You'll enjoy wandering the streets of New Glarus and browsing in the Swiss shops. Swiss-style food is available at the Swiss chalet-style New Glarus Hotel (100 6th Avenue).

The Swiss Historical Village (6th Avenue and 7th Street) features models of the first buildings in New Glarus and The Chalet of the Golden Fleece (2nd Street and 7th Avenue) contains more than 3,000 Swiss items.

HOURS: Swiss Cheese Shop—tour 9 a.m.-5 p.m. April through October (winter hours vary). Swiss Historical Village—9 a.m.-5 p.m. daily, May through October; closed November through April. Chalet of the Golden Fleece—9 a.m.-4:30 p.m., April through October; closed November through March.

FOR MORE INFORMATION: Call the Monroe Chamber of Commerce, (608) 325-3739.

ADMISSION: Swiss Cheese Shop: Adults 25¢; children under 18 years are free. Swiss Historical Village: Adults $2; children 6 to 12 years 50¢; children under 6 years free. Chalet of the Golden Fleece: Adults $1; children 6 to 11 years 50¢; children under 6 years free.

Green Bay: Adventures In American Traditions

Green Bay, Wisconsin

Driving Times: 2 hours from Milwaukee; 4 hours from Chicago; 6 hours from Minneapolis/St. Paul

Amateur historians who like to explore the great traditions of America's present and past will enjoy the **Green Bay area**. Visitors can wander through great moments in football history, witness the lifestyle of Wisconsin villagers in the 1800s, or hop aboard a steam locomotive that rode the rails during the train's Golden Age.

The **Green Bay Packer Hall of Fame** celebrates the spirit of one of the finest teams in the National Football League. Multi-media shows dramatize the achievements of such former Packer stars as Lambeau, Lombardi, and Starr, while game rooms allow fans to try their own hand on a mock football field. Of course, real fans will want to see the Packers in action across the street at **Lambeau Field**. An autumn visit should be planned in advance, because home games are usually sold out.

The past comes alive at **Heritage Hill State Park**, where actors costumed in the dress of 1871 guide visitors through buildings reconstructed to match the homes and businesses of yesteryear. Bark chapels of the late 1600s, like those where Catholic missionaries met Wisconsin Indians, are clustered near **Tank Cottage**, originally built in 1776. A **Victorian bandstand** hosts summer concerts of symphony and chamber music, while arts and crafts seldom seen today are

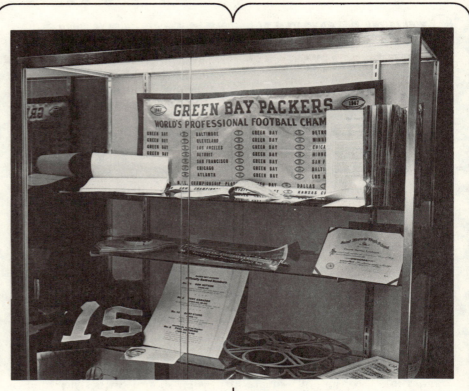

demonstrated at the park's **fall festival** in October and **"Spirit of Christmas Past"** celebration in November and December.

The folklore surrounding this nation's railroads becomes concrete at **Rail America**, the National Railroad Museum. Daytime tours carry passengers on an 1890-vintage coach past the Santa Fe "Big Boy" and more than 60 other locomotives and rail cars. At the Hood Junction Depot, there's a giant model train and many other exhibits of railroad memorabilia.

Docked right next to Rail America is Green Bay's latest visitor attraction, the *River Queen*. A one- or two-hour cruise along the Fox River is filled with stories of the region's past as told by the paddleboat guide. Green Bay visitors can learn more about native American history by taking a short drive southwest of the city to the **Oneida Nation Museum**, and the **Neville Public Museum** has displays on the natural history of northeastern Wisconsin.

Today's nature is preserved at the

Wildlife Sanctuary, where native waterfowl, birds, and animals nestle in a protected environment. The sanctuary is a good place for a family picnic, topped off by a stop at the mini-zoo. Across the street, children will find the excitement of bumper cars, pony rides, and a super slide at **Bay Beach Amusement Park**. Parents will enjoy the old-fashioned price of 10¢ per ride.

City entertainment is plentiful at the **Brown County Arena**, with its sporting events, concerts, and trade shows. The **Carlton Celebrity Room** features Las Vegas-style shows with top-name performers. For those with purchases in mind, the specialty shops of downtown **De Pere**, just outside Green Bay, should not be missed. Of course, Green Bay is at the base of the bay for which it is named, and it boasts of two harbors that boaters will want to explore. Winter sports-lovers will find snowmobile trails in two county parks and three downhill ski areas nearby: **Snowburst** and **Hilly Haven** in De Pere, and **Hidden Valley**, 18 miles south on I-43.

Wisconsin

Road racing gets under way at Elkhart, with actor Paul Newman at the wheel of car No. 33.

ZZZOOM! Road Racing in Elkhart Lake

Elkhart Lake, Wisconsin

Driving Time: 3 hours from Chicago; 1 hour from Milwaukee; 6½ hours from Minneapolis/St. Paul

Tucked in the placid surroundings of the Wisconsin countryside is a town made for the boldest, most daring drivers in the world. **Elkhart Lake**, home of Road America, is the site of five exciting weekends of sports car and motorcycle races each year.

Cars from around the world compete at this four-mile track, built in 1954 and known throughout the racing world as one of the most beautiful circuits. Racers charge at breakneck speeds along the course, winding through the kettles and hills that cover this region.

Actor/driver Paul Newman once made a film here. Every year, amateur and professional drivers bring more thrills to Elkhart Lake during the AMA Pro Series, June Sprints, Can-Am, Indy Car 200, and the Budweiser 500. An AM radio, set at 530, will give race fans flag-to-flag coverage of the races if their sight doesn't reach the remote turns.

After the races, there's much to enjoy in the Elkhart Lake area. A brat and beer at a local restaurant, or the outdoor enjoyment of Kettle Moraine Forest and lakes are only minutes away.

BEST TIME TO VISIT: June-August (racing season).
DIRECTIONS: From Chicago, take I-94 to Milwaukee, then I-43 north to Wis. Rt. 57 north, then 67 south to Elkhart Lake. From Green Bay, take Wis. Rt. 57 south to Wis. Rt. 67, then south on 67 to Elkhart Lake. From Minneapolis/St. Paul, take I-94 east to Wis. Rt. 82 east, to Wis. Rt. 23 east, to Wis. Rt. 67 north to Elkhart Lake.
FOR MORE INFORMATION: Write or call Road America, Elkhart Lake, WI 53020, (414) 876-3366.
ACCOMMODATIONS: Write or call Elkhart Lake Chamber of Commerce, Elkhart Lake, WI 53020, (414) 876-2922.

BEST TIMES TO VISIT: Summer, fall.
TRAVEL TIPS: If you want to see the Green Bay Packers play at home, call early to reserve tickets. Autumn colors begin in mid-September and last well into October. Dress in summer for temperatures in the 80s during the day and cooler nights. The Green Bay Area Visitor and Convention Bureau will help you plan your trip (see address below).
HOURS AND ADMISSIONS: Packer Hall of Fame — open 10 a.m.-5 p.m. daily, year round, $3.50. Heritage Hill State Park — weekends 10 a.m.-5 p.m. in May, September, and October, daily 10 a.m.-5 p.m. between June 1 and Labor Day, $2.25. Rail America — 9 a.m.-5 p.m. daily, May 1-October 1, $2.75. River Queen — tours daily at 10 a.m., 1:30 p.m. and 4 p.m., between Memorial Day and Labor Day, $4.50 and $6. Bay Beach Park — 10 a.m.-9 p.m. daily between June 1 and Labor Day. Wildlife Sanctuary — 8 a.m.-8 p.m. summer, 8 a.m.-5 p.m. winter.
DIRECTIONS: From Chicago, take I-94 to Milwaukee, then I-43 or Wis. 41 (longer route) to Green Bay. From Minneapolis, take I-94 east to Eau Claire, then Rt. 29 to Green Bay.
FOR MORE INFORMATION: Write or call Green Bay Area Chamber of Commerce, Box 969, Green Bay, WI 54301, (414) 437-8704. Green Bay Visitor and Convention Bureau, Box 3278, Green Bay, WI 54303, (414) 494-9507. Green Bay Packers Football, Box 3726, Green Bay, WI 54304, (414) 494-2345.

Wisconsin

Sauk City Area: A Menu Full Of Family Fun

Sauk City/Prairie du Sac, Wisconsin

Driving Time: 3½ hours from Chicago; 2 hours from Milwaukee; 5 hours from Minneapolis/St. Paul

Where can you see the circus all summer, tour a vineyard and taste its wines, enjoy a spectacular bike tour, and paddle through endless hours of canoe adventures — all within a 25-mile radius? In the **Sauk City/Prairie du Sac** region of Wisconsin, visitors find this and much more.

Springtime swells the waters of the **Wisconsin River**, which twists and turns through the Sauk City area, providing one of the Midwest's finest playgrounds for canoeing explorers. Navigating the meandering waters from the **Wisconsin Dells** to Prairie du Sac, then south again toward Spring Green, reminds the paddler of earlier days, when the Sauk Indians inhabited this land. Today, their culture is commemorated in the **Sauk County Historical Museum** in Baraboo, just 14 miles north of Sauk City and Prairie du Sac.

Baraboo, once the winter home of the Ringling Brothers Circus, now hosts the **Circus World Museum** between mid-May and mid-September. The young of all ages can witness all types of circus thrills in this 40-acre Big Top — spectacular outdoor aerial shows, live animal acts, and hysterical clown capers. For quieter moments, visitors can learn the living habits of an endangered bird species at Baraboo's **International Crane Foundation** or take a steam train ride through the Baraboo Valley at the **Mid-Continental Railway Museum**. (See the following article for information on Baraboo, Wisconsin.)

Winery at Prairie du Sac

There's no better way to see all the wonders of Sauk County than from the seat of a bicycle. The Wisconsin Tourism Office can provide you with detailed maps of **bikeways** that take you through some of the state's most dazzling scenery. The route skirts cliff-rimmed **Devil's Lake**, whose state park offers year-round camping with boating, swimming, fishing, and cross-country skiing. Farther south, the path crosses **Lake Wisconsin** via the free **Colsac Ferry**. Even cars can board the ferry, which connects the sides of Route 113 by a 10-minute ride across the water. **Natural Bridge** and **Mirror Lake** are other natural wonders that add to the area's beauty. Bird-watchers find special treats in Sauk County: sandhill cranes, woodpeckers, and red-shouldered hawks abound during warm weather at **Mazomanie Wildlife Area**. Winter brings American bald eagles to feed along the Wisconsin River.

Winter weather should not frighten tourists away from Sauk County. Fine cross-country skiing is available among the **Baraboo Bluffs** at Devil's Lake and **Mirror Lake State Parks**, as well as at several private trailgrounds. Snowmobiles are a common sight on the frozen waters of Lake Wisconsin, and **Christmas Mountain** at Wisconsin Dells offers downhill slopes. **Blackhawk Ridge Wilderness Recreation Area** in Sauk City has so much to offer year round that we've set aside a separate story for it among the shorter features.

Outdoor activities may be the main attraction in this region, but

Sauk City Area continued

tourists can find good entertainment, too. Country music lovers can enjoy the **Wisconsin Opry** (where Highway 12 joins I-90/94) six nights a week from late May until September. Matinee and evening performances of professional, classical theater are available from June until mid-October at Spring Green's **American Players Theatre**, just 20 miles west of Sauk City.

One of Prairie du Sac's most surprising offerings for visitors is the **Wollersheim Winery**, which has won national and international awards for several of its wines. Its vineyards grow next to an old stone house and the winery buildings are situated on a ridge that overlooks the Wisconsin River. A tour always ends in the tasting room, where visitors can sample the liquid fruit of the vine.

BEST TIMES TO VISIT: Spring, summer.
TRAVEL TIPS: Bicycles can be rented in the area, but must be returned to the rental site. Bringing your own bikes can save you from backtracking. Canoe and boat rental shops are plentiful.
HOURS: Wollersheim Winery — 10 a.m.-5 p.m. every day of the year. Sauk City Museum — Sunday and holidays, 2 p.m.-5 p.m., Memorial Day to Labor Day. Sauk County Historical Museum, Baraboo — daily 2 p.m.-5 p.m. from late May to mid-September. Wisconsin Opry — 8 p.m. six nights a week, late May to September. Circus World Museum, Baraboo — every day 9:30 a.m.-6 p.m. from mid-May to mid-September. Mid-Continental Railway Museum — 10:30 a.m.-5:30 p.m. daily from Memorial Day to Labor Day, Saturday and Sunday to mid-October.
DIRECTIONS: From Chicago, take I-90 west to Madison, then I-90/94 west to Rt. 60 west; take 60 west into Prairie du Sac and Sauk City. From Milwaukee, take I-94 west to Madison and follow preceding directions from there. From Minneapolis/St. Paul, take I-94 east, exit at U.S. 12, take 12 south to Rt. 60 east, and take 60 east into Sauk City.
FOR MORE INFORMATION: Write or call Sauk Prairie Chamber of Commerce, 468 Water St., Box B, Prairie du Sac, WI 53578, (608) 643-4168. Baraboo Area Chamber of Commerce, 124 Second St., Baraboo, WI 53913, (608) 356-8333. Sauk County, Box 46, Baraboo, WI 53913, (608) 356-5581. Circus World, 426 Water St., Baraboo, WI, 53913, (608) 356-8341. Wisconsin Dells Chamber of Commerce, Box 390, Wisconsin Dells, WI 53965, (608) 254-4321. For bike trail map: Department of Natural Resources, Box 450, Dept. B., Madison, WI 53701.

Wisconsin

An Outdoor Wonderland In Wisconsin

Driving Time: 3 hours east of Minneapolis/St. Paul, 9 hours northwest of Chicago

Hayward, Wisconsin

In any season the Hayward Lakes area of Wisconsin offers a myriad of opportunities for the outdoor enthusiast. The scenic beauty of the 200 lakes, rivers and streams has attracted visitors for years. Skiing in winter, sailing in summer—each season there's sure to be something exciting happening in Hayward.

Children will want to spend some time at **Historyland** (County Trunk B, one mile east of Hayward), where they can see a logging camp as it was many years ago and learn about the first Americans at the Indian Museum. The **Namekagon Queen** offers leisurely excursions along Lake Hayward and the Namekagon River. Each Tuesday evening there are authentic Chippewa Indian Pow-Wows, which are sure to entertain the whole family.

If you have a sweet tooth, be sure to check out the **Historyland Bakery** and the **Old Hayward Ice Cream Parlor**. Or, if you want a "lumberjack-style" meal, try the **Logging Camp Cook Shanty**. And for breakfast, the **Wannigan Pancake House** serves 10 tempting varieties of pancakes. In late July, **Historyland** hosts the Lumberjack World Championships, featuring log rolling, log scooping, tree topping and other events.

Another spot for family fun—especially animal lovers—is the **Wilderness**

Walk Recreational Park (Hwy. 27, three miles south of Hayward), which includes an animal farm and a western town. In the park you can watch farm animals and many unusual forest animals, such as fawns, porcupines, woodchucks, skunks, bobcats, etc. Some of the animals may be fed by hand. In the western town, get a glimpse of the old frontier life at the Crooked Creek Casino, Jail, Dodge House, Country Store, Mystery House and Blacksmith Shop. Before you leave, try your hand at panning for gold—you probably won't get rich, but you'll have fun doing it!

For those who like to browse, there are many unusual shops in the area featuring antiques and gifts. Stop in the **Namekagon General Store** and buy a pair of moccasins as a souvenir, or pick up a tree ornament at the **Jule Haus**, where it's Christmas all year round. But make sure you have time to take advantage of the outdoors. Of course, swimming and canoeing are activities you won't want to miss. Dads may want to go fishing and bring home a giant musky or bass. There are many motels in the area; the **Telemark Lodge** in Cable is a good choice for an overnight stay.

HOURS: Historyland: 10 AM to 8 PM daily, mid-May through mid-October; closed rest of year. Wilderness Walk Recreational Park: 10 AM to 5 PM daily, May through October.

FOR MORE INFORMATION: Call the Hayward Chamber of Commerce, (715) 634-8662.

ADMISSION: Historyland, free; Wilderness Walk Recreational Park:

DIRECTIONS: From Twin Cities, take I-94 east to U.S. Rt. 53 north at Eau Claire, Wisconsin. At intersection of Rtes. 63 and 53, take Rt. 63 north to Hayward.

Geese-Gazing Wonderland at Horicon Marsh

Horicon Marsh, Wisconsin

Driving Time: 3 hours from Chicago; 1½ hours from Green Bay; 1 hour from Milwaukee; 5½ hours from Minneapolis/St. Paul

Bird-watchers, grab your binoculars; photographers, load your film. A trip to **Horicon Marsh**, Wisconsin, in the autumn will fill your sight with the great gray wings of the graceful Canadian goose. More than 70,000 geese make a rest stop each year at this nature preserve, maintained by state and federal conservation offices. The season can begin as early as August's latter days and last as long as December, depending on the weather here and at the geese's northern home on Hudson Bay.

But there is more to see in the marshlands during this season and others. First, take a trip up **Conservation Hill** to the Horicon Marsh headquarters. From the high point there, you can get a good overview of the area. Then, talk with the local people for specific directions to the wild goose trails. The **Headquarters Trail** is marked, but there are four others — **Indermuehle Island, Federal Dike Road, East and West Side Impoundments,** and, for canoeists, the **Canoe Trail**. As you wander through the nature preserve, you're likely to see mallards, blue-winged teal, and wood ducks along the way. During summertime, coot, gallinules, egrets, and the great blue heron grace the marsh, which is also the nesting place for thousands of smaller songbirds.

Then, take a drive along Highway 49 and stop just east of Waupun, where the highway crosses the **National Wildlife Refuge.** At dawn or dusk, if you're quiet and patient, you'll probably catch sight of the plentiful wild animals that live along the wetland edge or in the clearings. Foxes, raccoon, oppossums, and white-tailed deer all make their home here. If you prefer not to walk, glide along the marsh surface on a **Blue Heron boat tour**, guided by commentary on area history and wildlife. Or, take the **Wild Goose Parkway** for an auto tour of the refuge perimeter. The way is marked by yellow signs.

If you're skilled with a canoe paddle, you'll be able to get an even closer look at the Horicon habitat. You can also paddle south through the narrow channels of the Rock River to **Lake Sinissippi**, where you can rent a larger boat if you'd like. There's fishing, swimming, and water skiing on the lake, and, during winter, ice fishing and snowmobiling are popular.

Campers can select from two county parks in the Horicon Marsh area: **Horicon Ledge Park**, two miles east of Horicon, or **Astico Park**, three miles east of Columbus, off State Highway 16. The **Playful Goose** has a private campground with an indoor heated pool.

Horicon Marsh is located in the center of Wisconsin's agricultural heartland. Pastoral scenes and picturesque villages blanket the countryside. Sights to see outside Dodge County include the **Danville Mill**, along the Crawfish River; the **Wagon and Carriage Factory**, maintained by the Village of Mayville's Historical Society; and the **Fox Lake Depot**, now a museum operated by the Fox Lake Historical Society.

Near Lake Sinissippi is the **Radloff Cheese Factory** of Hustiford. Visitors here can pick up some of the delicious cheeses that give Wisconsin its reputation as the dairy capital of the nation. Right in Horicon, meanwhile, the **Satterlee Clark House** is a fine example of Georgian architecture. Built around 1860, the Clark House is open for tours on select days between May and October.

BEST TIME TO VISIT: Fall (call ahead to learn the optimum time this year for viewing the return of the geese).

TRAVEL TIPS: Don't forget your binoculars and/or camera!

HOURS: Satterlee Clark House — May to October, 1:30 p.m.-4:30 p.m. on the second and fourth Sunday of each month. Wagon and Carriage Factory — same hours. Radloff's Cheese Factory — daily, 8 a.m.-5 p.m.

DIRECTIONS: From Chicago, take I-94 to Milwaukee, then U.S. 45 north to U.S. 41 north, to Wis. Rt. 33 west to Horicon. From Madison, take U.S. 151 north to Beaver Dam, then take Rt. 33 east to Horicon.

FOR MORE INFORMATION: Horicon Chamber of Commerce, Box 23, Horicon, WI 53032, (414) 485-2192. Horicon National Wildlife Refuge, Route #2, Mayville, WI 53050, (414) 387-2658. Horicon Marsh Canoe Outfitters, Highway 33, Horicon, WI 53032, (414) 485-4217. Big George's Marina (on Lake Sinissippi), Highway E, Lake Drive, Hustiford, WI, (414) 349-3550.

Wisconsin

Ice Age Hills, Wooded Paths In a Hiker's Delight

Kettle Moraine State Forest, Wisconsin

Driving Time: 2½-3 hours from Chicago; 1 hour from Milwaukee

The northern unit of **Kettle Moraine State Forest** is a long, narrow strip of wooded wilderness that hikers, campers, and backpackers can enjoy thoroughly in summer. In winter, dozens of cottages and motels in surrounding communities give the cross-country skier, hunter, and fisherman comfortable shelter after a day in the brisk outdoors.

This is unusual terrain, the result of glacial land formations left by the melting ice of the Ice Age. The "kettles" are depressions in the earth, some just a few feet across and some, like huge hollows, up to 200 feet deep. **Ice Age Park**, in the forest near Dundee, has a center where exhibits explain the topography of the region. Conical hills and outwash plains complement the kettles to make a fascinating labyrinth of trails for hikers and skiers.

Both within and outside the forest boundaries, there are nearly a dozen small lakes where swimming, fishing, and picnicking abound. Boaters can launch their vessels onto the clear waters of **Mauthe Lake, Long Lake, Crooked Lake,** and **Butlers Lake,** while campers can put up their tents or park their RVs at Long Lake or Mauthe Lake. There are boats to rent on the east and west shores of Long Lake. At Mauthe, you'll find a two-mile nature trail and the head of a 16½-mile trail for the overnight hiker. For a horseback ride along the hilly bridle paths, stop at the **Bar-N Dude Ranch** on the drive into Mauthe Lake.

During winter, the bridle paths become snowmobile trails that cover a 25-mile area. Hunters will find geese, duck, deer, and small game, while pike, northern, and pan fish can be caught in all of the area's lakes.

The northern tip of **Kettle Moraine —North** offers a change of pace from the hushed forest. In Greenbush, the **Old Wade House**, a stagecoach inn of the 1850s, gives the public a peek into the last century. From there, a short ride in a horse-drawn carriage takes visitors to the **Wesley Jung Carriage Museum**, home of a fine collection of restored carriages.

If you'd prefer to take a scenic drive in one of our modern carriages, go father north and west to Sheboygan Marsh and follow the acorn-shaped signs for a picturesque 12-mile auto tour of the Kettle Moraine region, particularly beautiful in autumn's colors. Two other attractions in the area are **Elkhart Lake** (see article in this section for more information) and Fond du Lac, at the base of Lake Winnebago.

Fond du Lac is just 20 miles west of the Wade House, at Greenbush along Route 23. The city is at the southern tip of Wisconsin's largest inland lake,

Lake Winnebago. Power boating, sailing, and water skiing are favorite activities here during summer months, and a 30-mile frozen surface in the heart of winter brings out the ice fishermen, ice boaters, and snowmobilers.

BEST TIMES TO VISIT: Summer, winter.

TRAVEL TIPS: Hunters and fishermen should check on license requirements with the Wisconsin Department of Natural Resources, P.O. Box 7921, Madison, WI 53707.

HOURS: Old Wade House — open May 1-October 31, 9 a.m.-4 p.m. on weekdays in May, June, September, October; 10 a.m.-5 p.m. on weekends during July and August. For more information on rates, call (414) 526-3271. Cross-country ski trail available here in winter months.

DIRECTIONS: From Chicago, take I-94 to Milwaukee, then take U.S. 41 and exit on Rt. 45 toward West Bend. Just outside Campbellsport, Rt. 45 intersects with Rt. 67; take 67 east into the state forest at the southwest end. If you want to go to the northern tip, from Milwaukee, take I-43 north to Rt. 57 north, then Rt. 23 west toward Plymouth and Greenbush. From Green Bay, take Rt. 57 south to 23 west.

FOR MORE INFORMATION: Wisconsin Conservation Department, Route 2, Campbellsport, WI 53010. Fond du Lac County, 160 S. Macy St., Fond du Lac, WI 54935, (414) 929-3135. Fond du Lac Area Association of Commerce, 207 N. Main St., Fond du Lac, WI 54935, (414) 921-9500. Elkhart Lake Area Chamber of Commerce, Box 41, Elkhart Lake, WI 53020, (414) 876-2922.

The Tallman House restoration

Janesville: A Trip Back to Civil War Days

Janesville, Wisconsin

Driving Time: 2 hours from Chicago; 1 hour from Milwaukee; 45 minutes from Madison

William Morrison Tallman came to Wisconsin in the 1850s, when the abolition of slavery was a burning issue. In Janesville, he built a home that he claimed was the largest and most elaborate house in the upper Midwest. Abraham Lincoln once stayed overnight in the guest chambers there, and no doubt, he and Tall-man discussed how to achieve their common goal of abolition.

The **Tallman House** has been restored, and its interior is open for public tours between May and October. Social customs and furnishings of the late 1800s are displayed in the Italianate structure. Its five levels feature three parlors, a basement kitchen, and even a top-floor observatory.

While in Janesville, visitors can canoe along the **Rock River**, browse for antiques in the town's numerous shops, or fish at the **Traxler Park Lagoon**. The lagoon is also the showcase on Sunday and Wednesday evenings for the Rock Aqua Jays, a team of top-notch water skiers who sponsor the annual **National Water Ski Show Tournament** each August.

Just 10 miles south of Janesville is **Beloit**, home of Beloit College, whose anthropology museum, art center, and observatory are worth a visit. The Bartlett Museum is another site of historical interest in Beloit. This Victorian farmstead has a one-room schoolhouse; Beloit's first fire engine; and exhibits of toys, dolls, and Indian artifacts.

BEST TIME TO VISIT: Summer.
HOURS: Tallman Restorations—May, September, October, weekends 11 a.m.-4 p.m., weekdays by appointment only for group tours; June-August, 11 a.m.-4 p.m. daily except Monday. Group tours by appointment.
ADMISSION: Adults, $3; students (K-12), $1.50; sr. citizens, $2.50. Rates are 50¢ less for group tours.
DIRECTIONS: From Chicago, take I-90 through Rockford and Beloit into Janesville. From Milwaukee, take Rt. 15 south to Elkhorn, then Rt. 11 west to Janesville. From Madison, take I-90 east to Janesville.
FOR MORE INFORMATION: Write or call the Rock County Historical Society—Tallman Restorations, Box 896, Janesville, WI 53547, (608) 752-4519; Janesville Chamber of Commerce, Box 998, Janesville, WI 53545, (608) 752-7459; Beloit Chamber of Commerce, Box 717, Beloit, WI 53511, (608) 365-8835.

Lake Geneva, Wisconsin: Fun For All Seasons

Lake Geneva, Wisconsin

Driving Time: 2 hours north of Chicago

A paradise for outdoor family fun, Lake Geneva, Wisconsin is 75 miles northwest of Chicago and offers adventure in any season. First, there's Geneva Lake, with its sparkling water and sandy beaches, which offers swimming, skiing, boating, fishing and sun-bathing. Children and parents alike will enjoy leisurely boat cruises leaving from Gage Marina, especially on Lady of the Lake, a twin smoke-stacked Mississippi paddle wheel. There's no better spot to skate or hook a tasty trout. In winter, how about snowmobiling on the wind-swept lakeshore? Ski enthusiasts have their pick of spots, including the Abbey Springs Ski Touring Center (South Lake Shore Drive, Fontana), Majestic Ski Area (South Shore Road), Interlaken Lodge (on Route 50), and more.

In the fall, the Lake Geneva area comes alive with brilliant golden hues of orange and red. Visitors come from miles around to enjoy the Lake Geneva Color Tour in October. If your family wants to explore the winding country roads, you might seek out the various antique shops in Lake Geneva, Williams Bay, Fontana or Delavan. During any season you can also see the scenery on bridle paths, hiking paths and bicycle trails around the lake.

At Lake Geneva, there's still more adventure. One of the attractions is the Wisconsin Winery (529 Main Street, Lake Geneva), which features half-hour tours. If you like

science, visit the Yerkes Observatory (Williams Bay), which has the largest lens ever constructed for a telescope. And try some of the food at Lake Geneva area restaurants. Just a few suggestions: Charley O's (12 West Geneva, Williams Bay), The Hayloft (760 S. Lake Shore Drive, Lake Geneva), Stevenson's III (Highway 67 West, Fontana), Popeye's (811 Wrigley Drive, Lake Geneva). If by chance

your family decides to spend more than a day, there are many resorts where you can continue your mini-vacation. One final tip: take some of that delicious Wisconsin cheese home with you.

FOR MORE INFORMATION: Call the Lake Geneva Chamber of Commerce, (414) 248-4416.
DIRECTIONS: From Chicago, take Tri-State Tollway (294-94) north toward Milwaukee, exit at Lake Geneva exit.

Wisconsin

Underground Chambers and The Valley Of the Elves

Blue Mounds, Wisconsin

Driving Time: 3½ hours from Chicago; 1½ hour from Milwaukee; 5½ hours from Minneapolis/St. Paul

Perhaps your family cannot afford plane fare to Oslo, but you can taste the magical flavor of Norwegian life with a trip to **Little Norway**, also named "Nissedahle" or Valley of the Elves by its founder. This outdoor museum is tucked into the southwest Wisconsin landscape at Blue Mounds.

Geologists call the region "driftless" because its terrain of carved hills, hollows, and valleys was left untouched by the glaciers of the Ice Age. The countryside reminded Norwegians of their homeland, and Midwest settlers like Osten Olson Haugen fashioned their new lodgings here. **Haugen's log houses** still stand at Little Norway, restored and filled with Norse artifacts and pioneer antiques.

The **Norway Building**, modeled after a 12th-century *stavkirke* (church), found its way here after Chicago's World Columbian Exposition in 1893. Today, guides garbed in bright Norwegian costumes show visitors the treasures of Little Norway — from an original manuscript of an Edvard Grieg composition to hand-carved skis.

More enchantments can be found at **Cave of the Mounds**, hidden for over a million years until a quarry blast on Brigham Farm in 1939 uncovered the underground marvel. Year-round tours enable visitors to see the cave's colorful formations, and theatrical lighting dazzles observers of its narrow passageways and jewel-like stone.

Every Saturday at 8 p.m. in July, the **Song of Norway Festival** fills the stage area at Cave of the Mounds with music. The audience brings chairs and blankets to gather around on the green for this dramatization of Edvard Grieg's life.

During warm weather months, **Blue Mounds State Park** offers swimming, hiking, camping, and scenic views from the highest point in southern Wisconsin. During winter, cross-country skiers will find trails open on a fee basis at Brigham Farm in Blue Mounds, while downhill slopes are available at **Tyrol Basin** in Mount Horeb.

Visitors can carry some of Norway back with them if they take time to shop in the neighboring town of **Mount Horeb**. There, import shops display the finest crafts of Scandinavia, and restaurants feature Norwegian specialties. Of course, fine Wisconsin cheeses and homemade bratwurst can also be found in the food stores here. In October, there is an Old World crafts demonstration, where weaving, woodcarving, and quilting are on display.

There are several inns in the Blue Mounds/Mount Horeb area, and you can find a wider selection just 25 miles away in **Madison**, the Wisconsin state capital. While there, trace the natural and human history of the region at the **State Historical Society Museum**. The city of Madison surrounds two lakes: **Mendota** and **Monona**. The lakeshore campus of the **University of Wisconsin** is a pleasant picnic spot, after a visit to the University Arboretum and Nevin fish hatchery.

BEST TIME TO VISIT: Summer.

TRAVEL TIPS: Bring a sweater or jacket when visiting the Cave of the Mounds; the temperature underground is always about 50° F. You'll also want that sweater for summer evenings in Blue Mounds, and visitors to the Song of Norway Festival should take chairs or blankets to ensure a comfortable lawn seat.

HOURS AND ADMISSIONS: State Historical Society Museum in Madison — open all year; free. Mount Horeb Area Museum — 1 p.m.-4 p.m. Saturday and Sunday, Memorial Day to Labor Day; free. Cave of the Mounds — open all year; for specifics, contact Brigham Farm, Blue Mounds, WI 53517, (608) 437-3355.

DIRECTIONS: From Chicago, take I-90 west to Madison, then U.S. 18 west to Mount Horeb and Blue Mounds. From Milwaukee, take I-94 west to Madison, then follow preceding directions. From Minneapolis/St. Paul, take I-90/94 east to Madison, then follow above directions.

FOR MORE INFORMATION: Call or write to Little Norway, Blue Mounds, WI 53517, (608) 437-8211. Tyrol BAsin, 3487 Bohn Rd., Mount Horeb, WI 53572, (608) 437-3076. Blue Mounds State Park, Blue Mounds, WI 53517, (608) 437-5711. Mount Horeb Area Chamber of Commerce, Box 84, Mount Horeb, WI 53572, (608) 437-8073. Madison Visitors Bureau, 425 W. Washington Ave., Madison, WI 53703, (608) 255-0701.

Wisconsin

A Rich Ethnic Past and a Modern City Skyline

Milwaukee, Wisconsin

Driving Time: 1½ hours from Chicago; 1½ hours from Green Bay; 1¼ hours from Madison

When the American Indians migrated westward from this lakeshore community, they left its name behind —Milwaukee. Some translate it as "gathering place by the waters," others as "meeting place of the rivers." Either translation is an apt description of the city whose first settlements were divided by the Milwaukee River as it flowed into Lake Michigan.

Many of those first white homesteaders were from Germany, and the culture they carried from the Old World still pervades much of Milwaukee. But since the turn of the century, German heritage has been joined by the ethnic traditions of Poles, Serbs, Greeks, Irish, Afro-Americans, and Italians, and a new urban American culture has grown up alongside the blend of Old World nationalities.

Visitors will want to experience both sides of Wisconsin's largest city. A **walking tour of Old World Third Street** will include a stop at **Usinger's sausage factory and shop**, where bratwurst and blood sausage are at their best. The heavy wood-carved interior of **Mader's** (1037 N. Third St.) hosts the lover of German cuisine, who will certainly want to sample the sauerbraten and cherry strudel. It was originally the Germans who made the beers that made Milwaukee famous. Two breweries still offer free tours—**Miller Brewing**

The Schlitz Brewery

Company (4251 W. State St.) and **Pabst Brewing Company** (901 W. Juneau Ave.). The **1893 mansion of Captain Frederick Pabst** is now a public museum, open between mid-March and November 30.

The **Milwaukee Public Museum** (800 W. Wells St.) recreates in its European Village Exhibit the streets of Old Milwaukee when the melting pot first began to simmer. There, the lifestyles, artifacts, and architecture of more than 30 cultures that settled Wisconsin are represented. Throughout the summer and fall, **ethnic festivals** enliven the city's parks with traditional music, food, and art. In November, one of the nation's largest ethnic fairs celebrates the season's holidays at the **Milwaukee Exposition and Convention Center and Arena (MECCA).**

The modern attractions of Milwaukee will keep visitors busy for days. The beauties of plant and animal wildlife are preserved and revealed in the carefully designed habitats of the **Milwaukee County Zoo** and the domes of the **Mitchell Park Conservatory**.

Just 10 minutes from downtown Milwaukee, the zoo is set on 184 acres of recreational land. More than 6,000 animals are grouped in habitats created to resemble their natural homes around the world. In the **Children's Zoo**, youngsters can pet all types of baby animals, and the family can tour the grounds by Zoomobile or miniature train.

At **Mitchell Park Conservatory**, the architectural wonders of the domes nearly match the horticultural sights. These three beehive-shaped conoidal structures are nearly as high as a seven-story building, and each houses 2½ acres of growing space for plants. The domes are designated as the Tropical, Arid, and Show Dome, where six different annual exhibits provide a grand flourish of color and greenery at any time of the year.

To get a view from on high of the rest of the city, climb to the 41st-floor **Skywalk in the First Wisconsin Center**. A clear sky will enable you to see for 30 miles, and perhaps you'll be able to pick out some of the interesting church architecture that graces greater Milwaukee. Frank Lloyd

Wisconsin

Wright drafted the plans for the **Annunciation Greek Orthodox Church** in Wauwatosa, whose bright-blue dome sits atop a Byzantine-styled structure. The campus of **Marquette University** is the home of the St. Joan of Arc Chapel, built during the 15th century near Lyon, France, and moved here in 1964. The **first Polish basilica** in North America stands on South Sixth Street in Milwaukee. St. Josaphat's Basilica, built from salvaged materials at the turn of the century, is noted for its majestic dome, stained glass, and woodcarving.

The **Milwaukee Art Museum** is located in the War Memorial, designed by world-renowned architect Eero Saarinen. A small admission fee admits you to collections of 20th-century European and American art, as well as 19th-century American and European painting, Renaissance art, and Haitian art.

There are several museums in the Milwaukee area for the eclectic hobbyist. The **EAA Air Museum Foundation** has on rotating display over 200 historic, sport, military, and special-purpose aircraft, as well as photographs and films. Bowlers might want to visit the **National Bowling Hall of Fame and Museum** in Greendale, where they'll find the world's only bowling-pin-shaped automobile. The museum's bowling memorabilia date back to the 1800s. Music lovers can see a huge assortment of music-playing machines, instruments, and written music at **Castle on Kilbourn**, which is also a finely restored Victorian mansion.

Life in the city would not be complete without the vast array of entertainment available there. **The Performing Arts Center** is a key showcase for Wisconsin's musicians, actors, and dancers. The Milwaukee Symphony Orchestra, Milwaukee Repertory Theater, Milwaukee Ballet Company, Florentine Opera Company, and Bel Canto Chorus—all make the center's stage their home. The **Pabst Theater** hosts many touring theatrical productions, concerts, and dance performances, and local theater groups have a variety of other stages in the city. Milwaukee's nightclubs offer a wide range of music—quiet jazz, quick Latin American rhythms, rock, folk, and popular music.

The world of sports has several outposts in Milwaukee. The **Milwaukee Brewers** make residents and visitors alike catch baseball fever at **Milwaukee County Stadium**. At the MECCA Arena, sports lovers can pick from the dazzling skating skills of the **Milwaukee Admirals** as they

compete in the IHL, or the home NBA games of the **Milwaukee Bucks** basketball team. The **Wisconsin State Fair Park Speedway** hosts five national championship races each year, and the **Green Bay Packers** play half their home games at Milwaukee County Stadium.

Amateur sportsmen and sportswomen have all varieties of outdoor facilities at their disposal in Milwaukee County. A **13,000-acre system of parks** provides for swimmers, tennis players, golfers, and skaters. **Downhill ski slopes** are available at three county parks, and cross-country trails can be found at six locations. **McKinley Marina** has boat-launching ramps which visitors can use on a fee basis, while **Grant Park** has an unimproved ramp available for free.

Emerald Isle Boatline and **Iroquois Boat tours** give visitors a chance to see the city from Lake Michigan.

The hungry tourist will find dozens of fine restaurants for snacks and scrumptious meals, but a few eateries that combine good dining with an unusual atmosphere deserve mention. The **Public Natatorium**, a restored 19th-century bathhouse, has continental cuisine and exotic dishes like Lion le Blanc. All tables overlook the antics taking place in a former bathhouse pool that now houses a trained dolphin show. **Karl Ratzsch's** is a classic German restaurant, whose waitresses wear lovely embroidered costumes, while a string trio soothes the dining crowd. Roast goose and liver dumpling soup are just two of the delightful menu items. About 16 miles outside the city is the **Woolen Mill Inn** in Cedarburg. Fresh baked goods add a homey touch to the hearty family fare.

BEST TIMES TO VISIT: Summer, fall, winter.

TRAVEL TIPS: Keep in mind the great variety of activities available here while you pack your wardrobe.

HOURS AND ADMISSION: Old World Third Street—most shops closed Sundays. Mader's Famous Restaurant — closed Monday; call 271-3377. Miller Brewing Company — 931-2153; closed Sunday and holidays. Pabst Brewing Company — 347-7328; hourly tours, call for times. Pabst Mansion—closed most major holidays; call for hours, 931-0808. Milwaukee Public Museum— 278-2700; open daily 9 a.m.-5 p.m., admission fee. Milwaukee County Zoo—open every day but New Year's, Thanksgiving, and Christmas; May-Labor Day, weekdays 9 a.m.-5 p.m., Sundays 9 a.m-6 p.m., rest of year daily 9 a.m.-4:30 p.m.; admission fee. Mitchell Park Conservatory (Domes)—summer hours, Saturday to Thursday 9 a.m.-8 p.m., Friday 9 a.m.-5 p.m.; Labor Day to Memorial Day, Monday to Friday 9 a.m.-5 p.m., Saturday and Sunday 9 a.m.-8 p.m. Milwaukee Art Museum — open Tuesday, Wednesday, Friday, Saturday 10 a.m.-5 p.m., Thursday noon-9 p.m., Sunday 1 p.m.-6 p.m., closed Monday; admission fee.

DIRECTIONS: From Chicago, take I-94 west to Milwaukee. From Green Bay, take I-43 south to Milwaukee. From Madison, take I-94 east to Milwaukee.

FOR MORE INFORMATION: Greater Milwaukee Convention and Visitors Bureau, 756 N. Milwaukee St., Milwaukee, WI 53202, (414) 278-2700. Its visitors' guide gives a very complete list of accommodations, shops, museums, and more.

Milwaukee's Music-Filled Summerfest

Milwaukee, Wisconsin

The Summerfest has become an exciting facet of Milwaukee's summer since it began in the late 1960s. The promoters of the 12-day festival in early July like to sum it up this way: "Music, food, music, dancing, music, fun, music." For families, a one-day excursion to Summerfest is well worth it.

The events take place along Milwaukee's lakefront, on grounds that the city has improved every year since the event's beginning. Landscaping and permanent structures have been added to make the site more appealing. It now resembles a village with paved streets, small cafes and arts and crafts shops. The facades are painted colorfully and more than 100,000 flowers planted.

One of the most important new additions for families is the **children's play area**, with swings, slides and a timerform tower — which has become one of the most popular features of the grounds. Also added were **Thrill-a-Minute Circus**, sports activities, comedy cabaret and folk stage.

Since its inception, the festival's staple has been **music**, which comes in all styles. Jazz, rock, pop, country, folk, bluegrass, symphony — there's something for every taste. Big-name acts are booked into the Summerfest every year. But to make sure you and your family see the acts you like, it's best to call or write ahead for the Summerfest schedule (see information that follows).

No one goes hungry at the Summerfest, either, There's **a wide variety of food** at rather reasonable prices, including the German fare that makes Milwaukee famous. But whether it's weinerschnitzel, sauerkraut, bratwurst, German potato salad — or fried fish, chicken, and tacos — you'll find what you want.

For all the attractions, the excitement of the Summerfest itself rates high. A few years ago promoters took a poll, asking fest-goers their favorite attraction: music ranked first, and "people-watching" second!

FOR MORE INFORMATION: Call the Greater Milwaukee Convention & Visitors Bureau, (414) 273-3950, or write the Bureau at 756 N. Milwaukee St., Milwaukee, WI 53202. **ADMISSION:** Adults, $5 (1983 prices), or $4 in advance; children, free when accompanied by adult in daytime hours, 50¢ each other times. Persons 60 and over, $1. **DIRECTIONS:** *From the west,* take I-94 east to I-794 exit and exit at the Civic Center/7th St. or Plankinton Ave. Continue east on St. Paul Ave. to Milwaukee St. and follow signs to Summerfest. *From the north:* take I-43 to I-794, follow preceding instructions from there. *From the south:* take I-94 north to the National Ave. exit, go east (right) to 1st St. Turn north (left) to Polk St.

Other Great Festivals In Milwaukee

MID-JUNE: Juneteenth Day, North Third Street, Milwaukee. Celebration of black culture, including arts and crafts, entertainment, food.

MID-JUNE: Lakefront Festival of Arts, Milwaukee Art Museum, on Lake Michigan. The Friends of Art of the Milwaukee Art Museum put on a weekend of concerts, art and family fun.

JULY: Greek Festivals, Annunciation Greek Orthodox Church and Sts. Constantine and Helen Greek Orthodox Church, Milwaukee, with orchestras, dancing, food and fun.

EARLY AUGUST: Wisconsin State Fair, State Fair Park in West Allis. Agriculture and food exhibits, music, top-name grandstand entertainment and a new midway make this one of the Midwest's top fairs.

MID-AUGUST: German Fest, Summerfest grounds, Milwaukee. German-American groups bring traditional music, dancing and culture, along with Old World foods, to Milwaukee in an event that adds to a great late-summer weekend.

LATE AUGUST: Irish Fest, Summerfest grounds, Milwaukee. Three days of Irish performers, Irish folk dancing, foods and activities for families.

LATE AUGUST: Fiesta Mexicana, Summerfest grounds, Milwaukee. Mexican music, crafts, dancing, cultural displays.

EARLY SEPTEMBER: Polish Fest, Summerfest grounds, Milwaukee. A four-day celebration of the music, dancing, food and traditions of Poland, including many exhibits.

THROUGH SEPTEMBER, WEEKENDS: Oktoberfest, Old Heidelberg Park, Glendale.

Wisconsin

An Arts and Crafts Village In an Old Cornish Miner's Town

Mineral Point, Wisconsin

Driving Time: 3½ hours north of Chicago; 2½ hours north of Milwaukee; 5 hours southeast of Minneapolis/St. Paul

At **Mineral Point, Wisconsin**, a craftsman fashions metal sculptures in a restored 19th-century blacksmith shop. A furnace once used for iron founding is now the tool of a glass blower, and cottages that once served as homes for Cornish miners are today a major historical attraction in Wisconsin's **Hidden Valley** region.

Mineral Point was a boomtown when workers wrenched lead ore from the mine shafts that reached deep into the rock and soil there. From the late 1820s through the 1840s, New World settlers from Cornwall, England, poured into the town to reap their fortunes from mining life. They built stone houses or dug "badger dwellings" into the ground. Their wives made pasties and saffron cakes to eat, and called them to meals by shaking rags out the door as a signal.

Today, some Mineral Point residents live in restored cottages still standing from those days, and visitors can tour the only surviving mine shaft, the **Merry Christmas Mine**. Cornish delights are part of the fare at restaurants like the **Walker House**, once a hotel for railroad workers. The State Historical Society offers tours of **Pendarvis**, a restoration project that includes a one-story cottage,

two- and three-story stone structures, log houses, and a kiddlywink, or old-time pub. The **Gundry House** serves as an example of a Victorian businessman's dwelling, complete with furnishings and mineral exhibits.

Shake Rag Alley displays more of life in the mid-1800s. There, visitors can see a quarry, a collection of mining tools, a hundred-year-old pottery, and **Ellery House**, the home of Mineral Point's cabinetmaker for three generations. Shake Rag Alley surrounds **Federal Spring**, where early settlers got all their water. Lovely landscaping and colorful flowers add to the beauty of this historic site.

Dozens of Mineral Point residents carry on the craft traditions of yesteryear. Lovers of handmade goods will be amazed by the orignal work of potters, weavers, jewelers, woodworkers, painters, and ceramic sculptors that can be found throughout the town in shops or in the homes of the artisans. The **Looms Weaving School and Gallery**, with its impressive collection of antique textiles and tools, gives demonstrations of spinning and weaving.

About seven miles north of Mineral Point is Dodgeville, home of the **Don Q Inn**, a 1914 barn that's been converted into a first-class supper club and motel. On the grounds at

Don Q is a flying museum and a 67-foot sculpture made of steel wagon wheels. A July series of **symphony concerts** is offered annually in the Dodgeville area, and a free **Corn Festival** celebrates the August harvest in Cobb, just 10 miles west of Dodgeville.

The **House on a Rock** is another major attraction in this area. Ten miles north of Dodgeville, this fascinating structure overlooks a spectacular view of the Hidden Valleys. Collections of stained-glass lamps, dolls, and music machines provide endless amusement for visitors. (See "House on a Rock" in this section.)

The outdoor enthusiast can enjoy the sandstone bluffs, deep valley, and sparkling lakes of **Governor Dodge State Park**, just north of Dodgeville on Route 23. Fishing, swimming, and boating are available here. Farther west, **Blackhawk Lake** has spacious camping sites, prime fishing spots, and sandy swimming beaches.

BEST TIMES TO VISIT: Summer, fall.

TRAVEL TIPS: Campsites are plentiful at Governor Dodge State Park, Blackhawk Lake, and private campgrounds. There are several motels in Mineral Point and Dodgeville, but an unusual lodging experience is available through Historic Retreats, Dodgeville, WI 53855.

HOURS: Shake Rag Alley tours — May-October, 10 a.m.-5 p.m. Pendarvis tours — May-October, 9 a.m.-5 p.m. Gundry House — Memorial Day-Labor Day, 10 a.m.-5 p.m. The Looms — May-October, 10 a.m.-5 p.m. The Foundry — May-October, 10 a.m.-noon and 1 p.m.-5 p.m. House on a Rock — 8 a.m.-one hour before dusk.

ADMISSION: Call for information.

DIRECTIONS: From Chicago, take I-90 west to Madison, then U.S. 18 west to Dodgeville, then U.S. 151 south to Mineral Point. From Milwaukee, take I-94 west to Madison, then follow preceding directions. From Minneapolis, take I-90/94 east to Madison, then follow above directions.

FOR MORE INFORMATION: House on a Rock, Spring Green, WI 53588. Shake Rag Alley, 18 Shake Rag St., Mineral Point WI 53465, (608) 249-0492. Don Q Inn, Box 199, Highway 23 North, Dodgeville, WI 53533, (608) 935-2321; toll-free in Wisconsin, (800) 242-2321, out-of-state, (800) 362-2950. Pendarvis, 114 Shake Rag St., Mineral Point, WI 53565, (608) 987-2122. Walker House, I Water St., Mineral Point, WI 53565, (608) 987-2788. Governor Dodge State Park, Dodgeville, WI 53533, (608) 935-2315. Dodgeville Chamber of Commerce, Box 70, Dodgeville, WI 53533, (608) 935-3151. Mineral Point Chamber of Commerce, 114 High St., Mineral Point, WI 53565, (608) 987-3707.

Wisconsin

Prairie du Chien: Historic and Scenic River Romp

Prairie du Chien, Wisconsin

Driving Time: 3 hours northwest of Chicago; 4 hours west of Milwaukee, 4 hours southeast of Minneapolis/St. Paul

This second-oldest European settlement in Wisconsin dates back 300 years, when French explorers Marquette and Joliet discovered the Mississippi River here.

Located where the Wisconsin River and the Mississippi meet in the southwestern corner of the state, **Prairie du Chien** is not only steeped in history but is also on the threshold of the Mississippi's most spectacular stretch as well.

The **Great River Road**, a network of roads and highways that most closely parallels the Mississippi, is at its best from Prairie du Chien northwest to Minneapolis/St. Paul. Great bluffs rise from the river's edge on both sides. The water winds back and forth from flood plain to rocky bluff, providing truly scenic thrills. And riverboat rides are available on the *Mississippi Queen* and the *Delta Queen*.

Men like Jefferson Davis, president of the Confederacy, and Zachary Taylor, 12th president of the United States, were once stationed at **Fort Crawford**, which currently houses the **Museum of Medical Progress** and the **Stovall Hall of Health**. Part of the museum contains relics of 19th-century medicine in Wisconsin, including displays of Indian herbal remedies, a reconstructed 1890s pharmacy, and dentist and physician's offices. Visitors to the Stovall Hall of Health can learn about their bodies from the Transparent Twins, life-sized, plastic female models, one showing 25 organs of the body and the other the 200-bone skeleton and the nervous system.

Villa Louis, off U.S. 18, is a lavish 19th-century mansion on historic St. Feriole Island. Originally owned by Col. H.L. Dousman, a fur trader and Wisconsin's first millionaire, the building still contains most of the original furnishings. Costumed guides conduct tours through the house from May through November.

Seven milles southeast on U.S. 18 lies **Wyalusing State Park**, where valleys, caves, waterfalls, and springs create a lovely view. Head six miles southeast on U.S. 18, then nine miles northeast on Route 60 to see **Kickapoo Indian Caverns**, where there's a centuries-old Indian skeleton, a Native American museum, relics of prehistoric man, and Indian handicrafts.

Thirty-five miles south via U.S. 18, Route 35, and Route 133, in Nelson Dewey State Park, rests **Stonefield**, a rock-studded, 2,000-acre farm established on the bluffs of the Mississippi River. **State Farm Crafts Museum** contains an interesting display of farm machinery. Your family can also take a horse-drawn carriage ride over a covered bridge to the reconstructed 1890 Stonefield Village, which has a blacksmith shop, a print shop, a general store, a school, a church, and 26 other buildings.

About 20 miles along the river at Potosi, visitors can take a tour of the **St. John Mine**. This lead ore mine follows natural caverns, some with stalactite-covered ceilings.

BEST TIME TO VISIT: Summer.

TRAVEL TIPS: Check out some of the area cheese factories located at nearby Fennimore, Lancaster, and Platteville.

HOURS: Museum of Medical Progress — open summer only; check locally for hours. Villa Louis — May-October, daily 9:30 a.m.-4:30 p.m. Stonefield Village — Memorial Day-Labor Day, daily 9 a.m.-5 p.m.; September-October, weekends. St. John Mine — tours, Memorial Day weekend-Labor Day, daily, 9 a.m.-5 p.m.; Labor Day-October, weekends 9 a.m.-5 p.m.

ADMISSION: Museum of Medical Progress — adults, $1; children 12 and under, 50¢. Villa Louis — adults, $3; children 5-17, $1; under 5, free. Stonefield Village — adults, $3.50; children 5-17, $1; under 5, free.

DIRECITONS: From Chicago, take I-90 to Madison, Wisconsin. From Madison, head east on U.S. 18 to Prairie du Chien. From Milwaukee, take I-94 west to Madison, then pick up Hwy. 18 west. From Minneapolis/St. Paul, take Minn. Hwy. 52 south to Rochester, I-90 east to La Crosse, Wis. Hwy. 35 south to Prairie du Chien.

FOR MORE INFORMATION: Call the Chamber of Commerce, (608) 326-8555, or write 211 S. Main St., Box 326, Prairie du Chien, WI 53821.

Wisconsin

Fun Near Wisconsin's Southern Gateway

Racine County, Wisconsin

Driving Time: 1½ hours from Chicago

Just across Wisconsin's southeast border with Illinois are several **Racine County** attractions that will fill a day-trip from Chicago with fun. Bring along your bicycles and a Racine county bike trail map (available at address listed below), and you can choose from 100 miles of roads with little traffic amidst rural scenery. Off-road trails with easy riding surfaces include the **Burlington Trail** along the Fox River and a five-mile route between Waterford and Wind Lake.

A drive into the city of Racine will be rewarded by a visit to **"Kringleville,"** the home of many Danish families who settled in the city. Kringle, an oval ring of pastry with pecans or other fillings, is the specialty of West Side bakeries like Lehmann's, Little Copenhagen, Bendtsen's, O & H, and Larsen's.

The **Wustum Museum of Fine Arts** in Racine is open seven days a week, free of charge. Special exhibits often feature regional artists. To learn more about Racine County's past, visitors can take a free trip through the **Racine County Historical Museum**. The architecture of Frank Lloyd Wright is a highlight of the **Johnson Wax Buildings**, and inside the Golden Rondelle Theatre there, free films like "The Living Planet," "To Fly," and "To Be Alive" offer good family entertainment.

Racine has sandy beaches and a harbor along Lake Michigan that allow for maximum summer enjoyment, while **Johnson Park** offers ice skating and cross-country skiing for winter sports lovers.

Call the Racine County tourist office for the dates of two of the area's biggest summer events: the **Salmon-a-Rama** and the **Kraut Festival**. During Salmon-a-Rama, thousands of fishermen compete for "The Big One." Even children are invited to try to hook the "Little Big One" at a small trout pond. Non-fishing visitors will find plenty to do at the festival's concerts, art fair, and sports show. The **Kraut Festival** in Franksville hosts the World Kraut Eating Championship, along with a dance and carnival.

North of Racine, along Seven Mile Road, an enormous **flea market** is set up during summer and fall months. At the Seven Mile Fair, visitors can find homecrafted decorations, antiques, fresh fruit, and much more. Parking is free. Ask local people for directions to **Quarry Lake Park** near Racine, where swimmers and snorkelers can enjoy the brisk, clear water.

In western Racine County, families can watch rural life at work with a trip to **Green Meadows Farm** near Waterford. Children help feed the animals and pick their own vegetables. The whole family can hop on a hayride in the fall, then pick free pumpkins from the fields. Meals and overnight accommodations are available for those who want the full flavor of farm life. A canoe trip along the Fox River can round out a trip to Waterford, with rentals from **Jim's Marina** on Milwaukee Street.

Just outside Racine County, west of Waterford, is the **East Troy Trolley Museum**. Railroad buffs will love the collections of electric railway locomotives, cars, and streetcars. Families can take a 10-mile ride on an electric trolley through the East Troy countryside.

BEST TIME TO VISIT: Summer.
HOURS: Wustum Museum—open daily, 1 p.m.-5 p.m., Monday and Thursday 1 p.m.-9 p.m.. Racine County Historical Museum—open Tuesday to Saturday 9 a.m.-5 p.m., Sunday 1 p.m.-5 p.m. Johnson'x Wax Golden Rondelle Theatre—call (414) 554-2154. Seven Mile Fair—summer months, Wednesday 8 a.m.-5 p.m., Saturday and Sunday 5 a.m.-5 p.m.; September and October, Saturday and Sunday only, 5 a.m.-5 p.m. Green Meadows Farm—contact Box 182, Waterford, WI 53185, or call (414) 534-2891. East Troy Trolley Museum—contact East Troy Depot, Box 726, East Troy, WI 53120, or call Milwaukee agent, (414) 332-7728.
DIRECTIONS: From Chicago, take I-94 west to Rt. 11 east into Racine. To Waterford and East Troy, exit I-94 at Rt. 20 and take 20 west into Waterford and East Troy.
FOR MORE INFORMATION: Racine Area Chamber of Commerce, Box 1526, Racine, WI 53403, (414) 633-2451; Racine County Tourism, 14200 Washington Ave., Sturtevant WI 53177, (414) 886-3366; East Troy Chamber of Commerce, 2085 Division St., East Troy, WI 53120, (414) 642-5271.

Racine is the "Capital of Kringles," which are Danish pastries.

A House Built On A Rock

Driving Time: About 4 hours northwest of Chicago, 6 hours east of the Twin Cities

Spring Green, Wisconsin

High atop Deershelter Rock, overlooking the breath-taking Wyoming Valley, is the world famous House on the Rock. Architect Alex Jordan began building it in the early 1940s, seeking to create a structure that would blend perfectly with it's lofty surroundings. He started the job by carrying stone and mortar in baskets to the top of the huge chimney-like rock, which rises 450 ft. above the valley!

The first room built was a studio workshop with a gigantic fireplace.

In the years since, this amazing house has grown to 13 rooms, each on a different level. From a distance the house appears to be part of this magnificent rock. Inside, the house is even more amazing: in every nook and cranny there is natural wood, stone, lush greenery and crystal-clear waterfalls.

But there is much more to see at House on the Rock. Visitors may cross the flying bridge to the Mill House, a mini-museum of antiques and unusual objects, such as suits of armor, dolls, and music machines from around the world.

The "Street of Yesterday" is next. The red-brick, 1880-style street lined with gas lamps features shops and quaint buildings of a bygone era: a Fire Station, Clock Shop, Woodcarver's Shop, Barber Shop, Toy Shop, Import Shop and an elegant home and carriage house.

The street resounds with melodies from the grand Gladiator Calliope, a musical wonder. And Esmerelda, the gypsy fortune teller, might reveal a secret or two about your future.

And a few miles away on Hwy. 23 is another artistic wonder, Taliesen, the summer home of famed architect Frank Lloyd Wright, where summer tours may be arranged. You might eat at the Spring Green Restaurant (2 miles south of Spring Green on Hwy. 23), which was designed by Frank Lloyd Wright. If you decide to stay overnight, the Hayloft Lodge (1 mile north of town on Rt. 14) is also close by.

HOURS: House on the Rock: 9 a.m. to dark, April through November; closed December through March. Taliesen Fellowship Buildings: 10 a.m. to 4 p.m., daily, early June through Labor Day.

ADMISSION: House on the Rock: Adults, $5; Children 7 to 12 yrs., $2.50; Children 4 to 6 yrs., $1; Children 3 yrs. and under free. Taliesen Fellowship Buildings, $3.

FOR MORE INFORMATION: Call the House on the Rock, (608)935-3639, or Taliesen, (608)588-2511.

DIRECTIONS: From Chicago, take I-90 northwest to Madison. Take Hwy. 12-18 west and pick up Rt. 14 west into Spring Green.

Wisconsin

A Family Playground— On the Water

Driving Time: 6 hours east of Minneapolis/St Paul; 5 hours northwest of Chicago

Wisconsin Dells, Wisconsin

Indian ceremonials, water ski shows, and breathtaking natural beauty are only a few of the attractions that make the Wisconsin Dells one of the Midwest's most popular family vacation spots. Clustered around the scenic shores of the Dells and Lake Delton are opportunities galore for adventure, excitement and lively entertainment.

One of the favorite performances is the **Tommy Bartlett Water Ski, Sky and Stage Show** on Lake Delton, where you'll see daring water ski and motorboat acts, trampoline artists, Aqua the Clown, and more. Another fascinating show is the **Stand Rock Indian Ceremonial**, featuring native songs, dances and stories performed and produced by the Dells Winnebago Indians. And if you're a country music fan, don't miss the **Wisconsin Opry**.

Younger family members will want to visit the summer wonderland of **Storybook Gardens**, where you'll see beautiful displays, ride on a mini-slide and train, and talk with live story-book characters. **Riverview Park** offers a variety of more than 20 rides, including Wisconsin's largest steel rollercoaster. You may want to take home a souvenir from the old-fashioned shops, candy kitchens or gift stores.

For auto buffs, there is the **Dells Auto Museum** displaying vintage autos from the early 20th century. Moms

and daughters are sure to enjoy the antique doll and toy collections there. And for a truly horrifying experience, visit the **Haunted Mansion or Future World**, a haunted house of the future. The spectacular **Xanadu** offers a real trip into the years ahead—a house of tomorrow built of 12 white polyurethane foam domes. Adults will marvel at the architectural innovations and children will delight in the maze of the Swiss Cheese playhouse.

Fascinating Indian artifacts are displayed at the **Winnebago Public Indian Museum** and **Parson's Indian Museum**. The Winnebago Museum has the nation's largest Indian-owned collection of relics, including ancient hunting, fishing and household items—some dating back 7,000 years. Also, souvenirs of the Battle of Little Big Horn and the Wounded Knee Massacre.

Finally, the natural beauty of the Dells area will come alive during a ride on a sea plane or the original **Wisconsin Ducks**, taking you over wooded trails and then splashing into the glistening waters of the Wisconsin River.

There are numerous motels in the area; you might try the **Chula Vista Resort** or **Birchcliff Lodge** (both on River Rd., Wisconsin Dells), or **Indian Trail** (1013 E. Broadway, Wisconsin Dells).

HOURS: Most attractions are open daily during June, July and August.
FOR MORE INFORMATION: Call the Wisconsin Dells Chamber of Commerce, (414) 254-4321 or (414) 254-8088.
DIRECTIONS: From Twin Cities, take I-94 east and south to Wisconsin Dells exits (Hwy. 12-16 or Hwy. 23).

Golf Greens, Fish-Filled Lakes at a Restful Resort

Green Lake, Wisconsin

Driving Time: 3½ hours from Chicago; 1½ hours from Milwaukee; 4 hours from Minneapolis/St. Paul

Green Lake, Wisconsin, is a resort community of classic style. Designed as a vacation spot for those who enjoy comfort and perhaps even luxury, the region is a haven for golfers, swimmers, boaters, fishermen, and hunters.

Prize trout and muskie are plentiful in the many lakes that grace the area. **Green Lake**, whose 237-foot depth makes it the deepest in the state, is a favorite spot for those who love a fishing challenge. The lake's clear waters are also a joy for the swimmer and the water skiier, and on many summer days, yachts glide across its 18-square-mile surface in full sailing regalia.

Back on land, golfers are in their element here with three well-groomed 18-hole courses, including one of the Midwest's most difficult and one of Wisconsin's most established. **Lawsonia Links** is widely known for its 91 traps and the steep elevation of nearly all of its greens, conditions that energize those who love a demanding game.

Another important feature of the Green Lake region is a type of terrain called **"wet lands."** Wild game abound in the ideal cover these areas provide. The hunter will have a field day trying to outsmart deer, pheasant, rabbit, geese, and other small game, while the trapper tries to coax beaver, mink, and fox from their lairs.

Summer is not the only time to enjoy Green Lake. Cross-country ski touring, ice fishing, and the peace of rural winter are major attractions for those who love an escape into snow-covered surroundings.

BEST TIME TO VISIT: Summer, although there are special winter attractions. Make your summer plans several months in advance.

ANNUAL EVENTS: June — American Legion Trout Boil; July — Wisconsin Grand Prix of Bicycle Races; late July — Green Lake County Free Fair; early August — Green Lake Chamber of Commerce Juried Art Fair; mid-August — Legion Trout Boil; September — Texas Chili Cookoff; October — Gene Edward Pro Am golf tournament; mid-October — Legion Trout Boil; February — Lions Club Fisheree; February — Antique Snowmobile Derby.

OTHER ATTRACTIONS: Camping, cross-country skiing, hayrides at Green Lake Center on Highway 23, open 8 a.m.-4:30 p.m., (414) 294-3323. Horseback riding, late April to early October at Lazy L Riding Stable, Route 2, (414) 295-3163.

DIRECTIONS: From Chicago, take I-94 to Milwaukee, then U.S. 41 to Fond du Lac, then Wis. 23 to Green Lake. From Minneapolis, take I-94 east to Mauston, then east on Wis. 82 until it connects with 23 east to Green Lake.

FOR MORE INFORMATION: Write or call Green Lake Area Chamber of Commerce, Box 386, Green Lake, WI 54941, (414) 294-3231. Get the annual Green Lake guide from Charles Bruce Heydon, Box 491, Green Lake, WI 54941. Heidel House, Box 537, Illinois Ave., Green Lake, WI 54941, (414) 294-3344.

Wilderness Wonderland: Blackhawk Ridge

Sauk City, Wisconsin

Driving Time: 3½ hours from Chicago; 2 hours from Milwaukee; 5 hours from Minneapolis/St. Paul.

A resort where families can enjoy the quiet sports, **Blackhawk Ridge** makes the best of its location along the Wisconsin River in Sauk City. Visitors can find acommodations there ranging from wilderness camping in tents or tent trailers to cabins, log houses, and modern apartment-style lodging.

Whether your family stays here or at a nearby country motel, you can use Blackhawk Ridge's recreational facilities on a fee basis. Its 600 acres have 25 miles of bridle paths for guided horseback riding. A two-hour "breakfast trail ride" includes a meal of sausage, eggs, biscuits, and coffee; the dinner ride features steak and potatoes over an open fire. The Blackhawk canoe base sits on the Wisconsin River below the last dam and dangerous eddies, making it a safe spot for the beginning canoeist. Canoe rental includes a shuttle service.

BEST TIMES TO VISIT: Spring, summer, winter.

DIRECTIONS: From Chicago, take I-90 west to Madison, then I-90/94 west to Rt. 60 west; take 60 west into Sauk City. From Milwaukee, take I-94 west to Madison and follow the preceding directions from there. From Minneapolis/St. Paul, take I-94 east, exit at U.S. 12, take 12 south to Rt. 60 east, and take 60 east into Sauk City.

FOR MORE INFORMATION: Call or write to Blackhawk Ridge, Box 92, Sauk City, WI 53583, (608) 643-3775; toll-free from Madison, (800) 767-3781.

Wisconsin

Festivals: All Seasons

Wisconsin

EARLY SEPTEMBER: WILLIAM TELL CELEBRATION, New Glaurus, tells the story in song and dance of the Swiss people's struggle for independence; includes ethnic entertainment, street dances, and an art show, with lots of good food, too. Call (608) 527-2921.

EARLY SEPTEMBER: CHEESE FESTIVAL, Blair, is a four-day celebration of the product that sustains the area's industry, with fiddling, tractor pulls, art exhibits and a beer garden. Call (715) 834-2781.

EARLY SEPTEMBER: RUSTIC LORE DAYS, Glenwood City, with displays of engines, arts and crafts, turkey shoots, parades and an outdoor roast of good country cooking. Call (715) 834-2781.

MID-SEPTEMBER: WINE AND HARVEST FESTIVALS, Cedarburg, 17 miles north of Milwaukee (just west of I-43). Ever wonder how they get the juice from grapes when they make wine? They'll show you one way to do it in this city's annual grape-stomping contest, a lively affair in which contestants are judged on the basis of fancy footwork and zany costumes. It begins Friday evening with a fish boil in the city park, continues Saturday with a farmer's market, art fair, ice cream social and the grape-stomping at the Stone Mill Winery, with more fun on Sunday. Call (414) 377-8020.

MID-SEPTEMBER: GOLDEN HARVEST FESTIVAL, Bainbridge, with visits to covered bridges and such good-old-days entertainment as hog-calling contests, three-legged races, square dances, fiddlers' competition. Call (715) 356-5266.

LATE SEPTEMBER: CHEESE DAYS, Monroe, 32 miles west of Janesville, off U.S. 81, 250 miles northwest of Chicago. The star attraction is cheese, so if you don't like it you might want to stay home. It opens on Friday night with a Cheese Ball and a cheese social, continues Saturday with an art fair, cheese factory tours, a parade, lots of entertainment through the day, and a Cheesemakers Ball on Saturday night. If you're not exhausted by Sunday, they hold a tour of historic homes, a carnival with tons of food, and tours of Idle Hour Mansion, an historic home that has been turned into a museum. All but the balls are free. Call (608) 325-3739.

MID-OCTOBER: DOOR COUNTY FALL FESTIVAL, Sister Bay, off Wis. Hwy. 42 at Wis. Hwy. 57, 270 miles north of Chicago. Picturesque Door County packs 'em in for a three-day streetfest, including a fish boil, parade, antiques auction, carnival, crafts show and the like. Admission is free. Call (414) 854-2812.

IOWA

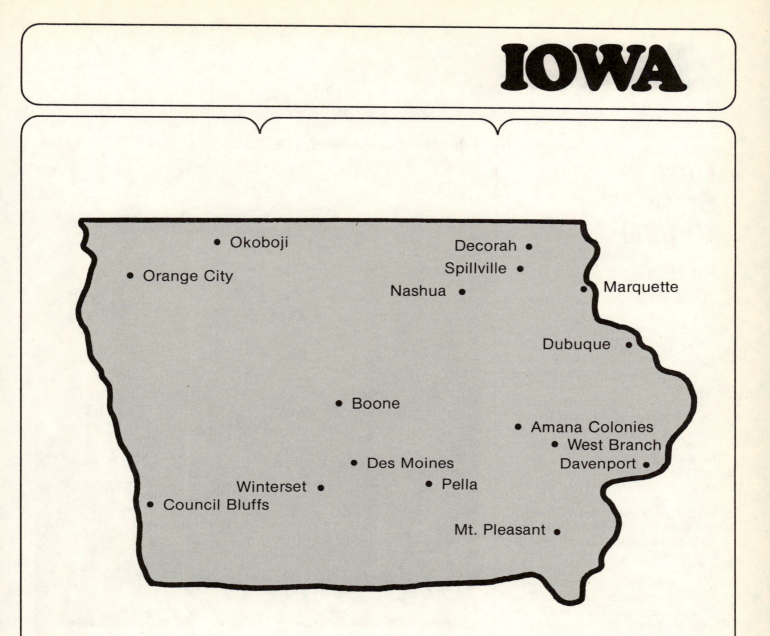

- Okoboji
- Orange City
- Decorah
- Spillville
- Nashua
- Marquette
- Dubuque
- Boone
- Amana Colonies
- West Branch
- Davenport
- Des Moines
- Winterset
- Pella
- Council Bluffs
- Mt. Pleasant

Iowa Vacations

Iowa's State Capital

Des Moines, Iowa

Driving Time: 2 hours from Iowa City

The largest city in Iowa, Des Moines offers a blend of historical, political, and educational sites and activities.

Rising 60 feet on the east bank of the Des Moines River is the dome of the city's **Botanical Center**. Nearly 1,000 species of plants from around the world are on display here. Trails lead past seasonal floral displays, an award-winning Bonsai collection, and a unique grouping of cacti.

The **Des Moines Art Center** has permanent displays of 19th- and 20th-century paintings and sculpture, as well as a variety of changing exhibits.

Children will love the hands-on learning experiences at the **Des Moines Center of Science and Industry**. The activity-oriented displays include a model railroad, computers, live animal exhibits, and planetarium shows.

At the **Living History Farms**, your family can experience farming as it was done by the pioneers. This 600-acre living agricultural museum features four farms: the **Ioway Indian Settlement of 1870**, displaying crops, homes, and skills of the Ioway Indians; the **Pioneer Farm of 1840**, including a log cabin and demonstrating early methods of farming; the **Horse-Powered Farm of 1900**, featuring farm life of that period; and the **Farm of Today and Tomorrow**, which is under construction. In addition, the **Living Farm** offers a town complete with old-time shops and an 1870 schoolhouse. On weekends, this

Iowa State Capitol building in Des Moines

is the site of various activities and special events, including music festivals and craft shows.

This prairie metropolis is home to many historic buildings, but none more unique than the English castle known as **Salisbury House**. An exact replica of a 42-room manor in Salisbury, England, the house is furnished in the Tudor style. Beautifully situated on 11 acres of woodland, Salisbury House is now the official residence of the Iowa State Education Association.

Another historic home is **Terrace Hill**, a Victorian mansion that is now the residence of the state's governor. The house, built in 1869 in the Second Empire style, is a recognized historic site.

No trip to Des Moines would be complete without a visit to the **State Capitol Building** and the **State Historical Building and Museum**. The State Capitol Building, a favorite spot with tourists, is readily identifiable by its large golden dome surrounded by four smaller domes. The building houses state offices, the **Supreme Court**, and the **Iowa House and Senate**. The State Historical Building and Museum, located across from the Capitol Building, contains a historical library, newspaper depository, census library, state historic museum, and the state archives.

If your interest lies more in buying antiques than just looking at them, stop by **Valley Junction**, located in West Des Moines, where you'll find

Iowa

one of the state's largest collections of antique and craft shops.

For a change of pace, your family might enjoy a trip to **Adventureland**, an amusement park located just outside of town. The offerings include separate theme areas, stage shows, a giant roller coaster, and 25 other rides.

Each year Des Moines is the site of many festivals and special events. Among them are the **Drake University Track Relays**, an officially sanctioned meet that provides a showcase for collegiate atheletes hoping to make the U.S. Olympic team, and the **Iowa State Fair**, one of the largest agricultural state fairs in the country. The fair's main attractions include name entertainment, horse shows, farm machinery exhibits, and a giant midway.

BEST TIME TO VISIT: Spring and summer.

HOURS: Botanical Center — 10:00 a.m.-6:00 p.m. Monday-Thrusday; 10:00 a.m.-9:00

6:00 p.m. Monday-Thursday; 10:00 a.m.-9:00 p.m. Friday; 10:00 a.m.-5:00 p.m. Saturday, Sunday, and holidays; closed Christmas, New Year's, and Thanksgiving. Art Center — 11:00 a.m.-5:00 p.m. Tuesday-Saturday; 12:00 p.m.-5:00 p.m. Sunday; closed Monday. Center of Science and Industry — 10:00 a.m.-5:00 p.m. Monday-Saturday; 1:00 p.m.-5:00 p.m. Sunday. Living History Farms — 9:00 a.m.-5:00 p.m. Monday-Saturday; 12:00 noon-6:00 p.m. Sunday; April 11-October 30. Salisbury House — tours may be scheduled 8:00 a.m.-4:30 p.m. Monday-Friday. Terrace Hill — 10:00 a.m.-2:00 p.m. Monday-Thursday; 1:00 p.m.-5:00 p.m. Sunday; closed legal holidays and during January and February. State Capitol Building — tours 8:00 a.m.-4:30 p.m. Monday-Friday, 8:00 a.m.-4:00 p.m. on weekends and holidays; no tours during June-August. State Historical Building and Museum — 8:00 a.m.-4:00 p.m. daily. Adventureland Park—weekends, April 30-May 26; daily May 27-August 28; weekends, until October 2. Valley Junction — 9:30 a.m.-5:00 p.m. Monday-Saturday. Drake University Track Relays — April 29-30. Iowa State Fair — August 10-20.

ADMISSION: Botanical Center — adults, 50¢; children 6 and over, 25¢; children under 6, free; student and senior citizen discounts available. Center of Science and Industry — adults, $3.00; children and senior citizens, $1.00. Living History Farms — adults, $5.00; senior citizens, $4.00; children, $3.00. Salisbury House — 12 and up, $1.00. Adventureland Park — 12 and up, $9.95; 4-11, $8.95; under 3, free; senior citizens, $6.95.

DIRECTIONS: From Iowa City, take I-80 west to Des Moines.

FOR MORE INFORMATION: Call the Des Moines Convention and Visitors Bureau, (515) 286-4960, or write Tourism Department, 800 High St., Des Moines, IA.

Living History Farms, Des Moines

Botanical Center, Des Moines

Historic Trading Center

Council Bluffs, Iowa

Driving Time: 2½ hours west of Des Moines

Council Bluffs has always been one of the country's leading trading centers, linking east with west, first by river and then by rail. Because of the important part it played in the development of the west, this city offers its visitors a number of sites of historic interest.

An appropriate beginning to any tour of this trading center is the **Lewis and Clark Monument**. Sitting high on the bluffs, the monument's stone marker depicts Lewis and Clark holding council with the Indians. The famed explorers, like the trappers and traders who followed, camped near here in 1804.

The **Pottawattamie County Jail** is a tribute to man's ingenuity. Built in 1855, this facility is one of the last remaining examples of the rotary or squirrel cage jails in the Midwest. Inside the jail is a three-story drum enclosed by a metal cage. There are three decks in the drum, each divided into 10 separate cells. Designed for efficiency, this revolving drum allows one man to guard more than 30 inmates.

Moving from the practical to the extravagant, it's time to tour the historic **General Dodge House**. This lavish home was built in 1869 by Grenville Dodge, the chief construction engineer for the Union Pacific Railroad and a former Civil War general. Carefully restored to its Victorian charm, the house has been designated a national landmark.

One-half hour north of Council Bluffs is the **DeSota Bend National Wildlife Refuge**, home to migrating geese and ducks. Late spring and early fall are ideal times for bird-

General Dodge House, Council Bluffs

watching. Your family may also get a glimpse of nesting bald eagles or some of the many other animals that inhabit the area. Here, too, are artifacts from the recently discovered steamboat, *Bertrand*. Excavation of the 100-year-old riverboat began a few years ago, after it was discovered buried under the Mississippi mud.

From September 2-5, Council Bluffs comes alive with the knee-slapping sounds of the frontier, during the **Old-Time Country Music Contest and Pioneer Exposition**. Although there is a list of scheduled events, the real excitement comes in the form of spontaneous music contests. Be sure to bring a lawn chair, as you'll want to move from place to place until you find music to suit your taste.

BEST TIME TO VISIT: Early fall.

HOURS: Pottawattamie County Jail — 1:00 p.m.-5:00 p.m. Saturday and Sunday, other times by appointment; closed holidays, January, and February. General Dodge House — 10:00 a.m.-5:00 p.m. Tuesday- Saturday, 1:00 p.m.-5:00 p.m. Sunday; closed Monday and January; night tours by appointment.

ADMISSION: Pottawattamie County Jail — adults, $1.00; children, 50¢. General Dodge House — adults, $3.00; children 6-16, $1.00; children under 6, free.

DIRECTIONS: From Des Moines, take I-80 west to Council Bluffs.

FOR MORE INFORMATION: Call the Council Bluffs Chamber of Commerce, (712) 325-1000, or write Suite 506, First Federal Savings and Loan Bldg., Box 1565, Council Bluffs, IA 51501.

Historic Town on the Mississippi

Dubuque, Iowa

Driving Time: 1½ hours east of Waterloo

Dubuque, Iowa's oldest city, was named for French Canadian Julien DuBuque, who founded it in 1788. From its humble mining and river town beginnings, it has grown to be the major Midwestern industrial center it is today. The people of Dubuque, proud of their city's history, are taking an active role in preserving and restoring their heritage. As a result, Dubuque offers a wealth of historic sites and buildings to visit.

There's no better way to start your tour than with the panoramic view of the city provided by the **Fenelon Place Elevator**. Grab a cable car downtown for a trip to the top of the bluffs and the three-state view. Operating since 1882, the elevator was built by a Dubuque banker to provide him with transportation from his hillside home to his place of business.

Once the ride is over, take a moment to browse through the unusual antique and craft shops in **Cable Car Square**. It's the perfect place to pick up a postcard or gift for someone back home.

After you've completed your shopping, head for the river. Tours of the **Port of Dubuque** provide visitors with historical information about the upper Mississippi while allowing them to see a modern river port in action. Located in the port's million-dollar complex is the **Upper Mississippi Riverboat Museum** and — the kids will love this — the *William M. Black*, one of the last steam-powered sidewheelers.

Old Shot Tower, in Dubuque, once used for molding lead shot

After completing the port tour, experience the excitement of life on the river by taking a ride on an authentic sternwheeler, the *Spirit of Dubuque*. Propelled by a paddlewheel, this 377-passenger riverboat offers afternoon excursions as well as romantic dinner cruises.

When it's time to eat, choose from one of the many elegant and historic houses that have been converted into popular restaurants and gathering places. The **Ryan House**, built in 1873 in the Italian villa style, has been turned into a fine restaurant, while the **Redstone**, a Queen Anne-style home once owned by wagonmaster August Cooper, is now a popular night spot.

Travelers who savor a touch of mystery may find the **Ham House Museum** intriguing. Many legends surround this 23-room mansion, built by Mathias Ham in 1857. Some say it is haunted, others link it to stories of murder, river pirates, and whiskey smugglers. Step into the past in rooms decorated in the Victorian style, or trace the city's beginnings through exhibits on early Dubuque history.

Those interested in art and architecture won't want to miss the **Old Jail Art Gallery**. This is the last known example of Egyptian Revival architecture in the country. The jail's cell block, dungeon, and exercise yard have been converted into artist studios and a gallery.

For a change of pace, take your family to visit **Crystal Lake Cave**, a glittering network of passages cut by underground streams. Here are anthodites or cave flowers, found in only one other cave in the country. The kids will enjoy wandering through the illuminated passageways which highlight the beautiful stalactites, stalagmites, and a small underground lake.

In June, the city celebrates its historical heritage with its three-day **Dubuquefest**. Music, food, and dance provide a lively backdrop to planned activities, including a parade, farmers' market, historical house tour, and water-thrill show.

BEST TIME TO VISIT: Early summer.
HOURS: Fenelon Place Elevator — daily, April-November. Port of Dubuque — 10:00 a.m.-6:00 p.m. daily, May 1-October 31. Ryan House — lunch, 11:30 a.m.-1:30 p.m. Monday-Friday; dinner, 6:00 p.m.-9:00 p.m. Tuesday-Thursday, 6:00-10:00 p.m. Friday and Saturday; reservations recommended. Spirit of Dubuque — 2:00 p.m. and 4:00 p.m. daily, late April and early October; 6:30 p.m. daily dinner cruises, May 1-September 2; 6:00 p.m. daily dinner cruises, September 6-October 31; reservations required. Ham House Museum — 10:00 a.m.-6:00 p.m. daily, May 1-October 31. Old Jail Art Gallery — 12 noon-5:00 p.m. Tuesday-Sunday. Crystal Lake Cave — 8:00 a.m.-6:00 p.m. daily, Memorial Day-Labor Day; 9:00 a.m.-5:00 p.m. weekends, May, September, and October. Cable Car Square — 10:00 a.m.-6:00 p.m.
ADMISSION: Fenelon Place Elevator — 25¢ one way, 50¢ round trip. Spirit of Dubuque — adults, $5.00; children 5-15, $3.50; children 3-4, $3.00 for sightseeing trips. Ham House Museum — adults, $2.00; children 7-15, $1.00. Crystal Lake Cave — adults, $3.00; children 6-12, $1.50.
DIRECTIONS: From Waterloo, take U.S. 20 east to Dubuque.
FOR MORE INFORMATION: Call the Dubuque Chamber of Commerce, (319) 557-9200, or write Fischer Arcade Building, 800 Locust St., Dubuque, IA 52001.

Iowa

Charming Old World Clocks

Spillville, Iowa

Driving Time: 1¼ hours northeast of Waterloo

The steady ticking of precision timepieces and the familiar melodies of American songs are the sounds that greet visitors to the **Bily Clock Museum**. Situated in a house once occupied by romantic composer Anton Dvorak, the museum contains an impressive collection of hand-carved clocks.

All the clocks displayed here were made by Joseph and Frank Bily, two Iowa farmers of Czech descent. Both self-taught carvers, the Bilys produced their priceless collection over a 45-year period.

The clocks are made of a variety of woods, and many feature unique mechanical figures. The brothers consider the 10-foot **"American Pioneer History"** clock to be their masterpiece. This timepiece plays *America the Beautiful* and consists of 57 panels depicting different events in the country's history. It also contains mechanical figures that portray the four ages of man.

The carved figures of the **"Parade of Nations,"** another clock, characterizes citizens of 36 different nations in their native costumes. The **"Village Blacksmith"** clock, built in 1942-43, plays *My Old Kentucky Home* and shows a farmer taking his plowshare to the blacksmith for repair.

After having finished looking at the clocks, stroll over to nearby **Riverside Park** to see the Anton Dvorak Memorial. Dvorak lived in America for two years, from 1892 to 1894. This trip inspired him to write his most famous work, the Symphony No. 9, "From the New World," and his "American" String Quartet No. 6.

BEST TIME TO VISIT: Summer and early fall.

HOURS: Bily Clock Museum — 10:00 a.m.-4:00 p.m. daily, April; 8:00 a.m.-5:30 p.m. daily, May-October; 10:00 a.m.-4:00 p.m. weekends, March and November; by appointment November-March.

ADMISSION: Adults, $2.00; children 7-12, $1.00; under 7, free.

DIRECTIONS: From Waterloo, take U.S. 63 north to New Hampton, then state 24 to Calmar, then U.S. 52 north to state 325; go east on 325 to Spillville.

FOR MORE INFORMATION: Call Rosalyn Poshusta, (319) 562-3569, or write Bily Clock Exhibit, Spillville, IA 52168.

Buried Treasure In Scenic River Towns

Marquette/McGregor, Iowa

Driving Time: 1¼ hours northwest of Dubuque

Located along the Mississippi, Marquette and McGregor provide Iowa a showplace in any season. The fall, when the bluffs, hills, and steep valleys are ablaze with autumn color, is particularly spectacular in these two scenic river towns.

Just three miles north of Marquette, on state 76, is Iowa's only national monument, **Effigy Mounds**. Here, over 190 prehistoric Indian mounds have been preserved, some of which are estimated to be 2,500 years old. Twenty-nine of the mounds are built in the shape of animals or birds, while the remainder are conical or linear in shape.

Take your family on a one-hour self-guided tour along **Fire Point Trail**. Along the way you'll see the **Little Bear Mound**, considered to be the largest bear effigy in the state. It measures 70 feet across the shoulders, 137 feet long, and five feet high. Other trailside sites include the **Hopewellian Mounds** and a spectacular view from the cliffs. After completing the tour, stop by the visitors center, where the museum and an audio-visual presentation provide an historical background about the site.

Seven miles west of McGregor is **Spook Cave**, an underground cavern accessible only by powerboats. Local guides will provide information on the discovery and exploration of the cave, and point out interesting formations during the 40-minute tour. A campground, beach, and stocked trout stream are located nearby.

BEST TIME TO VISIT: Late September and early October.

HOURS: Effigy Mounds National Monument — 8:00 a.m.-7:00 p.m. June-August, 8:00 a.m.-5:00 p.m. September-May; guided tours available on a regularly scheduled basis from Memorial Day to Labor Day. Spook Cave — 9:00 a.m.-4:00 p.m., May 1-Memorial Day, 9:00 a.m.-6:00 p.m. Memorial Day-Labor Day, 9:00 a.m.-4:00 p.m. September and October.

ADMISSION: Spook Cave — adults, $4.00; children 3-12, $2.00; children under 3, free.

DIRECTIONS: From Dubuque, take U.S. 52 west to Luxemburg, then north to U.S. 18, then east to state highway 360.

FOR MORE INFORMATION: Call Effigy Mounds National Monument, (319) 873-2356, or write Box K, McGregor, IA 52157. Call Spook Cave, (319) 873-2144, or write Bob and Ann Ruden, R.R. 1, Box 239, McGregor, IA 52157.

Iowa

Decorah Celebrates Scandinavia

Decorah, Iowa

Driving Time: 1¼ hours northeast of Waterloo

A taste of Scandinavia is what's in store for you when you visit **Decorah**, a city with a rich Nordic heritage. This picturesque town was originally settled by Norwegian immigrants, who brought with them many of the customs, foods, and arts and crafts of the old country. Today, Decorah is a center of Norwegian culture, with what many believe to be one of the finest ethnic museums in the country.

The **Vesterheim (American–Norwegian Museum)**, established in 1977, houses exhibits on Norwegian life, costumes, handicrafts, and tools that tell the story of the immigrants' life in America. Once a luxury hotel, the museum now includes a historic building section that features a restored stone mill, blacksmith shop, school, and Norwegian farmhouse.

In the last weekend in July, Decorah celebrates its Scandinavian heritage with the three-day **Nordic Fest**. Visitors are invited to view Norwegian handiwork and sample food from the smorgasbord. Traditional music, activities, and folk dancers dressed in authentic costumes provide the entertainment.

While in Decorah be sure to stop by the **Porter House Museum**, a Victorian home that houses a rare butterfly and insect collection. Some of the museum's other exhibits include stamps, coins, shells, and Indian relics. Take a stroll around the grounds to inspect the unusual crystal and rock wall surrounding the property. The museum has beautiful waterfalls, pools, and gardens.

BEST TIME TO VISIT: Summer and fall.
HOURS: Vesterheim, the Norwegian-American Museum — 9:00 a.m.-5:00 p.m. daily, May 1–November 1; 10:00 a.m.-4:00 p.m. November 1–April 30; closed major holidays. Porter House Museum — 1:30 p.m.-4:30 p.m. Saturday and Sunday, May-October (or by special appointment).
ADMISSION: Vesterheim, the Norwegian-American Museum — adults, $3.00; children 7-15, $1.25. Porter House Museum — adults, $1.50; college and senior high students, 75¢; 6-15, 50¢; under 6, free.
DIRECTIONS: From Waterloo, take U.S. 63 north to New Hampton, then state 24 east to Calmar, and finally state 52 north to Decorah.

FOR MORE INFORMATION: Call the Decorah Chamber of Commerce, (319) 382-3990, or write 102 E. Water St., P.O. Box 397, Decorah, IA 52101.

Herbert Hoover Library and Museum

West Branch, Iowa

Driving Time: 25 minutes east of Iowa City

The **Herbert Hoover National Historic Site**, situated in a 197-acre park in West Branch, just minutes from Iowa City, is the restored birthplace and home of the nation's 31st president, as well as the presidential library and museum.

The small cottage where Hoover was born still stands on its original location. The area around the home is being restored to recreate the late 19th-century farm community in which the president grew up. An authentic blacksmith shop, one-story frame schoolhouse, and Friends meetinghouse are already open to the public. The Friends, or Quakers, is a religious group, puritan in spirit, of which Hoover and his family were members.

North of the birthplace is the **Presidential Library and Museum**, housing the numerous papers and other documents Hoover collected during his 50 years of public service. Books, personal objects, and memorabilia are on display to the public, including Mrs. Hoover's world-famous porcelain collection. The archives provide scholars with valuable research material on Herbert Hoover and his times.

Hoover died on October 20, 1964, and was buried in a gravesite overlooking his boyhood home. Mrs. Hoover, who died in New York in 1944, is buried alongside her husband.

Before leaving town, take a minute to stop by the **West Branch Museum** on Main Street. Housed in an 1844

Herbert Hoover's birthplace cottage in the 33-acre park in West Branch. Hoover was the first president born west of the Mississippi River. The park also includes his father's blacksmith shop and the presidential library.

grocery store, the museum exhibits artifacts brought by the first Quaker pioneers. Other relics and a room from a pioneer home are also on display.

BEST TIME TO VISIT: Summer.
HOURS: Herbert Hoover National Historic Site — 8:00 a.m.-5:00 p.m. daily, except Thanksgiving, Christmas, and New Year's Day. West Branch Heritage Museum — 9:30 a.m.-4:30 p.m. weekdays and noon-5:00 p.m. Sunday; summer, anytime by appointment.
ADMISSION: Herbert Hoover National Historic Site — free. Presidential Library and Museum — $1.00.
DIRECTIONS: From Iowa City, take I-80 east to Exit 254.
FOR MORE INFORMATION: Call Herbert Hoover National HIstoric Site, (319) 643-2541, or write Box 607, West Branch, IA 52358. West Branch Heritage Museum, write 109 W. Main St., West Branch, IA 52358.

A Touch of Holland In Iowa

Orange City, Iowa

Driving Time: 1 hour northwest of Sioux City

Orange City's pride in its Dutch heritage is obvious throughout the city, from its historic buildings to its vast tulip gardens. Wander through **Kobes Gardens**, past the crystaline Reflection Lake, to the 100-year-old Love Seat and Altair Gate.

The park is beautifully landscaped with waterfalls, fountains, and a rock garden. In the spring, the garden comes alive with thousands of tulips in a rainbow of colors.

For a taste of Dutch life as it used to be, visit the **Old Mill**. Here grain, the staff of life, was ground to make bread. Inside the mill is the Dutch Room, living quarters of a typical Dutch family, furnished with antiques from the old country.

If you want to learn more about the founders of Orange City, visit the Heritage Room and Hoeven Room at the **Northwestern College Library**. The library contains materials that trace the founding and growth of this entire community.

During the third week in May, Orange City celebrates its Dutch heritage with its annual **Tulip Festival**. City residents dress in authentic Dutch costumes, there are two parades every day, and evening play performances every night. This year's festival will be held May 19-21.

BEST TIME TO VISIT: Early summer.
HOURS: Kobes Gardens — guided tours May 1 until frost. Heritage Room and Hoeven Room — open during library hours, Monday-Saturday.
DIRECTIONS: From Sioux City, take US. 75 north to state 10, then west to Orange City.
FOR MORE INFORMATION: Call the Orange City Chamber of Commerce, (712) 737-4510, or write 125 Central Ave. S.E., Orange City, IA 51041.

The "good old days" at Orange City's Tulip Festival

Mamie Eisenhower Birthplace

Boone, Iowa

Driving Time: 20 minutes west of Ames

Boone, a farming community in central Iowa, was the birthplace of one of America's best-loved first ladies, Mamie Doud Eisenhower. The quaint one-story frame house in which she was born has been carefully restored with furnishings from the Victorian era, including the family's original bedroom set.

Of particular interest is the display of **Mamie Eisenhower memorabilia and photographs** in the museum and library, located on the lower level. The museum's exhibits include a chronology of Mamie Eisenhower's life and such personal effects as her baptismal certificate, wedding announcement, and inaugural gown. The library offers books on both President and Mrs. Eisenhower, as well as family histories and political memorabilia.

BEST TIME TO VISIT: Summer and fall.
HOURS: Mamie Doud Eisenhower Birthplace — 1:00 p.m-5:00 p.m. Tuesday-Sunday, April-December; closed Mondays.
ADMISSION: Mamie Doud Eisenhower Birthplace — adults, $1.00; children 6-17, 50¢.
DIRECTIONS: From Ames, take U.S. 30 west to Boone exit.
FOR MORE INFORMATION: Call the Mamie Doud Eisenhower Birthplace, (515) 432-1931 or (515) 432-1896, or write Mamie Doud Eisenhower Birthplace, P.O. Box 55, Boone, IA 50036.

Pella:
City of
The Dutch

Pella, Iowa

Driving Time: 1 hour west of Des Moines

First settled in 1847 by Dutch refugees seeking religious freedom, this town still retains many of its Dutch customs. The Dutch influence is evident throughout the city, from the design of its buildings to its may tulip gardens. The **Pella Historical Village** features 17 restored buildings and antique exhibits. It includes a Dutch museum, gristmill, blacksmith shops, pioneer log cabin, even a wooden shoemaker. Frontier enthusiasts may want to visit the boyhood home of famed western lawman Wyatt Earp, also located here.

Each year in early May the community celebrates its Dutch heritage with its annual **Tulip Festival**. Thousands of brightly colored tulips provide a beautiful backdrop to the three-day event. Festival highlights include residents dressed in authentic Dutch costumes, an old-time street parade, the introduction of royalty, and the traditional street scrubbing. Before you leave be sure to see the huge windmill in the city's park and the lagoon made in the shape of a wooden shoe.

BEST TIME TO VISIT: Spring, summer. (The Tulip Festival is held May 12-14.)

HOURS: Historical Village and Wyatt Earp Boyhood Home — 9:00 a.m.-4:30 p.m. Monday-Saturday, April-September; closed holidays.

ADMISSION: Historical Village and Wyatt Earp Boyhood Home — adults, $2.50; children 12 and over, 50¢, children under 12, free.

DIRECTIONS: From Des Moines, take state route 163 west and exit at Pella.

FOR MORE INFORMATION: Call the Pella Chamber of Commerce, (515) 628-4311, or write 507 Franklin St., Box 145, Pella, IA 50219.

Iowa

A Trip Back To America's Early Days

Driving Time: 6 hours west of Chicago,
Amana Colonies, Iowa

With a quiet and peaceful charm of German heritage, the seven Amana Colonies in east-central Iowa preserve the hard-working traditional lifestyle of America's early days. Most of the 1,740 residents are descendants of the Community of True Inspiration who migrated to the United States from Germany and settled in Ebenezer, N.Y., and then in the Amana Colonies. Each year thousands of tourists are drawn to the area, exploring the villages and factories, restaurants, shops, and discovering antiques.

You won't find horse-drawn buggies, bearded men, or women in long frocks, but you will find history, tradition and good old-fashioned fun. The first Amana residents established woolen mills, furniture factories and meat-smoking shops that are still in operation. In each of the towns from **South Amana** to **Homestead** you'll find antiques and collectables, distinctive toys, pottery, cheese, wine, German-style food, handcrafted furniture and clocks, and much more. During July and August, one of the prettiest sites is the 200-acre **Amana Lily Lake**, between Amana and Middle Amana. Legend has it that Indians brought the bright-yellow lilies to the lake and harvested the tubers (stems) for food.

The lake is only part of the scenic beauty of the Amana region, where the Iowa River

winds through the forests and fields. Before you begin your tour you might want to stop at the **Museum of Amana History** in Amana to examine the historical exhibits and learn a bit about the Amana way of life. In **South Amana** be sure to stop at the **Amana Society Barn Museum**, which features a collection of miniature historic buildings being constructed by woodworker Henry Moore. The models recreate the lifestyle of pioneers in small towns at the turn of the century.

For an overnight stay, you'll find comfortable lodgings at the **Best Western Colony Haus Motor Inn** (south of I-80 exit 225 on R.R. 2, Williamsburg) or the **Holiday Inn** (I-80 exit 225). You'll find another worthwhile stop as you head back west on I-80 toward Des Moines.

Pella, Iowa, is a picturesque little town of 7,800 persons—a little Dutch island in the middle of 20th-century America. It was founded in 1847 by a Dutch Reformed minister, Henry Peter Scholte. Today, the population is still 90 percent Dutch. From the enchanting town square to the small white clapboard houses, Pella is quite a town. In fact, the famous Wyatt Earp spent his boyhood here, in a small house on Franklin St. Any time of the year you'll find many interesting sights in Pella. However, May is the best time to enjoy Pella's pride and joy—its tulips. The popular Tulip Festival is held each year on the second weekend in May.

HOURS: Museum of Amana History: 10 AM to 5 PM Monday through Saturday, noon to 5 PM Sunday, April 15 through Nov. 15. Amana Society Barn Museum: 10 AM to 5 PM Monday through Saturday, 1 to 4 PM Sundays, May through October. Most shops are open Monday through Saturday 9 AM to 5 PM; some are open Sunday.

FOR MORE INFORMATION: Call the Amana Colonies Travel Council, (319) 622-3051.

DIRECTIONS: From Twin Cities, take I-65-35 south toward Des Moines, Iowa. Pick up I-80 east toward Iowa City. Exit at Rt. 149 north; continue about 15 miles and turn right (east) on Rt. 6 to the Amanas. To reach Pella from the Amana Colonies, take I-80 west (toward Des Moines), exit Rt. 14 south and continue to Rt. 163 southwest. Take Rt. 163 straight into Pella (about 40 miles southwest of Des Moines).

An Historic, Festive River City

Davenport, Iowa

Driving Time: 1 hour east of Iowa City

Strategically located at a bend in the Mississippi River, Davenport grew to prominence as an agricultural machinery and trading center. Today, with three neighboring towns, it forms one part of the Quad Cities group and is especially known for its historical charm and popular festivals.

Begin your visit to Davenport with an exhilarating trip on a **Mississippi sternwheeler**, the *Julie N. Dubuque*. Whether your family is planning a fun-filled afternoon of sightseeing or a romantic evening cruise, the ship's panoramic view will keep you entertained. The 400-passenger riverboat makes two 1½-hour trips daily.

During the cruise you'll notice an island located in the Mississippi, **Rock Island Arsenal**, which is the largest manufacturing arsenal in the country. First established as a frontier fort in 1816, the island was later the site of a large Confederate prison camp during the Civil War. Both a national and a Confederate cemetery were established on the island after the war.

Today, Arsenal Island is the home of the **John M. Browning Memorial Museum**, an arms museum dedicated to the father of the automatic weapon. Here is housed one of the largest small-arm collections in the Midwest. Weapons on display date from before the Revolutionary War to the present.

If your family would like a real taste of life in a river town, visit the **Village of East Davenport**. Once an important logging and steamboat center, the village has been restored

Pres. Lincoln at the Civil War Festival in Davenport

to look as it did in the 1850s. The area's buildings and shops form Iowa's largest historical district and are now listed in the National Register of Historic Places.

In addition to its rich history, Davenport offers visitors a variety of festivals from which to choose. During the summer, Davenport hosts the four-day **Bix Beiderbecke Memorial Jazz Festival**. The 11-year-old festival draws jazz fans from around the country, as greats and near-greats come to jam. Money from the festival is being used to establish a Bix Beiderbecke memorial and museum and to provide scholarships to young musicians.

In September, the Village of East Davenport recreates the Civil War during its annual **Civil War Muster and Mercantile Exposition**. Some costumed residents reenact a battle of the Civil War, while others dressed as traders and Indians provide craft demonstrations. The event ends with a Grand Military Ball.

For a truly unique family experience, time your trip to see **Christmas in the Village**. Each year for one night in mid-December, the village's storefronts and shop windows become a stage as costumed volunteers recreate frontier and Victorian Christmas scenes. Thirty or more shop windows depict scenes of frontier life in the 1850s and '60s.

BEST TIME TO VISIT: Summer, fall, and early winter.
HOURS: Julie N. Dubuque — 1:00 p.m., 3:00 p.m., and 8:00 p.m. daily except Monday; 6:30 p.m. May 1-Labor Day; 1:00 p.m. and 3:00 p.m. Sunday, Memorial Day-Labor Day, extra Saturday night cruise at 9:30 p.m.; 6:00 p.m. Labor Day-October, extra Saturday night cruise at 9:00 p.m.; special Sunday morning dinner cruise at 10:30 a.m. May-October. John M. Browning Museum at Rock Island Arsenal — 11:00 a.m.-4:00 p.m. Wednesday-Sunday. Village of East Davenport — 10:00 a.m.-5:00 p.m. daily.
ADMISSION: Julie N. Dubuque — adults, $4.00; children, $2.00; other rates available.
DIRECTIONS: From Iowa City, take I-80 east to I-74 intersection.
FOR MORE INFORMATION: Call the Davenport Chamber of Commerce, (319) 322-1706, or write Davenport Area Convention and Visitors Bureau, 404 Main St., Davenport, IA 52801.

Iowa

Old Settlers, Threshers Center

Mount Pleasant, Iowa

Driving Time: 1 hour south of Iowa City

For five days each September, Mount Pleasant hosts the world's largest steam show, the **Midwest Old Settlers and Threshers Reunion**. The shriek of 100 steam-engine whistles, the chug of mighty iron horses, and the hum of threshers pierce the air during this agricultural festival.

The working exhibits thresh grain by steam and horse power, saw wood, press sorghum, and power a shingle mill. Live steam models, classic cars, and antique gas engines and tractors are at work, along with a narrow-gauge steam railway and five old-time electric trolleys.

Visitors can also see making soap, spinning, weaving, sawing wood, making brooms, carving, canning, and quilting. These and other demonstrations show how early Americans farmed, cooked, and lived before the advent of gasoline motors and electricity.

During the festival, visitors can also see and participate in barn dances, fiddlers' and check contests, songfests, daily vespers, and spelling bees. The **Schaffer Players**, America's only surviving traveling tent theater, and some of the biggest names in country music provide the entertainment.

After seeing the steam engines in action, your family won't want to miss the **Midwest Old Settlers and Threshers Heritage Museum**, just south of town. The building, which covers 1½ acres, houses one of the nation's largest collections of steam engines and other relics used by the early pioneers. Museum exhibits include steam-powered farm machin-

ery, agricultural artifacts, antique cars, horse-drawn vehicles, and a country kitchen.

The **Museum of Repetoire Americana**, located nearby, displays memorabilia of early folk and tent shows and repertory theater.

If you're looking for a place to stay while in town, stop by the **Harlan House**, the former home of James Harlan, a close friend of President Lincoln, now a popular hotel and restaurant. The older section of the building houses relics and memorabilia of the Civil War.

BEST TIME TO VISIT: Summer and fall. (The Midwest Old Settlers and Threshers Reunion is scheduled for September 1-5.)

HOURS: Midwest Old Settlers and Threshers Heritage Museum — 9:00 a.m.-5:00 p.m. daily, Memorial Day to five days before Labor Day. Museum of Repertoire Americana — by appointment only.

ADMISSION: Midwest Old Settlers and Threshers Heritage Museum — adults, $1.00; under 9th grade, free. Museum of Repertoire Americana — $1.00. Midwest Old Settlers and Threshers Reunion — adults, $5.00; children under 9th grade, free.

DIRECTIONS: From Iowa City, take U.S. 218 south to U.S. 34.

FOR MORE INFORMATION: Call the Mount Pleasant Chamber of Commerce, (319) 385-3101, or write 124 S. Main St., P.O. Box 109, Mount Pleasant, IA 52641.

Quaint Covered Bridges

Winterset, Iowa

Driving Time: 35 minutes southwest of Des Moines

What could be more romantic than a quaint **covered bridge**? It brings to mind pictures of courting couples in open-air buggies. You can almost hear the clippity-clop of the horses hooves on the wooden boards. The sight of a covered bridge is not one to be missed, and nowhere will you find more covered bridges than in and around Winterset, Iowa.

Of the original 16 covered bridges constructed in Madison County, seven are still standing. The 100-year-old structures, all within 12 miles of Winterset, were ordered covered by the county to protect them from the weather. Today, the bridges are recognized for their quaint charm and are listed in the National Register of Historic Places.

In the fall, on the second full weekend in October, Madison County holds its annual **Covered Bridge Festival**. During the two-day event, crafts people from around the county recreate life as it was in the late 19th century. Demonstrations include candle, cider, and rope making; muzzle loading; log splitting; and spelling bees. The festival also offers tours of houses and covered bridges, a farmers' market, quilt show, square dancing, horse racing, antique car parade, and country-western shows.

BEST TIME TO VISIT: Fall.
HOURS: Covered Bridges — open to the public year round.
ADMISSION: Covered Bridges — free.
DIRECTIONS: From Des Moines, take I-80 west to U.S. 169, then go to Winterset.
FOR MORE INFORMATION: Call the Chamber of Commerce, (515) 462-1185, or write Chamber of Commerce, Winterset, IA 50273.

More than a dozen covered bridges are located on off-the-beaten-track Iowa roads in Madison, Keokuk, and Marion Counties. Covered bridges were designed to give horses solid footing in snow or rain. They once charged tolls: 5¢ for a person on foot, 10¢ for a horse and rider, 15¢ for a vehicle drawn drawn by one animal.

Iowa

Little Brown Church In the Vale

Nashua, Iowa

Driving Time: 1 hour northeast of Waterloo

This charming little church was built on the site that provided the inspiration for the hymn, "The Church in the Wildwood."

William Pitts, a young music teacher, was on his way to visit his bride-to-be when his stagecoach stopped in Bradford for a rest. Struck by the beauty of the area, he imagined it the ideal setting for a pastoral church. Even after he returned home, this vision of the church in the vale remained, and inspired him to write a poem about his experience. The poem was later set to music and became, "The Church in the Wildwood."

Pitts was surprised years later when he returned to Bradford and found the town's people building a church on the site described in his song. The church, dedicated in 1864, is today a popular wedding chapel, with over 700 ceremonies conducted each year. A reunion is held the first Sunday in August for all couples married there, and everyone is invited to attend.

BEST TIME TO VISIT: First Sunday in August.

HOURS: Little Brown Church — open from early morning to late at night each day of the week; Sunday school 10:00 a.m., worship service 11:00 a.m. each Sunday.

DIRECTIONS: From Waterloo, take U.S. 218 north to Nashua, then go two miles east on state highway 346 to the church.

FOR MORE INFORMATION: Call John W. Christy, Pastor, (515) 435-2027, or write R.R. 1, Box 111, Nashua, IA 50658.

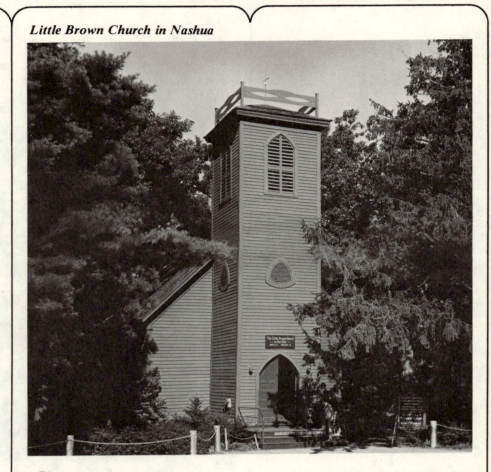

Little Brown Church in Nashua

Grotto Of the Redemption

West Bend, Iowa

Driving Time: 1 hour southwest of Fort Dodge

For a truly unique religious experience, visit the **Grotto of the Redemption** in West Bend; it portrays stories from the life of Christ and illustrates the fall and redemption of man.

The grotto, covering an entire city block, was begun in 1912 by Reverend Paul Dobberstein. He spent the next 42 years constructing the structure of concrete and ornamental stones from around the country. The area's nine separate grottoes are said to contain the largest collection of fossils, minerals, shells, and other petrified materials of anywhere in the world.

Construction on the grotto continues even today under the Reverend Louis Greving. You may wish to extend your family visit until after dark, to drive by when the illuminated grotto is most impressive.

BEST TIME TO VISIT: Summer and early fall.

HOURS: Grotto of the Redemption — 8:00 a.m.-5:00 p.m. daily, June-October 15; guided tours hourly.

ADMISSION: Grotto of the Redemption — suggested donation, adults, $1.00; children, 50¢.

DIRECTIONS: From Fort Dodge, take U.S. 169 to U.S. 18, then go west on U.S. 18 to state highway 15, then south to West Bend.

FOR MORE INFORMATION: Call the Grotto of the Redemption, (515) 887-2371, or write Reverend Louis Greving, Grotto of the Redemption, West Bend, IA 50597.

Reliving Pioneer Days

Oskaloosa, Iowa

Driving Time: 1 hour east of Des Moines

Once home to Indian tribes, the city was called "Oskaloosa" after an Indian maiden whose name meant "last of the beautiful." This thriving industrial and farming center boasts a unique combination of outdoor and historic activities.

Lake Keonah, located five miles east off state route 92, is an 84-acre lake with facilities for swimming, fishing, camping, picnicking, boating, and snowmobiling.

A national historic site, the **Nelson Pioneer Farm and Craft Museum,** recreates an authentic pioneer farm of the mid-1800s. It also includes a one-room schoolhouse, log cabin, country store, voting house, and historic museum.

The Nelson Pioneer Farm is also the home of an annual **Pioneer Craft Day Festival**, which is held on the third Saturday of each September.

BEST TIME TO VISIT: Summer and early fall.
HOURS: Nelson Pioneer Farm and Craft Museum — 10:00 a.m.-5:00 p.m. Tuesday-Saturday, from 1:00 p.m. Sunday, May to mid-October; no tours after 4:00 p.m.
ADMISSION: Nelson Pioneer Farm and Craft Museum — adults, $1.50; grades 1-12, 25¢; children under 5, free.
DIRECTIONS: From Des Moines, take state highway 163 east to Oskaloosa.
FOR MORE INFORMATION: Call the Nelson Pioneer Farm and Craft Museum, (515) 672-2989, or write the Chamber of Commerce, 124 N. Market St., Oskaloosa, IA 52577.

One of the Beautiful Lake Regions

Okoboji, Iowa

Driving Time: 2-1/3 hours north of Sioux City

An outdoorsman's delight, Okoboji offers something for everyone. Whether your family enjoys swimming, fishing, camping, boating, snowmobiling, or hiking, this area provides excellent facilities.

Situated in the Great Lakes region, this is among the most popular vacation spots in the state. Recognized by *National Geographic* as having one of the most beautiful blue water lakes in the world, Okoboji offers an incredible variety of things to do.

During the summer, the **Okoboji Theatre** premieres a new musical or Broadway play every week and hosts a variety of experimental and children's theatre productions.

The **Okoboji Winery,** built on the hills surrounding the lake, produces an interesting variety of table wines. Visitors are invited to take mini-tours of the facilities and sample wines in the tasting room.

If you time your trip right, your family can take part in one of Okoboji's exciting special events. In June, the region hosts the **Iowa Great Lakes Gunshow** (June 4-5) and the area **rugby championships** (June 18-19). Okoboji explodes with fireworks over July 4th, followed by a marathon race on July 23. During August, you can climb into a basket for a breathtaking view at the annual **Hot Air Balloon Race** or gape at the beautiful cars in the area's **Antique Auto Show**. The Iowa **Great Lakes Winter Game Festival** is held here in January; it features an exciting range of competitions, including skiing, ice skating, and broom ball.

BEST TIME TO VISIT: Summer.
HOURS: Okoboji Summer Theatre — June 14 to August 14. Okoboji Winery — daily, May 1-September 30.
DIRECTIONS: From Sioux City, take U.S. 75 north to Le Mars, then state 60 north to Sheldon, then U.S. 18 east to U.S. 71, then go north to Okoboji.
FOR MORE INFORMATION: Call the Iowa Great Lakes Area Chamber of Commerce, (712) 332-2107, or write Box A, Lakes Center, Arnolds Park, IA 51331.

Iowa

Year-Around Events in Iowa

A wondrous array of art fairs, craft shows, rodeos, ethnic festivals, and other year-around special events await families in Iowa:

• **FEBRUARY:** For cold weather enthusiasts, there is the **Winter Sports Festival** in Estherville. The Holiday Mountain Ski Area hosts a collegiate and open skiing competition. Other activities include snowmobile racing, ice skating, and ice sculpture competitions.

• **MAY:** More than 76 trombones will lead the big parade, when thousands of high school band students converge on Mason City for the annual **Northern Iowa Band Festival**. Where better to hold a band competition than in the hometown of Meridith Willson, author of "The Music Man"?

• **JULY:** A cavalcade of color dots the early morning sky over Indianola and heralds the beginning of the **National Hot Air Balloon Championships**. Hundreds of balloonists test their skill here every year in July. It is truly a spectacular sight, and not an event to be missed.

• **AUGUST**: Yippee, it's rodeo time! Sidney hosts the largest outdoor rodeo in the country. Top cowboys from across the nation perform along with top-name entertainment. Thrill to the excitement of bulldogging, calf roping, and bronc busting, as cowboys risk their lives for top honors.

• **MID-AUGUST:** Hotrodders won't want to miss the **National Sprint Car Championships**, held in Knoxville in mid-August. Featuring some of the best drivers and fastest cars in the country, the race guarantees excitement for everyone.

• **SEPTEMBER:** This is a big month for special events in Iowa. Mid-September is the best time to

Rodeo at Sidney, Iowa

tour the northeastern part of the state and take in the fall color-cade. Nowhere are the autumn colors more brilliant than in the hills and bluffs along the Mississippi.

• **SEPTEMBER:** Step into the past with a visit to the **Fort Atkinson Rendezvous**. The old frontier comes to life here late each September, when 19-century crafts are demonstrated, period military maneuvers are conducted, and costumed participants enact daily rituals.

• **LATE SEPTEMBER:** The **National Dairy Congress**, the state's largest cattle show, is held in Waterloo. Stroll among exhibits of horses and farm machinery or take in the saddle-horse show. Events like these make the Dairy Congress one of the best shows of its kind in the country. And what's a fair without a carnival? Let the kids choose from dozens of rides along the midway or try their skills at one of the numerous game booths.

MINNESOTA

International Falls

Ely

Grand Marais

Bemidji

Itasca Park

Grand Rapids

Walker

Two Harbors

Detroit Lakes

Hackensack

Duluth

Brainerd

Fergus Falls

Little Falls

Alexandria

Sauk Center

St. Cloud

Taylors/St. Croix

Stillwater

Minneapolis

St. Paul

Granite Falls

Shakopee

Redwood Falls

Valleyfair

Northfield

Redwing

Pipestone

Mantorville

Rochester

Minnesota Vacations

Minnesota

Minneapolis: City of Water

Minneapolis, Minnesota

Driving Time: 5 hours northwest of Chicago; 5 hours northwest of Milwaukee

Across the Mississippi from St. Paul lies Minneapolis — big, beautiful, almost brazen. And unlike St. Paul—its quiet, conservative brother — Minneapolis sports a let's-take-a-chance attitude that characterizes its business, cultural, and night life.

The city is a great place for vacationers of all ages. Within the city limits are **eleven lakes** that contain a wide variety of fish and are clean enough to swim in.

Unpolluted Minneapolis has one of the best park systems in the U.S. and its **153 parks** are havens of greenery. Some of the most scenic are around the city's lakes. The parks contain bikeways and hiking paths, flower gardens, wildlife areas (with deer and other animals), and facilities for numerous athletic activities.

Minneapolis also has a revitalized downtown with many fine stores. A year-round sports program, a symphony orchestra, and various theaters provide an excellent opportunity to enjoy the advantages of big city life.

The 775-foot, 57-story **IDS Tower** (80 S. 8th St.) dwarfs Minneapolis' former tallest building, the Foshay Tower, and there is a great view of the city from the observation deck on the 51st floor. The building serves as a striking focal point with its **Crystal Court**, shops, and restaurants. There's an information booth here, and the Minneapolis skyway system radiates in all directions from the second level of the Crystal Court.

Nicollet Mall in Minneapolis

The **Minnesota Transportation Museum** (W. 43rd St. and Queen Ave. S) offers rides in early 1900s electric streetcars along a reconstructed Como-Harriet line. Steam rail excursions, railway postal car demonstrations, and vintage buses are also available.

The whole family will enjoy the **Bell Museum of Natural History** (17th Ave. and University SE on the University of Minnesota campus). Dioramas show Minnesota birds and mammals in natural settings. Children will especially want to visit the "Touch and See Room," which encourages examination and comparison of the various biological exhibits.

The **Ard Godfrey House** (23 University Ave. SE on Nicollet Island) was built by a Maine millwright who came to Minnesota to open a mill at St. Anthony Falls. The building is an example of Greek Revival architecture in 1848. It once was a popular meeting place.

At **Tonka Toys Inc.** (53 Shoreline Blvd.), visitors have a chance to see how toys are manufactured during a tour of one of the nation's largest toy factories.

The **American Swedish Institute** (2600 Park Ave. S) is a 33-room turn-of-the-century mansion built by Swedish immmgrant Sven J. Turnblad. Currently a museum devoted to Swedish art and culture, the building contains artifacts of early Scandinavian settlers in the Midwest, a Swedish glass exhibit, antique furnishings, an art collection, and an import shop.

The **Minneapolis Grain Exchange** (400 4th St. S) is the world's largest cash grain market. Observers can view the action from a visitors' balcony.

The **Minneapolis City Hall** (5th St. and 3rd Ave. S) has the "Father of Waters" statue in its rotunda, carved from the largest single block of marble ever produced by Italian quarries.

St. Anthony Falls (Main St. SE and Central Ave.) provides an interesting view of the river's upper locks and dam. A renovated warehouse with shops and restaurants also stands at the site.

Costumed guide at Fort Snelling in Minneapolis

Stroll along **Nicollet Mall**, the world-famous downtown shopping promenade with a variety of shops, restaurants, museums, and art galleries. The mall is beautifully designed with spacious walkways, fountains, shaded trees, and flowers. No vehicles are allowed on the mall except for buses and cabs. A unique mini-bus takes visitors up and down the area.

The length of Nicollet Mall leads past **Orchestra Hall** and its beautiful **Peavey Plaza**; then the Loring Greenway takes you to Loring Park, the Walker Art Institute, and the equally famous **Guthrie Theater**. While downtown, youngsters will also want to visit the unusual **Children's Museum** (700 N. 1st St.).

The **Science Museum and Planetarium of the Minneapolis Public Library** (300 Nicollet Mall) is another favorite spot. There's a trading post, Minnesota Exhibit, Discovery Lab, a Creative Dynamics Center, and an Explore Store.

The **Butler Square Building** (6th St. and 1st Ave. N) is a restored office and retail complex that has won awards for architectural excellence.

The **Hennepin County Historical Museum** (2393 3rd Ave. S), located in an old mansion, houses a miniature turn-of-the-century village with 11 buildings. There are also 30 rooms of pioneer and Indian artifacts from the 1850s through the early 1900s.

At 24th Street in the next block stands the prestigious **Minneapolis Institute of Arts**, the **Children's Theater**, and the **Minneapolis College of Art and Design**.

Take Nicollet Avenue South to West Lake Street and to Lake Calhoun, where families can ride a replica of a sternwheel paddleboat. On the northwest shore of nearby Lake Harriet is the **Lake Harriet trolley** as well as the **Lake Harriet Garden Center** with a large rose garden display, perennials, and various species of trees.

Just a few blocks south of East Lake Harriet Boulevard, the tree-lined Minnehaha Parkway follows Minnehaha Creek east to **Minnehaha Park** on the banks of the Mississippi River. A self-guided tour through this historic and scenic 144 acres is rewarding. The tour includes Minnehaha Falls, immortalized by Henry Wadsworth Longfellow's "Song of Hiawatha." In winter, the falls become a spectacular ice sculpture.

The **Svenskarnas Dag** is held each year in the park in late June. The festival features various folk dancers, choirs, and performing groups from Sweden.

Minneapolis boasts the biggest summer festival in the U.S., the **Minneapolis Aquatennial**. It has land and water events, including parades and a hot-air balloon race.

Be sure to see **Valleyfair** (20 miles south on I-35, then nine miles west on MN 101 in Burnsville). It is an entertainment center with a turn-of-the-century theme. Rides include a 1920s carousel, a wooden roller coaster, corkscrew, and a log flume. There's also a petting zoo and live entertainment. (See complete write-up on Valleyfair in this section.)

BEST TIME TO VISIT: Year round.

TRAVEL TIPS: Driving around Minneapolis is fairly easy since its streets follow in numerical or alphabetical order. Numerous hotels and motels offer a wide variety of prices and accommodations. They are located in the downtown area, the 494 Freeway "Strip" near Met Stadium and Met Sports Center, and the airport area.

HOURS: IDS Tower observation deck — 10 a.m.-10 p.m. Monday-Thursday; 10 a.m.-11:30 p.m. Friday, Saturday; 10 a.m.-7 p.m. Sunday. Walker Art Institute — 10 a.m.-5 p.m. Tuesday-Saturday; after 5 p.m., special exhibition galleries only; Sunday from 11 a.m. Science Museum and Planetarium — 9 a.m.-5 p.m. Tuesday-Saturday, 1-5 p.m. Sunday. Hennepin County Historical Society Museum — 9 a.m.-4:30 p.m. Tuesday-Friday; 2-4:30 p.m. Saturday, Sunday; closed Saturday in June, July, August; closed holidays. Minneapolis Institute of Arts — 10 a.m.-5 p.m. Tuesday-Saturday, 10 a.m.-9 p.m. Thursday, noon-5 p.m. Sunday, closed December 25. Minneapolis College of Art and Design — 9 a.m.-9 p.m. weekdays, Saturday to 5 p.m., noon-5 p.m. Sunday. Minnesota Transportation Museum — 6:30 a.m.-dusk daily, Memorial Day-Labor Day; Saturday and Sunday only after Labor Day-October. Bell Museum of Natural History — 9 a.m.-5 p.m. Tuesday-Saturday, 1-5 p.m. Sunday, closed most holidays. Ard Godrey House — open for tours May 31-October 15. Tonka Toys — open by appointment Tuesday and Friday, February to November. American Swedish Museum — 1-4 p.m. Tuesday-Saturday, 1-5 p.m. Sunday, closed holidays. Grain Exchange — 9:15 a.m.-1:15 p.m. daily, closed holidays. City Hall — 8 a.m.-4:30 p.m. Monday-Friday except holidays. Lake Harriet Garden Center — 9 a.m.-10 p.m. mid-June to September is best time to visit. Queen of the Lakes Cruise from Harriet Island — 1-4 p.m. and 6-8:15 p.m. daily, May-September, leaves every 45 minutes; open holidays. Valleyfair — daily mid-May to Labor Day; weekends, September.

ADMISSION: IDS Tower observation deck — adults, $2; sr. citizens and children 5-15, $1.50. Walker Art Institute — there may be a fee for some exhibits. Science Museum and Planetarium — free. Hennepin County Historical Society Museum — free. Institute of Arts — adults, $2; 12-18, $1; under 12 and sr. citizens, free. College of Art and Design — free. Minnesota Transportation Museum — adults, 40¢; under 2, free. Bell Museum of Natural History — free. Ard Godfrey House — adults, $1; students, 25¢; sr. citizens, 50¢. American Swedish Museum — adults, $2; students and sr. citizens, $1; 6-21, 50¢; under 6, free. Grain Exchange — free. Lake Harriet Garden Center — free. Queen of the Lakes Cruise — adults, $1; children, 50¢. Valleyfair — adults, $8.45; 4-11, $7.95; under 4, free.

DIRECTIONS: From St. Paul, take I-94 west to Minneapolis.

FOR MORE INFORMATION: Call the Minneapolis Convention and Tourism Center, (612) 348-4313, or write 15 S. 5th St., Minneapolis, MN 55402.

Minnesota

St. Paul: The Quiet Twin

St. Paul, Minnesota

Driving Time: 5 hours northwest of Chicago

At the great bend of the Mississippi, near the point where the waters of the Mississippi and Minnesota Rivers meet, St. Paul and its twin city, Minneapolis, form a mighty northern metropolis.

A terraced city of diversified industry and lovely homes, St. Paul boasts 30 lakes within 30 minutes' distance as well as more than 90 parks.

For an exciting combination of art, architecture, and government, be sure to tour the **Minnesota State Capitol** (Aurora and Park Aves.). One of the largest self-supporting marble domes in the world, it is very similar in design to St. Peter's in Rome. Designed by architect Cass Gilbert, this handsome building contains many fine pieces of sculpture, paintings, and decorations.

At the **Minnesota Historical Society Building** (690 Cedar St.), just east of the capitol, visitors will find exhibits on many aspects of the state's history, including an outstanding special exhibit on the Great Lakes fur trade.

The **Landmark Center** (75 W. 5th St.), the restored 1894 Old Federal Courts Building, is a breathtaking, designated landmark resplendent in columns and marble with period art and huge fireplaces. The center now houses programs for performing and visual arts as well as civic activities.

The **James J. Hill House** (take John Ireland Blvd. from the capitol across the freeway past the St. Paul Cathedral to Summit Ave.) is one of the largest and best preserved of St. Paul's mansions. Guided tours of the

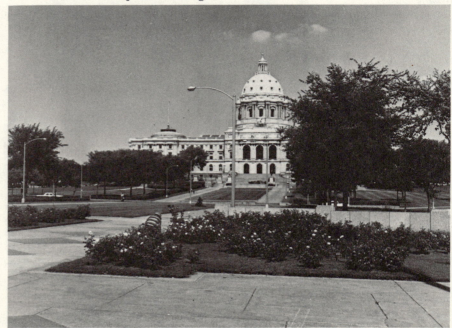

Minnesota State Capitol building in St. Paul

home introduce your family to the life and time of Hill, whose Great Northern Railroad was for many years the backbone of northwestern settlement and growth.

The **St. Paul Arts and Science Center** (30 E. 10th St.), a multi-million dollar facility, combines a theater for the performing arts, an auditorium, a gallery of the Minnesota Museum of Art, and a rooftop lounge. Also in the building is the **Science Museum of Minnesota**, where various programs and hands-on exhibits occupy three floors. The **William L. McKnight–3M Omnitheater** is the most advanced audio-visual theater in the world, with a 7,300-square-foot tilted, domed screen that surrounds the viewer.

Visitors might drive down Cedar Street to Kellogg Boulevard and spend some time just watching the riverboat traffic on the Mississippi River from the vantage of Kellogg Park. **Harriet Island** (drive across the Wabash St. Bridge, turn right at Nagaski St.) is the embarkation point for sightseeing cruises on a stern-wheel paddleboat. Your family will feel the nostalgia of a less hurried time.

The **Alexander Ramsey House** (265 S. Exchange St.), the home of Minnesota's first territorial governor, still contains most of its original 1870s furnishings.

The **Minnesota Museum of Art** (305 St. Peter at Kellogg Blvd.) has exhibits that include Oriental works, contemporary prints and drawings, and crafts displays.

Como Park (Lexington Park and W. Como Blvd.) boasts a turn-of-the-century greenhouse with flora and fauna from all parts of the globe. In addition to a zoo, visitors will find picnic grounds, athletic fields, an amusement park for children, and boat, canoe, and bike rentals.

Indian Mounds Park (Earl St. and Mounds Blvd. in Dayton's Bluff section) has more than 25 acres containing prehistoric burial grounds for Sioux chiefs. There are picnic facilities, a ballfield, and a view of the Mississippi.

The **Minnesota State Fair** is held each year during the 12 days before Labor Day at the State Fairgrounds (Como and Snelling Aves.). More than one million visitors see a thrill show, a horse show, and an all-star revue.

Minnesota

Mississippi Queen riverboat

The **Gibbs Farm Museum** (go west on Larpenteur Ave., north of the fairgrounds) is a living-history truck farm where the fields are tilled just the way they were in the 1870s. The Ramsey County Historical Society operates the farm.

The **F. Scott Fitzgerald home** (599 Summit Ave.) is not open to the public, but visitors can drive by and picture themselves in the age of *The Great Gatsby*.

Fort Snelling State Park (six miles southwest at the junction of MN 5 and 55) offers picnicking, boating, swimming, fishing, hiking, a nature center, and cross-country skiing. In the park stands **Historic Fort Snelling**, an old stone frontier outpost. The original army buildings have been restored; and from late spring to early fall, daily pageantry re-enacts the lives of frontier families.

A must-see is the **Minnesota Zoological Garden**, with its domed Tropical Garden, in nearby suburban Apple Valley. The 500 acres are connected by a monorail so the 1,200 animals and 2,000 plant varieties can be seen easily in open, landscaped exhibits.

The last week of January and the first week of February is the time of the **St. Paul Winter Carnival**, biggest winter celebration in the U.S. It features everything from the Winnipeg-to-St. Paul "500" Snowmobile Race, dog sled races, ski-jumping championships, ice-fishing competitions, and ice-carving contests. The Winter Carnival Queen contest, Ice Capades, a gigantic Winter Carnival parade, and much, much more help warm participants during the generally sub-zero wintry weather.

West of St. Paul lies **Lake Minnetonka**. This beautiful lake in an urban setting is one of the best all-around fish producers in the state. It's flecked by dozens of bays and inlets along its 92 miles of shoreline. There are many lakeshore restaurants and boat rentals are available.

Or your family may wish to visit another popular suburban lake, **White Bear Lake**, which has two public beaches and great fishing. In the winter, fishing shacks dot the lake's icy surface.

BEST TIME TO VISIT: Year round.

TRAVEL TIPS: Be sure to get a detailed map of the city, since St. Paul's streets follow no numerical or alphabetical order.

HOURS: State Capitol — 9 a.m.-5 p.m. Monday-Friday, 10 a.m.-4 p.m. Saturday, 1-4 p.m. Sunday; closed January 1, Easter, Thanksgiving, December 25; 45-minute guided tours of capitol from main entrance information desk. Historical Society Building — 8:30 a.m.-5 p.m. Monday-Saturday, 1-4 p.m. Sunday; closed January 1, Easter, Thanksgiving, December 25. Landmark Center — 8 a.m.-5 p.m. Monday-Friday, Thursday to 8 p.m.; Saturday from 10 a.m., Sunday from 1 p.m., galleries closed Monday; closed January 1, December 25. Cathedral of St. Paul — 6 a.m.-5 p.m. daily. Science Museum — 9:30 a.m.-9 p.m. Tuesday-Saturday, 11 a.m.-9 p.m. Sunday and Monday April 12-Labor Day. Ramsey House — 10 a.m.-4 p.m. Monday-Friday, March-Demcember; 1-4:30 p.m. Saturday and Sunday. Museum of Art — 10 a.m.-5 p.m. Tuesday-Friday, 11:30 a.m.-5 p.m. Sunday, closed holidays. Como Park — 8 a.m.-8 p.m. daily, summer; 8 a.m.-4 p.m. daily, winter. Gibbs Farm Museum — Tuesday-Friday 10 a.m.-5 p.m., mid-April to December; noon-4 p.m. Sunday. Historic Fort Snelling — 11 a.m.-8 p.m. daily, June-Labor Day; 9 a.m.-5 p.m. Monday-Friday, Labor Day-October; 11 a.m.-8 p.m. Saturday and Sunday. Minnesota Zoological Garden — 9:30 a.m.-4:30 p.m. daily, November-March; 9:30 a.m.-5 p.m. April-May; 9:30 a.m.-6 p.m. June-August; 9:30 a.m.-5 p.m. September-October.

ADMISSION: State Capitol — free. Historical Society Building — free. Landmark Center — free. Science Museum-Omnitheater — adults, $5.50; sr. citizens and children under 13, $4; exhibit halls only: adults, $3; sr. citizens, $2; children under 13, $2. Ramsey House — adults, $1.50; children under 16, free with adult. Museum of Art — donation. Gibbs Farm Museum — adults, $1.50; sr. citizens, $1.25; 13-19 $1; under 13, 50¢. Historic Fort Snelling — adults, $1; 6-16, 25¢; under 6, free with adult; over 65, free. Minnesota Zoological Garden — adults, $3; 12-16 and sr. citizens, $1.50; 6-11, $1; under 6, free.

DIRECTIONS: From Minneapolis, take I-94 east to St. Paul.

FOR MORE INFORMATION: Call the St. Paul Chamber of Commerce, (612) 222-5561, or write Suite 701, N. Central Tower, 445 Minnesota St., St. Paul, MN 55101.

Minnesota

Duluth: Lake Superior Gateway

Duluth, Minnesota

Driving Time: 3½ hours north of Minneapolis/St. Paul

Hugging the eastern slopes of the preglacial Sawtooth Mountains and the western tip of Lake Superior, Duluth is a world port with a busy and picturesque harbor. At night, the city and harbor lights illuminate the landscape like an immense jeweled necklace against the mountainous shoreline.

The harbor and lake can be viewed from **Skyline Parkway Drive**, which extends 27 miles along the bluffs on the Lake Superior shore. **Enger Tower** (Skyline Dr. and 18th Ave. W) provides a commanding view of the city.

Every September, bird-watchers gather at **Hawk Ridge** (northeastern most extension of Skyline Dr.) to observe, photograph, and study the largest migration of hawks, owls, and eagles in the nation.

Another sight to boggle the eyes of visitors is the unique **Duluth Aerial Lift Bridge**, connecting Minnesota Point. The bridge lifts 38 feet in less than one minute to let ships through.

The **Canal Park Marine Museum** (Minnesota Point at Aerial Bridge) provides a landlubber's glimpse of sea life, with ship models, relics of shipwrecks, reconstructed ship cabins, and exhibits relating to the maritime history of Lake Superior and Duluth harbor. Visitors can also see ships entering and leaving the harbor.

Minnesota Park Point Recreation Center has a playground, picnic tables, boat ramp, and swimming facilities.

At **Leif Erikson Park** (11th Ave. E and London Rd.) stands a statue of

the Norwegian explorer and a half-sized reproduction of the sailing vessel in which he and his crew of Norsemen supposedly made the first voyage by Europeans to the North American continent.

On the first Saturday in August, visitors can participate in one of the state's most popular events, the **International Folk Festival**. Gaily costumed nationality groups display and sell their craft work and food specialties. The festival climax is a two-hour stage program of music and dance from around the world at Leif Erikson Park.

Glensheen (300 London Rd.), a mammoth 39-room mansion on the shore of Lake Superior, was built by Duluth business magnate Chester Adgate Congdon around the turn of the century. Tour guides escort visitors into an era of ornate, hand-carved woodwork, tapestried walls, stained glass windows, and exotic light fixtures of brass, crystal, and silver.

The **St. Louis County Heritage and Arts Center** (506 W. Michigan St.) was originally Union Depot. The building includes the A.M. Chisholm Museum, which has natural and cultural history exhibits, and the St. Louis County Historical Society, which houses exhibits of northern Minnesota history. Also in the building is the Museum of Transportation and Industry, which contains more than 2,000 feet of track with antique rail cars and other railroad memorabilia.

Youngsters and adults alike will enjoy the **Fairmont Park Zoo** (72nd and Grand Ave. W, on MN 23), which has more than 300 animals from all over the world. Picnic facilities are also available.

Minnesota

Spirit Mountain Recreation Area (9500 Spirit Mountain Place, seven miles south on I-35 near the Boundary Ave. exit) offers tennis, swimming, picnicking, hiking, camping, and skiing.

Jay Cooke State Park (southwest via MN 23, 210, adjoining the gorge of the St. Louis River) boasts 8,155 acres of rugged country where families can have picnics or go fishing, camping, cross-country skiing, and snowmobiling.

The **Duluth-Superior Excursions** (foot of 5th Ave. W and waterfront) offers a two-hour boat tour of Duluth Harbor and Lake Superior on the *Vista King* and *Vista Queen*.

From Duluth towards Canada, U.S. 61 provides a scenic drive along Lake Superior's north shore.

BEST TIME TO VISIT: Summer.
TRAVEL TIPS: If members of your family suffer from hay fever, make sure they come to Duluth in the summer. The pollen count is always very low here.
HOURS: Canal Park Marine Museum — 10 a.m.-9 p.m. daily, May 15 to October 15; 10 a.m.-6 p.m., April-May 14, October 16-December 15; 10 a.m.-4:30 p.m. Friday, Saturday, Sunday, December 16-March; closed January 1, Thanksgiving. Minnesota Park Point Recreation Center — daily, May-September 15. Glensheen — 10 a.m.-4 p.m. Thursday-Tuesday, mid-May to mid-October; rest of year, Monday, Tuesday, Thursday, Friday, tours at noon and 2 p.m.; 1-4 p.m. Saturday and Sunday; closed January 1, Easter, Thanksgiving, December 25. Leif Erikson Park — daily, May-September 15. St. Louis County Heritage and Arts Center — 10 a.m.-5 p.m. daily. Museum of Transportation and Industry — 10 a.m.-5 p.m. daily, May-September; 10 a.m.-5 p.m. Saturday, 1-5 p.m. Sunday, October-May; closed January 1, Easter, Thanksgiving, December 25. Fairmont Park Zoo — 10 a.m.-8 p.m. daily, May-September; 10 a.m.-4 p.m. October-April. Duluth-Superior Excursions — 9:30 a.m.-9:30 p.m., trips every two hours, May, June, Labor Day to mid-October; 9:30 a.m.-7:30 p.m., trips every hour, July-Labor Day.
ADMISSION: Canal Park Marine Museum — free. Minnesota Park Point Recreation Center — free. Leif Erikson Park — free. Glensheen — adults, $4; under 17, $2. St. Louis County Heritage and Arts Center — adults, $2.25; sr. citizens, $1.75; 6-17, 75¢; under 6, free. Fairmont Park Zoo — adults, $1.50; 6-12, 50¢; under 6, free. Duluth-Superior Excursions — adults, $4.95; under 12, $2.25.
DIRECTIONS: From Minneapolis/St. Paul, take I-94 east to U.S. 61 north to I-35 north to Duluth.
FOR MORE INFORMATION: Call the Duluth Area Chamber of Commerce, (218) 722-5501, or write 325 Harbor Dr., Duluth, MN 55802.

Fishing In the North Country

Detroit Lakes, Minnesota

Driving Time: 4 hours northwest of Minneapolis/St. Paul

If your family is looking for a splendid fishing and resort area, then **Detroit Lakes** is the place to go. There are 412 lakes, in separate chains, within a 25-mile span.

Fort Detroit (three miles west via Hwy. 10) is the largest deer park in Minnesota, with almost 100 tame deer waiting to be hand-fed. Bears and buffalos are also on the grounds. Visitors can take stagecoach and pony rides. Other attractions include a Tom Sawyer tree house, a gravity-mystery house, and a fish pond.

The **Becker County Historical Society Museum** (915 Lake Ave.) contains an outstanding collection of Viking, Indian, and pioneer artifacts.

The **Tamarac National Wildlife Refuge** has 18 lakes, abundant wild rice, and other aquatic vegetation. There's no shortage of grouse, beaver, and deer. And a flyway sanctuary exists for thousands of ducks and geese. Fishing and picnic areas are available.

The **Detroit Mt. Ski Area** (three miles east of MN 34) offers a double chair lift, two T-bars, six rope tows, a ski school, equipment rentals, and snowmaking.

BEST TIME TO VISIT: Summer.
HOURS: Fort Detroit — 9 a.m.-7 p.m. daily, May 17-September 15, holidays; rest of May and September to 5 p.m. Becker County Historical Society Museum — 2-5 p.m. Monday-Friday, except holidays. Tamarac National Wildlife Refuge — daylight hours daily. Detroit Mt. Ski Area — 11 a.m.-5 p.m. Wednesday, Thanksgiving-late March; 10 a.m.-9 p.m. Thursday-Friday; 9:30 a.m.-8 p.m. Saturday, Sunday.
ADMISSION: Fort Detroit — adults, $1.75; under 11, $1.25. Becker County Historical Society Museum — free. Tamarac National Wildlife Refuge — free.
DIRECTIONS: From Minneapolis/St. Paul, take I-94 northwest to Fergus Falls. Pick up U.S. 59 north to Detroit Lakes.
FOR MORE INFORMATION: Call the Detroit Lakes Regional Chamber of Commerce, (218) 847-9202, or write P.O. Box 348, Detroit Lakes, MN 56501.

Minnesota

Northfield: James' Gang Shootout

Northfield, Minnesota

Driving Time: 1¼ hours south of Minneapolis/St. Paul

Once called the "Holstein Capital of America," Northfield is still the center of farm-wealthy Rice County. Located on the banks of the scenic Cannon River, Northfield is the home of **Carleton** and **St. Olaf's colleges**. Carleton has long ranked with the Ivy League schools as one of the finest liberal arts colleges in the nation. There are hiking trails in its 455-acre arboretum.

St. Olaf's for decades has been renowned worldwide for its superb choir. Campus visitors can see the

Steensland Art Gallery and the archives of the **Norwegian-American Historical Association**. If members of your family are hungry, they can eat at the public dining room.

Northfield is probably best remembered for the time on September 7, 1876, when the Jesse James gang unsuccessfully tried to hold up the First National Bank in the **Scriver Building** (408 Division). The restored structure currently houses the Northfield Chamber of Commerce and the Northfield Historical Society, which has a museum there.

The **Defeat of Jesse James Days**, held each September, is a community festival with athletic contests, art exhibits, and a carnival. The main event is a reenactment of the famous bank raid that led to the demise of the James-Younger gang.

The **Northfield Arts Guild** in the historic YMCA building contains exhibits of local and regional arts and crafts. Both the gallery and the gift shop are on the first floor. Upstairs are administrative offices, an art

classroom, a private studio, and a recital room. Musicals are held in August and September.

Nerstrand Woods State Park (12 miles southeast, off MN 246) is 1,073 acres of heavily wooded area with a picturesque prairie creek, 11 miles of hiking trails, five miles of snowmobile trails, six miles of cross-country skiing trails, 62 modern campsites, and many picnic areas.

BEST TIME TO VISIT: Summer.
HOURS: Carleton College Arboretum — tours available with advance notice. Steensland Art Gallery — 1-5 p.m. Monday-Friday, 2-5 p.m. Saturday and Sunday. Scriver Bldg. — 9 a.m.-5 p.m. Monday, Tuesday, Wednesday, Friday; 5-9 p.m. Thursday; 10 a.m.-5 p.m. Saturday; closed Sunday. Northfield Arts Guild — 10 a.m.-5 p.m. Tuesday-Sunday, open holidays.
ADMISSION: Carleton College Arboretum — free. Steensland Art Gallery — free. Scriver Bldg. — donation. Northfield Arts Guild — free.
DIRECTIONS: From Minneapolis/St. Paul, take I-35 south to Northfield.
FOR MORE INFORMATION: Call the Northfield Area Chamber of Commerce, (507) 645-5604, or write 22 Bridge Sq., Box 198, Northfield, MN 55057.

Minnesota

Little Falls: Land of Lindbergh

Little Falls, Minnesota

Driving Time: 2 hours northwest of Minneapolis

Little Falls got its name from the Mississippi River rapids, which are now harnessed by a dam in the center of the city.

The **Lindbergh Home and Interpretive Center**, at the southern edge of town, preserves the boyhood home of aviator Charles Lindbergh. The house is in its original condition and contains the original furnishings of the Lindbergh family. In the entrace hall hangs a decorative map of Lindbergh's 1927 solo flight from New York to Paris in the monoplane *Spirit of St. Louis*. Costumed guides give tours and the Interpretive Center contains many artifacts of three generations of Lindberghs. There's also a slide show, and a book and souvenir shop.

Lindbergh State Park (1½ miles southwest on Lindbergh Dr.) is actually named after Lindbergh's father, who was a prominent U.S. congressman. The park has 52 modern campsites, a pioneer group camp, picnic areas, and two miles of foot trails.

The **Charles A. Weyerhaeuser Memorial Home** (two miles southwest of town via Lindbergh Dr.), a museum and resource center for Morrison County history, contains many interesting exhibits.

Smuda's Zoo (south of Lindbergh Park and across from the Weyerhaeuser Museum) is a privately owned zoo with 50 varieties of birds and other animals from all over the world. Canoe rentals are also available.

Pine Grove Municipal Park (west on MN 27) is filled with beautiful

virgin white pine timber. There's playground equipment, picnic facilities, and a shelter cabin. Also in the park is the **Pine Grove Municipal Zoo**, which contains buffalo, elk, bear, deer, wolves, and small native animals.

Another site worth looking at is the **Dewey-Radke Mansion** (west on Hwy. 27), a restored and refurnished house built in 1893.

BEST TIME TO VISIT: Summer.
HOURS: Lindbergh Home and Interpretive Center — 10 a.m.-5 p.m. daily, May-October 31. Weyerhaeuser Memorial Museum — 10 a.m.-5 p.m. Tuesday-Sunday; winter, closed Sunday; closed January 1, Thanksgiving, December 25. Pine Grove Municipal Park — 9 a.m.-9 p.m. daily, May-September. Dewey-Radke Mansion — 11 a.m.-5 p.m. Monday-Friday, June-September; noon-7 p.m. Saturday and Sunday.
ADMISSION: Lindbergh House and Interpretive Center — free. Weyerhaeuser Memorial Museum — free. Pine Grove Municipal Park — free. Dewey-Radke Mansion — free.
DIRECTIONS: From Minneapolis/St. Paul, take U.S. 10 northwest to Little Falls.
FOR MORE INFORMATION: Call the Little Falls Chamber of Commerce, (612) 632-5155, or write 310 NE 1st St., Little Falls, MN 56345.

Ely: Canoer's Paradise

Driving Time: 2 hours north of Duluth

A vacation and resort community, Ely is in the heart of the **Superior National Forest** and is also the gateway to **Boundary Waters Canoe Area Wilderness**, one of the world's finest canoeing areas. The wilderness, most of it accessible only by water, is a canoer's paradise, with more than 1,000 miles of canoe routes and more than 2,000 managed campsites.

Canoes, equipment, and supplies can be obtained at **Bill Rom's Canoe Outfitters** (629 E. Sheridan St.) and **Quetico-Superior Canoe Outfitters** (20 miles northeast on Moose Lake). Vacationers may also want to obtain information about the **Tom and Woods' Moose Lake Wilderness Canoe Trip** (20 miles northeast on Moose Lake).

The area is also renowned for its great fishing. The thousands of lakes are widely heralded producers of walleye, northern pike, lake trout, and smallmouth bass.

Voyageur Visitor Center (half mile east on MN 169) contains exhibits of Indians, miners, and voyageurs. There's also wildlife and geology displays, and the park naturalist presents evening programs.

The **Greenstone outcropping** (13th Ave. E and Main St.) is the only surface ellipsoidal greenstone in the U.S., judged to be more than two billion years old.

BEST TIME TO VISIT: Summer.
HOURS: Boundary Waters Canoe Area Wilderness — travel permits required for each party, May to November 15. Voyageur Visitor Center—6 a.m.-8 p.m. daily, May-September.
ADMISSION: Boundary Waters Canoe Area Wilderness — travel permits, free. Voyageur Visitor Center — free.
DIRECTIONS: From Duluth, take U.S. 53 north to Hwy. 169 northwest to Ely.
FOR MORE INFORMATION: Call the Ely Chamber of Commerce, (218) 365-6123, or write 1600 E. Sheridan, Ely, MN 55731.

Minnesota

Northland Vacation Paradise

Bemidji, Minnesota

Driving Time: 3 hours northwest of Duluth

Bemidji, on the shores of beautiful Lake Bemidji, is a vacation paradise of lakes and forests. It's the site of many logging and Indian trails, wooded shorelines, and scenic rivers. Once strictly a summer vacation area, Bemidji now plays host to winter sports enthusiasts, spring anglers, fall hunters, and nature-lovers.

To the north lies **Red Lake**, the largest body of water wholly within one state. Here visitors may see the Chippewa sawmill, fisheries, and the burial grounds at Ponemah. Saum is the site of a restored one-room school. Also, a few miles north is the **Continental Divide**, where water flows north to the Hudson Bay and south to the Gulf of Mexico.

Lake Bemidji State Park, just north of the city limits (six miles northeast off U.S. 71), is a small 337-acre park with swimming, fishing, hiking, boating, camping, and picnic areas.

There are five state forests nearby; to the east is the beautiful **Chippewa National Forest** with thousands of acres of pines and lakes. Visitors can go mushroom and berry picking, wildlife-watching, cross-country skiing, snowmobiling, and camping.

Bemidji has an excellent park system, with 11 parks containing a total of approximately 150 acres. Public beaches are maintained at **Diamond Point, Nymore,** and **Cameron Parks**.

Bemidji is the birthplace of **Paul Bunyan**, and various attractions celebrate his exploits. On U.S. 71 stand huge replicas of the mythical lumberjack and his mascot, Babe, the Blue Ox.

Bemidji celebrates Paul Bunyan, too.

Nearby, on the shores of Lake Bemidji, the **Bunyan House Information Center** (3rd St. and Bemidji Ave.) houses a collection of Bunyan tools and artifacts with amusing descriptions. There's also the nationally famous "Fireplace of States," which is made from stones from every state in the Union, Canadian provinces, and many foreign countries.

The **Historical and Wildlife Museum** (3rd St. and Bemidji Ave.) features the John G. Morrison Collection of Indian artifacts, authentic reproductions of Minnesota birds and animals in their native habitat, as well as the Beltrami County Historical Society collection.

The **Paul Bunyan Water Carnival** is held each July 4th weekend. The festival consists of a water show, parade, beauty pageant, and fireworks.

BEST TIME TO VISIT: Summer.
TRAVEL TIPS: Bemidji can get crowded during the summer months, so make your vacation reservations early.
HOURS: Bunyan House Information Center — 8:30 a.m.-8:30 p.m. daily, Memorial Day-Labor Day; 8:30 a.m.-4:30 p.m., Monday-Friday, rest of the year. Historical and Wildlife Museum — 8:30 a.m.-8:30 p.m. daily, Memorial Day-Labor Day; 8:30 a.m.-4:30 p.m. Monday-Friday, rest of the year.
ADMISSION: Bunyan House Information Center — free. Historical and Wildlife Museum — adults, $1.25; under 18, 50¢; family, $2.50
DIRECTIONS: From Duluth, take U.S. 2 northwest to Bemidji.
FOR MORE INFORMATION: Call the Bemidji Chamber of Commerce, (218) 751-3540, or write 3rd and Bemidji Ave., Box 806, Bemidji, MN 56601.

Minnesota

Middle Falls on the Pidgeon River

Striking Outdoor Scenery

Grand Rapids, Minnesota

Driving Time: 3½ hours north of Minneapolis/St. Paul

Grand Rapids, seat of Itasca County, is at the western end of the **Mesabi Iron Range**. A number of open-pit mines nearby have observation stands for the public. The forested area surrounding the town includes more than a thousand lakes. Four of them (Crystal, Hale, Forest, and McKinney) are within the city limits.

Scenic State Park (40 miles north on MN 38, then east) is a primitive area that has two lakes, Coon and Sandwich. Camping, picnicking, boating, fishing, swimming, hiking, cross-country skiing, and snowmobiling are available.

Vacationers can go swimming at **Blandin Beach** (10th Ave. W and 5th St. on Forest Lake). There's a beach house, diving raft, tower, and playground.

If your family prefers canoeing, they can go south on the Mississippi River or north on Bigfork waters to **Rainy Lake**.

Sugar Hills (14 miles southwest on U.S. 169) is an all-year recreation complex of 100 acres filled with lakes and forests. Vacationers can go fishing, swimming, boating, skiing, or play water sports.

The **Forest History Center** (three miles southwest via U.S. 169) provides displays of man's interaction with the forest from prehistoric Indian times to the present and on into the future. The center also includes an authentically reconstructed turn-of-the-century logging camp typical of such camps once common in northern Minnesota.

Not far from the logging camp is a mid-1930s ranger cabin and fire tower where a uniformed ranger shows the tools and discusses techniques of early forest protection.

Included on the grounds of the center is a short woodland trail where visitors are encouraged to take leisurely strolls through the forested area.

BEST TIME TO VISIT: Late spring, summer, early fall.
TRAVEL TIPS: Grand Rapids is noted for its pretty autumns. Drive on any of several fall color routes and witness Mother Nature at her colorful best.
HOURS: Blandin Park — 9 a.m.-8:45 p.m. Monday-Saturday, mid-June to late August; Sunday, holidays from 1 p.m. Forest History Center — 10 a.m.-5 p.m. daily, May-October.
ADMISSION: Blandin Park —free. Forest History Center — free.
DIRECTIONS: From Minneapolis/St. Paul, take U.S. 169 north to Grand Rapids.
FOR MORE INFORMAITON: Call the Grand Rapids Area Chamber of Commerce, (218) 326-6619, or write Grand Rapids, MN 55744.

A Famous Lighthouse And Fishing

Two Harbors, Minnesota

Driving Time: 2 hours north of Duluth, 5½ hours north of Minneapolis/St. Paul

Two Harbors is an important ore-shipping terminal. Your family can observe ore-loading operations from **Paul Van Hoven Park** or from **Fisherman's Point**.

Gooseberry Falls State Park (14 miles northeast on U.S. 61) offers picnicking, fishing, hiking, camping, cross-country skiing, and snowmobiling. A trout-laden stream rushes over five waterfalls and through a magnificent woodland. Visitors can cool their feet or take a swim at the foot of a waterfall on the north side of the park bridge.

A few miles north, travelers will find one of Minnesota's best-known landmarks, **Split Rock Lighthouse**, perched on a cliff over 100 feet above Lake Superior. For nearly 60 years the huge lens at the top of the tower flashed across some of the most dangerous inland navigable water in the world. Visit the tower, the fog signal building, and a restored keeper's home where guides tell about life at this remote station in the years when it could be reached only by water.

Your family can lunch in Silver Bay or buy snacks for a picnic at **Palisade Head**. Palisade Baptist Church is a landmark to watch for before turning off to the 350-foot rock cliff that provides an awesome view of Lake Superior and the jagged Sawtooth Range.

BEST TIME TO VISIT: Summer, fall.
HOURS: Gooseberry Falls State Park — open all year. Split Rock Lighthouse — open all year.
ADMISSION: Split Rock Lighthouse — free.
DIRECTIONS: From Duluth, take U.S. 61 north to Two Harbors.
FOR MORE INFORMATION: Call the Two Harbors Area Development Corp., (218) 834-3846, or write Box 39, Two Harbors, MN 55616.

Minnesota

International Falls: Land of Voyageurs

International Falls, Minnesota

Driving Time: 6 hours north of Minneapolis/St. Paul

International Falls, at the northernmost point in the central part of the state, is a major point of entry between Canada and Minnesota. The city is a crossroads for sportsmen, hunters, and fishermen traveling to and from the great walleye waters of Rainy Lake in **Voyageurs National Park** (off U.S. 53) and huge, muskie-filled **Lake of the Woods**, some 70 miles to the west.

The main body of land in the park is **Rainy Lake's Kabetogama Peninsula**, accessible only by water or by air. There are many fine resorts and campgrounds in the area, which offers superb fishing, boating, and canoeing.

The French-Canadian voyageurs transported furs by canoe through this forested lake country. To enjoy it fully, your family will have to travel the same way, as there are no roads to the interior of the park. Many of the most beautiful lakes, in fact, can be reached only by foot.

Of the park's 219,000 acres, more than one-third are water. Four large interconnected lakes dominate the park, and 26 smaller lakes dot the landscape. Hundreds of small, rocky islands are scattered over the bigger lakes.

The park lies in the southern portion of the Canadian Shield. The ancient sediment that comprises the shield represents some of the oldest rock formations in the world.

Perhaps nothing so symbolizes the park's enduring primitive character as the presence of its wolves. The park is in the heart of the only region in the continental United States

where the eastern timber wolf still survives.

The **Koochiching County Historical Museum** in Municipal Park has exhibits, photographs, and artifacts that provide historical background on the area. Children will especially enjoy the 25-foot statue of Smokey the Bear in the park.

Visitors can picnic, swim, and enjoy a fine sand beach at **International Falls City Beach** (3½ miles east on MN 11).

Near the **Grand Mound Interpretive Center** (17 miles west via Hwy. 11) are several ancient Indian burial mounds, the largest being the Grand Mound, which has never been excavated. The Interpretive Center offers an audio-visual program, a sound system exhibit, and a half-mile trail to the mound site.

International Falls is one of the nation's major centers of the wood

industry, dominated by the immense mills of the Boise-Cascade Paper Co. Tours of the paper mills are available to visitors.

BEST TIME TO VISIT: Summer.
TRAVEL TIPS: Find out about the ranger-guided tours at Voyageurs National Park. Children can enjoy various planned activities geared especially for them. Activities include evening campfire programs, nature walks, and blueberry safaris.
HOURS: Koochiching County Historical Museum — 9 a.m.-6 p.m. Monday-Saturday, Memorial Day-Labor Day; 2-5 p.m. Sunday, holidays, rest of year; research center, open by appointment. Grand Mound Interpretive Center — 10 a.m.-5 p.m. daily, May-October; weekends November-April. Boise-Cascade Mill Tours — 8:30 a.m., 10 a.m., 1 p.m. Monday-Friday, June-August; closed holidays.
ADMISSION: Koochiching County Historical Museum — adults, 50¢; children, 25¢. Grand Mound Interpretive Center — free. Boise-Cascade Mill Tours — free.
DIRECTIONS: From the Twin Cities, take I-35 north to U.S. 53 north to International Falls.
FOR MORE INFORMATION: Call Greater International Falls Area Chamber of Commerce, (218) 283-9400, or write Box 169, International Falls, MN 56649.

Grand Marais: Getting Away From It All

Grand Marais, Minnesota

Driving Time: 1 hour northeast of Duluth

Because of its cool climate, pollen-free air, excellent lake and stream fishing, abundant wildlife, ample camping, and breathtaking wilderness, Grand Marais remains a leading resort area. The town, perched on the north shore of Lake Superior in northeast Minnesota, resembles the tip of an arrow and is known as the "Arrowhead Country."

The **Grand Portage National Monument** (1 mile northeast on U.S. 61) was a fur post that has been restored to its 18th-century appearance to recall when it was the boisterous center of voyageur activity.

Some of the region's outstanding scenery is in **Cascade State Park**. The Cascade River flows through this beautiful 2,300-acre park and pours into Lake Superior over a series of dazzling waterfalls. The park is well equipped with hiking trails, campgrounds, fireplaces, and picnic facilities.

Grand Marais is the jumping-off point for a shunpike over **Gunflint Trail** into the wilderness area of **Superior National Forest**. Arrowhead and Sawbill Trails also are located in the Superior National Forest region of the North Shore Drive. Both are worth a trip.

The Gunflint Trail leads some 60 miles over a hardtop road through a primeval forest to the Canadian border. Travelers will find hundreds of lakes where camping, picnicking, fishing, and canoeing are available. (Boundary Waters Canoe Area Wilderness, part of the forest, is perhaps the finest canoe country in the U.S.)

BEST TIME TO VISIT: Summer.
TRAVEL TIPS: Take some of the side roads off the main highways and trails. They lead to fish-laden lakes and spectacular scenery.
HOURS: Grand Portage National Monument — 8 a.m.-5 p.m. daily, mid-May to mid-October. Gunflint Trail and Superior National Forest — year round.
ADMISSION: Grand Portage National Monument — free. Superior National Forest camping — $3-$4/site/night.
DIRECTIONS: From Duluth, take U.S. 61 northeast to Grand Marais.
FOR MORE INFORMATION: Call the Tip of the Arrowhead Association, (218) 387-1330, or write Box MT, Grand Marais, MN 55604.

Center Of Lake Country

Fergus Falls, Minnesota

Driving Time: 4 hours northwest of Minneapolis/St. Paul

Fergus Falls, in central Minnesota, is the seat of Otter Tail County. A map of the area shows more blue than green, reflecting the hundreds of lakes that are there for your family's pleasure. There are five lakes within the city's limits. Numerous parks and a host of recreational facilities, such as tennis courts, hockey rinks, beaches, and exercise areas, are scattered throughout the city.

Lake Alice, sometimes called the "Lake on the Hill," rests in the center of town on a hilly tract that provides many pleasant drives. Geese and ducks feed and breed there throughout the warm months.

Families can picnic, swim, play golf on an 18-hole course, or sunbathe on a beach at **Pebble Lake City Park** (southeast on U.S. 59).

Another popular recreation site is **DeLagoon Park** (one mile south on U.S. 59), which also provides picnicking, swimming, boating, fishing, and camping.

Otter Tail County Historical Museum (1110 W. Lincoln Ave.) contains artifacts of local and county history, including replicas of a one-room schoolhouse, a general store, and a trapper's cabin.

BEST TIME TO VISIT: Spring, summer.
HOURS: Pebble Lake City Park — 1-9 p.m. daily, early June-late August. DeLagoon Park — daily, mid-May to October. Otter Tail County Historical Society Museum — 11 a.m.-5 p.m. Monday-Friday, 1-4 p.m. Saturday and Sunday; closed holidays.
ADMISSION: Pebble Lake City Park — free. DeLagoon Park — free. Otter Tail County Historical Society Museum — adults, $1; children, free.
DIRECTIONS: From Minneapolis/St. Paul, take I-94 northwest to Fergus Falls.
FOR MORE INFORMATION: Call Fergus Falls Chamber of Commerce, (218) 736-6951, or write 202 S. Court, Fergus Falls, MN 56537.

Minnesota

Pipestone: Hiawatha Holiday

Pipestone, Minnesota

Driving Time: 4½ hours southwest of Minneapolis/St. Paul

The city of Pipestone is located on the edge of "Coteau des Prairies," a long ride of land running almost 200 miles northwest to southeast. It is along this ridge that prehistoric glacial activity occured, leaving a soft, reddish stone layer found by early Indians. Some of the red granite from the quarries shows up in Pipestone's public buildings.

Pipestone also plays host to visitors on their way to **Pipestone National Monument**, a prairie area of 283 acres. The quarries were sacred ground for Indian tribes, who used the red stone to carve ceremonial pipes used in significant ceremonies. Visitors can still watch Indians fashion peacepipes and demonstrate other crafts at the Upper Midwest Indian Cultural Center.

Established as a national monument in 1937, Pipestone protects the remaining red stone and preserves its use by Indians. The **Visitor Center** has exhibits, slides, and a self-guided tour booklet. A three-quarter-mile circular trail leads travelers to many points of interest, including Lake Hiawatha; Old Stone Face, a natural profile in a quartzite ledge; and beautiful Winnewissa Falls. During the growing season, many of the plants, trees, and shrubs along the trail are identified with labels that also describe their use by Indians.

If your family is in the area during the last two weekends of July or the first weekend of August, don't miss the **"Song of Hiawatha" Outdoor Pageant** performed in the natural amphitheater near the monument.

Hiawatha pageant in Pipestone

Quarry Lake fronts the stage, with three huge granite boulders, named the Three Maidens, as a backdrop. Reenacting Longfellow's famous poem, the program uses elaborate lighting equipment which highlights the costumed players and reflects across ripppling water and colorful stone ledges.

The first floor of the **Pipestone County Museum** (113 S. Hiawatha) contains three galleries forming a chronological walk through Pipestone County history. The second floor has a research library and reading room, a Native Americans Gallery, Pipestone County Photo Gallery, and other exhibits.

Ask about the walking tour of the historic district. Be sure to see the restored Calumet Hotel, with its massive stone walls, both inside and out.

Travel south to **Split Rock Creek State Park** on MN 23, a 238-acre recreation area with 17 modern campsites, a pioneer group camp, picnic grounds, a swimming beach, lake fishing, a half-mile hiking trail, and 1½ miles of snowmobile trails. There is an abundance of wildflowers, and the area is also a haven for waterfowl and aquatic birds.

BEST TIME TO VISIT: Summer.

TRAVEL TIPS: Bring a sweater or jacket to the Song of Hiawatha Pageant, which is held outdoors. Even though the performances are offered in mid-summer, evenings can still get chilly.

HOURS: Upper Midwest Indian Cultural Center — 8 a.m.-9 p.m. daily, Memorial Day-Labor Day; rest of year to 5 p.m. Visitor Center — same hours as the Indian Cultural Center; closed January 1, December 25. Pipestone County Museum — 10 a.m.-noon and 1-5 p.m. Tuesday-Saturday, September-May; 10 a.m.-5 p.m. Monday-Saturday, 1-5 p.m. Sunday, June-August. Split Rock Creek State Park — open all year.

ADMISSION: Upper Midwest Indian Cultural Center — free. Pipestone County Museum — free. Split Rock Creek State Park — standard fees.

DIRECTIONS: From Minneapolis/St. Paul, take U.S. 169 southwest to U.S. 75 west to Hwy. 23 south to Pipestone.

FOR MORE INFORMATION: Call Pipestone Chamber of Commerce, (507) 825-3316, or write 117 Eighth Ave. SE, P.O. Box 551, Pipestone, MN 56164.

St. Cloud: Pleasant Sojourn

St. Cloud, Minnesota

Driving Time: 1½ hours southwest of Minneapolis/St. Paul

Noted for its granite quarries, St. Cloud was the northern boundary of Mississippi River navigation during the mid-1800s.

At **Riverside Park** (Riverside Dr. SE) stands a monument to Zebulon Pike, the discoverer of the nearby Beaver Islands in 1805 during his exploration of the Mississippi. There are gardens, a wading pool, tennis courts, picnic facilities, and lighted cross-country skiing trails.

Visit **Eastman Park** (Ninth Ave. and Division St.) and see graceful swans and paddleboats skimming Lake George in the summer. Activities include picnicking, sun bathing, and swimming in the Olympic-sized municipal pool. During the winter, hockey players and figure skaters criss-cross the lake. A new warming house offers shelter from the cold.

Waite's Crossing (Eighth St. N) is a monument that marks the point where the Sauk River was forded by pioneers in oxcarts en route to the Red River Valley.

The **Mississippi River County Park** (north of Sartell on County Rd. 1) includes a nature and tree plantation area, a six-acre native prairieland exhibit, and cross-country skiing and snowmobile trails.

Your family can also find picnic space, playgrounds, hiking trails, a swimming area, a boat ramp, and fishing at **Warner Lake County Park** (five miles south of St. Augusta, just off County Rd. 75).

The **Stearns County Historical Society** (501 Mall Germain) contains historical books, old photographs,

Hiawatha and Minnehaha in Pipestone pageant

newspaper articles, oral interviews, and family histories. The society also offers a 15-site walking tour past historic homes and landmarks.

St. Cloud State University (Third Ave. S) has such points of interest as a planetarium, the Minnesota Wildlife Museum, a greenhouse, and the Museum of Anthropology.

St. John's University (15 minutes west on I-74) is located on the grounds of St. John's Abbey, the largest Benedictine monastery in the world. The university is situated among 2,400 acres of woods and lakes, with trails for hiking and cross-country skiing. The campus is dominated by the spectacular Abbey Church, with its 110-foot bell tower. Designed by Marcel Breuer, the church is renowned for its unique architecture.

The **College of St. Benedict** (in St. Joseph, seven miles west on U.S. 52) is the second largest Catholic women's college in the world. The Benedicta Arts Center, an award-winning fine arts building, features theater, music and art exhibits, concerts, lectures, and films.

The **Powder Ridge Ski Area** (16 miles southwest on MN 15) has two chair lifts, one J-bar, two rope tows, snowmaking, a ski school, equipment rentals, and a restaurant.

BEST TIME TO VISIT: Summer, winter.
HOURS: Stearns County Historical Society — call the society at (218) 253-8424 for hours. St. Cloud University — 8:30 a.m.-4 p.m. Monday-Friday except holidays; closed late August, late December, early March, early June. College of St. Benedict — call (218) 363-5901 for schedules. Powder Ridge Ski Area — 10 a.m.-10 p.m. Monday-Friday, late November-April; Saturday, Sunday, holidays from 9 a.m.
ADMISSION: Stearns County Historical Society — free. St. Cloud University — free. Powder Ridge Ski Area — adults, $7-12; under 12, $5-10.
DIRECTIONS: From Minneapolis/St. Paul, take Hwy. 10 southwest to St. Cloud.
FOR MORE INFORMATION: Call St. Cloud Chamber of Commerce, (218) 251-2940, or write 20 S. 4th Ave., Box 487, St. Cloud MN 56751.

Minnesota

Brainerd: Paul Bunyan Country

Brainerd, Minnesota

Driving Time: 2½ hours northwest of Minneapolis/St. Paul

Sometimes called the "hometown of Paul Bunyan," Brainerd hugs the Mississippi River banks at the geographical center of the state. Within a 30-mile radius are nearly 500 clean, blue lakes that help to make this one of Minnesota's most popular vacation areas. In addition to superb boating, fishing, and swimming, the area offers eight golf courses, horseback riding, roller skating, bowling, and hundreds of fine restaurants, resorts, motels, and campgrounds.

One of the most popular attractions in Brainerd is the **Paul Bunyan Amusement Center** (one mile west at junction of MN 210 and 371), where a 26-foot animated Paul Bunyan and a 15-foot Babe, the Blue Ox, greet visitors. There are lumber exhibits, trained animals, picnic grounds, an amusement park, and helicopter rides.

Another top attraction, **Lumbertown USA** (four miles north on MN 371, then eight miles west on County 77, Pine Beach Rd.), is a replica of a typical old Minnesota lumber town of the 1870s. Travelers will find more than 30 buildings, including a general store, country schoolhouse, mess hall and bunk house, a saloon, and a museum of fire pumpers. Visitors can ride a replica of an original Northern Pacific train or board an old paddlewheel boat.

The **Crow Wing County Historical Museum** (Laurel and 4th Sts., in the basement of the courthouse) contains an unusual array of pre-Civil War clothing through the 1930s, uniforms, weapons, household goods,

Indian artifacts, logging and railroad equipment, hand tools, and an extensive collection of rare and interesting photographs.

Another highly acclaimed museum in the area is the **Minnesota State Historical Society Indian Museum**, located on the Mille Lacs Indian Reservation (south of Garrison on Hwy. 169). It features life-sized displays of Indian camps as well as artifacts and historical photographs of native Minnesota Indians.

At **Deer Forest**, 10 miles away in Nisswa, visitors can feed and pet tame deer and other native animals in a natural wooded setting. Next door sits **Storybook Land**, which depicts famous fairy tales in attractive displays.

Auto-racing fans won't want to miss events at **Brainerd International Raceway,** where road and drag races are held in the summer.

The **Paul Bunyan Arboretum** (Hwy. 210 west to NW 7th St.) is a nature center with plants, trees, and shrubs native to the area. There's hiking in summer, cross-country skiing in winter.

Tourists can see turn-of-the-century mining artifacts at **Croft**

Mine Park (just north of Crosby).

The **Paul Bunyan Festival** in late September commemorates the logging heritage of the Brainerd area. Part of the events include the Great American Lumberjack Show featuring five World Class lumberjacks competing against each other in various exhibitions.

BEST TIME TO VISIT: Summer.
TRAVEL TIPS: Brainerd is noted for its fishing. If your family is the competitive type, check with the Brainerd Area Chamber of Commerce for information on various fishing tournaments offered throughout the year.
HOURS: Paul Bunyan Amusement Center — 9 a.m.-10 p.m. daily, May 29-September 6. Lumbertown USA — 10 a.m.-6 p.m. daily, mid-June to Labor Day; 10 a.m.-4:30 p.m., late May to mid-June and after Labor Day to mid-September. Crow Wing County Historical Museum — 1-5 p.m. Monday-Friday, June-August; Tuesday and Friday, September-May; closed holidays. Deer Forest Storybook Land — 9 a.m.-9 p.m. daily, May-October. Brainerd International Raceway — call for race dates.
ADMISSION: Paul Bunyan Amusement Center — 50¢ per person. Lumbertown USA — adults, $1.50; 5-12, 75¢; under 5, free. Crow Wing County Historical Museum — free. Deer Forest Storybook Land — call (218) 963-4776 for fees. Brainerd International Raceway — call for prices.
DIRECTIONS: From Minneapolis/St. Paul, take U.S. 10 northwest to Hwy. 371 north to Brainerd.
FOR MORE INFORMATION: Call Brainerd Area Chamber of Commerce, (218) 829-2838, or write 6th and Washington Sts., Brainerd, MN 56401.

World's oldest rock at Granite Falls

Pioneer Indian Life

Granite Falls, Minnesota

Driving Time: 2 hours southwest of Minneapolis/St. Paul

At Granite Falls, the **Yellow Medicine County Museum** (½ mile from the center of town via MN 67) has a delightful collection of artifacts, several pioneer buildings, and some of the world's oldest rock, which dates back 3.6 billion years.

Just south of Granite Falls is the **Upper Sioux Indian Agency.** This was one of two administrative centers established to serve the Dakota (Sioux) and teach them the farming methods used by pioneer settlers. Most of the buildings here were destroyed in an uprising, but one remaining structure, a brick duplex, has been restored and opened to the public.

In the state park area, an interpretive center explains the natural history of the region. The park is located on the peaceful banks of the Yellow Medicine River.

BEST TIME TO VISIT: Summer.
HOURS: Yellow Medicine County Museum — 1-5 p.m. Tuesday-Saturday, May-October; open holidays. Upper Sioux Indian Agency State Park — open all year.
ADMISSION: Yellow Medicine County Museum — free. Upper Sioux Indian Agency State Park — standard fees.
DIRECTIONS: From Minneapolis/St. Paul, take U.S. 212 southwest to Granite Falls.
FOR MORE INFORMATION: Call Granite Falls Chamber of Commerece, (612) 564-4039, or write Community Center, Granite Falls, MN 56241.

Itasca Park: Mississippi Source

Driving Time: 3 hours northwest of Duluth; 5 hours northwest of Minneapolis/St. Paul

Itasca, Minnesota's most popular state park, is only 30 miles south of Bemidji on Hwy. 71.

This 32,000-acre park includes the **source of the mighty Mississippi River**, where it begins its 2,552-mile journey to the Gulf of Mexico. At the source of the Mississippi, visitors can walk barefoot across the little stream and hardly get their feet wet.

More than one million people a year come to the park to marvel at its unspoiled natural beauty. The world's largest Norway pine, 115 inches around and 120 feet high, is located here. Miles of marked hiking trails wind through the quiet, peaceful forest where wildlife can be seen. Indian burial mounds, old log cabins, eagle nests, walleye fishing, swimming, camping, and dining facilities at historic **Douglas Lodge** are but a few of the things to see and do.

The **University of Minnesota's School of Forestry's** biological station operates in the park during the summer. It has laboratories and an arboretum. Exhibits show nearly every animal and plant native to the state. A naturalist program provides self-guided and guided hikes, car tours, and evening movies on the history and the attractions of the area. Inquire at the entrance gates for details.

The park is 21 miles north of Park Rapids, a popular resort area.

BEST TIME TO VISIT: Summer.
DIRECTIONS: From Duluth, take U.S. 2 to Hwy. 200 west to Walker. Pick up Hwy. 34 to Park Rapids and then take U.S. 71 north to Itasca State Park.
FOR MORE INFORMATION: Call Park Rapids Chamber of Commerce, (218) 732-4111, or write Box 249, Park Rapids, MN 56470.

Minnesota

Redwood Falls: Waterfall Wonderland

Redwood Falls, Minnesota

Driving Time: 2 hours southwest of Minneapolis/St. Paul

Redwood Falls is in a beautiful setting on a high bank of the **Redwood River**. It is surrounded by gorges and bluffs. The river drops 140 feet in three miles in a series of waterfalls. The town is probably best remembered as being the birthplace of Sears, Roebuck and Co.

At the city's northwest edge is **Alexander Ramsey Park**. Winding streams, rock cliffs, deep gorges, beautiful woodland, a small zoo, a playground, and other recreational equipment for children are found in its 200 acres.

The **Lower Sioux Agency and Interpretive Center** (nine miles east via MN 67 and County 2) has exhibits that trace the history of the Dakota Indians in Minnesota from the mid-16th century through the present day.

BEST TIME TO VISIT: Spring, fall.
HOURS: Lower Sioux Agency and Interpretive Center — 9 a.m.-5 p.m. daily, April-October.
ADMISSION: Lower Sioux Agency and Interpretive Center — free.
DIRECTIONS: From Minneapolis/St. Paul, take U.S. 169 southwest to Hwy. 19 west to Redwood Falls.
FOR MORE INFORMATION: Call Redwood Falls Area Chamber of Commerce, (507) 637-2828, or write Box 397, Redwood Falls, MN 56283.

Writer's Boyhood Home

Sauk Center, Minnesota

Driving Time: 2½ hours northwest of Minneapolis/St. Paul

Literary-minded travelers should make it a point to stop off at Sauk Center, the boyhood home of Sinclair Lewis. The first American to win the Nobel Prize for literature, Lewis based his novel *Main Street* on his early experiences here.

The **Sinclair Lewis Boyhood Home** (612 Sinclair Lewis Ave.), the author's restored house, is filled with original antique furnishings.

The **Sinclair Lewis Interpretive Center** (junction of I-94 and U.S. 7) explains the history of Sauk Center and the Lewis family. Many original manuscripts and letters shed light on the author, his life, and his works. A tour includes an 18-minute slide presentation on the novelist's life.

BEST TIME TO VISIT: Summer.
HOURS: Sinclair Lewis Boyhood Home — 10 a.m.-6 p.m. Monday-Saturday, 1-6 p.m. Sunday, Memorial Day-Labor Day. Sinclair Lewis Interpretive Center — 8 a.m.-8 p.m. daily, Memorial Day-Labor Day.
ADMISSION: Sinclair Lewis Boyhood Home—adults, $1; children, 50¢. Sinclair Lewis Interpretive Center — free.
DIRECTIONS: From Minneapolis/St. Paul, take I-94 northwest to Sauk Center.
FOR MORE INFORMATION: Call Sauk Area Chamber of Commerce, (612) 352-5201, or write Box 222, Sauk Center, MN 56378.

Panfish Capital Of the World

Alexandria, Minnesota

Driving Time: 2½ hours northwest of Minneapolis/St. Paul

A steady stream of tourists are continuously attracted to Alexandria's 214 fish-filled lakes and more than 90 resorts and campgrounds.

Kensington Runestone Museum (206 N. Broadway) has as its title display a greywacke boulder with runic inscriptions of a 1362 date, supporting the belief that Vikings explored North America long before Columbus' discovery of the New World. Other fascinating artifacts of 14th-century origin include weapons and implements found along the route of the Vikings through Minnesota waterways. There are also restored log cabins, farm tools, horse-drawn machinery, and an old country schoolhouse.

Lake Carlos State Park (10 miles north, off MN 29) has 1,250 acres that lie within the scenic Leaf Hills region. Diverse aquatic and upland habitats account for the abundance of wildlife in the park, which is dominated by the rolling, wooded landscape along the sandy shoreline of Lake Carlos.

BEST TIME TO VISIT: Summer.
HOURS: Kensington Runestone Museum — 9 a.m.-5 p.m. Monday-Friday, Saturday to 8 p.m., Sunday from 10 a.m.; closed January 1, Thanksgiving, December 25.
ADMISSION: Kensington Runestone Museum — adults, $2.25; sr. citizens, $1.50; 11-17, $1; under 11, free.
DIRECTIONS: From Minneapolis/St. Paul, take I-94 northwest to Alexandria.
FOR MORE INFORMATION: Call Alexandria Chamber of Commerce, (612) 763-3161, or write 206 N. Broadway, Alexandria, MN 56308.

Sweetheart Days in Hackensack

Hackensack, Minnesota

Driving Time: 4 hours north of Minneapolis/St. Paul

Hackensack is a provisioning point for **Long Pine Playground**, an area of 648 lakes and nearly 500 resorts in Minnesota's Arrowhead Country. This village claims fame as the home of Paul Bunyan's sweetheart, Lucette Diana Kensack. A large statue of her stands on the shores of Birch Lake. Sweetheart Day, held each year during the second Wednesday in July, celebrates the legendary visits of Paul Bunyan to his girlfriend with a full day of family activities, including parades, pageants, races, contests, and a carnival.

BEST TIME TO VISIT: Summer.
DIRECTIONS: From Minneapolis/St. Paul, take I-94 to U.S. 10 to Hwy. 371 to Hackensack.
FOR MORE INFORMATION: Call the Hackensack Chamber of Commerce, (218) 675-6135, or write Civic Association, Hackensack, MN 56452.

Woods and Water Adventure

Walker, Minnesota

Driving Time: 2½ hours west of Duluth; 3½ hours north of Minneapolis/St. Paul

Located at the foot of **Chippewa National Forest** and the southwest shore of Leech Lake, Walker is ideal for families who like woods and water. **Leech Lake** is famed among fishermen for its large walleyes and record catches of northerns and muskies.

A major annual event is **Muskie Derby Days,** held during the first week of August. Dozens of muskies, some as big as 43 pounds, are entered for prizes.

Several hundred summer resorts are scattered along Leech Lakes's hundreds of miles of shoreline. Points of interest in the area include a forest lookout tower, an Indian burial ground, the **Wildlife and Indian Arts Museum and Aquarium, Deer Valley Farm,** the **Chippewa Indian Reservation**, and a monument to the Battle of Sugar Point, the state's last Indian fight.

Snowmobiling and cross-country skiing are popular sports here.

BEST TIME TO VISIT: Summer, winter.
DIRECTIONS: From Duluth, take U.S. 2 west to Hwy. 200 west to Walker.
FOR MORE INFORMATION: Call the Walker Chamber of Commerce, (218) 547-1313, or write Box G, Walker, MN 56484.

Minnesota

St. Croix: Outdoor Paradise

Taylors Falls, Minnesota
St. Croix Falls, Wisconsin

Driving Time: 1 hour northeast of Minneapolis/St. Paul; 8 hours northwest of Milwaukee

Situated on bluffs high above the St. Croix River are the historic towns of **Taylors Falls**, Minn. and **St. Croix Falls**, Wisc. As one of the last wild rivers in the midwestern United States, the St. Croix looks much as it did years ago when settlers traveled to the area. Lush forests and spectacular rock configurations form breathtaking scenic views all year round—but especially in the fall when the trees are ablaze with color.

Years ago, the French explorers named the river St. Croix (sacred cross) because of a gigantic cross-like rock formation on the river bank. Boat tours of the area are available. On them you'll learn interesting historical facts and see unique natural rock creations such as Devil's Chair, Lion's Head and "The Old Man of the Dalles"—a rock face that looks like an old man. (Boat trips early May through mid-October from Minnesota Interstate Park or the Trading Post near the Minnesota-Wisconsin Bridge.)

If you want a do-it-yourself tour, rent canoes for a half day or more (Minnesota Interstate Park). Of course, the river is full of catfish, sturgeon and smallmouth bass.

Back on land, children and adults will enjoy a popular new summer sport at the **Wild Mountain Ski Area** (north of Taylors Falls on Rt. 16). The

Alpine Slide offers a scenic chair lift ride up the ski hill followed by a thrilling ride down through hairpin turns, around curves and along straightways.

In downtown Taylors Falls, the shady, tree-lined streets offer a look into the past. The streets of the **Angels Hill District**, just above the Taylors Falls commercial section, are lined with white clapboard houses built in the 1850s and 1860s by a group of St. Croix Valley settlers who wished to recreate a New England village. The **W.H.C. Folsom House** on Government Road is open to the public daily during the summer and early fall. Built in 1854 by a politician, the pine lumber structure reflects the Federal and Greek Revival architectural style. In Taylors Falls, there are also many unusual antique shops, intriguing art galleries and stores full of uncommon items.

Across the river in **St. Croix Falls, Wisc.**, visit the **Blanding House Museum of Dolls** (one mile east of town on Old Cemetery Road), which has more than 500 dolls. A good spot to

camp for the night is **Wildwood Park** (3 miles west of Taylors Falls on Hwy. 8). The area features modern camping facilities and a deer park and animal farm for children.

HOURS: Folsom House: 1 to 4:30 p.m., Memorial Day through October 15. Alpine Slide: weekends mid-April to Memorial Day and Labor Day to November; daily Memorial Day through Labor Day. Blanding House Museum of Dolls: 1 to 5 p.m. daily, May through October. Muller Scenic Boat Tour: May through Oct. 15.

FOR MORE INFORMATION: Call Taylors Falls Commercial Club, (612) 465-3811; St. Croix Falls Chamber of Commerce, (715) 483-3606, or Chisago County Guide and Tourism Service, (612) 257-5371.

ADMISSION: Folsom House: Adults, $1; children 6 to 12 yrs., 50¢; under 6 yrs. free. Alpine Slide: Teens and adults, $2; children 7 to 12 yrs., $1.25. Blanding House Museum of Dolls: Adults, $1; children, 50¢; children under 5 yrs. free. Muller Scenic Boat Tour: Half-hour trip—adults and teens 12 yrs. and up, $2; children and pre-teens 3 to 11 yrs., $1.25. Hour trip—adults and teens 12 yrs. and up, $3; children and pre-teens, 3 to 11 yrs., $2; children under 3 yrs. free. (All prices subject to change.)

Back to The Days of Merry England

Shakopee, Minnesota, Renaissance Festival

Driving Time: One-half hour south of Minneapolis/St. Paul

If you've wanted to visit an English hamlet, but couldn't get to England, your wish can come true! You can visit the **Renaissance Festival**, 25 miles south of the Twin Cities in Shakopee. Picture your family members munching on gigantic roasted turkey legs or joining the cheers of a crowd watching armored knights battle with gleaming silver swords. If it sounds like a scene straight from the Renaissance, it is. You might even see old Will Shakespeare penning some of his famous couplets— or Queen Guinevere telling tales to her ladies-in-waiting.

Founded 10 years ago, the fair is a faithful reproduction of a bustling English marketplace that existed more than 400 years ago. Lords and ladies leisurely stroll the grounds in festive costumes, while merchants hawk their wares just as they did back in Merry Old England. The handcrafted goods include pottery, ceramics, stained glass, woodcarvings, ironwork, brass rubbings, clothings, costuming and more. Throughout the six-week period, workshops are held— an easy way to become a true Renaissance citizen by learning several new crafts: leatherworking, macrame, etc.

Young and old may participate in various games such as

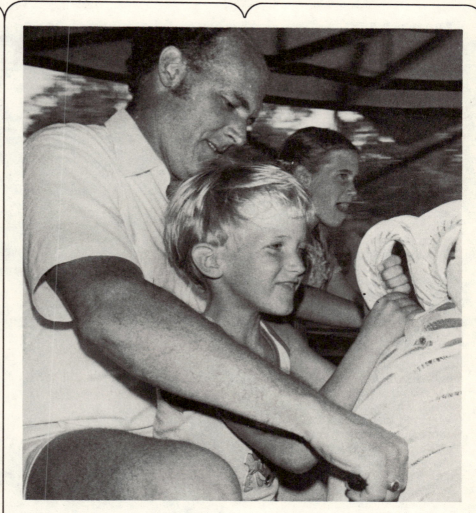

King Arthur's Joust, fencing, archery and Jacob's Ladder, just to name a few. Entertainment is at its best with numerous theatrical performances of Shakespearean works and commedia-style antics

While engaging in all the frivolities, be sure to try the Renaissance food—truly fit for a king. A sample menu might include Quiche Lorraine, Sweet Buttered Popovers, Corn on the Cob, Spinach Pye and Fresh Fruit. Quite a dinner, even for fat old King Henry VIII! You never know what will happen at the Renaissance Festival as jugglers, craftsmen and comedy players vie to the chance to

amuse and return you to a simpler age when knighthood was in flower.

HOURS: 9:30 a.m. to 7 p.m. each Saturday and Sunday mid-August through mid-September (exact dates change each year).

FOR MORE INFORMATION: Call the Festival Office, (612) 445-7361.

ADMISSION: Adults, $6.75; children 5 to 12 yrs., $2; children under 5 yrs. free. Discounts available for tickets purchased in advance and group rates. (Prices subject to change.)

DIRECTIONS: From the Twin Cities, take Hwy. 169 to Shakopee and continue 4 miles southeast to fair site. Or take Hwy. 35 south to Hwy. 101 west to Shakopee; go 4 miles southwest on Rt. 169 to fair.

Minnesota

Red Wing: Outdoors Adventure!

Red Wing, Minnesota
Driving Time: 1 hour south of Minneapolis/St. Paul

Just at the point where the Mighty Mississippi widens to become **Lake Pepin**, is **Red Wing**, a town where the past meets the present.

For the outdoorsman, there's no better place—especially so close to the Twin Cities. Just 46 miles southeast of St. Paul, the town provides opportunities for every outdoor activity from boating and swimming in summer to skiing and snowmobiling in winter—and everything in between. For hikers and nature-lovers, there's the spectacular **Barn Bluff** walking trail. The two-mile trek has markers explaining the area's history and ecology. And for more history, there's the **Goodhue County Historical Museum** (1166 Oak St.) featuring historical collections and memorabilia. To see more of the area from the river, take a two-hour trip offered by **Red Wing Excursions.**

The city is named for Sioux Indian leaders who bore the title **"Red Wing."** The chief's title was derived from an Indian symbol of a swan's wing stained scarlet. For many years, Indians remained around the Red Wing area, but following the Treaty of 1851 the Red Wing band moved to a reservation on the Minnesota River. Hazen Wakute, who died in 1950, was the last descendant of the famous chiefs.

Because of the area's scenic beauty, there are many routes you can take to enjoy nature, especially in the fall when the trees are so colorful. One pos-

sibility: drive south on U.S. 61 and turn left on road marked **"Frontenac State Park."** Tour the park and then turn left to **Old Frontenac,** a picturesque little community of southern colonial mansions overlooking Lake Pepin.

Another route: take U.S. 63 across the Eisenhower Bridge and turn right on Wisconsin 35. The route offers gorgeous views of Lake Pepin and visits to charming river towns. Drive as far as Nelson, Wisconsin, take Wisconsin 25 and cross to Wabasha, Minn. Take U.S. 61 back to Red Wing.

For skiiers, the **Welch Vil-** lage is a popular spot. (Go 12 miles northwest on U.S. 61, then 3 miles south to Welch.) During warmer weather visitors can go tubing on the Cannon River. Also, one-half to four-day canoe trips are available from Welch Village.

HOURS: Goodhue County Historical Museum: 1 to 5 p.m. Tuesday through Sunday.

FOR MORE INFORMATION: Call the Red Wing Area Chamber of Commerce, (612) 388-4719.

ADMISSION: Goodhue County Historical Museum: Adults, 50¢; children, 25¢. (Prices subject to change.)

DIRECTIONS: From Twin Cities, take Rt. 10-61 south and east to Red Wing.

Minnesota

Stillwater: Remembering The Past

Stillwater, Minnesota

Driving Time: ½ hour east of Minneapolis St. Paul

Once the center of the lumbering industry, Stillwater is a picturesque town perched on the banks of the St. Croix River. From the quaint shops lining **Main Street** to the austere simplicity of the Hay Lake School, Stillwater exhibits a dedication to its humble beginnings in pioneer days.

A walking tour of the downtown area would be a good way to explore the historical city. Shop at **Thatchentree, Cat's Meow** or **Hickory Dickory Dock** for unusual gifts, distinctive antiques, furniture, stained glass, toys, homemade German food and fine clothing. For lunch, try **Kane's Brick Alley;** and for an afternoon snack, the famous Stillwater taffy. You can watch it being made in the windows of the **Gerber Piano and Organ Store** (Main Street near Olive). If you're really hungry, have lunch at the **Madcapper's Saloon** (Main St.), which serves "the biggest sandwich in town." In fact, there are many interesting spots to eat in Stillwater: among them are **The St. Croix Boom Co.** (317 S. Main) and **The Freighthouse Saloon** (305 S. Water St.).

More artifacts of local heritage are on display at the **Washington County Historical Museum** (602 N. Main St.), once the warden's home at a former prison site. It has a lumberjack room, pioneer kitchen, antique furniture and

momentoes of lumbering days. And at the **Historic Corner**, there's an Old Log House, Hay Lake School, and the Swedish Monument, a tribute to the Swedish immigrant settlers of the 1850s.

During the last half of the 19th century, Washington County was the center of much activity in Minnesota because of the area's social, economic and cultural progress. To learn more of area history, you can take a river tour aboard the "Discovery" riverboat (St. Croix Cruise and Charter Co., 408 E. Chestnut). And if you're there during the warmer months, the fishing is great in **Lake St. Croix** for bass, walleye and muskie. Another great tour is available at the **Goggin Candy Co.** (902 S. Fourth St.); call for an appointment, (612) 439-1516. If your family spends the night, there are excellent accommodations at the **Lowell Inn** (102 N. Second St.).

If you're traveling on a Tuesday, you may wish to visit **Cedarhurst Mansion** in southern Washington County (6940 Keats Ave., Cottage Grove), a 26-room mansion with a 100-foot veranda.

For a scenic drive from Stillwater, head in the other direction to **Taylors Falls**. Take the St. Croix Scenic Highway (MN 95) north for 30 miles—you'll see some beautiful sights.

HOURS: Washington County Historical Museum: 2 to 5 p.m. Tuesday, Thursday and weekends, May through October and by appointment; closed holidays and November through April. Historic Corner: 1 to 5 p.m. Saturday and Sunday, May through November or by appointment. Cedarhurst: tours 11 a.m. and 1 p.m. each Tuesday.

FOR MORE INFORMATION: Call the Stillwater Chamber of Commerce, (612) 439-7700, or Cedarhurst Mansion, (612) 459-9741.

ADMISSION: Washington County Historical Museum and Historic Corner: 25¢ to 50¢ depending on age; children under 6 yrs. free. Cedarhurst: $2.25 per person. (Prices subject to change.)

DIRECTIONS: From Twin Cities, take Hwy. 36 straight west to Stillwater. To reach Cedarhurst from Stillwater, take Hwy. 95 south and west to County Road 20; go west to Cedarhurst. From Twin Cities, take 494 to U.S. 110 to Rt. 61 south. Take 61 to County Road 22 (70th St.) and go to County Road 19. Cedarhurst is at junction of County Roads 19 and 20.

Minnesota

Reliving The "Good Old Days"

Mantorville, Minnesota

Driving Time: 40 minutes south of Minneapolis/St. Paul

A visit to Mantorville is a voyage back in time. A nationally-registered historic place, the town is named for two of its first pioneers, Peter and Riley Mantor, who settled there in 1854 attracted by the rich agricultural land, water supply, limestone deposits and forest lands. The County Seat of Dodge County, Mantorville boasts the only **boardwalk** in the state.

Each year visitors flock to Mantorville to enjoy the quiet, country charm, to browse in the antique shops and to sample some old-fashioned home cooking at **Carlson's Cafe** or **Hubbell House** (on Main Street boardwalk). Across the covered bridge on the Zumbro River is Mantorville. More than 200 gas lights lend a special charm to each street, from Walnut to Main. Guided tours are available at the tour center on Main Street boardwalk, but you may want to take a leisurely tour on your own.

All along the boardwalk are unusual shops featuring crafts, antiques, jewelry, leathergoods, toys, western gear and numerous collectibles. At the **Dodge County Historical Society Museum** (Main and Seventh sts.) there are exhibits of historical documents, photographs, period clothing and other area artifacts. Nearby is the **one room school** and the **Restoration House** (Main and Sixth sts.), which was built in 1857 as a courthouse. The building recently

has been restored to its original condition by the Mantorville Restoration Association.

For lunch, the most popular spot is **Hubbell House**, famous for its superb cuisine. The building, constructed in 1854, was originally a log hotel.

Each year on the weekend following Labor Day, Mantorville residents turn out for the **"Marigold Days"** celebration, featuring parades, art shows, a flower show, a flea market, dancing, hymn singing and more good fun (a "water fight," for example).

Another interesting stop on your tour of Hiawathaland is **Wasioja**, a historic hamlet of about 75 persons (1 mile north of Mantorville and 3 miles west on City Road 16). The main

attraction is the **Doig House**, built by a Scottish family of master stone cutters more than a century ago. The house has been refurnished in period furnishings. There is also an antique shop connected to the house.

HOURS: Some shops closed Sundays. Dodge County Historical Society Museum, School House: noon to 5 p.m. Tuesday through Saturday, 1 to 5 p.m. Sunday, May 31 through October 31; closed Mondays. Hubbell House: open Tuesday through Sunday, lunch and dinner. Restoration House: 1 to 5:30 p.m. Tuesday through Sunday; closed Mondays.

FOR MORE INFORMATION: Call the Mantorville Tour Center, (507) 635-5132, or City Hall, (507) 635-5170.

ADMISSION: Museums: 50¢.

DIRECTIONS: From the Twin Cities, take Hwy. 52 south to Hader exit, go south to Hwy. 57 to Mantorville.

Minnesota

The Fascinating World of Medicine

Rochester, Minnesota

Driving Time: 1 hour, 20 min. from Minneapolis St. Paul

From the hustle and bustle of city streets to the scenic beauty of the surrounding countryside, **Rochester** offers much of interest to visitors.

Each year thousands of visitors tour the facilities of the world renown **Mayo Clinic** and its **Medical Museum,** which offer a glimpse into the world of medical science. The famous clinic was established around the turn of the century by the Drs. C.H. and W.H. Mayo. The medical museum features numerous exhibits and films designed to instruct visitors on the structure and functions of the human body, and on methods of dealing with physical problems. One of the most popular attractions is "The Incredible Machine," a 25-minute film highlighting all the body systems.

Tours of Mayowood, the Mayo family home, are available through the Olmsted County Historical Center (corner of Salen Road and Hwy. 122). The restored mansion features 40 rooms filled with period furnishings. (No parking is available; the mansion may be reached by bus only.) The Olmsted County Historical Center features interesting exhibits ranging from Norwegian furniture to early spinning and weaving equipment.

For city folks who want a taste of rural life, the Chamber of Commerce (212 First Ave. S.W.) offers tours of a typical Minnesota farm. Another stop should be the **Oxbow Park and Zoo** (Rt. 14 west of Rochester) where you'll see many unusual wild animals native to Minnesota. And a special treat for children is summer theatre for children presented by the Mayo Park by Rochester Civic Theater (August through May).

There are many motels in Rochester providing comfortable lodgings, among them the **Holiday Inn-Downtown** (220 S. Broadway). For an elegant continental dinner, try the **Elizabethan Room at the Kahler Hotel** (20 S.W. Second Ave.); for more conventional fare, **Hoffman House at the Best Western Midway Motel** (1516 16th St. S.W.).

An interesting side trip is available at nearby Spring Valley, where the breathtaking **Mystery Caves** (32 miles south of Rochester) are located. Discovered in 1937, the formation is the upper Midwest's largest cave. Its highlights include the "disappearing river" in the subterranean Turquoise Lake, and the lustrous colorful rock creations that constantly change with the passage of time. A scenic picnic and camping area is included in the Mystery Cave grounds.

HOURS: Mayo Clinic Tours: 10 a.m. and 2 p.m. Monday through Friday. Mayo Medical Museum: 9 a.m. to 9 p.m. Monday through Friday; 9 a.m. to 5 p.m. Saturday; 1 to 5 p.m. Sunday. Olmsted County Historical Center: 9 a.m. to 5 p.m. Monday through Friday; noon to 4:30 p.m. Saturday and Sunday; closed holidays. Mayowood Tours: 1 and 3 p.m., Saturday and Sunday in April; Wednesday, Thursday, Saturday and Sunday in May, September and October; Tuesday, Wednesday, Thursday, Saturday and Sunday in June, July and August. Farm Tour: 1:45 p.m. Thursday, June through August—call for reservations. Mystery Caves: 1-hr. tours 10 a.m. to 4 p.m. daily Memorial Day through Labor Day; 10 a.m. to 4 p.m. weekends only, May and September.

FOR MORE INFORMATION: Call Rochester Area Chamber of Commerce, (507) 288-0201, or Spring Valley Mystery Caves, (507) 937-3251.

ADMISSION: Mayo Clinic Tours and Medical Museum free. Mayowood: Adults and teens 17 yrs. and up, $2.50; children, pre-teens and teens 5 to 16 yrs., $1.50; under 5 yrs. free. Olmsted Country Historical Museum: free. Spring Valley Mystery Caves: Adults and teens, $3; children and pre-teens 6 to 12 yrs., $1.50; under 6 yrs. free. (Prices subject to change.)

DIRECTIONS: From Twin Cities, take Hwy. 52 southwest to Rochester.

Minnesota

Valleyfair: Area's First Theme Park

Driving Time: 45 minutes from Minneapolis/St. Paul

A day of excitement, entertainment, and just plain fun awaits you at Valleyfair, the Upper Midwest's first "theme" park. The turn-of-the-century atmosphere incorporates thrilling rides, games, and a variety of delightful shows and other attractions.

Meet John Phillips Ohoompapa and the charming **Chocolate Moose**. They and their friends around the park are guaranteed to put a smile on everyone's face with their antics.

Near the entrance, you'll want to see the **Antique Carousel**, handmade in 1923. This popular attraction is still running, pleasing hundreds of kids every day. Farther along, the antique car rides let kids drive around the park while mom and dad ride. There are a half-dozen or so kiddie rides, too, for the youngest kids.

Valleyfair
Theme Park

Continued

For the more adventurous, how about the **Corkscrew**? It climbs to a height of 85 feet and makes two full 360° loops, reaching speeds of 50 miles per hour. And if that isn't enough, there are two more roller coasters, including the wooden "High Roller," which travels over one-half mile of track and reaches speeds of nearly 60 miles per hour on its 70-foot descent.

On a hot day, there's nothing like the **Log Flume**, which carries you in a hollowed-out log through swirling rapids to a splash-down descent of nearly 50 feet. There are at least a dozen other rides, too, all guaranteed to give you all the white-knuckled excitement you can possibly want.

When you're ready to take a break from the rides, how about a show? Take a stroll to the **Marine Arena**, where two blue Atlantic bottlenosed dolphins will delight and amaze you as they go through their paces. Or see the **Mississippi Road Showboat Review** in Valleyfair's Amphitheater. The many talented singers and musicians are sure to please. And at four other stage areas in the park, entertainment ranges from bluegrass to barbershop quartet to the John Phillips Ohoompapa Band.

When you get hungry, there are four restaurants, dozens of snack stands, an ice cream parlor and more to satisfy you. And what amusement park is complete without an arcade where you can try your hand at more than a dozen challenging games? Before you leave, you'll also want to visit Grandpa's Farm, where you can feed and pet friendly farm animals.

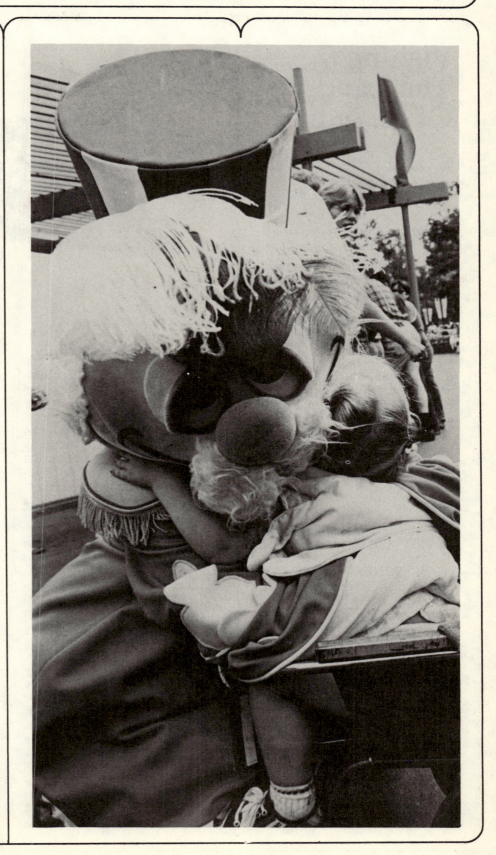

Minnesota

Visiting The Land Of the Indians

Pioneerland:
Jeffers Petroglyphs
Lower Sioux Agency
New Ulm

Driving Time: 2 hours south-
west of Minneapolis/St. Paul

If you'd like to learn the history of early Minnesota Indians, visit the Jeffers Petroglyphs and Lower Sioux Agency in **Pioneerland**, southwest of the Twin Cities. Long before pioneers came to the Cottonwood River Valley, Indians roamed the prairies and left mysterious carvings on the ancient rocks. Now called the Jeffers Petroglyphs, the almost 2,000 carvings are the largest petroglyph group in the state. Many of the other carving sites have been destroyed.

Archeologists and anthropologists believe that the petroglyphs date from the Late Archaic-Early Woodland period (3,000 B.C. to 500 A.D.) and the Late Woodland period (900 to 1750 A.D.). Many of the carvings are representations of plains animals: bison, rabbits, wolves, turtles, and elk, etc. Anthropologists say the primitive art could have been connected with some of the early Indian legends.

But no matter the significance of these carvings, a tour of the area is an intriguing experience. There are 18 different sites depicting activities such as warfare and hunting. You'll also learn about the land and how archeologists determine the age of the carvings.

Just a few miles north is another opportunity to learn about

those early Americans: the **Lower Sioux Agency in Redwood Falls**. The agency was established after the 1851 treaties between the U.S. government and the Dakota Indians. The agencies were actually small pioneer communities that were the centers of the surrounding reservations. At the interpretive center there are displays and exhibits telling the story of the Indians—their life on reservations, war on the plains, the Battle of Wounded Knee, and more.

Before heading back to Minneapolis-St. Paul, stop in the quiet community of **New Ulm** — a bit of old Germany. Explore the town, and drop in at the **Harkin Store** (8 miles northwest on Hwy. 21). It's probably the only chance you'll ever have to see merchandise at such low prices: brooms, 40¢ each; flour, 2¢ per pound.(Sorry, the goods aren't for sale.) Those were the good old days! The store was originally part of the bustling village of **West Newton**, abandoned soon after the railroad was built near New Ulm. Also, 14 miles on U.S. 14, there are the

ruins of **Fort Ridgely** and the interpretive center. A good place to stop for lunch in New Ulm is **Veigel's Kaiserhoff**, a fine German restaurant with reasonable prices.

HOURS: Lower Sioux Agency: 10 a.m. to 5 p.m. daily April 1 through Oct. 31; 10 a.m. to 5 p.m. Wednesday through Sunday, Nov. 1 through March 31. Jeffers Petroglyphs: 10 a.m. to 5 p.m. daily May 15 through Labor Day; open September and October only for groups with reservations. Harkin Store: 10 a.m. to 5 p.m. daily May 1 through Sept. 30. (Hours subject to change; call ahead.)
FOR MORE INFORMATION: Call the Minnesota Historical Society, (612) 726-1171, or the New Ulm Chamber of Commerce, (507) 354-4217.
ADMISSION: All free.
DIRECTIONS: From the Twin Cities take U.S. 169 (becomes Rt. 60) southwest to U.S. 71 at Windom. Go north on U.S. 71 past Rt. 30 to County Rd. 2; turn right to Petroglyphs. To reach Redwood Falls, take U.S. 71 north 20 miles. To reach New Ulm from Redwood Falls, take U.S. 71 south again to U.S. 14; turn left on U.S. 14 (east) and take it straight to New Ulm. Or take Rt. 67 southeast to Rt. 4 south; take Rt. 4 to U.S. 14 east (shorter route, but roads not as good).

MISSOURI

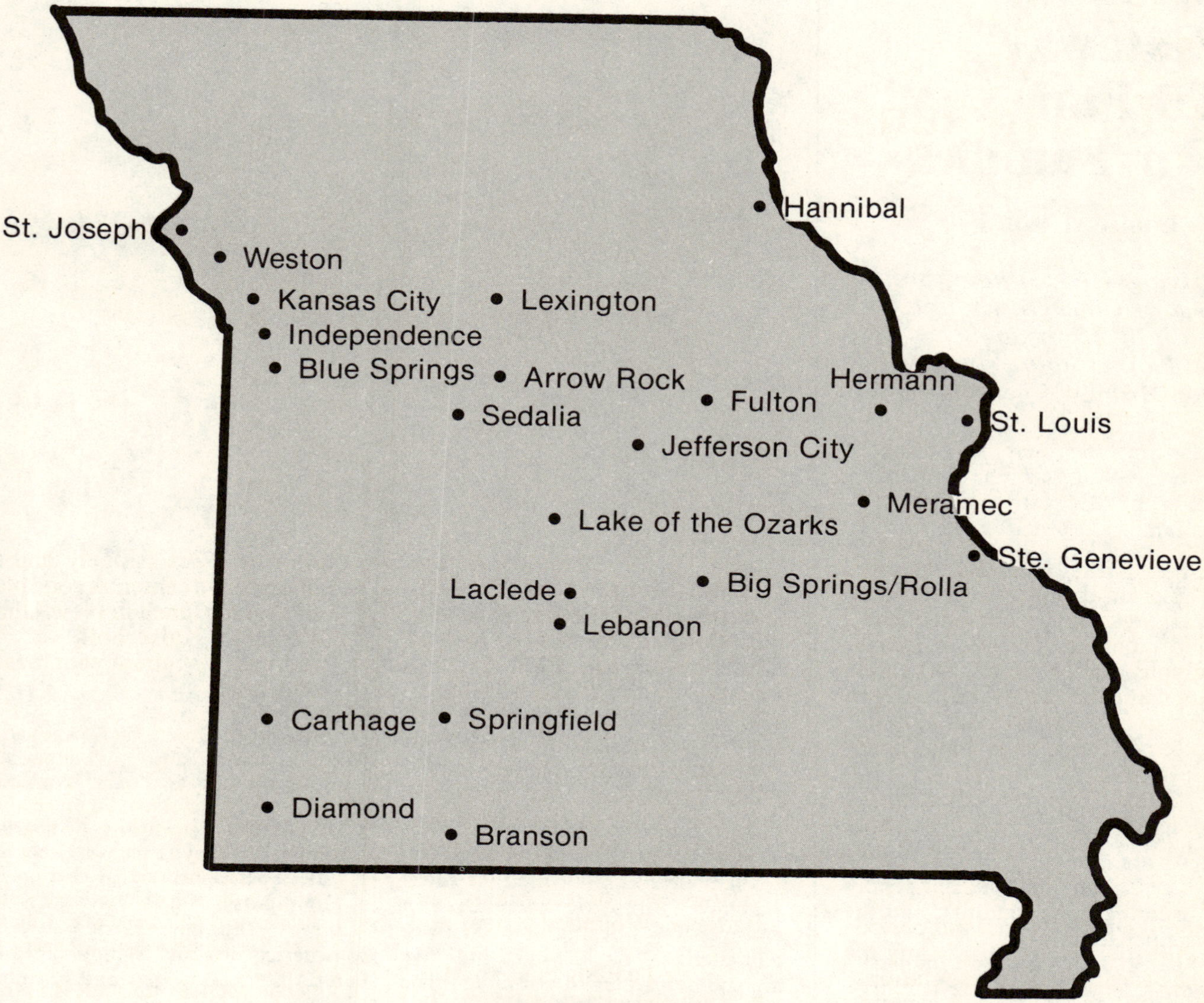

St. Joseph •

• Weston

• Kansas City   • Lexington

• Independence

• Blue Springs   • Arrow Rock

• Hannibal

• Sedalia

• Fulton   Hermann •

• Jefferson City

• St. Louis

• Lake of the Ozarks

• Meramec

• Ste. Genevieve

Laclede •   • Big Springs/Rolla

• Lebanon

• Carthage   • Springfield

• Diamond

• Branson

Missouri Vacations

Missouri

St. Louis: 'Gateway' To Fun For Families

St. Louis, Missouri

Driving Time: 6 hours southwest of Chicago; 12 hours south of Minneapolis/St. Paul; 5 hours south of Des Moines

For travelers, there's no getting the "blues" in St. Louis. The city remains one of the Midwest's most attractive for families, no matter the form of entertainment sought, be it art, music, or a trip to the zoo.

Forest Park (bounded by Skinker, Kingshighway Blvd., and Oakland Ave.) was once the site of the 1904 World's Fair and is now home to many of the city's major attractions. Here is the **McDonnell Planetarium** (5100 Clayton Rd.), one of the nation's foremost astronomical facilities. Exhibits on astronomy, geology, physics, and space and daily sky shows are offered. Highlights of the facility include the Foucault pendulum, holography exhibits, and the Laserium Light Show.

The **St. Louis Zoo**, on the park's south side, is one of the country's finest. The 83-acre complex houses more than 2,000 animals in their native habitat. The zoo's garden-like atmosphere makes walking a pleasure, but if you tire you can always catch the Zooline Railroad to your next destination. Not-to-be-missed sights include the bird aviary, Big Cat Country (home to great cats), and the Children's Zoo with its close-up views for kids.

On top of Art Hill stands the **St. Louis Art Museum**, another structure inspired by the 1904 World's Fair. The art museum specializes in American and European paintings

The St. Louis Arch

but maintains exhibits on treasures collected from around the world.

Plant-lovers should visit the **Jewel Box** (Wells and McKinley Drs.), a conservatory housing unique flower and plant displays. Major holidays are the best times to visit here (lilies are displayed during Easter, poinsettias during Christmas). After making the rounds of the conservatory, walk or drive around Forest Park, a botanical garden in itself, with streams, ponds, lakes, and winding, wooded walkways.

Not far from the park stands the imposing **Cathedral of St. Louis** (4431 Lindell Blvd. at Norsted Ave.), home church of the St. Louis Archdiocese. The cathedral's architecture carefully blends Romanesque and Byzantine styles and houses an outstanding collection of mosaic art.

A short drive from the cathedral,

the **Missouri Botanical Gardens** (2101 Tower Grove Ave.) beckons with spectacular floral displays. Highlights include "Seiwa-En," the largest Japanese garden in North America, with its islands, lakes, waterfalls, footbridges, and tea house; and the Climatron, a geodesic-domed greenhouse. For the footweary, the gardens have a miniature railroad, and for the hungry, the Greenery Restaurant.

Just south of the downtown area is the **Anheuser-Busch Brewery** (610 Pestalozzi St.), a company whose name — and fortune — has become linked with St. Louis. The Busch family built Busch Stadium on the riverfront and owns the World Champion St. Louis Cardinals. Tour this National Historic Landmark and taste-test the famous "suds"; the package includes the Clydesdale horses and the old brewhouse, too.

Missouri

On the city's outskirts lies **Grant's Farm** (10501 Gravois Rd.), showplace of Anheuser-Busch. Built on land once farmed by President Ulysses S. Grant, it features Grant's original cabin and its famous gun-barrel fence, plus other sundry attractions. (Admission to the farm area is free; however, reservations are required to attend this popular attraction.)

Six Flags Over Mid-America (30 miles southwest off I-44 at the Allentown Rd. exit) lays claim to being the Midwest's largest amusement park, with more than 100 rides spread across a lush, 200-acre countryside setting. Thrill-seekers will love the "Screaming Eagle" and the "Jetscream" roller coasters, as well as the park's recreation of a white-water rafting trip, "Thunder River."

Music of every kind is offered at Six Flags, from Broadway melodies at the Palace to good-time country at

Miss Kitty's Saloon. Kids will gravitate to the "Farmyard Frolics" and adults to the celebrity stars of the Old Glory Amphitheater. "Goodtime Hollow" is a specially designed amusement park for small fry.

Festivals And Events In St. Louis

Special events scheduled for the city include:

• The **Annual International Festival** (Memorial Day weekend), in which dozens of nationalities display the foods, dancing, and customs of their native lands.

• The **Annual National Ragtime and Traditional Jazz Festival** (mid-June) on the *Goldenrod Showboat*, a week-long event featuring legendary jazz greats and the best ragtimers the city has to offer.

• The **Veiled Prophet Fair** (early July), started in 1878 by a group of local businessmen to celebrate the Veiled Prophet of Khorassan and his court. The show includes a parade, fireworks, entertainment, food, sports events, and the crowning of the festival's queen.

BEST TIME TO VISIT: Summer and fall.

HOURS: McDonnell Planetarium — open daily except Monday; closed Thanksgiving, Christmas, New Year's Day and Easter. St. Louis Zoo — 9 a.m.-5 p.m. daily, closed Christmas and New Year's Day. St. Louis Art Museum — 10 a.m.-5 p.m. Wednesday-Sunday, 2:30 pm.-9:30 p.m. Tuesday, closed Christmas and New Year's Day. Jewel Box — 9 a.m.-5 p.m. daily. St. Louis Cathedral — 6 a.m.-7 p.m. April-October, rest of year to 6 p.m. Missouri Botanical Gardens — Garden, 9 a.m.-7:30 p.m. May-October, 9 a.m.-5 p.m. November-April, closed Christmas; Climatron, 10 a.m.-7:30 p.m. May-October, 10 a.m.-5 p.m. November-April, closed Christmas. Anheuser-Busch, Inc. — 9:30 a.m.-3:30 p.m. Monday-Friday, September-May; 9 a.m.-3:30 p.m. Monday-Saturday, June-August; closed major holidays. Grant's Farm — at selected hours (9, 10, 11 a.m. and 1, 2, 3 p.m.) daily except Mondays, June-August; Thursday-Sunday, mid-April to May, September to mid-October; reservations are required. Six Flags Over Mid-America — 10 a.m.-10 p.m. June-August; Saturday and Sunday, April-May, September-October. Al Baker's — 5 p.m.-midnight, closed Sunday and major holidays. Cheshire Inn — 7 a.m.-10 p.m. weekdays, 7:30 p.m.-midnight Saturday, 8:30 a.m.-10 p.m. Sunday. Port of St. Louis — 5 p.m.-11 p.m. daily, closed major holidays. Top of the Sevens — 11:30 a.m.-2:30 p.m. and 5:30 p.m.-11 p.m. weekdays, 5:30 p.m.-11 p.m. Saturday, closed Sunday.

ADMISSION: St. Louis Zoo — animal shows 45¢; children's zoo 45¢, zoo train 90¢. Missouri Botanical Gardens — adults, $2.50; 6-16, $1; children under 6, free; Train ride, 75¢. Six Flags Over Mid-America — one-day ticket $11.50; children under 3, free.

TRAVEL TIPS: St. Louis boasts some of the best shopping centers in the Midwest, including Plaza Frontenac (Lindbergh and Clayton Rds.), 20 minutes from downtown, for fashions and gifts; WestPort Plaza, with its boutiques, restaurants and nightclubs; and Maryland Plaza, featuring cobblestone streets, old-fashioned street lamps and a lovely fountain.

ACCOMMODATIONS: There are many excellent hotels and motels, a few of which are: the Breckenridge Inn (1335 S. Lindbergh Blvd.); the Cheshire Inn & Lodge (6300 Clayton Rd.); and the Sheraton Plaza (900 Westport Plaza).

EATING OUT: Some local favorites are Al Baker's, 8101 Clayton Rd., for Italian and Continental; the Cheshire Inn, 6300 Clayton Rd., for traditional American dishes in an Old-English atmosphere; Port of St. Louis, 15 N. Central, for seafood; and the Top of the Sevens, 7777 Bonhomme Ave., Clayton, for Continental, French-Creole.

FOR MORE INFORMATION: Call the St. Louis Visitor's Center, (314) 241-1764, or write 330 Mansion House Center, Suite 211, St. Louis, MO 63103.

Missouri

Kansas City: Big City With Small-Town Appeal

Kansas City, Missouri

Driving Time: 6 hours west of St. Louis; 7 hours southwest of Des Moines

Kansas City offers the advantages of a large metropolitan area while retaining a small town's friendly atmosphere. If you like art museums, great restaurants, professional sports, and terrific shopping but don't want the hassle of big cities, you'll find Kansas City appealing.

The city began as a trading post and has blossomed into one of the world's great agri-business capitals. Every Tuesday, Wednesday, and Thursday, the **Kansas City Livestock Exchange** (16th and Gennesse Sts.), holds its cattle auctions. The frenetic bidding begins early each morning as thousands of cattle and hogs change hands. If you've never seen a commodities exchange in action, drop in at the **Board of Trade** (4500 Main St.), where the world's largest winter wheat market is in session each weekday.

Although this city's roots are rural, its residents have a keen appreciation of the fine arts. This is evident everywhere in the architecture, broad boulevards, and well-planned parks. The **Nelson Gallery** (4525 Oak St. at 45th St.), the city's celebrated art museum, contains one of the country's most comprehensive collections. The origin of art, from ancient Sumerian times (3,000 B.C.) to the present, is traced in exhibits that include the Burnap Collection of English pottery, the Kress Collection of Italian sculpture and paintings, and the Starr Collection of miniatures. Here, too, is the famous Chinese and In-

The Screamroller at Kansas City's Worlds of Fun

dian art collection for which the gallery has an international reputation.

Just four blocks from the Nelson Gallery is the **Country Club Plaza** (47th and Main Sts.), America's first shopping center. The striking Spanish-styled plaza is populated with statues, and murals. One of the best places to shop, **Halls,** is often described by promoters as "more an experience than a department store."

Hallmark, the greeting card company, is headquartered here, and tours of its manufacturing facilities are available at company headquarters (25th and McGee St.). The tour covers the many steps involved in producing a card—embossing, die cutting, foil stamping, and silk screening.

Crown Center (2440 Pershing Rd.), a Hallmark redevelopment project, consists of eight restaurants, two hotels, a shopping center, apartments, and an outdoor square used for special events.

The **Liberty Memorial and Museum** (100 W. 26th St., near Union Station), the only museum devoted to World War I, recreates the days of the doughboys with displays of weapons, maps, uniforms, and other military artifacts. (Grab the elevator to the top of the memorial, 217 feet up, for a panoramic view of the city.)

Other family-oriented attractions in or near Kansas City are:

• **Worlds of Fun** (12 miles northeast of I-435 Exit 54 between Parvin Rd. and N.E. 48th St.), a theme park on the city's outskirts. The park, divided into five international theme areas, features 110 rides, including the "Orient Express," billed as the world's "largest" steel roller coaster; the Screamroller, another roller coaster; and the "River City Rampage," a free-wheeling gondola. Other attractions: music and dance revues, super star concerts, animal acts, as well as a narrow gauge railroad, schooner, sidewheeler paddleboat, restaurants, and boutiques.

• **Oceans of Fun** (12 miles northeast of I-435 Exit 54), a huge recreational water park, covers more than 60 acres. Imagine an oceanfront re-

Missouri

sort in the Midwest with everything from body surfing to sun-bathing! (Eat your heart out, California!) The park boasts of three 400-foot water slides and wave-making machines at "Surf City" that allow inland surfers to test their skills. There are bathhouse facilities with private showers and dresssing areas — everything is provided, except suntans. Food is available at Cap'n Cook's Nook and a daily water ski thrill show is staged at Buccaneer Bay. The beach extends around the length of the bay.

• **The Kansas City Zoo**, with its unique "African veldt area" (veldt is a grassland with few trees), is home to zebras, ostriches, elephants, rhinos, and gnus, who live together harmoniously wandering the premises. Elephant and pony rides, a miniature railroad, a children's zoo, an ape house, and the great cat walk are among the zoo's attractions.

• For the sports-minded there's action at the twin-stadium **Truman Sports Complex** (I-435 and I-70), which is home to the baseball Royals and the football Chiefs. Kansas City's other two professional sports teams, the Kings (basketball) and the Comets (soccer), play at **Kemper Arena**.

Special Events, Festivals In Kansas City

Special and seasonal events abound in the city. In the summer, the **Starlight Outdoor Amphitheatre** has Broadway musicals. Fall brings to town the **American Royal Livestock, Horse Show and Rodeo**, the nation's largest combined horse and livestock show and the largest quarterhorse show.

BEST TIME TO VISIT: Summer or fall.
TRAVEL TIPS: Among the city's most popular restaurants: American Restaurant (25th at Grand), with specialties that include poached salmon and shrimp sauteed in fennel butter; Jasper's (405 W. 75th St.), superb veal Francais cappeli and lobster Livornese; La Mediterranee (4742 Pennsylvania), French cuisine; and Stempenson's Apple Farm (Lee's Summit Rd.), with country cooking and legendary apple fritters.

Historic Blue Springs Celebrates Its Past

Blue Springs, Missouri

Driving Time: 20 minutes southeast of Kansas City

Missouri Town 1855 (22807 Woods Chapel Rd., Blue Springs), a group of original western Missouri buildings, is the highlight of a visit to Blue Springs. The 17 buildings, dating from the 1820s to the 1860s, have been brought from various parts of the state to the east side of Lake Jacomo and restored. These antebellum structures bring an old frontier town to life.

The original 19th-century structures include homes, barns, stagecoach stop, blacksmith shop, livery stable, law office, and church. Gardens, livestock, and furnishings complete the 1850s atmosphere.

Overlooking the Missouri River is **Fort Osage** (22807 Woods Chapel Rd.), a reconstructed frontier fur-trading post first built in 1808. Captain William Clark (of the Lewis and Clark Expedition) supervised the construction of the post, which included blockhouses, officers quarters, soldiers barracks, stockade, and a trading post. Information concerning the fort and the important part it played in the region's development is detailed in the adjoining museum.

BEST TIME TO VISIT: Summer.
HOURS: Missouri Town 1855 — 9 a.m.-7 p.m. daily, Memorial Day-Labor Day; 9 a.m.-5 p.m. rest of year; closed New Year's Day, Thanksgiving, and Christmas. Fort Osage — 9 a.m.-7 p.m. daily, Memorial Day-Labor Day; 9 a.m.-5 p.m. rest of year; closed New Year's Day, Thanksgiving, and Christmas.
DIRECTIONS: From Kansas City, take I-70 east to Rt. 7, then go south to Blue Springs.
FOR MORE INFORMATION: Call Missouri Town 1855, (816) 795-8200, or write 22807 Woods Chapel Rd., Blue Springs, MO 64015.

Reliving Civil War Days In Lexington

Lexington, Missouri

Driving Time: 1 hour east of Kansas City

Lexington is the site of the Civil War conflict known as the "Battle of the Hemp Bales" (named for the movable breastworks used by Confederate soldiers). It was here, on September 18-20, 1861, that Union troops under the command of Col. James A. Mulligan were defeated by the Confederate troops of Maj. Gen. Sterling Price in one of the largest and most important battles of the war. Today, the battlefield is part of the **Battle of Lexington State Historic Site** (at Rt. 13A and Utah St.), along with a beautiful antebellum mansion.

Anderson House, built in 1853, overlooks the battlefield. The home served as a field hospital in the midst of the battle and changed from Union to Confederate control many times during the bloody conflict. The building has been preserved along with its original furnishings, and today serves as a museum for Civil War relics.

To learn more about the battle and the city of Lexington, visit the **Lexington Historical Museum**. Originally built as a church in 1846, the building houses a museum containing Civil War exhibits, steamboat models, pony express items, relics of the Battle of Lexington, and photographs of the city.

BEST TIME TO VISIT: Summer.
HOURS: Battle of Lexington Historic Site — noon-4 p.m. Monday-Saturday; noon-6 p.m. Sunday; closed New Year's Day, Easter, Thanksgiving, and Christmas. Lexington Historical Museum — 10 a.m.-4:30 p.m. daily, mid-April to mid-October; closed New Year's Day, Thanksgiving, and Christmas.
ADMISSION: Battle of Lexington State Historic Site — adults, $1; children 6-12, 50¢; under 6, free.
DIRECTIONS: From Kansas City, take I-24 east to Lexington exit.
FOR MORE INFORMATION: Call the Chamber of Commerce, (816) 259-3082, or write 1211 Main St., Box 457, Lexington, MO 64067.

Missouri

Lake of the Ozarks: Missouri's Summer Vacationland

Lake of the Ozarks, Missouri

Driving Time: 4 hours southwest of St. Louis

Lying deep in Missouri's sleepy hill country, the Lake of the Ozarks ladles out scenic beauty and downhome hospitality. Since it was formed in 1931, when Union Electric dammed the Osage River, this lake has become a year-around vacation destination for sportsmen and nature-lovers.

Lake of the Ozarks was nicknamed the "dragon-lake" for its serpentine shoreline. To see it all, take an excursion boat, seaplane, or helicopter sightseeing trip. The **Tom Sawyer** (east end of Bagnell Dam on U.S. 54), a replica of an old-time paddle-wheeler, has leisurely cruises of the lake; seaplane and helicopter rides are available at the same site. If it's too crowded there, go to nearby **Casino Pier** (Business Rt. 54 at Bagnell Dam), where the *Larry Don* and *Commander* excursion boats offer sightseeing cruises every hour on the hour during the day, and dinner dances nightly.

In the same area is **Bagnell Dam**, a 148-foot-high and half-mile-long structure that impounds more than 600 million gallons of water. Tours are available, on which you'll see the dam's water plant and learn how flowing water creates electricity. Today, Bagnell provides energy to many of the state's major cities.

The area near Bagnell Dam can best be seen from the air, via the **Ozark Sky Ferry** (landing strip near the dam), which provides a scenic

trip over the wooded countryside. Attractions near the dam include: The **Ozark Water Slide** (junction of Rt. 59 and Business 54); the **Missouri Aquarium** (U.S. 54, one mile south of Bagnell Dam), where the kids can feed the carp; the **Indian Burial Cave** (four miles south of Bagnell Dam on U.S. 54, then east on State D), where 1,500-year-old Indian skeletons have been discovered.

From Bagnell Dam, steer south on U.S. 54 to **Osage Beach**, the largest resort area in the Ozarks. Some of the lake's finest restaurants and accommodations are located here, including the state's largest park.

Lake of the Ozarks State Park (Rt. 34, south of Osage Beach) offers 16,762 acres packed with sports activities and scenic beauty. The facilities include two public beaches, bridle paths, and a scenic campgrounds for tents or trailers; there are also boat-launching facilities, outdoor fireplaces, and picnic areas for meals along the lake — as well as more trails than you'll have time to hike. The **Ozark Caverns**, beneath Lake of the Ozarks State Park, is a great respite from summer heat.

For a change of pace, take in the water ski thrill show at **Fort of the Osage** for a program of precision group skiing, ski jumping, and der-

ring-do on hang-gliders. Round out the day on the adjacent midway of the Fort of the Osage Frontier Theme Park. (The heart-stopping rides will keep the weary awake.)

The next stop, southward on U.S. 54 is **Camdenton**, hub of the Ozark Lake region. For romantics, popular **Bridal Cave** and its beautiful onyx formations have been an aphrodisiac: more than 750 weddings have taken place inside the cave. Even newly-weds are impressed with the cave's brilliantly colored onyx formations.

Newly-weds may want to pass up Camdenton's **Kelsey's Antique Car Museum**, but car lovers won't: it's a throwback to the days when cars were more than EPA ratings. On display are steam, electric, and gas-powered models, including the finest four-wheeled vehicles ever to grace America's highways and pollute its air — everything from the dashing Stutz Bearcat to the practical Stanley Steamer. All are squeaky clean and hum with clocklike efficiency.

South of Camdenton, reposing on the Niangua arm of the lake, is **Ha Ha Tonka State Park**. Hearty souls can hike the scenic trails, past caves and natural springs and natural rock bridges, or explore the ruins of a 60-room mansion destroyed by a 1942 fire. (Picnic among the geological wonders, then visit the Colosseum, a natural pit theater on the grounds.)

No trip to the Ozarks would be complete without a day spent boating on the lake. Whether you prefer a sailboat's tranquility or a motorboat's rip-roaring power, the area's resorts and marinas have it. Expert water skiiers are available for lessons; if you prefer a more leisurely pace, rent a pontoon boat.

Whatever the vessel, you'll want to spend some time anchored in one of the lake's hundreds of coves, a popular pastime with local residents. There your family can fish, swim, or have a shipboard picnic. (For a more permanent arrangement, rent one of the lake's houseboats.)

The fishing in the Lake of the Ozark region is among the finest in the state. It's open season year-round for catfish, crappie, walleye, and largemouth and smallmouth bass, and the shoreline is dotted with fishing docks that are covered in the summer and heated in the winter. If you're lured by trout, head for **Troutdale Ranch** in Gravois Mills (a fishing license is required, but is available in most area shops and stores).

BEST TIME TO VISIT: Summer or fall.
ACCOMMODATIONS: Various price ranges and styles include the Holiday Inn (Rt. 1, two blocks south of Bagnell Dam on U.S. 54); Howard Johnson's (three miles south of Bagnell Dam at U.S. 54 Business); Lodge of the Four Seasons (one mile south of Bagnell Dam, three miles west of Business 54 on State and County HH); Millstone Lodge (Rt. 1, six miles east of State 5 on State Rd O., 25 miles north of Camdenton). In Osage Beach, choose from among: the Best Western Lake Chateau (one block west of Grand Glaze Bridge on U.S. 54); Osage House (Lake Rd. 54-30, 1½ mile north of Grand Glaze Bridge); Point Breeze (two blocks south of Grand Glaze Bridge on U.S. 54, then ¼ mile northwest on Lake Rd. 54-37); Marriott's Tan-Tar-A (two miles southwest of Grand Glaze Bridge on U.S. 54, then two miles west on county KK).
EATING OUT: Some of the area's fine restaurants include Bentley's Restaurant and Pub (two miles south of Bagnell Dam on Business 54), where prime rib is a favorite; Millstone Lodge Dining Room (at Millstone Lodge), specializing in trout, steak, and ribs; and the Toledo Room (at the Lodge of the Four Seasons), with rack of lamb, fettuccine alla Alfredo and chateaubriand. In Osage Beach, try the Brass Door (Rt. 2, three blocks south of Grand Glaze Bridge on U.S. 54), for crab legs and Omaha beef, or the Potted Steer (west end of Grand Glaze Bridge on U.S. 54), for fried lobster, smoked game hen and Dover sole.

Famous Winston Churchill Memorial

Fulton, Missouri

Driving Time: 2½ hours west of St. Louis

The campus of **Westminster College** (7th and Westminster Ave.), in Fulton, was the site of one of Winston Churchill's most famous speeches, "Sinews of Peace." It was here on March 5, 1946, that Churchill declared: "From Stettin in the Baltic to Trieste in the Adriatic, an Iron Curtain has descended across the continent.

To honor this great man and his historic speech, the college purchased an 800-year-old English church and had it shipped to Fulton to serve as a memorial. The historic **Church of St. Mary Aldermanbury** was first built in the 17th century, destroyed in London's Great Fire in 1666, and later rebuilt by Christopher Wren. Destroyed again in 1940 by the blitz during World War II, the remains of the church were purchased by the college in 1966. The building was then reassembled, the destroyed portions replaced, and rededicated in 1969.

Today, the centuries-old church houses a museum and library containing Churchill and Wren memorabilia, including letters, photos, manuscripts, paintings, books, and documents relating to World War II.

BEST TIME TO VISIT: Summer.
HOURS: Winston Churchill Memorial and Library — 10 a.m.-5 p.m. daily, April-October; 10 a.m.-4 p.m. Monday-Friday, November-March; noon-5 p.m Saturday and Sunday; closed New Year's Day, Christmas, and Thanksgiving.
ADMISSION: Winston Churchill Memorial and Library — adults, $1.50; children 10-16, 75¢; under 10, free.
DIRECTIONS: From Columbia, take I-70 east to junction with I-54, then go south to Fulton exit.
FOR MORE INFORMATION: Call the Chamber of Commerce, (314) 642-3055, or write 209 Callaway Bank, 5th and Court Sts., Fulton, MO 65251.

A Trout Fishermen's Paradise

Lebanon, Missouri

Driving Time: 4 hours west of St. Louis; 2 hours east of Kansas City

Rainbow trout fishing is the chief attraction at **Bennett Springs State Park** (12 miles west on Rt. 64) near Lebanon. The trout fishing season, which runs from March through October, offers both beginning and expert anglers excellent prospects in the waters flowing from Missouri's sixth-largest spring.

All you need is a fishing license, fly rod, and waders to enjoy everything this clear, swift-running stream has to offer. The park offers a range of accommodations that include cabins, campgrounds, and trailer hookups. The park has a dining lodge and concession stand, and there's a country store with all the fixin's for a fine picnic.

While there, visit the park's fish hatchery, nature museum, and talk to the resident naturalist. Every year the park becomes more popular due to its proximity to the Lake of the Ozarks and the spring's excellent fishing.

BEST TIME TO VISIT: Spring and summer.
HOURS: Bennett Springs State Park — daily; trout fishing, March-October.
DIRECTIONS: From Springfield, take I-44 north to Lebanon, then go west on Rt. 64 to Bennett Springs State Park.
FOR MORE INFORMATION: Call the Chamber of Commerce, (417) 532-4338, or write 255 N. Jefferson, Lebanon, MO 65536.

Missouri

Mark Twain 'Lives Again' In Historic Hannibal

Hannibal, Missouri

Driving Time: 2½ hours north of St. Louis

Mark Twain's boyhood home

Mark Twain once lived in Hannibal and, in a sense, he still lives on — in the memories of local residents and merchants who cater to a thriving tourist trade in this pleasant river town in northeastern Missouri's wooded, rolling hills. The great humorist-writer, whose real name was Samuel Clemens, borrowed a lot from his home city and put that local color into his best books, including the classic, "The Adventures of Tom Sawyer."

The town has done its best to preserve the local scenes that inspired Twain's best work. There **Twain's home**, a modest, two-story frame house at 208 Hill Street, built by his father in 1843 and filled with authentic furniture of the 1840s-1850s. Adjacent to the house is the **Mark Twain Museum**, with its collection of Twain memorabilia — first edition books, manuscripts, photographs, and personal items of Twain and his family.

Across the street is the **Haunted House of Hill Street** (215 Hill St.), a haunted house and wax museum that might have delighted Twain himself — though doubtless he would have disapproved of seeing his own figure in wax. The supernatural theme is carried out in "skull" and "corpse" rooms, and in the ghostly graveyard of the Haunted House. (Have a friend accompany you here!)

Down the street, the **Pilaster House-Grant's Drug Store** (at Hill and Main Sts.) is a reminder of the Twain family's misfortunes. The Twains lived here after losing their own home. Today, the building houses a restored old-time kitchen, drug store, doctor's office, and the room in which Twain's father died. Next door, the **Tom Sawyer Dioramas Museum** (323 N. Main) is filled with hand-carved, three-dimensional scenes from "Tom Sawyer" and Hannibal of the 1840s.

Also part of the Hill Street scene: the **home of Laura Hawkins** (211 Hill St.), the model for the character Becky Thatcher, with a Twain bookstore and souvenir shop in its lower level and period furniture in its upper level; and the **Clemens' law office**, where Twain's father once held forth as the local justice-of-the-peace and which later became the inspiration for courtroom scenes in the author's books.

If you have time, pause to have your picture taken in front of the famous **bronze statue of Tom Sawyer and Huckleberry Finn** at Main and North Streets. Then drive two miles south (off Rt. 79) to see the famous **Mark Twain Cave**, where, in Twain's vivid imagination, treasure was found, Tom and Becky Thatcher were lost, and Injun Joe died. (Guided tours of this national landmark leave the visitors center every 15 minutes. Guided tours are also offered at the nearby **Cameron Cave**, with its mazelike passageways.)

House and architecture buffs will find much of interest in Hannibal, especially in the elegant mansions just south of the city. **Garth Woodside Mansion** (south via U.S. 61, exit at Warren Barrett Dr.), a Victorian marvel built by a friend of Mark Twain's in 1871, has a flying staircase, several Italian marble fireplaces, and beautiful furniture and accessories. The **Rockcliffe Mansion** (1000 Bird St.), a lumber magnate's turn-of-the-century mansion, is a reminder of how the "other half" used to live — splendid art nouveau riverfront manse rated one of the best of its kind. (This was Twain's address on his last trip to town in 1902. Both mansions are listed in the National Historic Register.) Another building of architectural interest, **Stonecroft Manor** (2400 Caro Lane), is a stone farmhouse complete with Victorian furniture and an English herb garden.

Just north of Hannibal, the **Civil War Fort and Barkley Railroad Station** (one mile northwest via U.S. 61 exit at Huck Finn Shopping Center) was once a base for Union soldiers. The fort's museum exhibits cavalry equipment, spurs, Indian relics, and farm equipment.

Missouri

Festivals, Special Events In Hannibal

The city has a variety of special events based on its rich history:

• **"Tom Sawyer Days"** are held during the week of July 4th and include the "National Fence Painting Contest," "The Tom and Becky Contest," and frog jumping and river raft races.

• The annual **Autumn Folklife Festival** is held the first weekend in November and highlights native and historic crafts.

• The **Clemens Outdoor Amphitheatre** presents a two-hour pageant based on Mark Twain's life and characters during the summer months.

BEST TIME TO VISIT: Summer and fall.
HOURS: Many attractions are open from 8 a.m. to 4-6 p.m. in the summer with slightly shorter hours in the other seasons. For complete times, call or write to the local information numbers listed below.
ADMISSION: The Sternwheeler, Twainland Express, and Mark Twain Cave — $4-$5 for adults; children about half that. Other admissions are in the $1-$2 range.
TRAVEL TIPS: For a complete tour of Mark Twain's Hannibal, pick up the "Twainland Express Sightseeing Tour" next to the Twain Home and Museum for a 60-minute, 12-mile guided tour around the significant spots. More apropos perhaps is the tour offered by the sternwheeler *Mark Twain*, docked at the Center Street Landing, with one-hour cruises and chatter about river lore. In the evening, the riverboat has a "Prime Rib Dinner Cruise," with music, dancing, a cash bar, and a band. Accommodations in Hannibal include: the Best Western Hannibal House (3603 McMasters Ave.), the Best Western Mark Twain Motor Inn (612 Mark Twain Ave.), or the Holiday Inn Twainland (U.S. 61 at Market St.), which features a tropical Holidrome. Local restaurants of note: the Country Kitchen (4793 McMasters Ave. on U.S. 61), with a varied family menu; Fern's Restaurant (U.S. 61 and Rt. 41), hearty meals and homemade pies; and the Ole Planters Restaurant (316 N. Main), offering "home-cooked meals at reasonable prices." Favorite haunts of souvenir hunters are: Aunt Polly's Handcrafts (323 N. Main), with a selection of locally made quilts; Aunt Polly's Attic Antiques and Uniques (215 N. Main), with its primitive furniture and glassware collections; and the Hannibal Tintype Co. (322 N. Main), which will photograph your family in period costumes for a fee.
DIRECTIONS: From St. Louis, take U.S. 61 north to Hannibal exit.
FOR MORE INFORMATION: Call the Hannibal Tourism Commission, (314) 221-2477, or write P.O. Box 624, Hannibal, MO 63401

Where Ragtime Got Its Start

Sedalia, Missouri

Driving Time: 3½ hours west of St. Louis; 3 hours east of Kansas City

Don't be surprised if you hear the mournful sounds of "The Entertainer" or the syncopated rhythm of the "Pineapple Rag" as you enter this town, for this is Sedalia, the birthplace of ragtime music. Composer Scott Joplin lived in Sedalia at the turn of the century, and it was here that he wrote and played the "Maple Leaf Rag," launching the ragtime era of music.

The **Sedalia Ragtime Archives** (1900 Clarendon Rd. in the State Fair Community College Library) honors Joplin and ragtime music with original sheet music and piano rolls from the Maple Leaf Club, a local saloon that catered to railroad men in the late 1800s. The exhibits trace the career of this talented black pianist and composer from his lowly beginnings to his tragic end. Tapes of entertainer Eubie Blake explain the man and his music. Once you've completed your tour of the archives, go to the corner of Lamine and Main Streets to see the monument the city has erected to mark the site of the Maple Leaf Club, where Joplin's music first began the ragtime craze.

Sedalia is also the site of the **Missouri State Fair**, held here each year since 1901. The fair, held every August, is one of the largest agricultural expositions in the country. It features nationally prominent musical entertainment, horse and auto racing, and midway attractions.

BEST TIME TO VISIT: Summer.
HOURS: Sedalia Ragtime Archives 8 a.m.-8 p.m. Monday-Thursday, 8 a.m.-4 p.m. Friday; closed holidays.
DIRECTIONS: From Columbia, take I-70 west to junction with I-65, then go south to Sedalia.
FOR MORE INFORMATION: Call the Chamber of Commerce, (816) 826-2222, or write 113 E. 4th St., Sedalia, MO 65301.

America's Greatest General's Boyhood Home

Laclede, Missouri

Driving Time: 1½ hours east of St. Joseph

Laclede, a farming community in north-central Missouri, is perhaps best known as General John (Blackjack) Pershing's boyhood home (11 miles north of U.S. 36 on Rt. 5), the only man every to become a six-star general within his lifetime.

The "rural gothic" home of this World War I hero is today a state historic site featuring a nine-room house built in 1858. Tour this historic home with its period furnishings and examine this extraordinary man's papers and other personal effects.

Pershing State Park (two miles west of Laclede on U.S. 36) is a 1,836-acre memorial to the city's favorite son. This lovely wooded area is perfect for picnicking and camping; it also provides excellent facilities for swimming, hiking, and fishing. The park is also the site of the **Pershing Balloon Derby** in August, one of the nation's largest such races.

Thirteen miles south of Laclede you'll discover the town of **Sumner**, home of the **Swan Lake National Wildlife Refuge** (on Rt. 139). In the spring and again in the fall, this park becomes a resting area for one of the country's largest flocks of Canadian geese.

Bring your binoculars and camera, as this park offers a wealth of wildlife photo possibilities.

BEST TIME TO VISIT: Summer.
HOURS: General Pershing's Boyhood Home — 10 a.m.-4 p.m. daily; closed New Year's Day, Easter, Thanksgiving, and Christmas. Pershing State Park — daily. Swan Lake National Wildlife Refuge — daily.
ADMISSION: General Pershing's Boyhood Home — adults, 50¢; children 6-12, 25¢.
DIRECTIONS: From St. Joseph, take I-36 east to Laclede exit.
FOR MORE INFORMATION: Call the Pershing Boyhood Home, (816) 963-2525.

Missouri

Meramec's Magnificent Caverns

Sullivan, Missouri

Driving Time: 1-1/3 hours west of St. Louis

Where can you find the stunning beauty of natural rock formations combined with the lore of the history of the Wild West? Answer: the **Meramec Caverns**, just three miles south of Sullivan.

The caverns, which have a long and somewhat mysterious history, consist of five separate levels with ceilings of varying thicknesses, causing some of the world's most varied and colorful rock formations — a veritable geological treasure house.

Without having seen it firsthand, you'd have a hard time picturing the cave's beauty. Every turn in the trail leads from one room of astonishing beauty to another. In the Jungle Room, the dense growth of rock seems to come to life before your eyes; in the Echo Room, the sound of your voice reverberates off the Crystal Pool's colorful formations.

The cave's formations have been named for the images they bring to mind. The **Wine Table**, a natural onyx rock formation, appears to be a perfectly balanced, three-legged wine table. **Mirror Lake**, in another part of the cavern, offers an illusion of another kind: it reflects the cavern's height in its depths, creating the illusion of a vast watery canyon. This phenomenon has earned it the nickname, "Miniature Grand Canyon of the Caverns."

Perhaps the most majestic of the cave's formations is the **Stage Curtain**. Estimated to be 70 million years old, it is considered the single largest formation of its kind in the world, measuring 70 feet high, 60 feet wide, and 35 feet thick.

Meramec's beauty is just one aspect of its appeal. These caves have also played a role in regional history. Discovered in 1716, the caverns were used by copper and lead miners. Later, during the Civil War, they were reopened by the North and used as a gunpowder-manufacturing station, complete with an "underground railroad" for thousands of fleeing slaves.

The gunpowder plant subsequently was captured by Quantrill's pro-Confederacy raiders, led by Jesse and Frank James, Frank Dalton, and the Younger brothers — all of whom later became notorious outlaws. The caverns were used by these outlaws as a hideout in the 1870s, until they were followed there by a posse after a train robbery. After a three-day gun battle, the gang escaped by following an underground river — a route that remained a mystery until its discovery in 1940.

There was no further exploration of the caverns until 1933, when a noted "caveologist," Lester B. Dill, discovered the caverns' upper levels. In 1935, the caves were opened to the public; today, they rank among the state's most popular tourist attractions.

Meramec State Park, a short drive from the caverns, is one of Missouri's largest and most scenic state parks. Within its boundaries are 20 caves, numerous springs, and a large game reserve. The Meramec River has excellent boating, swimming, and fishing areas. There's also a nature museum, hiking trails, a resident naturalist, and a full range of facilities that include cabins, camping areas, trailer hook-ups, and a dining lodge.

Just 20 minutes away, **Onondaga State Park** features daily tours of its spectacular onyx cave. Also found here are beautiful campsites on the Meramec River, swimming, canoe rentals, picnic sites, and even a country store.

BEST TIME TO VISIT: Summer.

TRAVEL TIPS: If you're looking for a place to stay, consider the Best Western I-44 (307 N. Service Rd., just off I-44, one block south on Rt. 185) or Zeno's (209 N. Service Rd., just off I-44, one block south on Rt. 185), both located in Sullivan. Zeno's Steak House (next to Zeno's) has an excellent Italian-American menu.

The concrete walkways and spectacular lighting system make a visit to the Meramec Caverns safe and enjoyable, without diminishing the natural beauty. Remember, however, that even on hot summer afternoons aboveground, it's a cool 60 degrees underground, so a light jacket or wrap is recommended.

HOURS: Meramec Caverns — 8:30 a.m.-7:30 p.m. daily, June-August; 9 a.m.-5 p.m. rest of year; closed January, February, Thanksgiving, and Christmas. Onondaga Cave State Park — 8 a.m.-7 p.m. daily, Memorial Day-Labor Day; closed Thanksgiving and Christmas.

ADMISSION: Meramec Caverns—adults, $5; children 5-11, $2.50; under 5, free. Onondaga Cave State Park — adults, $5; children 5-11, $2.50; under 5, free.

DIRECTIONS: From St. Louis, take I-44 west to the Sullivan exit.

FOR MORE INFORMATION: Call the Sullivan Chamber of Commerce, (314) 468-3314, or write Box 536, Sullivan, MO 63080.

Arrow Rock: The Whole Town's Now A Museum!

Arrow Rock, Missouri

Driving Time: 3½ hours west of St. Louis

Many towns in Missouri tout their historic buildings or districts, but only one can claim the entire city as a State Historic District — and that's Arrow Rock. Once a prosperous stop on the Santa Fe Trail, the town fell on hard times. Now revived, this picturesque river town is experiencing a migration of another kind — an influx of tourists.

Arrow Rock was the backdrop for a movie, "Tom Sawyer," and it's easy to understand why once you've seen it. Nearly 40 buildings from the mid-1800s have been preserved, and many are open to the public. The best way to explore the town is on foot, so pick up a guide map at the Information Center (Main St., across from the Old Tavern) and set off.

Among the stops along the way: the **restored log courthouse**, the first in Salina County; the popular **John Sites Gunshop and House**; the **print shop**, with its newspaper museum; and the **Country Doctor Medical Museum**, with its patent medicines, home remedies, and tonics. Along the way, too, is the **home of Dr. John Sappington**, discoverer of quinine.

For foot-weary, thirsty travelers, a welcome sight is the **Arrow Rock Tavern**, built in 1834 and once a bustling settlers hangout. Between refreshments, look over the tavern's museum, with its Civil War antiques and exhibits that include letters, Indian relics, collections of Americana, and pioneer artifacts.

Trout fishing at Bennett Springs

Another stop is the **George Caleb Bingham House**, a three-room home constructed by the artist in 1837 and now a National Historic Landmark. Bingham, a self-taught painter, is best known for his Missouri scenes detailing lives of ordinary people.

The town's 90-year-old **Lyceum Summer Theatre** (Morgan St.), refurnished in the style of 19th-century American theaters, draws talented actors, directors, and designers each summer. (Performances are held nightly Wednesday through Saturday during the summer, with matinees Wednesday, Saturday, and Sunday. Reservations are not required, but are strongly suggested.)

Not far from Arrow Rock, the **Van Meter State Park** (22 miles northwest on Rt. 41, then west and north on Rt. 122) was once the home of the Missouri Indians, from whom the state got its name. This archeological site contains relics dating from 10,000 B.C. and some old Indian earthworks known locally as the "Old Fort." In addition to its historic treasures, Van Meter has excellent facilities for camping, picnicking, fishing, and even a playground.

Boonville, a city on the Missouri River about 20 minutes east of Arrow Rock on I-70, was the point where wagon trains obtained provisions for the long journey west over the Santa Fe Trail. This city was also the site of the state's first Civil War battle, fought on June 17, 1861. Like Arrow Rock, Boonville has a theatrical tradition. It's home to one of the country's oldest surviving theater buildings, **Thespian Hall**. Built in 1855, the building has been restored to its vintage-1901 appearance. Tours of the theater and information on spring and fall concert series are available on request. (The third week of every August the Hall hosts the *Missouri River Festival of the Arts*, which offers a variety of musical performances, including opera, orchestras, and band concerts.)

BEST TIME TO VISIT: Summer.
HOURS: Old Tavern — 11 a.m.-7 p.m. Tuesday-Sunday; closed January 1-31 and major holidays. George Caleb Bingham House — 10:30 a.m. and 1:30 p.m. Monday-Saturday, 1:30 p.m. Sunday, Memorial Day-Labor Day; by appointment the rest of the year. Arrow Rock Lyceum — performances nightly and Sunday afternoon, Memorial Day-Labor Day.
ADMISSION: Arrow Rock Tavern — adults, 50¢; children 6-12, 25¢. George Caleb Bingham House — adults, $1.50; children under 12, 50¢; this includes a tour of all the houses and businesses in the Arrow Rock State Historical Site.
DIRECTIONS: From Columbia, take I-70 west to Rt. 41, then go north to Arrow Rock.
FOR MORE INFORMATION: Call the Arrow Rock State Historic Site, (816) 837-3309.

Missouri

Ste. Genevieve: Missouri's Oldest City

Sainte Genevieve, Missouri

Driving Time: 1 hour southeast of St. Louis

Canadian fur trappers and lead miners seeking their fortunes founded this town in the early 1700s. Commercially, it once rivaled St. Louis but was later bypassed as a major trading post. Now enough remains of its French heritage — in the vertical log houses, country French inns, and its old Catholic church — to make it an interesting byway for the traveler. In all, more than 40 buildings remain from that 1700s to early 1800s era.

The **Sainte Genevieve Museum** (Merchant St. and Dubourg Pl.) exhibits land grants (this was part of the Louisiana Territory) and other historic documents. Here, too, are the giant salt tubs used by the early settlers to distill salt from water; a display of stuffed birds by John J. Audubon once an area resident; and a variety of relics and artifacts left by the Osage Indians.

Bolduc House (123 S. Main St.), a 1770 French colonial considered the most authentic house of its kind, once sat on the riverbank two miles to the south. Like the rest of the town's structures, it was moved right after a flood in 1785. Inside, you'll find a restored frontier kitchen and period furnishings. Outside, there's a formal herb garden that supplied the kitchen with the herbs and spices that make French cooking so special. A stockade fence, much like the one that once protected the whole town from Indians, circles the house.

Green Tavern Inn (St. Mary's Rd. nearby), built in 1790 by a friend of George Rogers Clark, was once a popular hangout for colonists in Louisiana Purchase days. The inn's

Bolduce House in Ste. Genevieve

architectural features include a sapling roof, a triangular fireplace that opens into three rooms, and a fake wall to hide children and womenfolk during Indian attacks. Additional anti-attack features included front steps that pull in and windows shaped to allow lookout perches.

The French-colonial **Amouraux House** (St. Mary's Rd.), of 1770 vintage, contains period furniture and an antique doll and toy collection. A stone's throw away is the **Guilbourd-Valle House** (4th and Merchant Sts.), a 1798-restored vertical log house furnished with French antiques. Surrounded by a brick wall with an elegant iron gate, the house has a formal rose garden and slave quarters in the rear.

The **Church of Sainte Genevieve** (49 Dubourg Pl.), built in 1759, still holds Mass every Saturday and Sunday. An enormous, red-brick structure, it's adorned with colorful stained-glass windows and lovely 17th-century French paintings. Three of Upper Louisiana's French governors are buried beneath the church.

To sample the city's heritage, attend Sainte Genevieve's French Day celebration, the *Jour de Fete a Ste. Genevieve*. On the agenda are an historic house and museum tour, arts and crafts demonstrations, strolling French street singers, and fine cuisine.

BEST TIME TO VISIT: Summer.
TRAVEL TIPS: Start any tours at the visitor information center on Third St.; brochures and maps of the town's historic buildings are available there. Stop for lunch at the Old Brick House (3rd and Market), so named because it is the oldest brick building west of the Mississippi (1790); let your family gorge itself on its famous smorgasbord. A number of historic restaurants offer excellent meals: the Anvil Restaurant and Bar (46 S. Third St.), built in 1850, for charbroiled steak, fresh seafood, and channel catfish; Oberle's Restaurant (950 Ste. Genevieve Dr.) specializes in smoked meats, fried chicken, and liver dumpings; and the Sainte Genevieve Restaurant (Main and Merchants Sts.), 1800s vintage, excellent catfish. If you stay in St. Genevieve during the festival, make reservations early. The finest hotel in town is the tiny country-French inn, St. Gemme Beauvias (78 N. Main), with eight guest rooms furnished with antiques and one of the finest French luncheons in town. Another hotel, the Sainte Genevieve (Main and Merchants Sts.), late 1800s, offers a restaurant and bar.
HOURS: Ste. Genevieve Museum — 9 a.m.-11 p.m. and noon-4 p.m. April-November; noon-4 p.m. November-March; closed Thanksgiving, Christmas, and New Year's Day. Bolduc House—10 a.m.-4 p.m. Monday-Saturday, 11 a.m.-5 p.m. Sunday, April-October. Green Tavern Inn — 10 a.m.-5 p.m. daily. Old Brick House — 8 a.m.-8 p.m. daily. Amoureaux House — 10 a.m.-5 p.m. daily; closed Thanksgiving and Christmas. Guilbourd-Valle House — 10 a.m.-5 p.m. daily; closed Thanksgiving, December 25-January 1. Church of Sainte Genevieve — 6 a.m.-8 p.m. daily. Anvil Restaurant and Bar — 11 a.m.-10 p.m. Monday-Saturday. Oberle's Restaurant — 7 a.m.-10 p.m. Monday-Thursday, 7 a.m.-11 p.m. Friday and Saturday. Sainte Genevieve Restaurant — 7 a.m.-9 p.m. weekdays, 4 p.m.-10 p.m. Saturday, 8 a.m.-3 p.m. Sunday, Christmas, Memorial Day, New Year's Day. Inn St. Gemme Beauvias — 11 a.m.-2 p.m. daily.
ADMISSION: Fees for various houses and museums range from about $1 for adults to 50¢ for children.
DIRECTIONS: From St. Louis, take I-55 southeast to Rt. 32. Go east on 32 to Ste. Genevieve.

Missouri

Missouri's State Capitol building in Jefferson City

George Washington Carver's Birthplace

Diamond, Missouri

Driving Time: 1 hour north of Kansas City

The **George Washington Carver National Monument** (two miles west of Diamond on Rt. 5, then one-half mile south) near Diamond honors the birthplace of the distinguished teacher, humanitarian, and scientist (1860-1943), who began life as a slave on the farm of Moses Carver.

Despite his humble beginnings, Carver attended Simpson College in Iowa and later received a master's degree from Iowa State Agricultural College. As head of the Department of Agriculture at Tuskegee Institute, Carver worked to develop agricultural products for use in the South, where the land had been destroyed by the one-crop farming system. He is perhaps best known for his work with the peanut and the over 300 products he developed from it. He also is

credited with creating products from the soybean and sweet potato, and for educating the South's small farmers on the importance of developing these crops for market.

While at the monument, attend the audio-visual presentation on Carver's life at the visitor center, then browse through the museum and see memorabilia of the man. A short (3/4-mile) trail leads your family to the birthplace cabin site, where you can admire a statue of Carver as a boy by Robert Amendola. Then continue up the path to the restored 1881 **Moses Carver House** and the family cemetery, all the while enjoying the natural scenic beauty of Carver's youth.

In recognition of his contributions to the nation and to American frontier history, this memorial to Carver was declared a national monument in 1943. President Franklin D. Roosevelt praised Carver, saying that his life and work were an "inspiring example to youth everywhere."

BEST TIME TO VISIT: Summer.
HOURS: George Washington Carver National Monument — 8:30 a.m.-5 p.m. daily; closed New Year's Day and Christmas.
DIRECTIONS: From Joplin, take I-44 east to the junction with I-72, then go south to Diamond; the monument is two miles west of Diamond on County V, then ½ mile south.
FOR MORE INFORMATION: Call the George Washington Carver National Monument, (417) 325-4151.

'Jeff City': Missouri's State Capital

Jefferson City, Missouri

Driving Time: 2 hours west of St. Louis

The **state capitol** (High St. and Broadway), built of Carthage stone and overlooking the Missouri River, is the most prominent landmark in Jefferson City, seat of the state's government since 1821. The present capitol is the third in the state's history; sadly, the two preceding structures were destroyed by fires in 1837 and 1911. The building includes murals by famed American artist Thomas Hart Benton and other paintings that depict Missouri's history, natural environment, and turbulent Civil War era.

On your way to the governor's mansion, stop by **Jefferson Landing State Historic Site** (Water St.), an authentic mid-1800 riverboat landing. The Lohman Building (1839), one of the landing's three buildings dating from the mid-1800s, offers exhibits and an audio-visual presentation on the history of Jefferson City and the Missouri River.

A visit to the state capital might also include a stop at the executive mansion. The 1871 building (100 Madison St.) was designed in Renaissance Revival style by architect George I. Barnett and features antiques, a winding staircase, and beautiful needlepoint rugs.

BEST TIME TO VISIT: Summer.
HOURS: State Capitol — 8 a.m.-5 p.m. daily, tours on the hour; closed New Year's Day, Easter, Thanksgiving, and Christmas. Jefferson Landing State Historic Site — 8 a.m.-4:30 p.m. daily, tours on the hour; closed New Year's Day, Easter, Thanksgiving, and Christmas. Missouri Executive Mansion — tours on Tuesday and Thursday at 10 a.m., 11 a.m., and 1 p.m.; closed holidays.
DIRECTIONS: From Columbia, take I-63 south to Capital exit.
FOR MORE INFORMATION: Call the Jefferson City Area Chamber of Commerce, (314) 634-3616, or write 213 Adams St., Box 776, Jefferson City, MO 65101.

Missouri

St. Joseph: The Pony Express Rides Again

St. Joseph, Missouri

Driving Time: 1 hour north of Kansas City

Early on April 3, 1860, a solitary horse and rider left Pike's Peak stables in St. Joseph, Missouri, with a single mission in mind — to get the mail to Sacramento, California, 2,000 miles away, faster than it had ever been delivered before. Thus began one of America's greatest adventure stories—the Pony Express.

More was at stake than just a mail contract. Unless the government was able to provide California with regular postal delivery, many feared the state would leave the Union. So for two years, from 1860 to 1861, when the telegraph ended the need for the Pony Express, riders for the Central Overland Express battled nature and hostile Indians to bring the mail in on time.

The **Pony Express Museum** (914 Penn St.), which honors these fearless riders, is located in the old Pike's Peak stables, eastern terminus of the Overland line. The stables include a restored blacksmith and wheelwright shop, as well as a variety of other exhibits. On display are replicas of the saddle and mochila used by the riders, maps, and other information explaining the routes they used and the hazards they encountered. The museum also highlights some of the company's greatest riders, including such legends as Buffalo Bill, Johnny Fry, and Cyclone Charlie Thompson.

North of the red-brick Pony Express stables, the **Pony Express Memorial Statue** immortalizes in bronze the spirit and rugged individ-

ualism of these heroic frontiersmen. The statue has become the symbol of St. Joseph and is very popular with photographers.

The **Patee House Museum** (12th and Penn Sts.), a former hotel, was once used as the St. Joseph headquarters of the Pony Express. Now a western museum, it contains pioneer exhibits, frontier shops, a train depot, wood-burning engine, and more.

The **Jesse James Home Museum** (12th and Penn St.) is located next door to the Patee House Museum. Here the famous outlaw was gunned down in 1882 by a former associate. The museum contains the house's original furnishings as well as exhibits on the life and times of the desperado.

Down Penn Street, the **Society of Memories Doll Museum** displays more than 600 different dolls and other toys. The museum exhibits antique dolls, toys, doll houses, and mechanical miniatures from in and around the St. Joseph area.

Across town, the **St. Joseph Museum** seeks to preserve art of another kind, that of the American Indian. This collection contains over 5,000 Indian artifacts, including Pomo feather baskets, quilted moccasins of the Iroquois, and copper masks from the Haida. The museum also houses an extensive natural history collection, presenting "wildlife" in their natural habitats, everything from the American bald eagle to the Alaskan brown bear.

The museum is situated in the 1879 **Wyeth-Tootle Mansion**, a 43-room Gothic sandstone with lovely Tiffany windows. Today, the mansion serves as a community center.

BEST TIME TO VISIT: Spring and summer.

TRAVEL TIPS: Accommodations in St. Joseph: the Ramada Inn (4016 Fredrick Blvd.), the Great Western Hospitality Pony Express (1211 N. Belt Hwy.), or the Holiday Inn (4312 Frederick Ave.). Good local restaurants include the Swiss Chalet (3101 N. Belt Hwy.), for veal Stalder, bratwurst, and European pastries, and the Pony Express (1211 N. Belt Hwy. in the Great Western Hospitality Pony Express), for charcoal-broiled steaks, home-fried chicken, and prime rib. If you prefer camping, there's the Lewis and Clark State Park (19 miles southwest on U.S. 59, then two miles southwest on Rt. 45), with facilities for camping, picnicking, boating, swimming, and fishing.

HOURS: Pony Express Museum — 9 a.m.-5 p.m. Monday-Saturday, April-September; 2 p.m.-5 p.m. Sunday and holidays. Patee House Museum — 10 a.m.-5 p.m. Monday-Saturday, June-August; 1 p.m.-5 p.m. April-May; 1 p.m.-5 p.m. Saturday-Sunday only, September-November. Jesse James Home Museum — 10 a.m.-5 p.m. Monday-Saturday, June-August; 1 p.m.-5 p.m. April-May; 1 p.m.-5 p.m. weekends only, September-November. Society of Memories Doll Museum — 1 p.m.-5 p.m. Tuesday-Sunday, May 30-October. St. Joseph Museum — 9 am.-5 p.m. Monday-Saturday, April-September; 1 p.m.-5 p.m. Tuesday-Saturday, rest of year; 2 p.m.-5 p.m. Sundays and holidays; closed Thanksgiving, December 24, 25 and 31, and New Year's Day. Swiss Chalet — 11:30 a.m.-2 p.m. and 5 p.m.-10 p.m. daily, 11 a.m.-2:30 p.m. and 5 p.m.-10 p.m. Sunday. Pony Express — 6:30 p.m.-10 p.m. daily.

ADMISSION: Pony Express Museum — adults, 50¢; children, 25¢. Jesse James Home Museum — adults, $1; 6-16, 50¢; children under 6, free. Society of Memories Doll Museum — adults, $1; 6-12, 50¢; children under 6, free. St. Joseph Museum — adults, 50¢; children, 25¢. (Prices subject to change.)

DIRECTIONS: From Kansas City, take I-29 north to the St. Joseph exit.

FOR MORE INFORMATION: Call the Chamber of Commerce, (816) 232-4461, or write to Suite 500, First Federal Bldg., 7th and Felix, St. Joseph, MO 64501.

Sampling Hermann's German Heritage

Hermann, Missouri

Driving Time: 2 hours west of St. Louis

German immigrants founded this riverside town, having been reminded of their native Rhineland by the neighboring hills and valleys. They built up a wine business that by the turn of the century made Missouri this country's second-leading wine-producing state, a title that was ravished by vine disease and prohibition. Today, Hermann's wine industry is coming back and so are visitors, who are looking for a taste of the "old country."

Historic buildings abound here. The **Hermann Museum** (4th and Schiller Sts.), in the Old German School Building, contains artifacts, relics, local handicrafts, and Missouri riverboat lore. While there, look in on the huge internal mechanism that powers the town's clock.

A number of 19th-century houses built of native stone and clay are scattered around town, including the 1846 **Klenk House** (301 Gellert St.), with its smokehouse and summer kitchen; **Scharnhorst-Eitzen House** (Wharf St.), with its authentic period furnishings; and an 1860s hotel, the **White House** (232 Wharf St.). Also worth seeing by house buffs are the **Heney-Langendoeffer House** (2nd St.), the **Graf House** (Mozart St.), and the 1871 **Reiff House**, which is now a bank.

Hermann's wines can be tasted at two of the best local wineries. The **Stone Hill Winery** (on Rt. 1) offers one-hour guided tours of its wine cellars, museum, and exhibits on grape-growing and wine-making. In addition to red, white, and rose, Stone Hill has a variety of fruit wines. The winery has been declared a National Historic Site. At the **Hermannhof Winery** (330 E. First St.), a 150-year-old establishment, wines aren't the only product to savor; there are also delicious sausages and cheeses. Ten wine cellars and the sausage smokehouse are also on the agenda. Next door, the **Cooperage Craft Center** (338 E. First St.) provides demonstrations of pioneer arts and crafts

The city's popular special events, Maifest and Winefest, are tied to the traditional folklore and industries. Each year, on May 21-22, the whole town and the surrounding area's populace turn out for the **German Maifest**, welcoming spring with bratwurst, sauerkraut, beer, and German music and dancing in a traditional beer garden. Each October, an **Octoberfest** (or "Winefest," as the local wine-makers prefer to call it) attracts throngs for wine-tasting, craft demonstrations, and more music and dancing.

BEST TIME TO VISIT: Summer and fall.
TRAVEL TIPS: For accommodations, your best bet is Jefferson City, the state's capital, about 45 miles away: the Ramada Inn (1510 Jefferson Hwy.), the Rodeway Inn (319 W. Miller St.), and the Holiday Inn-Downtown (422 Monroe St.). Try some of that good German cooking in the town's restaurants: the Vintage 1847 Restaurant (Rt. 1), in a former carriage house and stables; the Hermannhof Weinstube (330 E. First St.), a restored national historic site; and the Calico Cupboard (4 Schiller St.), in the historic district and furnished with antiques.
HOURS: Historic Hermann Museum — 10 a.m.-5 p.m. daily, April-November; December-March by appointment. Stone Hill Winery — 8:30 a.m.-dusk, Monday-Saturday; noon-5 p.m. Sunday; closed Thanksgiving, Christmas, and New Year's Day. Hermannhof Winery — 9 a.m.-6 p.m. Monday-Saturday; noon-6 p.m. Sunday; closed Christmas, New Year's Day, Easter. Vintage 1847 Restaurant — 11:30 a.m.-8:30 p.m. daily, 11 a.m.-10 p.m. Saturday and Sunday. Hermannhof Weinstube—9:30 a.m.-5:30 p.m. Monday-Saturday; noon-5:30 p.m. Sunday. Calico Cupboard — daily, April-November.
ADMISSION: Historic Hermann Museum — adults, 50¢; children 12-18, 25¢; under 12, free. Hermannhof Winery — adults, $1.50; children under 13, free. Stone Hill Winery — adults, $1.50, children under 12, 50¢; preschoolers, free.
DIRECTIONS: From St. Louis, take I-70 west to Rt. 19, then go south to Hermann.
FOR MORE INFORMATION: Call the Historic Hermann Information Center, (314) 486-2057, or write German School Building, 4th and Schiller Sts., Hermann, MO 65041.

Carthage: City Built Of Marble

Carthage, Missouri

Driving Time: 2 hours south of Kansas City

Carthage, in the southwest corner of Missouri, was the site of the first major Civil War battle west of the Mississippi. Confederate guerrilla raids extensively damaged the town during the battle. Among the guerrillas was Carthage native Belle Shirley, who later became known as outlaw Belle Starr.

Other famous early residents of this city include Annie Baxter, the first woman in the country to win elective office (she became county clerk in 1890), and well-known ragtime composer and musician James Scott, who began his musical career here in 1906.

In the 1880s, Carthage opened its now-famous **marble quarries**. The marble was used to construct several Victorian buildings in Carthage, including the stately courthouse in the city's historic town square. The **Jasper County Courthouse** (Courthouse Square), built in 1894, features a mural by Lowell Davis, "Forged in Fire," depicting the city's history. Near the courthouse, the **Historic Square**, bounded by Main, Grant, 3rd, and 4th Streets, is populated by Victorian buildings made of Carthage marble.

The town's many lovely Victorian homes are open to tourists. The 1887 **Hill House Mansion** (1157 S. Main) is today a 20-room Victorian museum

BEST TIME TO VISIT: Summer.
HOURS: Jasper County Courthouse — 8 a.m.-5 p.m. Monday-Friday; closed holidays. Hill House Museum — 1 p.m.-5 p.m. daily.
ADMISSION: Hill House Museum — adults, $2.50; senior citizens, $1.50; children, 6-12, $1; under 6, free.
DIRECTIONS: From Kansas City, take U.S. 71 south to Carthage.
FOR MORE INFORMATION: Call the Carthage Chamber of Commerce, (417) 358-2373, or write 407 S. Garrison, Carthage, MO 64836.

Missouri

Traveling Missouri's Scenic Waterways

Big Springs Region, near Rolla, Missouri

Driving Time: 2½ hours southwest of St. Louis

In a state known for its scenic beauty, the Big Springs region is No. 1 in "rustic splendor." Blending pristine forests, clear streams, natural springs, and rolling hills, this area has a character all its own.

This is genuine rural America — a network of small towns, each with its own particular history and charm. To experience Big Springs, you must travel, but that presents no problem because getting there is half the fun. The place to begin the tour is Rolla (at the intersection of I-44 and U.S. 63).

Outdoor enthusiasts will enjoy the many state parks and forests this area offers. Fishermen will be challenged by the trout streams at **Montauk State Park** (35 miles south on U.S. 63, two miles south on Rt. 137, then 10 miles east on County VV). The streams' fish, bred at the park's hatchery, are hard to hook and even harder to land. In another part of the park, an old gristmill grinds flour the way it did in the old days. The facilities allow hiking, picnicking, and overnight stays.

Iron mining was the area's main industry. To learn more about this tough occupation, visit the **old 1826 ironworks** at nearby Meramec State Park. Here your family can inspect the iron ore deposits and the 1857 blast furnace used to make pig iron.

The heart of this park is **Meramec Springs**, providing its streams with more than 96 million gallons of fresh water every day. Have a picnic lunch beside the stream or wander through the park's nature center and along its scenic trails, sampling the park's pleasures — fishing, a campground, museum, and children's playground.

At the headwaters of the Gasconade, **Big Piney and Little Piney Rivers**, is the headquarters of the **Mark Twain National Forest** (southwest via I-44 and U.S. 63), with some of the state's best hunting and fishing. The park has excellent facilities for camping, water sports, and picnicking.

To continue your family's tour of the Big Springs region, drive east on I-44 to **St. James**, the next stop. This town was founded to provide a home for the ironworkers of Meramec Springs, many of them European immigrants who brought with them the love of wine-making. Today, wine has replaced iron mining as the major industry. Plan to tour **local wineries** and sample their offerings. Some suggestions: the Heinrichshaus Winery (Rt. 2), specializing in European-style table wines; the St. James Winery (540 Sydney St.), with a full range of Missouri wines; and the Rosati Winery (Rt. 1), Italian wines.

Leaving the vineyards of St. James, head south for Graniteville and the **Elephant Rocks State Park** (take Rt. 8 southeast to Potosi, then south on Rt. 21 to Graniteville). This route will lead to the northern edge of the Mark Twain National Forest and then past the world's largest lead-mining district. Elephant Rocks State Park was named for its huge, picturesque, red granite boulders estimated to be 1.2 billion years old. Hikers can tackle mile-long National Recreation Trail circling the park's formations; rockhounds will like the 22 trail markers written in English and Braille describing each of the park's natural features.

Continuing south on Route 21, you'll find **Fort Davidson**, site of a bloody Civil War battle. In the 1864 encounter, 1,000 soldiers became casualties in 20 minutes of fierce fighting.

Farther south on Route 21, take the Route 49 turnoff west and you'll be at the foot of **Taum Sauk Mountain**, the state's highest point. Here, the 20-mile Taum Sauk backpacking trail leads over the 1,772-foot mountain (don't try it unless you're in tip-top shape, it's tough). Less adventurous souls may prefer **Johnson's Shut-Ins State Park**, a popular spot with campers. The Shut-Ins were formed by the erosion of the Black River's rock shelf over eons (thus exposing some of the oldest rock in Missouri). Take time to examine the rocks and climb around. The park's canyon-like rapids provide the perfect backdrop for picnickers and fishermen; swimming and hiking are excellent at this park.

A tour of the Big Springs region should end with a visit to **Van Buren**, home of the **Ozark National Scenic**

Riverways. Here, the National Park Service has sought to preserve more than 134 miles of the Current and Jack Fork Rivers in their natural state. For adventurers, the chief attraction of the Big Springs area is white-water canoeing. One of the most popular access points is at **Big Springs**, just south of town. The springs, the largest in the state (276 million gallons a day), provide an excellent staging area for a float trip. A number of rental firms and outfitters can provide guidance and equipment.

BEST TIME TO VISIT: Summer and fall.

TRAVEL TIPS: Accommodations in Rolla include the Holiday Inn (Martin Spring Dr., one-quarter mile west of U.S. 66, I-44 exit at Rolla), featuring a cafe, pool, and bar with nightly entertainment; and the Howard Johnson's Motor Lodge (1½ miles west at junction of U.S. 66 Business and I-44), with an indoor-outdoor pool, whirlpool, sauna, and 24-hour cafe. Family-style dining can be found in Rolla at Chub and Jo's Restaurant (704 Pine St.) or, for more elegant surroundings in an historic home, eat at the Carney House Restaurant (1102 Pine St.) for steaks and German food. In St. James, there's the Barn Bar-B-Q (308 N. Jefferson), with its family-style barbecue and salad bar, or the Jefferson Restaurant (I-44 and Rt. 68) for smorgasbord with homemade soup and pies. In the Van Buren area: the Deer Run Inn (three miles northwest on County M) has a cafe, golf course, bar, private beach, and boat rental; and the Hawthorne (on U.S. 60) has a pool, playground, and air-conditioned rooms.

HOURS: Meramec Spring Park — daily, sunrise to sunset. Chub and Jo's Restaurant — 5:30 a.m.-7:45 p.m. daily. Howard Johnson's — 24 hours a day. Heinrichshaus Winery — 9 a.m.-6 p.m. Monday-Saturday, noon-6 p.m. Sunday. St. James Winery — 8 a.m.-8 p.m. Monday-Saturday, summer; 8 a.m.-6 p.m. Monday-Saturday, winter; noon-6 p.m. Sunday year round. Rosati Winery — daily. Barn Bar-B-Q — 11 a.m.-7 p.m. Monday-Friday. Jamestown Restaurant — 6 a.m.-8 p.m. daily. Elephant Rocks State Park — 7 a.m.-5 p.m. daily, for trail; 7 a.m.-10 p.m. daily, summer, for picnic area; 7 a.m.-5 p.m. daily, for trail; 7 a.m.-10 p.m. daily, summer, for picnic area; 7 a.m.-7 p.m. daily, winter, for picnic area. Fort Davidson — 7 a.m.-10 p.m. daily. Johnson's Shut-Ins State Park (Taum Sauk Trail) — 24 hour daily. Ozark National Scenic Riverways — 24 hours daily.

ADMISSION: Meramec Spring Park — museum, 25¢; $1-$5/season; parking.

DIRECTIONS: From St. Louis, take I-44 southwest to Rolla.

FOR MORE INFORMATION: Call the Rolla Chamber of Commerce, (314) 364-3577, or write 901 Elm St., Rolla, MO 65401. Call Elephant Rocks State Park, (314) 697-5395; Johnson's Shut-Ins, (314) 546-2450; or the Superintendent, Ozark National Scenic Riverways, (314) 323-4236, or P.O. Box 490, Van Buren, MO 64683.

Old River City Relives Its Glory Days

Weston, Missouri

Driving Time: One-half hour northwest of Kansas City

The glory that was the old South can be relived in **Weston**, a former river city now best known for its historic district of antebellum houses and businesses. Once a trading center to rival St. Louis, the city was beset by a number of disasters — floods, fire, and the Civil War — from which it never recovered.

The city's 16-block **Historic District** provides a taste of life as it was before the Civil War. You can almost hear the sounds of carriage wheels on the pavement, the rustle of hoop skirts, and the shouts of men as they load cargo on the riverboats. Over half the town is included in the Historic District, giving it the country's highest concentration of historic buildings.

Before the Civil War, Weston was a major trading center for hemp and tobacco. Today, the city retains its title, "Tobacco Capital of the West," with auctions at the largest tobacco market west of the Mississippi (357 Main). More than six million pounds of leaf change hands here each year.

Weston is also the site of the country's oldest and smallest continuous distillery. Built by Ben Holladay in 1856, the **McCormick Distilling Company** (1¼ miles south via Rt. JJ) produces some of the South's finest whiskey.

BEST TIME TO VISIT: Summer.

TRAVEL TIP: A popular place to eat with the locals is the America Bowman Keeping Room (500 Welt St., Kansas Rt. 92 to Missouri Rt. 45, Rt. 45 to Rt. JJ west to Main behind City Hall), which specializes in sugar-cured ham, seafood, and prime rib.

HOURS: Tobacco Auction — Thanksgiving to February, call for times and places. McCormick Distilling Co. — 9 a.m.-4:30 p.m. daily, mid-March to November; closed holidays.

DIRECTIONS: From Kansas City, take I-29 north to Rt. M, then go west to Weston.

FOR MORE INFORMATION: Call the Historic Weston Commission, (816) 386-5235, or write P.O. Box 97, Weston, MO 64098.

Missouri

Branson: Good Times, Ozark Style

Branson, Missouri

Driving Time: 4 hours south-west of St. Louis; 3 hours southeast of Kansas City

Rolling green hills, sparkling streams, and crystal-blue lakes have made the Ozark Mountains resort town of Branson a popular vacation spot. Thousands of people flock here each summer to fish, swim, or camp.

Branson inspired author Harold Bell Wright, who wrote *Shepherd of the Hills*, a novel that became the fourth-best seller of all time. The book recreates the saga of the homesteading Matthews family, and the town has kept the saga alive for tourists.

Wright's story can best be relived via a "Jeep-train" at the Shepherd of the Hills Farm (seven miles west of Branson on Rt. 76). Some highlights: **"Old Matt's Cabin,"** with its period furniture and pioneer relics; **Inspiration Point**, where Wright camped while writing the book; and the **Memorial Museum**, with its Ozark Mountains handicraft displays. The hour-long tour includes visits to an old mill and a working still — the latter also the inspiration of other local legends. In nightly performances from May to October, local actors recreate the *Shepherd of the Hills* story at the Old Mill Theatre, located on the farm's grounds.

At **Silver Dollar City** (nine miles west of Branson on Rt. 76), talented mountain folk recreate pioneer life. This 1880s-style Ozark mining town offers visitors the thrills, "dangers," and rollicking life of the old frontier. A steam train is pursued by robbers, "Rube Dugan's Diving Bell" takes daring tourists beneath Lake Silver's waters, and an ore car races to escape a flooding mine. As if that weren't

Old Matt's Cabin

enough, saloons explode with gunfire, and dance halls vibrate with the sound of music and raucous comedy. Silver Dollar City also has a children's petting zoo and some of the best country food in "them-thar" parts.

Many tour services ply their trade in the Branson area: **Ozark Mountain Sightseeing, Inc.**, offers bus tours to the Shepherd of the Hills Pageant and the Passion Play in Eureka; **Sammy Lane Pirate Cruise and Water Pageant**, one-hour cruises on Lake Tanycomo with a "pirate attack" and a stop at a gold mine; **Ducks Land and Water Tours**, 90-minute treks in World War II amphibious vehicles; and *Zebulon Pike Excursion Boat*, daily sightseeing and dinner cruises on Table Rock Lake.

By far, the area's most popular drawing card is **Table Rock Lake** (four miles west of Branson on Rt. 76), then seven miles south on Rt. 165). Formed when the U.S. Army Corps of Engineers built a dam on the White River, the lake boasts some of the state's finest sport fish-

ing, especially for large- and small-mouth bass. **Table Rock State Park** (five miles west on Rt. 76, then south on Rt. 165) has wooded campgrounds near the lake plus rustic hiking trails, mountaintop picnic grounds, and sunlit coves.

Music has always been close to the hearts of the Ozarks' mountain people. Cut off from the "outside" world, they relied on their own resources for entertainment. The result: a hand-clapping, knee-slapping brand of music, a tradition carried on in the country, folk, and hillbilly stage shows in the Branson area. The best of them include **Presley's Mountain Music Jubilee** (four miles west on Rt. 76), one of the longest-running country music and comedy stage shows; the **Foggy River Boys Music Show** (two miles west on Rt. 76), a country show with quartet harmony; and **Baldknobbers Hillbilly Jamboree** (three miles west via Rt. 76), a show blending the sounds of country and hillbilly music.

Branson also has a number of annual special events, and it's worth timing your trip there to take them in. The **Ozark Mountain Crafts Festival** (April 30-May 22) and the **Fall National Crafts Festival** (September 17-October 23) feature some of America's best artists. The **Mountain Folks Music Festival** (June 11-19) throbs to the beat of folk, mountain, and country msuic, and the **Mountain Clog Dancing Festival** (June 17-19) determines the area's best at this lively form of country dancing.

The region's people pride themselves on their independence and self-reliance. These qualities are reflected in one of the state's most unusual colleges, the **School of the Ozarks**. Here, every student is required to work for his or her own room and board by doing various campus jobs. A miniature train at the school's entrance provides campus tours. Also on the premises: the **Edwards Mill**, a water-powered gristmill, and the **Ralph Foster Museum**, which displays artifacts of Ozark pioneers and Indians.

BEST TIME TO VISIT: Summer and fall.
TRAVEL TIPS: Accommodations in the Branson area are available at the Best Western Mountain Ozark Lodge (half-mile west of Silver Dollar City on Rt. 76); the Holiday Inn (two miles west on Rt. 76); the Roark Motor Lodge (403 North on U.S. Business 65); and the Music Country Motor Inn (3½ miles west on Rt. 76). The best in country cooking is available at Candlestick Inn (1½ miles east on Rt. 76, on Mt. Branson), which features steak, seafood, and prime rib; Dimitris (420 E. Main St. on Lake Tanycomo), with its view of the lake and delicious seafood dinners; and C.L.'s, at the Mountain Oak Lodge, for excellent catfish and barbecued ribs.
HOURS: Shepherd of the Hills Farm — 9 a.m.-6 p.m. mid-April to late October. Shepherd of the Hills Play — most nights from May through October (call for reservations and dates), showtime 8:30 p.m. before Labor Day, 7:30 p.m. after. Silver Dollar City — 9:30 a.m.- 6 p.m. April 30-June 10; 9 a.m.-8 p.m. June 11-August 20; 9:30 a.m.-6 p.m. August 21-October 23. School of the Ozarks — tours 10 a.m., 1:30 p.m., and 3:30 p.m. daily, mid-April to October; no 10 a.m. tour Sundays. Edwards Mill — 8:30 a.m.-4:30 p.m. Monday-Saturday; 1 p.m.-5 p.m. Sunday; closed Thanksgiving, Christmas, and New Year's Day. Ralph Foster Museum — 9 a.m.-4:50 p.m. Monday-Saturday; 1 p.m.-4:50 p.m. Sunday; closed Thanksgiving, Christmas, and New Year's Day. Ozark Mountain Sightseeing — daily, April-October. Sammy Lane Pirate Cruise and Water Pageant — 9:30 a.m.-6:30 p.m. daily, May-October. Ducks Land and Water Tours — daily, mid-May to October. Presley's Mountain Music Jubilee—Monday-Saturday, late April-late October, Sunday of Memorial Day weekend, July 4th and Labor Day weekend. Foggy River Boys Music Show — nightly except Monday, May-October; no Monday or Tuesday performances in May; special shows Labor Day weekend. Baldknobbers Hillbilly Jamboree — 8 p.m. nightly except Sunday, May-October. Candlestick Inn — 5 p.m.-10 p.m. daily; closed Sunday, Easter, Thanksgiving, December 23 through January 10. Dimitris — 5 p.m.-10 p.m. daily, closed November to mid-March. C.L.'s at the Mountain Oak Lodge — 7 a.m.-2 p.m. and 5 p.m.-10 p.m. weekdays; closed late October-April.
ADMISSION: Shepherd of the Hills Farm — adults, $4; children 6-12, $2; under 6, free. Shepherd of the Hills Play — adults, $7.50-9.50; children, half price. Silver Dollar City — adults, $12.95 plus tax; children 5-10, $9.95; under 5, free. Ralph Foster Museum — adults, $2; children, free. Sammy Lane Pirate Cruise and Water Pageant — adults, $4.75; children 2-12, $2.75; under 2, free. Ducks Land and Water Tours — adults, $5; children 3-12, $3; under 3, free. Presley's Mountain Music Jubilee — adults, $5; children under 12, $2.50. Foggy River Boys Music Show — adults, $5; children under 11, $3. Baldknobbers Hillbilly Jamboree — adults, $5; children under 12, $2. (Prices subject to change.)
DIRECTIONS: From Springfield, take U.S. 65 south to Branson exit.
FOR MORE INFORMATION: Call the Branson/Lakes Area Chamber of Commerce, (417) 334-4136, or write P.O. Box 220, Branson, MO 65616.

Springfield: The Best Of the City And Country

Springfield, Missouri

Driving Time: 3½ hours southwest of St. Louis

Springfield, Missouri, is known as the "Gateway to the Ozarks," and the city fathers would like every southbound tourist to consider it as such.

The city has two major museums. The **Springfield Art Museum** contains exhibits of American and European paintings and sculpture, but perhaps is best known as host of Watercolor U.S.A. This annual event draws the country's finest artists to the city each June. To experience the Victorian era's charm and elegance, visit the **Museum of the Ozarks** in historic Bentley House, an 18-room, Queen Anne-style mansion decorated with furniture and accessories of the period.

The **Dickerson Park Zoo**, dedicated to preserving and promoting rare and endangered species, is home to a rare elephant herd.

In the mood for music? The two-hour show at the **Ozark Mountain Jamboree** mixes lively country, blues, and gospel music by the Blue Mountain Cousins.

Tours of the Ozark mountain country around Springfield might begin with the **Fantastic Caverns** (five miles northwest on I-44, then north 1½ miles to U.S. 13), the only cave in America through which you can drive a vehicle. A Jeep-drawn trailer known as the "Time Machine" provides a rolling 45-minute look at the cave's "secrets": rock formations millions of years old, stalactites, stalagmites, and shimmering onyx curtains in a rainbow of natural colors.

Nearby **Crystal Cave**, which provided shelter for the Osage Indians, entices visitors with lovely crystals and other rock formations.

Buena Vista's **Exotic Animal Paradise** (12 miles east of Springfield on I-44) has more than 3,000 wild animals and birds along a nine-mile drive. Roaming freely through the park's natural settings are such creatures as the white-tailed gnu, the South American vulture, the Bengal tiger, and the stump-tailed monkey.

About 40 miles away is the restored home of **Laura Ingalls Wilder**, author of the *Little House on the Prairie* books, which inspired the popular TV series. This 19th-century home has the writer's manuscripts and family mementoes displayed in an authentic 19th-century setting.

The **Wilson Creek National Battlefield** (head west on U.S. 60 from Mansfield, go through Springfield to Rt. ZZ, then to the battlefield) was the site of a major Civil War encounter. In August 1861, Confederate forces seized Springfield in the Battle of Wilson Creek; a year later, the North won it back, but a prolonged and bitter guerrilla war ensued. (One of the Union's scouts was "Wild Bill" Hickok, later a famous U.S. marshal.) Pick up self-guided tour maps at the park's entrance and you're on your way.

BEST TIME TO VISIT: Summer.
TRAVEL TIPS: For overnight lodgings, recommended are the Hilton Inn of the Ozarks (3050 N. Kentwood), the Holiday Inn (2720 N. Glenstone Ave.), and Howard Johnson's (2610 N. Glenstone Ave.). Worthy local restaurants are the Golden Lion (102 Battlefield Mall), the Shady Inn (524 W. Sunshine St.), and the Wicker Works (3333 S. Glenstone Ave.).
ADMISSION: Museum of the Ozarks — adults, 12,; senior citizens, 75¢; children under 12, 25¢. Dickerson Park Zoo — adults, $1.50. Ozark Mountain Jamboree — adults, $4. Fantastic Caverns — adults, $5.95; children up to $1, $2.95. Crystal Cave — adults, $4; children 6-12, $1.25; under 6, free. Buena Vista's Exotic Animal Paradise — adults, $5; children under 12, $3. Laura Ingalls Wilder-Rose Wilder Home and Museum — adults, $2.25; children 3-11, $1; under 3, free if carried.
DIRECTIONS: From St. Louis take I-44 southwest to Springfield exit.
FOR MORE INFORMATION: Call the Springfield Convention and Visitors Bureau, (417) 862-5567, or write P.O. Box 1687, 320 N. Jefferson, Springfield, MO 65806.

Missouri

Independence: Historic Home Of America's 33rd President

Independence, Missouri

Driving Time: 15 minutes east of Kansas City

This historic frontier city played host to wagon trains lumbering west and to Mormons heading for Salt Lake City. Today, however, it's best known as the hometown of America's most outspoken president, Harry S. Truman. Years ago, when President Truman's term ended, he and his wife, Bess, set out in their family car and drove home to Independence — and remained there until they died.

The best place to soak up Truman lore is at the **Harry S. Truman Library and Museum** (U.S. 24 and Delaware St.), where Truman's papers, books, and personal effects are displayed. Other exhibits illustrate the important decisions Truman made, including the bombing of Hiroshima. There's also a replica of Truman's White House office, a frontier mural by Missouri artist Thomas Hart Benton, and in the courtyard, Truman's gravesite.

At **Independence Square Courthouse**, the courtroom and office used by Truman as judge of Jackson County have been restored. A 30-minute film describes Truman's early years and political career.

From 1945 to 1952, the **Truman Home** (219 N. Delaware St.), a fine example of Victorian architecture, served as the summer White House during Truman's incumbency. The local train station, last stop on the former president's famous whistle-stop campaign, might be a fitting last stop on your Truman itinerary.

The **Church of Jesus Christ of Latter-Day Saints**, which is asso-

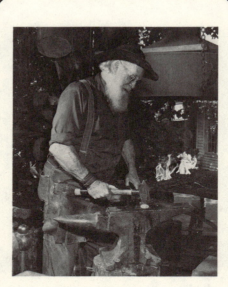

ciated with the Mormon Church in Salt Lake City, maintains a visitors center. It provides insights into the religion and the 1830-1839 "Mormon Wars" in Missouri. These clashes between Mormons and other pioneers lasted until Brigham Young led their exodus to Utah.

Many homes built in the city's boom times during the 1800s still stand today. The 1827 **Old Log Courthouse** (100 Kansas) served as the county's first tribunal; it was constructed by slaves for a total of $150. The **Pioneer Spring Cabin** (Truman and Noland Rds.), now restored to its 19th-century simplicity and replete with pioneer relics, once served as an outlaw hideout.

The 1859 **Marshal's Home, Jail and Museum** (217 N. Main St.) was a headquarters for the Confederate army, and its jail once played host to such outlaw luminaries as Frank James and the Younger brothers. The complex includes a restored marshal's quarters, limestone jail, regional museum, and an 1865 one-room schoolhouse. Another noteworthy local structure is the **Bingham-Waggoner Estate** (313 W. Pacific), a 19-acre site that was the home of renowned Missouri frontier artist George Caleb Bingham. (The Waggoner family that brought you "Queen of the Pantry" flour later called it home.)

Fort Osage (11 miles east of town on U.S. 24 to Buckner, then three miles north to Sibley) is a reconstruction of the original 1808 fort built by William Clark (of Lewis and Clark fame). Officers' quarters, barracks, a museum, and a trading post are all part of it.

The city's Independence Day celebrations include costumed residents reliving the Civil War at the Truman Museum and McCoy Park, with square dancing, entertainment, and food.

BEST TIME TO VISIT: Summer.
TRAVEL TIPS: Accommodations in Independence include Howard Johnson's East (4200 S. Noland Rd.) and Ramada Inn East (4141 S. Noland Rd.). Among the better restaurants for families are Sam Wilson's Meat Market (3720 Noland Rd.), for pan-fried chicken, steak, and barbecue; and V's Restaurant and Vineyard Lounge (10819 E. U.S. 40) for Italian dishes.
HOURS: Harry S. Truman Library and Museum — 9 a.m.-7 p.m. Memorial Day-Labor Day; 9 a.m.-5 p.m. rest of year; closed Thanksgiving, Christmas, and New Year's Day. Harry S. Truman Courtroom and Office — 9 a.m.-5 p.m. Tuesday-Saturday, 1 p.m.-5 p.m. Sunday; closed Sunday, March-December; closed Thanksgiving, Christmas, and New Year's Day. World Headquarters, Reorganized Church of Jesus Christ of Latter-Day Saints — 9 a.m.-5 p.m. Monday-Saturday, 1 p.m.-5 p.m. Sunday; closed Thanksgiving and Christmas. Mormon L.D.S. Visitors Center — 9 a.m.-9 p.m. daily. Log Courthouse — by appointment, April-October. Pioneer Spring Cabin — 10 a.m.-noon and 2 p.m.-4 p.m. Monday, Tuesday, and Thursday-Saturday, 3 p.m.-5 p.m. Sunday; closed holidays. 1859 Marshal's Home, Jail, and Museum — 9 a.m.-5 p.m. Monday-Saturday, June-August; 10 a.m.-4 p.m. Tuesday-Saturday, September-May; 1 p.m.-5 p.m. Sunday; closed holidays. Bingham-Waggoner Estate — by appointment year round. Fort Osage — 9 a.m.-7 p.m. Memorial Day-Labor Day; 9 a.m.-5 p.m. rest of year; closed Thanksgiving, Christmas, and New Year's Day. Sam Wilson's Meat Market — 11:30 a.m.-2:30 p.m. and 5:30 p.m.-10 p.m. Monday-Thursday; 11:30 a.m.-2:30 p.m. and 5 p.m.-11 p.m. Friday and Saturday; 11:30 a.m.-9 p.m. Sunday. V's Restaurant — 11 a.m.-10:30 p.m. Monday-Thursday, 11 a.m.-midnight Friday and Saturday.
ADMISSION: Harry S. Truman Library and Museum — adults, $1; children under 16, free. Harry S. Truman Courtroom and Office — adults, 25¢; children under 16, free. 1859 Marshal's Home, Jail, and Museum — adults, $1; children under 12, free with adult. Bingham-Waggoner Estate — adults, $1.50; children under 12, free.
DIRECTIONS: From Kansas City, take I-70 east to Independence exit.
FOR MORE INFORMATION: Call the Department of Tourism, (816) 836-8300, ext. 300, or write 103 N. Main St., Independence, MO 64050.

$7.95

Midwest
FAMILY VACATION BOOK

225 Great Ideas for Vacations Close to Home — in Any Season

- **Facts** on where to go, how to go, when to go
- **Information** on what to do when you get there
- **Advice** on when to go, where to stay, what to see
- **Tips** on what to do while you're there
- **Pictures** of what you'll see when you get there
- **Ideas** on travel in eight midwestern states: Ohio, Michigan, Indiana, Illinois, Wisconsin, Iowa, Minnesota, Missouri

No matter when you travel — spring, summer, fall or winter — the Midwest FAMILY VACATION BOOK will show you where to go and how to have the most fun on close-to-home vacations. Unusual places, fascinating things to do and see, right in America's Heartland. Enjoy reading it, enjoy using it, and enjoy your vacations more!

ISBN 0-937416-03-7